A NOBLE THING

THE NATIONAL TRUST
AND ITS BENEFACTORS

*The way to have is to spend… lavish generosity pays,
as well as being delightful. The thing is to give, give, give.
You always get back more than you give.*

WALTER SICKERT

A NOBLE THING

THE NATIONAL TRUST AND ITS BENEFACTORS

MERLIN WATERSON

SCALA

PAGES 2–3: Fold Head Farm in the hamlet
of Watendlath, at Borrowdale, Cumbria.
The farm was bought in the 1960s with
bequests and a donation from an
anonymous benefactor.

CONTENTS

IN MEMORY OF MY PARENTS

ACKNOWLEDGEMENTS

D URING THE TWENTIETH CENTURY there was an unprecedented transfer of property in Britain from private ownership into the hands of a single charitable institution. This extraordinary transaction was largely unplanned and unforeseen, even by the beneficiary, the National Trust for Places of Historic Interest and Natural Beauty. In 1945 the Trust owned 112,000 acres and had a membership of 7,850. By the time it celebrated the centenary of the National Trust Act in 2007, membership had risen to 3.5 million, the acreage owned to 617,000, and the Trust had in its care 37,000 buildings, 4,000 historic monuments and 235 gardens and parks. What had taken place, almost by stealth, was a social and cultural revolution on a huge scale. Only relatively recently has the significance of this transfer begun to attract the serious interest of political and social historians. Was it last gasp expediency on the part of a landed aristocracy taxed nearly to extinction; or philanthropy; or a mixture of both? Was it socialism by the back door? Were many of the most significant benefactors in fact middle class, imbued with a tradition of public service? Or is the continuing generosity apolitical and classless: the expression of what is generous and – to use the word Beatrix Potter applied to the National Trust – 'noble' in the human spirit? Or is it all of those things and more? This book, which concentrates on the period 1940 to 2010, attempts to answer some of those questions.

During my 33 years on the staff of the National Trust, I worked first, from 1970 to 1981, as Historic Buildings Representative in the West Midlands and Wales; then from 1981 to 2001 as Regional Director for East Anglia; and latterly as Director of Historic Properties. In that time I met many of its benefactors. Most were generous not only to the Trust, but to me personally. Their generosity took various forms: encouragement to research their sometimes distinguished, sometimes painful family histories; to rearrange rooms they had known and used since childhood; and to write about their houses, collections, and gardens. This was often combined with generous hospitality, the recollection of which brings to mind sunrise over Snowdonia and the Menai Strait, seen from the upper floor of Plas Newydd on Anglesey; toast and peanut butter teas at Erddig near Wrexham (followed once by some of the worst food poisoning I have ever experienced); and hanging pictures acquired by the donors of Dudmaston in Shropshire. One of my reasons for gathering together this long gallery of portraits of benefactors is to record their generosity. I have had to be selective, choosing to write about the gifts that seem to me to be revealing or amusing. The omissions may puzzle or enrage some readers, who will find that many of their favourite properties are not given their due.

Most benefactors would not expect, or thank me for, a piece of uncritical hagiography. I discussed with many of them their motives and the reasons for their generosity to the National Trust. These are, I believe, worth recording, not least because they are so various, just as the social backgrounds of the donors I have written about are varied. This is a collection of portraits which has not been hung to conform to a museum curator's tidy sense of 'schools' and chronology. Equally, it would be disingenuous to pretend that continuities and connections, complexities and contradictions, have not been traced deliberately.

One reason for that complexity is that my relationship with the Trust's donors was itself never entirely disinterested. It is one of the themes of this book that generosity rarely is. The benefactors with whom I had dealings were, after all, landed with an official of the National Trust who was not of their choosing; and they may well have found him tiresome and bumptious. And yet, far more often than not, they were extraordinarily kind and forgiving. I hope they might see this book as an extended acknowledgement of those kindnesses. I would particularly like to thank the late Sir John Acland, the Marquess and Marchioness of Anglesey, Nicholas and Diana Baring, Lord Bridges, the late Mildred Cordeaux, Tam and Kathleen Dalyell, Lord Egremont, Lady Gibson and the late Lord Gibson, the late Lady Labouchere, the late Lady Mander, John Miller, Lord Rothschild, the late Sir Joshua Rowley, the late Bill and Mollie Smith, the late Sir John Smith, Lady Smith, the late John Workman, and the late Philip Yorke.

I have tried to test my own recollections and interpretations by talking to, or corresponding with, friends, former colleagues and many others. Those who have been helpful include Michael Argent, Richard Ayres, Frances Bailey, David Bett, Caroline Bowyer, Philip Broadbent-Yale, Professor Ronald Buchanan, Chris Calnan, Anthea Case, Giles and Ginnie Clotworthy, Warren Davies, Jane Gallagher, Simon Garnier, Ian Gow, Elizabeth Green, Stewart Grimshaw, Laurence Harwood, Richard Haslam, Lord Hemingford, Sukie Hemming, Richard Hill, Elizabeth Jacobs, Dame Jennifer Jenkins, Gareth Jones, Sarah Kay, Ian Kennaway, Maureen Kimberley, Valerie Lewis, Liz Luck, Ian Macquiston, The Hon. Michael McLaren, Peter and Fiona Marlow, Jeremy Musson, Gerard Noel, John Powell, Julian Prideaux, John Sales, Dame Rosalind Savill, David Sekers, John Sinclair, Cyril Southerland, the late Michael Trinick, Angus Wainwright and Keith Zealand. Several have kindly commented on sections of the book which draw on their recollections. I am particularly grateful to Martin Drury, Oliver Garnett and Dame Fiona Reynolds who read the book in draft, suggested improvements and provided numerous insights. The mistakes that remain are mine and not theirs.

Some of the material on National Trust benefactors was gathered when I was working on my book, *The National Trust: The First Hundred Years*, which was produced for its centenary in 1995. As part of the research for the book, Samantha Wyndham travelled round the country interviewing and recording numerous benefactors and former staff, many of whom are no longer alive. Very often these interviews gave me insights that had to be distilled in a general history into a sentence or two. The interviews are, I always believed, a precious resource, and I wanted to be able to return to and re-use them. Their quality is partly attributable to the easy rapport between the interviewer and her source. For this book she has tracked down unfamiliar illustrations and has left her yellow correction slips clustered like swallowtail butterflies on page after page of my typescript. The interviews with relatives of Ferguson's Gang were recorded and transcribed by her and also involved Sue Herdman and Alison Dalby. We interviewed Penelope Adamson, Joanna Bagnall, Judy Boyt, Ray Gallet, Jean Gladstone, Michael Maine, Claire Riche and Kitty Turnbull, who provided a mass of fresh information for my second chapter and have patiently answered a string of subsequent questions.

For access to the Trust's files and other records I am grateful to Peter Griffiths, Sue Saville, Iain Shaw, Nino Strachey and Cloe Tapping. The staff of the National Archives of Scotland in Edinburgh have been exceptionally helpful, as have the staff of the London Library.

Andrew Motion has kindly allowed me to quote from his poem about Orford Ness, 'Salt Water'. Seamus Heaney gave me permission to use his address at the opening of Sutton Hoo. I am also grateful to Michael Bloch for allowing me to quote from the books of James Lees-Milne; to David Gentleman for permission to reproduce one of the posters he designed for the campaign against the proposed Petworth bypass; and to Dennis Creffield for the use of his evocative picture of Orford Ness.

Writing a book about generosity is, of course, an extremely selfish activity, during which I have been humoured, indulged and tolerated more than I deserve. Those who have been generous in their response include my agent Andrew Hewson, my publisher David Campbell at Scala, their editorial director, Oliver Craske, his assistant Zoe Charteris, the designer Nigel Soper, the National Trust's publisher, John Stachiewicz and the head of its picture library, Chris Lacey and Chris Rowlin. They have all been unfailingly helpful and a delight to work with. I am also grateful to Michael Russell, who gave me much needed encouragement. My wife Imogen has been a patient critic and my daughter Natasha a brutal one. For guidance on the study by anthropologists of different traditions of giving and the relevant literature I am indebted to my sister, Roxana Waterson. She and I have concluded that the reliability of oral testimony needs to be questioned, whether you are interviewing a Toraja headman or a dowager duchess.

St John (Bobby) Gore, the Trust's Historic Buildings Secretary from 1973 to 1981 and Adviser on Paintings, used sometimes to plagiarise P.G. Wodehouse and say of staff at the properties that 'without their help I could have managed in half the time'. In my case I could not have got started without the assistance of those I have mentioned and those I have failed to acknowledge; nor would I have finished. I hope that those who have helped me will not feel that their kindness has been poorly repaid.

Merlin Waterson, Saxthorpe, Easter 2010

1

INTRODUCTION:
THE DONORS' LUNCH

WHEN THE AFTERNOON SUN reaches into the south transept of Iona Abbey, off the west coast of the island of Mull, it falls across two white marble effigies of George, 8th Duke of Argyll, in the robes of the Order of the Garter, and his third wife, Ina. The figure of the Duke was installed in 1912, although he died in 1900 and was buried in the Argyll Mausoleum at Kilmun on the shores of Holy Loch. How did this strangely incongruous intrusion into the Benedictine ruins of Iona come about?

The explanation can be found in a Deed of Trust dated 1899, a year before the 8th Duke's death, a copy of which hangs in the transept. The Deed explains that the Duke had 'found myself proprietor of the Island of Iona' and had 'laid out a considerable sum in preserving the Cathedral from further decay, and have so strengthened and repaired the walls that it is now nearly fit to be re-roofed.' There follows a statement which may seem surprising:

> … although the said architectural remains may be safe in my hands and in the hands of my immediate successors, yet the vicissitudes of personal position and character in those to whom such property may descend offer a very imperfect security for the protection, or for the appropriate use, of buildings of such great historic interest to the whole Christian world.

The 8th Duke had good reason for doubting the security of private ownership, even at a time of considerable national prosperity. Although his family had been virtual rulers of Scotland for much of the eighteenth century, the 6th Duke was a friend of the Prince Regent and a wastrel who came close to bankrupting his vast inheritance. His successors struggled to repair the damage, and so knew all about the consequences of 'vicissitudes of character'. The solution for Iona was for the 8th Duke to 'transfer my right of property and ownership… to a public trust… to hold it inalienably.' The bleak assessment of his successors' vulnerabilities was justified. Rosneath, the great neo-classical house of the Dukes of Argyll, designed by Joseph Bonomi on the Firth of Clyde, was in 1961 finally released from the indignity of being the centrepiece of a caravan park. This huge classical building needed two hundred pounds of explosive to blow it apart. The 8th Duke could scarcely have imagined such extreme consequences of 'vicissitudes of personal position'.

Beatrix Potter in 1913 at her Lake District farmhouse, Hill Top, bequeathed to the National Trust on her death in 1943. She wrote: 'The Trust is a noble thing, and – humanly speaking – immortal. There are some silly mortals connected with it; but they will pass.'

Rosneath Castle in Scotland, photographed in 1961 with the surrounding caravan park, shortly before the house was demolished.

This book is about what motivates the owners of precious possessions – sacred buildings, great works of art, historic houses, and treasured artefacts – to give them away. It touches on why one generation may be fiercely acquisitive, only for another to dispose of its inheritance, sometimes with great generosity and at others with wilful recklessness.

The examples generally come from my own experience of dealing with those who have given generously to the National Trust. Some are, or were, the owners of great estates. But I have also included accounts of people who were not rich, such as a schoolmaster, a gardener, and an off-shore fisherman, who believed that something precious to them was best safe-guarded by donation to some form of public body or trust.

Such generosity is timeless, and seems to appear in different guises in every age, from the creation of medieval almshouses to the endowing of hospitals and universities in recent centuries. The motives for such conspicuous generosity have usually been mixed, as one senses from the images of pious donors who appear in so many Renaissance altarpieces.

Generosity may be timeless, but the climate of giving changes, subtly at some moments, decisively at others. As far as gifts to the National Trust are concerned, there was one such shift in attitude in the middle years of the last century, as has been chronicled in the diaries of James Lees-Milne. He described how the owners of many great houses, immediately before and after the Second World War, chose to pass their inheritance over to the Trust. His account records his own crucial role in what Simon Jenkins, writing in *The Times* in 1992, called 'the noblest nationalisation'.[1] As I try to explain in Chapter 4, Lees-Milne's diaries give very little idea of the contributions of others, and at times present a distorted picture, as he acknowledged. I have tried to correct the impression he sometimes gives that the Trust's benefactors were all faded aristocrats facing punitive taxation.

Not only are Lees-Milne's recollections inevitably partial, but they also deal much less authoritatively with changes in attitude after his retirement from full-time employment with the National Trust in 1951. My own experience suggests that during the closing decades of the twentieth century, attitudes to philanthropy altered as society itself changed. The acquisition by the Trust in 1947 of an estate such as Attingham Park in Shropshire was made possible by the generosity of Thomas, 8th Lord Berwick, guided and encouraged by his wife, Teresa. Only a few hundred people would have even been aware that the gift had been made. The comparison with the purchase in 2002 of Tyntesfield, a High Victorian country house in north Somerset, could not be more striking. The estate was bought at market value, thanks to the enthusiasm and generosity of over 77,000 individual donors and the support of grant-aiding bodies, principally the Heritage Lottery Fund. By the end of the period between these two acquisitions, the National Trust had found itself the custodian of the largest composite collection of works of art in single ownership in the world.

Lees-Milne was principally concerned with great houses and admitted that he suffered from agoraphobia. Places such as Gull Rock in Cornwall and Orford Ness in Suffolk were not for him, still less the fate of a Norfolk fishing boat, which to its owner was a beautiful and cherished thing, charged with historical significance. As Secretary to the National Trust's Country Houses (later Historic Buildings) Committee, Lees-Milne had few dealings with donors who wanted to give things which were neither grand nor beautiful. It was generosity from relatively modest sources which made possible the acquisition of properties such as Sheringham Park in Norfolk and Sutton Hoo in Suffolk.

By the 1970s, the Trust had become extremely wary of major acquisitions that might impose huge financial burdens. Erddig near Wrexham and Plas Newydd on the Isle of Anglesey were two of the last properties to be accepted before the introduction of a formula devised by a future Chairman, Lord Chorley, which established the financial basis for more realistic endowments. The need for hefty endowments changed the way large properties were given to the National Trust. Financial worries might have prevented the Trust from taking on further houses, had the National Heritage Memorial Fund (NHMF) not been set up in 1980, with trustees anxious to see estates such as Canons Ashby in Northamptonshire, and Belton House and Calke Abbey in Derbyshire, given a secure future. When the trustees of the NHMF were made responsible for distributing the Heritage Lottery Fund in 1994, it might have seemed that the opportunities for the Trust would be legion. But other influences have been at work: the climate for giving has changed profoundly, and so too have tax incentives. It might be more realistic to refer to tax *dis*incentives, as is touched on in my concluding chapter, which deals with the Goodison Report of 2004 and its attempt to explain to the Government why the donation of works of art to museums and to the National Trust lags behind what happens in some other European countries and in the United States.

The unexpected and unprecedented public response in 2002 to the efforts to save Tyntesfield as an entity might seem to point to a new and enlightened phase of giving. This makes it all the more disappointing that today there seems to be little of the imagination and vision of Governments immediately before and after the Second World War, which made possible the legislation supporting both the National Trust's Country Houses Scheme and the National Land Fund. By contrast, the generosity of the general public is on a scale that would have been unthinkable fifty years ago. Today's donors are, more than ever before, the thousands who respond to the Trust's appeals for help.

Exactly what influences this new generation of benefactors, and why they choose to use the National Trust as the conduit for their generosity, is not easy to pin down. Sweeping generalisations about their motives can be misleading, and it seems more fruitful to consider a few examples of giving, where evidence is reasonably detailed and clear, although sometimes veiled by reticence. The Trust and its donors have tended to be diffident about their generosity, far more so than would be the case in the United States, for instance. Here the tradition of discretion over such matters means that anthropologists and social historians are more likely to record and analyse the traditions of making and receiving gifts in other cultures, from ancient Greece to the Pacific islands, than they are to assess the changing patterns of giving in our own society. The few portraits that I have tried to capture, of a varied and sometimes eccentric collection of benefactors, may help to explain at least some of the motives of the Trust's donors.

In most of its publications, the National Trust refers to 'donors' and 'donor families' as if they were a single species, without mutations. To do so may be tactful, but can also be confusing. Many of those I describe were generous in an entirely disinterested way. It is the nature and manner of that generosity which prompted Beatrix Potter to describe the Trust, in a letter to its Chairman, as 'a noble thing, and – humanly speaking – immortal. There are some silly mortals connected with it; but they will pass.' She used the royalties from her children's books to fund a succession of gifts of property in the Lake District, but would have been the first to acknowledge that her generosity was by no means disinterested. During her lifetime she managed those properties as she believed was for the best; and any interference from the National Trust's Regional Agent or forester would occasion a withering letter to the Chairman. As early as 1902 Beatrix Potter had been involved in the efforts to give Brandelhow, a hundred acres of woods and parkland on the shores of Derwentwater in the Lake District, the protection of National Trust ownership, and she had probably heard about the working men who contributed to the public appeal. One was a factory worker from Sheffield, who sent 2s.6d. with a note saying, 'All my life I have longed to see the Lakes. I shall never see them now, but I should like to help keep them for others.' Such generosity could scarcely be more simple and unselfish.

Some of the donors of great estates were motivated by a similar wish to see others benefit from things of beauty, but because the scale of the gift was so considerable, the nature of their generosity was more complicated. The interests of other family members, their closeness, their strengths and their weaknesses, had to be considered. Issues of taxation usually had to be taken into account. In many cases, properties came to the Trust in lieu of tax, and so might seem not to be gifts at all. The Cadbury family, who were Quaker philanthropists and benefactors of the Trust in the West Midlands, regarded charitable giving which involved avoiding tax as spending public money, for public benefit.[2] But even when great houses were acquired by the National Trust in the 1970s and 1980s, often taking advantage of tax concessions and with very large grants from public funds, there was invariably an element of gift, and the Trust had no compunction about referring to the family involved as 'donors'.

Ickworth in Suffolk came to the Trust in lieu of death duties in 1956 with Theodora, Marchioness of Bristol, the wife of the 4th Marquess, providing an endowment from her own substantial fortune, which came from Victorian railway building. The motives of this perceptive, public-spirited benefactor were straightforward. The successor to the title and to the Ickworth estates was her nephew Victor, who from an early age showed signs of being profoundly disturbed. On a visit to the village post office as a child he had tried to wring the necks of the ducks belonging to the postmistress. In 1939 he was sent to prison for robbery with violence.

His son John, the 7th Marquess, was a pathetic but vicious drug addict, who after spells in prison died at the age of 44. Ickworth, the Marchioness perceived, needed to be protected.

In 1985 the solution for Calke Abbey in Derbyshire involved the house, contents and most of the estate being offered to the Treasury in payment of Capital Transfer Tax, and with the Harpur-Crewe trustees making a contribution to match the £1 million raised by the National Trust's appeal. Often such transfers involved a continuing right of occupation, the terms of which were recorded in a memorandum of wishes. The generosity was consequently scarcely disinterested, but real nonetheless.

There will be those who think it is bad form to scrutinise these degrees of generosity at all closely. Among the most reticent are those who have been most generous, for instance the late Simon Sainsbury, whose Monument Trust came to the rescue of scores of houses and their collections. Ostentatious philanthropy, like ostentatious wealth, used to be thought vulgar. In an age of celebrity-giving, this seems to be no longer the case. Trying to plot these changes in attitude is relatively uncharted territory as far as our own society is concerned; and this is where the work of anthropologists can be so instructive.

Beatrix Potter, *View up the Newlands Valley*, 1903.

There is a huge literature on the nature of giving in remote societies. Most of the contributors acknowledge their debt to the writings of Marcel Mauss (1872–1950) and to his book, *Essai sur le Don*, published in France in 1924, and translated into English in 1954, and again in 1990, as *The Gift*.[3] For anthropologists it has become something of a sacred text. An anthropologist's rigour could usefully be applied to a comparison between the gifts of the British landed aristocracy in the mid-twentieth century and those of the chiefs of, say, Melanesia, Polynesia and Papua New Guinea; or to societies where Hindu law applies. The attempts by anthropologists to analyse the motives for giving may, however, provide a vocabulary for describing philanthropy in this country.

In some societies, for instance in the South Seas, the gift is seen as a form of transaction between self-interested individuals and is expected to be reciprocated. It is a form of contractual obligation: the unreciprocated gift debases the recipient. At church services in Samoa the donation made by each member of the congregation is announced and is a way of establishing the donor's wealth and status. Failure to contribute appropriately would inevitably mean a loss of social position. In many Hindu societies, the opposite is true: the gift can be a form of purification and any reciprocation or material benefit would cancel the desired effect. For many Buddhists

The Rotunda at Ickworth in Suffolk: the house was transferred to the National Trust in lieu of death duties in 1956, and endowed by Theodora, Marchioness of Bristol.

a gift motivated by self-interest belongs to the profane world and salvation lies through the gift that is unreciprocated: virtue depends on the giver being disinterested.

There are obvious parallels with our own conventions of giving. At the crudest level there is the Chicago economist's belief that 'there is no such thing as a free lunch.' The expectation that generosity will be rewarded was expressed with characteristic overstatement by the painter Walter Sickert when he advised a friend that 'the way to have, is to spend… lavish generosity pays, as well as being delightful.'[4] Throughout his life Sickert put his theory to the test; and my chapter on Attingham Park explains how the collections there, and the artist himself, benefitted.

Then there are the various Christian attitudes to giving, from the medieval sale of indulgences and redemption through good works, to post-Reformation attitudes to charity. The greatest of the Christian virtues is charity, and charitable giving which is voluntary and unrequited. 'When you do some act of charity, do not let your left hand know what your right hand is doing; your good deed must be secret,' advocates chapter 6 of Matthew's Gospel. Jewish teaching identifies eight levels of charity, the second of which is to give to the poor without knowing to whom one gives, and without the recipient knowing from whom he receives. In these regards the Sheffield worker contributing to the Brandelhow appeal in 1902 was acting charitably in the purest sense.

If there is an anthropology and a theology of giving, then there is also a politics of giv-

The Drawing Room at Calke Abbey in Derbyshire, acquired by the National Trust in 1985 in lieu of taxes, and endowed by the trustees of the Harpur-Crewe Estate, public organisations, an anonymous benefactor and money raised by a public appeal.

ing. This will not surprise those who, like the historian David Cannadine, regard the National Trust as 'the pursuit of politics by other means.'[5] The founders of the Trust would not be surprised by this identification with politics. As a young man, long before he devised a constitution for the National Trust and drafted its first Act of Parliament, Robert Hunter wrote an essay for the Commons Preservations Society, in which he expressed radical views, which many, then and since, would have found profoundly shocking:

> … the position of the landowner is peculiar. Land is not made by any man, but exists in a limited quantity. Any one who has power over a portion of it has a share in a monopoly; is enjoying something which cannot be increased indefinitely, and out of the enjoyment of which he is consequently keeping someone else. This share of a limited commodity having been conferred upon him, it must in reason have been conferred in trust to be used for the benefit of the remainder of the community. If this idea was not present at the time of the original gift, it must have arisen as a just appreciation of the duties of man to man became prevalent.[6]

Some of the great landowners who have been generous to the Trust would understand or even share Hunter's view. Many others would not, and indeed might feel threatened by it. When Sir Charles Trevelyan announced, in a broadcast of 1937, that he intended to give his Wallington estate in Northumberland to the Trust, he told his listeners:

George Bernard Shaw realigning his revolving writing hut, in the garden of Shaw's Corner in Hertfordshire, his home from 1906, which he gave to the National Trust in 1944.

To me it is natural and reasonable that a place such as this should come into public ownership, so that the right to use and enjoy it may be for ever secured for the community. As a Socialist, I am not hampered by any sentiment of ownership. I am prompted to act as I am doing by satisfaction at knowing that the place I love will be held in perpetuity for the people of my country.[7]

Some future donors, such as the playwright George Bernard Shaw, who donated his house to the Trust in 1944, gave more strident voice to their socialist principles. There was a hostile reaction to both Trevelyan and Shaw among many landowners. Others, such as the Carew Pole family of Antony in Cornwall, were more moderate and saw the National Trust as a halfway house. In his speech of 1934, which launched the Trust's Country Houses Scheme, Philip, 11th Marquess of Lothian, referred to 'the new order of planned private enterprise which is increasingly coming to replace both the unrestricted individualism of the early capitalistic era and the universal socialisation of early socialist thinkers.' His views were similar to those of the post-war Chancellor of the Exchequer, Hugh Dalton, who confided that the acquisition of properties by the National Trust was as near as the country would allow the nationalisation of land to go.[8] He described the National Trust as a typically British example of 'Practical Socialism in action.'[9] Dalton, like Lothian, was a considerable benefactor, noting in his diary on 11 September 1950: 'Ruth and I … agreed to streamline our Wills. I leave all to her and all, if she dies first, to the National Trust – subject to King's having Rupert [Brooke]'s letters to me.' He also unlocked the generosity of others through the creation of the National Land Fund, established in 1946 with an initial allocation of £50 million, from the sale of surplus military equipment. The Fund was to help with the setting up of National Parks and for the acquisition of countryside and historic buildings by the National Trust, so providing a memorial to those who had given their lives in the war. The Fund had a major impact, although Dalton was frustrated that more use was not made of it. He wrote in 1948 there should be no qualms about using the reserve 'so long as it is spent on the National Trust and not on the precious owners.'[10]

Andrew, 11th Duke of Devonshire, photographed by his grandson, William Burlington.

To mark its Centenary in 1995, the National Trust held a lunch for major benefactors in the Grosvenor House Hotel in Park Lane. What may seem an incongruous venue was chosen because the inaugural meeting of the Trust had been held at Grosvenor House by invitation of Hugh, 1st Duke of Westminster, who was an admirer of one of the founders, Octavia Hill. It was an occasion that prompted the Duke to predict: 'Mark my words, Miss Hill, this is going to be a very big thing.' The building which provided the infant National Trust with such an elegant cradle was demolished in 1927 to make way for the luxury flats and hotel where – in rather coarser surroundings – the Trust celebrated its birth and adult achievements.[11]

The sequel was memorable. In 2001 there was another lunch for donors and their descendants, held this time at Spencer House in St James's, impeccably restored by Lord Rothschild, whose cousin, James de Rothschild, had bequeathed Waddesdon Manor in Buckinghamshire to the Trust in 1957. After Lord Rothschild's welcome, there was the opportunity for discussion. Contributions rapidly became a succession of complaints. Following the devastating damage to Uppark in 1989, open fires in the entrance hall of another house had been forbidden until the chimney flue had been lined; when would the Trust find the money to do the work? Were its investments ethical? Why were consultants involved at great expense? The mood of the gathering turned sour. At this moment, the Duke of Devonshire indicated that he wished to speak. He was over eighty and virtually blind, but had lost none of the politician's sense of timing. 'In the course of my long life, I have done many foolish things,' he began, and then paused for what seemed a long time. 'I have also done one supremely wise one. In 1959 I decided that Hardwick Hall should go to the National Trust. No praise is too high for the way they have looked after it since then.'[12]

Some of those present may have felt that the Duke's position

The High Great Chamber at Hardwick Hall in Derbyshire, which was transferred to the National Trust in lieu of death duties in 1959.

was rather different from theirs. He had parted with Hardwick Hall, but at least he still had Chatsworth. If this was thought, it was certainly not said, and the atmosphere of the ensuing lunch could not have been more benign. Many would have recognised that the Duke and Duchess of Devonshire had, over half a century, transformed public attitudes to houses such as Chatsworth, which had come to be regarded not as an exclusive symbol of privilege, but as a supreme work of art to be shared and enjoyed by everyone.

My own professional involvement with the National Trust had begun thirty years earlier, in 1970. I still have the letter from the Historic Buildings Secretary, Robin Fedden, in his cursive, elegant handwriting, in response to my enquiry about working for the Trust: I am in London only for 24 hours, but shall be back on July 6th. Do please telephone and make a date to come and see me after that.

Fedden was a mountaineer, and the author of books on subjects ranging from Syrian castles to the history of suicide. One of his passions was skiing, among the Cedars of Lebanon on Jebel Makmel, or in the sand dunes near Cairo – where he was photographed by Lee Miller – or in European resorts, about which he wrote for *Country Life*. During the war he registered as a conscientious objector and used his fluent Arabic to set up the Friends' Ambulance Unit in Syria. He had first encountered the future Chairman of the Trust when they were both working in Cairo, and Randal McDonnell was 'beneath palm trees and a full moon, dancing… with a hermaphrodite' (as he recalled at the Chairman's retirement party). Fedden's prose style was, like the man himself, spare and apparently effortless. In 1968 he wrote a history of the National Trust, *The Continuing Purpose,* which has never been bettered.

I was to discover that Fedden often dealt with his office responsibilities in 24-hour bursts between expeditions: for instance, to the Tigris, to the Andes, or to Snowdonia for a little ice-climbing in the gullies, which he would combine with visits to Trust properties. When we met, he no doubt concluded that my lack of the necessary administrative experience was a problem; but this seemed to be compensated for by a period studying carpet weaving in southern Iran. I was in due course granted a formal interview for the position of Historic Buildings Representative in the West Midlands and North Wales.

Long after the interview I learnt that there was only one other applicant, probably with considerably more knowledge and experience. At that time, however, the Trust was divided into two camps: on the one hand there were the Land Agents, who were thoroughly professional and experienced managers of property; and on the other the Historic Buildings Representatives, who were aesthetes and sometimes of questionable administrative competence. The latter had been labelled by one of the rising stars of the Trust's committees, John Smith, as 'the lilies', in order to distinguish them from 'the boots' or Land Agents. I was to be interviewed by Fedden (theoretically a 'lily', but at least a regular user of climbing boots), the Trust's Area Agent in the West Midlands, Gerard Noel (very much a riding boots man), and the Secretary (later Director-General), Jack Boles (neither a 'lily' nor a 'boot', but with the engaging manner of a bright young tutor sent to improve some not always responsive pupils).

The other candidate, for all his many and no doubt outstanding qualities, made the disas-

Robin Fedden, Historic Buildings Secretary of the National Trust from 1951 to 1973, photographed by Lee Miller on sand skis in Egypt in 1937.

trous mistake of coming to the interview wearing a bright yellow tie with a stain on it. As far as Noel was concerned, this was nailing colours to the mast. But the other two had to be persuaded. The questions I was asked were not those used today by professional head-hunters. Fedden enquired, with his carefully deployed stutter: 'Do you h-h-h-hunt, shoot or fish?' The nearest I had come to any of these was a little coarse fishing. 'It doesn't really matter, but it gives you something to talk about with the s-s-s-squires.' My answer to Fedden's next question, whether I had private means, was equally negative and unsatisfactory. 'Ah, you will not make your f-f-f-fortune working for the Trust.' I must have been a severe disappointment, but in spite of my replies, that yellow tie got me the job.

I was to start work on 16 November 1970, on a salary of £900 a year (there was a deduction of £600 if I chose to live in a National Trust house or cottage). Fedden was right. During the next thirty years, I failed to make my fortune in any conventional, financial sense. But he had written in his letter of appointment: 'I hope you find the work as interesting and stimulating as I have always done;' and indeed I did. One of the greatest pleasures – not unmingled with crises and doubts – was dealing with a succession of great houses that came to the Trust in the 1970s. Dealing with their donors was a large part of that pleasure.

THE PUBLICAN
AND THE MASKED LADIES
Sir Clough Williams-Ellis, Bill Stickers and Red Biddy

A N I N S C R I P T I O N O N T H E Belfry Tower designed by Clough Williams-Ellis for Portmeirion, in north Wales, describes its creator as 'Architect and Publican'. The tower was built, the inscription records, in 1928, using stones from a twelfth-century castle which was:

> … finally razed *c.*1869 by Sir Wm Fothergill Cook inventor of the Electric Telegraph 'lest the ruins should become known and attract visitors to the place.' This 19th-century affront to the 12th is thus piously redressed in the 20th.

Clough found much that affronted him architecturally. His response was not just to wring his hands, but to show how things could be done better.

Clough's designs, which began playfully in 1905 and were still playful in the 1970s, are increasingly seen to be highly original and a bridge spanning pre- and post-modern architecture. His many books now have a lasting place in the literature of conservation. What have not been sufficiently understood and recorded are his contributions to the work of different conservation organisations, the generosity of his gifts to the National Trust, and the largely unacknowledged part he played in what became known as the Trust's 'Country Houses Scheme'. The extraordinary success of this initiative is usually attributed to Lord Lothian and James Lees-Milne. Both in effect took up a cause for which Clough Williams-Ellis was the early advocate: a John the Baptist figure who was eloquent, handsome, and dressed not in animal skins but in tweed, canary-yellow stockings and flamboyant neckties.

His discovery of Portmeirion was partly the result of his passion for island-hopping, initially in his sloop *Twinkler* and then in the Loch Fyne ketch *Scott*. It led him to purchase the islands of St Tudwal off the Llŷn peninsula, partly to protect them from unsuitable development, but also to provide an anchorage in Cardigan Bay. The peninsula of Aber Iâ, as it was then known (Clough found the name 'chilly' as the Welsh means 'ice mouth'), gave him much more than a well-protected quay where the estuaries of Traeth Mawr and Traeth Bach meet. Its dramatic hillsides and benign climate were the perfect setting for the romantic, extended folly which Clough set about building for his own and other people's pleasure, and which he named Portmeirion. His first designs for the hotel-village are dated 1925,

Sir Clough Williams-Ellis at Portmeirion in north Wales, photographed by Bruno de Hamil in 1973.

Portmeirion from the gazebo, with a view over the estuaries of Traeth Mawr and Traeth Bach.

and he was still delighting in embellishments shortly before he died in 1978.

To his mid-twentieth-century critics, Clough was guilty of at least two unforgivable sins. First of all he was a polymath: an architect with a thriving practice and the ability to attract commissions large and small; a prolific writer on buildings and landscapes, whose books reached a mass audience; and a pioneer environmentalist who championed good design and planning, whether for a new town, a remote cottage, a country house, or for his own *jeu d'e-sprit*, Portmeirion. An even deadlier sin to many was his apparent frivolity. He may have shared an enthusiasm for great architecture with Sir Nikolaus Pevsner, but in most other respects he was a most un-Pevsnerian figure. He would quote the philosopher Don Marquis:

> The purpose of the universe is to play. The artists know that, and that play and art and
> creation are different names for the same – a thing that is sweats and agonies and ecstasies …

This insistence on the sharing of pleasure, of playfulness and wit, went with a genuine modesty about his own buildings, which he summed up in a speech at his 80th birthday party at Portmeirion in 1963:

> … it's not as though I was an 'important' architect who just <u>had</u> to be recognised, because I
> am demonstrably and emphatically nothing of the kind – no great work of mine stands out
> against the sky in splendour to excite men's wonder. I shall never even appear in Banister
> Fletcher or any such reference work – I have merely had a perfectly lovely hobbyhorsical time
> designing and building all sorts of lesser things that pleased me. Whence Portmeirion and
> such like trivia.[1]

Today Clough's architectural achievements are taken more seriously than he ever imagined. His skilful mixing of styles from different periods and countries, sometimes within a classical framework, and often to picturesque effect, found him a place in Charles Jencks's *The*

Language of Post-Modern Architecture, published in 1977, the year before Clough's death. His working life of over 60 years meant that his early buildings reflect Arts and Crafts ideals, followed by responses to modernism; but ultimately his own highly personal version of eclectic classicism prevails. Always ready to irritate the purists, he enjoyed playing tricks with scale, for instance by placing very small windows high in a façade or tower, and he often used strong Italianate colour without being unduly deferential to different architectural elements. In spite of being easy to disparage and hard to pin down, many of his best buildings, including most of Portmeirion, are now listed as being of national significance.

Clough's books about architecture and conservation were more influential than his buildings. *The Pleasures of Architecture*, which he wrote with his wife Amabel, was published in 1924, and was one of the first books on the subject to reach a mass audience. Four years later *England and the Octopus* appeared, quickly ran through several editions, and now ranks, with the later books of John Ruskin and with Rachel Carson's *Silent Spring*, as one of the most powerful and influential polemics on the threats to the natural and historic environment. Clough saw uncontrolled, badly designed development reaching out into the countryside like the tentacles of an octopus, hence the title of his book.[2] Like Ruskin, he was aware of just

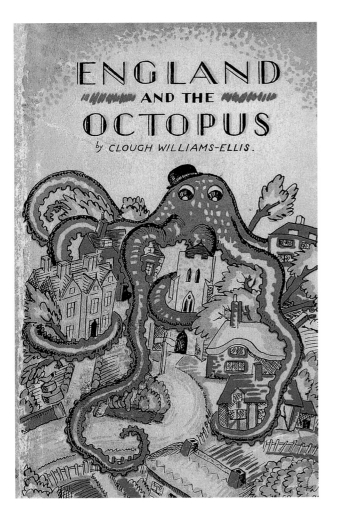

The front cover of the dust-jacket on the first edition of *England and the Octopus*, written by Clough Williams-Ellis and published in 1928.

how much ugliness and destruction could be spawned by unrestrained free-market capitalism. In a chapter entitled 'Donkeys, Drones and Ostriches,' he lays much of the blame at the feet of those responsible for education, not least at universities with little excuse for insensitivity and ignorance. He acknowledged, 50 years later, that it was 'an angry book, written by an angry young man', and much of his rage was directed at the greed and fecklessness of many of the owners of country houses and estates.

Another chapter, entitled 'The Great House: Its Conservation and Conversion,' made several measured and constructive proposals to safeguard a representative number of great buildings. Clough suggested that the editor of *Country Life* should be asked to draft a list of country houses which 'really deserve protection as national monuments'. He then advocated that 'the scheduled house would enjoy substantial remissions from rates and tax: it would carry very definite privileges with it as well as obligations.' The message was heeded, both in the offices of *Country Life* and more widely. Its future editor, Christopher Hussey, is the subject of the chapter which follows.

Clough was never a rich man, but he was prepared to back his pen with his own hard-earned money. In 1922, when a proposal to demolish

Stowe in Buckinghamshire – a house and park on which Vanbrugh, Kent, Gibbs and Adam had worked – was reported in the press, *Country Life* observed negatively that it had outlived its usefulness; while *The Times* merely noted that such buildings assumed a certain grandeur once ruined. Clough, invited to write about its architectural and landscape importance in *The Spectator*, struck his own very different note, emphasising its beauty and historical significance. His article was read by the Reverend Percy Warrington, who saw that abandoned country houses could be bought very cheaply and adapted for use as public schools. Stowe was to be the best-known of his group of schools, with its grand façades calculated to appeal to traditionally-minded parents.

Clough was appointed architect to the school, with a brief to adapt the existing buildings and design new ones. For the governors, the educational needs of the pupils were paramount, and in spite of Clough's protestations, they decided to sell at auction the Grand Avenue, stretching for nearly two miles from the Buckingham Lodges, past the Corinthian Arch, and on towards the lake and the house itself. Clough appreciated that the park at Stowe was at least as historically important as the house, and that there was a very real danger that the southern end of the avenue would appeal to builders keen to create housing estates on the edge of Buckingham. In desperation he attended the auction and bought the avenue himself. Unlike the rival bidders, he acquired not a potential asset, but an expensive conservation liability. Eventually he was able to sell it on at a loss to a group of benefactors of the school, and in 1990 it was transferred, with most of the rest of the park, to the National Trust. The long-term repair and protection of Stowe, made possible by an anonymous gift of £1.8 million, a public appeal, and grants from the National Heritage Memorial Fund and the Heritage Lottery Fund, could scarcely have been justified if it had been deprived of its southern approach and parkland. In that respect, Clough was one of the saviours of Stowe.

He was also directly generous to the National Trust in Wales. During a royal visit, George VI asked him about ownership of the land around Snowdon. 'Actually that bit belongs to me, but you can keep that under your crown,' he replied to the monarch, pointing with his cane. In 1938 he decided that the 314 acres he owned at Llyn Gwynant, on the south-west side of Snowdon, should be given to the Trust, with protective covenants over a further fifty-six acres to prevent development. He also gave restrictive covenants over land near the Aberglaslyn Pass in 1941.

Shortly after *England and the Octopus* was published it was read by Margaret (Peggy, as she preferred to be known) Pollard, who had moved to Cornwall shortly after her marriage in 1928 to Frank Pollard, a sailor and novelist. Before their marriage Peggy Gladstone – she was a great-niece of the Prime Minister W.E. Gladstone – had a brilliant academic career at Cambridge, where she and Frank met. Her decision to read oriental languages was to satisfy a demanding mother, who was herself an accomplished linguist and whom Peggy held in awe: the migraines which she suffered for most of her life ceased on the day her mother died.[3] Peggy specialised in Sanskrit and was the first woman in the university to achieve first-class honours in both parts of the oriental languages tripos. She then studied Russian and translated many of the hymns of the Eastern Orthodox Church. Her academic career may suggest a dowdy bluestocking, but she was nothing of the kind. In fact she maintained that

Peggy Pollard, the founder of Ferguson's Gang, a generous group of anonymous National Trust benefactors in the 1930s.

she wore stockings for the last time when she was presented to George V and vowed she would never wear them again. Peggy was a musician of professional ability, playing the organ and later the harp; a talented painter and embroiderer; and a writer of poetry, plays, and humorous verse. She was beautiful, and she would sometimes dress like a debutante, at other times like a Russian peasant; and she kept goats, on the breeding of which she became an authority.

In Peggy Pollard, Clough the polymath had more than met his match, as he later acknowledged. In her copy of *England and the Octopus* he wrote: 'To Peggy Pollard, to whom I would have Dedicated this Angry Little Book had she been known to me when I wrote it.'[4] She had fallen in love with him from afar when she attended one of his lectures. Clough was wearing his usual bow tie and yellow stockings and looked, she thought, ' like a bird of paradise'.[5] Peggy's response to Clough's impassioned plea for the protection of places of beauty was to set about raising money for the National Trust in highly eccentric ways, at the same time harnessing previously undreamt-of levels of public support. It was the beginning of Peggy Pollard's double life. She became Bill Stickers (as in 'Bill Stickers will be prosecuted'), the leader of the mysterious and faintly sinister Ferguson's Gang.

Notice of the gang's intentions came in the form of a card, handed into the Trust's head office in Buckingham Palace Gardens, which read:

We ain't so many – we ain't so few
All of us has this end in view –
National Trust – to work for you.
Green grass turning to bricks and dust –
Stately homes that will soon go bust –
No defence, but the National Trust.
Looking at rural England thus –
George and Dragon is changed for us,
Into St Clough and the Octopus.[6]

The gangsters recruited by Bill Stickers included a musician, given the name 'Sister Agatha', the 'Lord Beershop of the Gladstone Islands', otherwise known as the 'Bloody Bishop', who had studied at the Slade, 'Kate O'Brien the Nark' and 'Red Biddy', so called because of her Marxist convictions. All were women, were Peggy Pollard's friends, and took a vow that as members of Ferguson's Gang their real names would be kept secret. The name Ferguson was a convenient red herring and could be bestowed on any man who could be useful to them. In 1939 the war brought their activities to a halt; and it was not until the 1970s that their true identities began to emerge.

The member of the gang to lead the most unconventional life was 'Red Biddy' or, as she was known professionally, Dr. Rachel Pinney: general practitioner, child psychologist, CND campaigner and inmate of Holloway Prison. Her father was a distinguished soldier (and less than ideal father),

Members of Ferguson's Gang at Shalford Mill in Surrey. All adopted fictitious names to preserve their anonymity: Rachel Pinney (left) was 'Red Biddy'; Brynhild Jervis-Read (centre) was 'Sister Agatha'; and Peggy Pollard (right) was 'Bill Stickers'.

Major-General Sir Reginald Pinney, KCB. The draw towards medicine came from her mother's side of the family: Lady Pinney's father, Henry Head, was a highly regarded neurologist. Until her marriage she was a Quaker - which may account for Rachel's later pacifism – and it was probably her husband's career that prompted a move to the Church of England. Rachel's academic record was chequered: she was sent down from Bristol University, where she was supposed to be studying philosophy but failed to attend lectures or supervisions. It was not until 1940 that she began to read medicine at Sheffield University, finally passing the exams at the ninth attempt. By then she had three children by her Italian husband, Luigi Cocuzzi, whom she had married in 1934. The two led largely separate lives, Luigi returning periodically to Italy. When their eldest child, Karin, was found to be seriously neglected and suffering from rickets, she was entrusted to another member of the family. As Rachel's political views gradually changed, so did her Ferguson's Gang *nom de guerre,* and she was latterly known as 'White Biddy'. A photograph of her in the gang's minute book shows that she was shorter than other members, with hunched shoulders, stumpy legs (a family characteristic) and dark, tousled hair.

The assumption that all the gang were rich society girls was incorrect. Sister Agatha – her real name was Brynhild Catherine Jervis-Read – trained as a hospital almoner and spent most of her professional life as a senior administrator of the Red Cross. Her father did not believe in inherited wealth and gave her nothing. To try to obstruct her relationship with her music teacher, who was already married, he sent Bryn to Australia; but she defied him and returned. After her father's death they were able to marry and Bryn devoted much of her considerable energy to helping young musicians.

The early meetings of the gang, organised by Bill Stickers and Sister Agatha, took place at Shalford Mill, an eighteenth-century watermill in Surrey. This derelict building was acquired and endowed for the National Trust by the gang in 1932. It was restored by its first tenant, the architect John Macgregor, who was christened 'The Artichoke', partly because the gang's dinners at the mill, sent down from Fortnum and Masons, often included artichokes, and partly to mock his profession. Macgregor was an architect much favoured by the Society for the Protection of Ancient Buildings and the National Trust. His children used to eavesdrop on the gang's all-night vigils, with their chanting of Latin, dancing and the reciting of Peggy's poems.

The way Ferguson's Gang delivered their gifts to the Trust had a touch of genius about it. Having carefully alerted the press beforehand, a member of the gang would arrive at the Trust's headquarters heavily disguised. On 1 February 1933 *The Times* carried an article under the headline 'Masked lady weighed down with silver'. The report continued:

WE FERGUSONS GANG

With loyal assurance of our de ~ votion and future endeavour, Do thus discharge our debt to the ..... National Trust.

An illuminated manuscript with seals, signed by the members of Ferguson's Gang, and delivered to the National Trust with £200 in 1933.

The eighteenth-century Old Town Hall at Newtown on the Isle of Wight, given in 1933 by Ferguson's Gang, and photographed for their minute book, or so-called 'Boo', because the 'k' would not fit on its cover.

On January 13, when the day about Victoria was slipping into an unpleasant evening, cold and wet, a taxicab stopped outside 7 Buckingham Palace Gardens. A lady, heavily masked, got out and announced herself to the commissionaire as 'Red Biddy' of 'Ferguson's Gang'. She was bent with the weight of a heavy bag and desired to see the Secretary, with whom, without lifting her mask, she deposited £100 in silver… she left, as she had come, recognised by no-one.

The visit is also recorded in the 'Boo', as the minute book of meetings of the gang was called. 'Red Biddy' gave her own account:

I goes up to the door and says to the man at the door – Ear's my card – please give it to the Secretary of the National Trust – Well e looks at me suspicious like and sez av yer got an appointment? – I sez 'no, but the Secretary will see me when e sees my card'…

The perilous condition of Newtown Old Town Hall – a name for the gang to savour – on the Isle of Wight probably came to their attention through John Macgregor. The eighteenth-century building was bought in a state of dereliction by the gang in 1933, and given to the National Trust on the understanding that it would be restored. The gang visited it in 1935, enjoying a picnic of chicken mousse, Russian salad and plenty of white wine on the way. Evocative photographs of the building, suffocated with ivy, were taken during the inspection and duly found their way into the 'Boo'.[7]

The money for the Old Town Hall was delivered to the National Trust by ''erb the Smasher' in November 1933, an event that was again reported in *The Times*. 'The Smasher', who was never a fully paid-up member of the gang, was in fact Peggy Pollard's extremely handsome brother, Bobby. He owed his name to his physical attributes in the eyes of the gang members, rather than to any destructive tendencies. In 1935, when the Trust was invited by the BBC to make one of its regular appeals, the task was entrusted to Ferguson's Gang, and in turn to 'The Smasher'. ''erb' arrived masked, in a dinner jacket, and delivered an extremely polished broadcast, which began:

I am Ferguson of Ferguson's Gang. I appeal to you tonight for the National Trust. That means for the beauty of England; for all that is left of the England that belongs to you and me and is vanishing under our eyes. The land held by the National Trust is your land and nobody else's. The cliffs that you buy for the National Trust will be open for you to walk on. Nobody can turn you out of the woods and fields that are held for you by the National Trust. But no Government grant supports the work of the Trust; it is kept going by your efforts and mine. And it urgently needs more members to help in its battle against the Octopus; the Octopus, whose tentacles, in the shape of jerrybuilt estates and ribbon development, are stretching like a pestilence over the face of England.

A few lines of one of Peggy's poems followed. The broadcast ended:

Do anything but watch the Octopus at work and say 'why doesn't somebody do something about it?'

It then reminded listeners that they could become members at 2s 6d a year, or could simply send a donation to 'Ferguson, c/o the National Trust'.

The Trust promptly recruited 600 new members. The amount raised, over £900, exceeded almost all the BBC's other appeals that year. Peggy wrote to congratulate her brother immediately afterwards:

dear erb,
ere is your first rite-up. I ope you will be pleased. They ave got the money wrong as they did before when they said Red Biddy had 1000 half crowns in one of the papers, but still it is a good riteup… I am thinking of trying if Ferguson will take the boodil next year, they ort 2 noe that Ferguson is no Socighety lady, but a ily placed public oftial with a beard.

This may refer to her husband Frank, who sported a beard of buccaneering proportions, served as a Captain in the Royal Navy during the war, and became a county councillor. Peggy was with him in 1930 when his *Bellatrix* sank and she sent a telegram home saying 'yacht lost in north sea all saved'.

Ferguson's Gang's fundraising to buy Mayon and Trevescan Cliffs, between Sennen Cove and Land's End in Cornwall, exceeded their earlier donations, and brought their total contributions to more than £3,500. By 1936, when the cliffs were successfully acquired by the National Trust, Peggy Pollard was enmeshed in learning revival Cornish and performing at the Gorsedd, the gathering of Cornish bards, at which she played the harp. When she became a bard herself in 1938 she took her name, Arlodhes Ywerdhon, from the rock also known as the Irish Lady, which rises from the sea just below Mayon Cliff. Cornish legend has it that a shipwrecked lady, stranded there in a storm, reappears with a lantern when the rock is lashed by gales.

Peggy the romantic could abruptly return to Peggy the author of songs and light verse. The successful acquisition of Mayon Cliff prompted verses which begin:

> Up on the cliffs by Mayon Castle,
> What 'as you seen to make a fuss?
> Up on the cliffs by Mayon Castle
> There I seen the Octopus!
>
> What was the Octopus a-doing?
> East of the Longships as you go?
> E'd some bricks and a load o' concrete
> For to start on a bungalow…

There was also a brisk, practical side to Peggy, which made her an efficient secretary of the Council for the Preservation of Rural England (CPRE, later renamed the Campaign for the Protection of Rural England) in Cornwall from 1935 to 1945.

Behind all the false names, the disguises and the light verse there was a deeply serious purpose. Between them Clough Williams-Ellis and Peggy Pollard managed to convey the urgent need to protect the countryside and to fix in the public's mind that the National Trust was a crusading organisation that could play a major role in that cause. In 1947 Clough published 'On Trust to the Nation', an account of the properties of the National Trust with lively illustrations by Barbara Jones, in which he praised 'Ferguson's Gang – a benignly melodramatic secret society that has brought off a number of minor *coups* on the Trust's behalf in what can only be called a spectacularly stealthy fashion.'[8]

During the years that she was involved in the antics of Ferguson's Gang, Pollard was also enabling the National Trust to buy Predannack Wartha, on the Lizard Peninsula, using money that came to her through a legacy, and acknowledged in the Trust's Annual Report of 1937 as the gift of Mrs G. F. G. Pollard. She was the principal contributor towards the purchase of Trevan and Pennywilgie Points in Lundy Bay the same year. In 1939 land on the Helford River was purchased by the Trust, with her gift again made in the name of Mrs G. F. G. Pollard. When the Trust appealed for funds to buy Rosemullion Head, she persuaded a benefactor who wanted to be anonymous to transfer much of the money needed to her, and she then wrote the cheque. Sometimes she allowed her generosity to be acknowledged. At others she preferred what she called 'my little bit of anonymous immortality'.

There is an account of Predannack in Peggy Pollard's quirky and personal *Cornwall,* published in 1947, with illustrations by Sven Berlin, as part of a series called *Vision of England,* edited by Clough and Amabel Williams-Ellis. Pollard writes of its rare and diverse flora and the damage resulting from its continuing military use after the end of the war. She does not mention that she had purchased part of it for the National Trust. By then Ferguson's Gang had dispersed and Peggy Pollard's double life was over.

Rachel Pinney's career, meanwhile, lurched from crisis to crisis. She became a member of the Campaign for Nuclear Disarmament in 1961 and that year took part in the Direct Action Committee's walk from London to Holy Loch. As a result of her CND activities she was sent to prison in Staffordshire. On her release she opened a peace café in the Fulham Road. She also continued to work as a general practitioner until 1970, when her recklessness over the care of a patient brought her national notoriety. Concerned for the welfare of a fourteen-year-old boy, Matthew Collins, who had been deserted by his father and whose mother had suffered a severe nervous breakdown, Pinney arranged for a friend to take the child to Canada. When questioned by the police, she refused to say where he was. The Detective Chief Inspector who then arrested Pinney described her house as 'an abode of educated filth'. Her court appearance was widely reported in the press and she was duly sent to Holloway for abduction. On her release she became involved in the treatment of autism, publishing an influential book, *Bobby: Breakthrough of an Autistic Child,* in 1983. Long divorced, in 1989 she appeared in a television programme, *Women like Us,* in which she declared herself a lesbian. Rachel Pinney died in 1995, still committed to her belief that the purpose of her brave, chaotic life was to 'find something only I can do, and do it somewhat'.

The friendship between Clough and Peggy was an enduring one. To celebrate his 80th birthday in 1963 and the opening of the new piazza at Portmeirion, a masque was written in an Elizabethan style and in verse that must surely be by Peggy Pollard. In it Briaraeus the Octopus proclaims:

I'll seize this place, and level all its groves;
For me alone the thought of profit moves;
A supermarket and a bowling alley
Are fairer in my sight than any valley.

Hercules comes to the rescue, and after much absurdity the Octopus is slain. The piazza is duly opened to the sound of trumpets and the chanting of the chorus:

O potent CLOUGH! Our rustic lay
Shall celebrate this happy day.[9]

When Peggy visited Portmeirion in the 1970s, Clough ensured that bells rang out from the campanile on her arrival. Both lived well into their nineties. In 1971 Clough published his autobiography, *Architect Errant,* in which he divulged that Ferguson's Gang was Peggy Pollard's creation. After his suspicions about the true identity of Bill Stickers were aroused, 'Peggy

Epphaven Bay (left) and Lundy Beach (right) on the north Cornish coast: forty acres surrounding Epphaven Bay were bought for the National Trust by Peggy Pollard and Ernest Hedgman in 1937.

herself at last confessed and gave me leave to reveal, though I have become privy to other equally anonymous and beneficent ploys that are still under the seal of secrecy.'[10] Like its author, *England and the Octopus* also had a long life. A new edition appeared in 1975, the royalties of which Clough shared equally between the CPRE and the National Trust (another, facsimile edition was commissioned in 1996 by Fiona Reynolds, when she was director of the CPRE). Clough had resigned from the Trust's Committee for Wales in 1970, at the age of 88 and after 30 years of active involvement in its work. The preface to the 1975 edition again violates Ferguson's long-observed pact of secrecy, particularly on the part of Bill Stickers, who had previously insisted that 'I ave always preferred 2 be enonymous.' Clough referred to Peggy Pollard as 'the once leader of a notorious, yet beneficent secret society called "Ferguson's Gang"', and added that she 'could be counted on for witty topical comments… when I was fighting the menace of ribbon-building'.[11] He then included her poem, 'The Jerry-Builder':

The jerrybuilder lay dreaming
In his golden fourposter bed;
He dreamt of an endless ribbon
Of bungalows pink and red,
With fancy work on the gables
To every purchaser's choice:
And he dreamt in the back of his conscience,
He heard Old England's voice:

Don't build on the By-pass, Brother:
Give ear to our last appeal!
Don't advertise where it tries the eyes
And distracts the man at the wheel.
You've peppered the landscape brother
And blotted out half the sky:
Get further back with your loathsome shack,
Let the By-pass pass you by!

The jerrybuilder made answer:
'I'm English. I wants me rights.
Wot are the By-pass fields to me
But desirable building sites?
I've peppered the landscape proper,
But me pocket 'as to be filled.
If I wants to build on the By-pass,
I'm bloody well going to build!'

Don't build on the By-pass brother:
It won't suit anyone's book;
An endless street is nobody's treat,
With roofs wherever you look.
Before you smother the country
We only hope you'll die:
You ought to be hung with the ribbons you've strung…
Let the By-Pass pass you by!

They swung out a big new By-pass
When the first was a choke full street:
The glorious day isn't far away
When London and Liverpool meet,
And nothing remains of England
Where the country used to be
But roads run straight through a housing estate
And a single specimen tree.

Don't build on the By-pass Brother;
Allow us a breath of air:
We like to see an occasional tree,
More so as they're getting rare;
You're poisoning all the country
Like a dirty bluebottle fly:
Don't clutter the tracks with your loathsome shacks
Let the By-pass pass you by![12]

Writing to Peggy in July 1971, Clough said he was sending an advance copy of *Architect Errant*, even though it had numerous printer's errors, because:

> … you ought to have this imperfect one (which for that very reason will no doubt become exceedingly valuable!) ahead of other beneficiaries, as you strove so nobly to bash my shapeless heap of stuff into relatively readable shape.[13]

When in 1978 he published his autobiography, *Around the World in Ninety Years*, he dedicated it to 'Peggy Pollard. My most gallant comrade-in-arms in uncounted conservation battles, for her generous help in the shaping of this book.' By then she was living in a Cornish tin-miner's cottage, with an earth floor, no heating, and two large organs at either end of its main room. After Frank Pollard's death in 1968, and as they had no children, she gradually disposed of most of her possessions to support an order of black nuns in South Africa and other causes, usually anonymously. But she never completely turned her back on the modern world. When she thought Clough was inclined to neglect the needs of his fellow creatures by 'over-stressing the claims of landscape,' she wrote:

> Pomona loves the orchard,
> And Liber loves the vine,
> And Clough he loves an old façade
> And an unspoilt skyline.
> But the citizen wants gas-works
> Electric wires on high
> And light and drains and telephones
> God help me – So do I![14]

The final chapter of Peggy Pollard's *Cornwall* sums up some of her contradictions and idiosyncrasies. In her 'Vision for Cornwall' she briskly advocates the need for rural employment, for the proper care of woodland, for new building which respects the materials, scale and simplicity of a strong vernacular tradition. She then indulges her passion for goats, wishing that 'the moors may be overrun with herds of Toggenburgs'; and she concludes, 'let there be goats on the croft land of the cliffs, among the heather and the blue squills; lop-eared, languid-eyed Anglo-Nubians… and sturdy white Saanens.' Her agreement to write the book, in response to Clough's invitation, was on two conditions: that she could survey Cornwall 'as though through the eyes of a goat'; and that the author's fee should be paid to charity.[15]

THE EDITOR
AND THE STATESMAN

Christopher Hussey and Scotney Castle;
Philip, 11th Marquess of Lothian and Blickling Hall

WHEN IN 1922 *Country Life* reacted to the possible destruction of Stowe with such casual indifference, it was reflecting the prevailing attitude to Georgian architecture and to country houses. Both were anachronisms. In the 1920s its readers were assumed to be interested in medieval buildings, and particularly in Tudor and Jacobean manor houses, which were thought (usually wrongly) to be relatively untouched by what Ruskin called 'the foul tide of the Renaissance'. By the time Christopher Hussey joined the staff of *Country Life* in 1921, on graduating from Oxford, a shift towards a more scholarly and sympathetic approach to Georgian architecture was already being fostered by the magazine's principal writer on country houses, Avray Tipping. Hussey was a friend of Clough Williams-Ellis, and like Clough, the full extent of his influence on conservation and the National Trust has not been sufficiently acknowledged. Both were generous benefactors.

One of Hussey's closest friends at Eton was Ralph Dutton, who shared his interest in country houses and gardens. Dutton also wrote elegantly about architecture, not just in England but in France and other European countries. Sacheverell Sitwell was another Eton friend, with whom Hussey founded the Magnasco Society for the study of the Grand Tour and the collections of Italian pictures which resulted. Virtually all the members of this circle of friends were fluent writers who would influence and change public attitudes to the value of historic buildings.

In 1927, a year before the appearance of *England and the Octopus*, Hussey published a book which was a model of scholarship, and which marked a turning point in the study and appreciation of landscape history. *The Picturesque: Studies in a Point of View* explains how, in the late eighteenth century, writers, painters and patrons came to look at landscape in a different way, not just as a matter of utility, but as a branch of aesthetics. The shock of the moment when Hussey discovered this artistic turning point is described in the book's early pages:

> It happened in the library of a country house (Scotney Castle) built, in 1837, by my grandfather. Through the windows of that room you see, in a valley below, a castle, partly ruined, on an island in a lake.... I had often agreed that it formed a perfect picture, which has time and again been copied by my family, myself included, in watercolours, some of which are hung, with other examples of the family talent, on the staircase.[1]

The moment of revelation came when his eye fell on the library shelf which contained Sir Uvedale Price's *On the Picturesque*, of 1794, and *Essays on the Picturesque*. These books not only explained the aims of many of the architects and landscape designers of the eighteenth and early nineteenth centuries, including those who had shaped the gardens at Scotney, but also suggested to Hussey how contemporary buildings could be more sympathetically planned and enriched.

In the early 1930s, and under Hussey's influence, *Country Life* began to change its stance on the continuing dispersal of country house collections and the demolitions which frequently followed. Its editorials swung from resigned lamentation over the destruction of country houses to the championing of their preservation. The issue of 25 January 1930 marks the beginning of what was to be a measured but carefully researched, sustained and persuasive argument that the nation was, through its taxation policies, destroying a valuable part of its cultural and architectural history. The article deplored 'the dispersal abroad of well-nigh priceless collections,' and drew attention to the benefit that would be lost when the parks, woods and open spaces of country house demesnes, which had been open to the public for centuries, were given over to 'ugly building estates'. It was one thing to recognise that industry and agriculture were depressed; and quite another to conclude that in times of economic hardship there was no place for the preservation of beautiful countryside and buildings.

The depression of the early 1930s hit *Country Life*, as it did most areas of national life. In a draft letter of April 1930 in the archives at Scotney Castle and probably intended for the chairman of *Country Life*, Hussey refers to the magazine being ' in financial difficulties ' and

John Piper, *The Old Castle at Scotney*, 1976 (detail).

'run on a cheese-paring basis'. He reluctantly agreed to forego an increase in his salary and then, when he was still in his early thirties, accepted the joint position of architectural and general editor, partly to help the magazine through 'the bad times'. This put Hussey in a very dominant position at *Country Life* and he remained an 'Olympian figure who managed to create an unnerving silence around him'.[2] His aloofness was partly the consequence of a speech impediment, which caused misery at school and which encouraged him to communicate in other ways. From an early age he wrote with confidence, developing an easy prose style and producing poems and light verse. His drawings included caricatures and studies of architectural subjects. All his life he painted competent topographical watercolours of the houses he visited, partly to develop his visual memory and partly to provide a record for the family albums. Hussey was never the person to provide the public voice for a campaign – he and his wife Betty, who also had a stutter, used to tease each other when they had difficulty expressing themselves – but his administrative ability, his writing and his position at *Country Life* gave him influence and authority.[3]

Under the heading 'Large Ideas for Small Estates', the issue of *Country Life* published on 5 April 1930 included an article on the recent creation of Portmeirion, then less than five years old, but with most of its key features, including the citadel and the campanile, already fitting snugly into its precipitous valley, and with walls zig-zagging down to the estuary. Hussey, the author of the article, saw Portmeirion as an inspired rediscovery of the principles of picturesque design, and he was generous in his praise:

> A pastiche conglomeration such as the acropolis at Portmeirion might easily have been an architectural horror. Set down in words, the idea of dumping a bright Italian village on the Welsh coast is scarcely promising. It would probably not have occurred to anybody but Mr. Williams-Ellis, and, if it had, have produced a series of distressing discords. Actually it is a personal expression of Mr. Ellis's peculiar genius.[4]

The article suggested that 'the distressed landowner' would do well to look to Portmeirion for ways in which an estate might be revived by building new shops and cottages, and by providing accommodation 'for this increasingly roofless and mobile generation'. Hussey writes as admiringly of Clough's 'provocative little book', *England and the Octopus*, as he does of Portmeirion itself. Exactly what the two of them discussed when Hussey visited to prepare the article will probably never be known; and most of Clough's records and letters were destroyed in a fire in 1951. What is clear, however, is that Clough's suggestion that the editor of *Country Life* be asked 'to submit a draft list' of those houses worthy of preservation did not fall on deaf ears.

Hussey must have been putting the finishing touches to his Portmeirion piece at the time that he was embarking on a series of three articles on Blickling Hall in Norfolk. He visited the house when Philip Kerr, who had become 11th Marquess of Lothian in 1930, was grappling with the problem of what to do, not just with Blickling, but with four other houses. Kerr was also faced with death duties that could only be met by selling off parts of his inheritance.

As his biographer J.R.M. Butler wrote, Kerr 'had foreseen his approaching destiny with anything but enthusiasm'.[5] After Oxford, and a first-class degree in Modern History, he had worked in southern Africa as part of the group of talented young men brought together by Lord Milner to formulate plans for rebuilding after the Boer War. In 1916 he had become private secretary to the Prime Minister, Lloyd George, and in 1919 had drafted the preface to the Treaty of Versailles. He left Downing Street in 1921 to pursue a career in journalism and as secretary of the Rhodes Trust, which made him responsible for awarding grants to enable foreign students to study at Oxford. At the time he inherited the Lothian estates from his cousin, the 10th Marquess, he was well known and respected politically, with a wide circle of influential friends both in government and the press. He was an idealist, used to thinking independently and to having his views taken seriously at the highest levels.

Lord Lothian, with a cat called 'Crisis', shortly after his arrival as British Ambassador in Washington in 1939.

By upbringing and temperament Kerr was deeply religious, and in early life he was a devout Roman Catholic, as were his mother, who was the daughter of Henry, 14th Duke of Norfolk, and his father.[6] The loss of his Catholic faith was gradual and painful. In 1914, when he was seriously ill as the result of a burst appendix, Kerr was introduced to Christian Science by Nancy Astor, whose husband Waldorf had been a contemporary at New College. Nancy had already helped him to recover from a nervous breakdown – or what he called 'brain fag' – when he had stayed with the Astors at St Moritz the previous year.[7] She was to continue to be a profound influence in his life, personally, politically and through a shared interest in the work of the National Trust.

There had been an earlier crisis in Kerr's life. In 1911 he had been much in love with Lady Beatrice Cecil, daughter of the 4th Marquess of Salisbury.[8] The one family was staunchly Catholic, the other Anglican. In December of that year, Kerr wrote to Nancy Astor to tell her that the position he had found himself in was 'the most damnable thing on earth', and that it had been 'relieved only by the extraordinary kindness of my friends',[9] Kerr and 'Mima' Cecil, as she was known, agreed to a separation while he was abroad for six months, and on his return the relationship was not resumed. Both Kerr's faith and his affections were to influence his thinking about the future of Blickling; and consequently that of other country houses.

The irony of his position once he became the Marquess of Lothian in 1930 was that in principle he approved of death duties, which he realised would in time,

> … involve the complete destruction of the old territorial position. I think this is a good thing from the national point of view, provided the state will create an alternative system for supplying capital to agriculture.[10]

When Lloyd George wrote to congratulate him on his succession, he replied wryly that he found himself owing the Exchequer 'almost 40% of the capital value of a mainly agricultural estate,' and added:

In my capacity as an ordinary citizen I think highly of these arrangements, but as an inheritor of a title and estates thereto they will prove somewhat embarrassing.[11]

His solution was to find radical new uses for three of his houses and estates – Ferniehurst, Newbattle and Blickling – with the aim of allowing others to benefit from them.

Ferniehurst Castle stands above the River Jed in the Scottish borders, not far from Monteviot, which in 1930 was occupied by his aunt, the dowager Marchioness. Lothian proposed that she should continue to live there; while Ferniehurst was to be let to the Scottish Youth Hostels Association. Newbattle Abbey, in Midlothian, is a largely seventeenth-century house built out of the ruins of a twelfth-century Cistercian abbey, with an important collection of pictures (including a portrait of John Donne, acquired by the National Portrait Gallery in 2006). Lothian's solution for Newbattle was to let it to the universities of Scotland for use as an adult education college.

The house for which Lothian devised the most radical use was Blickling Hall. In 1930, when Christopher Hussey visited to prepare his articles for *Country Life*, Blickling was let to tenants, although Lothian had it in mind to use it for gatherings of his political friends, or 'moots,' as he called them. In the short term, and with considerable regret, he met some of the £300,000 he owed in death duties by selling, in New York, some of the most valuable books from its outstanding library, including the very rare Anglo-Saxon *Homilies* of 971, and

The Long Gallery at Blickling Hall in Norfolk.

167 other volumes. He was well aware that the next round of death duties was likely to lead to further depredations. As he was later to write:

> … heirs sell their securities or their books or their valuables before they break up their estates. But once sold these assets cannot be used a second time.[12]

These were exactly the issues which were exercising Hussey; and the Blickling estate encompassed most of what makes country houses culturally significant.

'The suddenness and completeness with which the scene bursts upon the eye strikes a simultaneous chord rather than a scale of impressions,' wrote Hussey of the first view visitors have of Blickling. Its yew hedges and Dutch gables flank the forecourt like guards of honour, protecting the bridge across the dry moat. The Jacobean towers and bays of warm red brick are in perfect symmetry, with a backdrop of ancient and ornamental trees. It is the house where Anne Boleyn was reputed to have spent her childhood. Blickling's treasures included the works of art collected by John, 2nd Earl of Buckinghamshire, when he was Ambassador to the Court of Catherine the Great at St Petersburg between 1762 and 1764. Blickling's twentieth-century role was to be no less significant than its romantic past.

The south front of Blickling Hall, acquired by the National Trust in 1942 under the will of Philip, 11th Marquess of Lothian.

The timing of Hussey's visit and Lothian's agonising over the sale of Blickling's finest books happened to coincide with changes in the National Trust. The Chairman, John Bailey, died in 1931 and was succeeded by the astute and politically adept Lawrence, 2nd Marquess of Zetland. The Secretary of the Trust, Samuel Hamer, retired in 1933 and Donald MacLeod Matheson was appointed. His sister, Hilda Matheson, had been Nancy Astor's political secretary and was now director of talks at the BBC. She knew Lothian well, as did Donald Matheson, who had participated in some of his 'moots'. A few years before, the National Trust – with its tiny membership of less than 3,000, its ailing Chairman and aged Secretary – could scarcely have responded positively and energetically to a new role as guardian of country houses at risk.

The Trust's early efforts to protect country houses had proved highly problematical. Kanturk Castle in County Cork had been acquired in 1900, but was now effectively 'out of bounds' in the Irish Republic. Barrington Court in Somerset had come close to bankrupting the Trust in the years after its acquisition in 1907; and the nearby Montacute House, transferred by the Society for the Protection of Ancient Buildings in 1931 and devoid of furniture, was proving a financial worry. With hindsight it appears that in the early 1930s there was a

moment when the National Trust had to decide whether or not to transform its role and so the whole organisation: it was facing 'a tide in the affairs of men, which taken at the flood leads on to fortune'. Instead of keeping to the relative safety of the shallows, Zetland and Matheson resolved to take the Trust out into the current of concern about the future of country houses, with Hussey and Lothian giving encouragement and practical support.

Anyone more interested in self-promotion than Hussey might have wanted to be perceived as the champion of the country house cause. That was neither in his character, nor with his speech-impediment was it something he was equipped for. Still less did he wish to be regarded as a proselytising aesthete, as James Lees-Milne was shortly to project himself. As well as being a scholar and writer, Hussey saw himself as a Kentish squire, devoted to public service and to his herd of Sussex cattle. His purchase in the 1950s of William Maw Egley's *Hallo Largess!* with its depiction of the idealised landowner and his family distributing gifts to his agricultural labourers, says much about Hussey's attitude to rural life.[13] He was also sufficiently shrewd and politically aware to realise that, coming from a landed family, he might appear self-interested, whereas anonymous editorials in *Country Life* could be read as the voice of enlightened and public concern. During the much publicised events of the coming months, others made the centre-stage speeches, with Hussey as *répétiteur* and Zetland as stage manager.

Zetland's reasons for letting others take on the role of advocate may have been similar to Hussey's: he appreciated that the National Trust was best seen as responding to external demands, rather than promoting itself. He may also have known that he was not the person to win over a national audience. Robert, 1st Lord Chorley, who observed him at work, described him as:

William Maw Egley, *Hallo, Largess! A Harvest Scene in Norfolk*, 1860, now hanging at Scotney Castle in Kent.

… a slightly dandified figure who looked rather as if he wore a corset; his voice was rather unattractive and his delivery somewhat pompous. Indeed, as a speaker he had little ability either to make his subject attractive or to hold the attention of his audience, all of which disadvantages were underlined by an irritating gesture he made by a jerking movement of the head repeated continually.[14]

As a committee chairman, however, Chorley thought him unsurpassed; and as Secretary of State for India between 1935 and 1940, he had the ear of the Cabinet. There was also common ground with Lothian, who had served as Under-Secretary of State for India between 1931 and 1932, and who entertained Jawaharlal Nehru at Blickling in 1938. The India Office was shared territory and most of Zetland's correspondence about the Country Houses Scheme was on India Office notepaper.

It must have been with Zetland's encouragement that the director of the Courtauld Institute, Professor W.G. Constable, spoke at a National Trust dinner in 1933 on the need for preferential taxation to protect the finest country houses. The following year, on 19 July, the Trust's Annual General Meeting was held in the Inner Temple, at which Lothian gave an address under the title, 'England's Country Houses: the case for their preservation'. Unlike Zetland and Hussey, Lothian was a compelling public speaker. The speeches he made when he was Ambassador in Washington were recorded, and his naturally attractive voice still comes over as unpompous, avoiding political oratory, and with touches of informality and humour that won over audiences on both sides of the Atlantic. At the time of the Trust's meeting in 1934, he was 52, physically attractive, with an athletic build – he played tennis well and had a golf handicap of plus two – and swept-back hair which became unruly when, in moments of concentration or exasperation, he ran his fingers through it.

Lothian told the National Trust's audience that country houses were 'under sentence of death, and the axe that is destroying them is taxation'. They were reminded of the steady rise in death duties since their introduction by Sir William Harcourt in 1894:

> Under the Finance Act of 1904 the maximum rate of Estate Duty was 8 per cent; after the Budget of 1909 up to 1914 the maximum rate was 15 per cent, from 1919 to 1930 the maximum rate was 40 per cent, and from 1930 to the present day the maximum rate has been 50 per cent... death duties and surtax as a form of taxation have come to stay. There is indeed much to be said for them as an instrument of social justice, though far more careful study should be made of their practical effect.

He challenged the Trust to assess the scale of the problem and propose solutions. 'So far as I know,' he said, 'the only accurate and detailed body of knowledge on this subject is that in the possession of *Country Life*.' Without actually naming Hussey, he went on:

> The proprietors of that journal have been kind enough to prepare for me a list of the country houses which in their expert opinion are of real historic interest and artistic merit. It is an extremely interesting list, a copy of which I shall be very glad to hand to the officers of the Trust.

At Lothian's request, the list had been divided into 'big' houses, such as Blenheim Palace, Castle Howard, Haddon Hall, Hatfield and Knole, and smaller houses.

> According to *Country Life*, therefore, and I know of no better judges, there is in this country an unique treasure of about 60 large and 600 smaller dwelling houses of real historic interest.... It is surely not an unmanageable proposition to set to work to preserve them.

He then came to what he called 'practical steps'. Some of his proposals, such as allowing for the establishment of tax-free maintenance funds for privately owned historic houses, were eventually enacted. Lothian noted the absurdity of having legislation to preserve ancient monuments by scheduling, but not extending this protection to buildings which are lived in: 'The Commission [on Ancient and Historical Monuments]... is allowed to interest itself in houses only when they have become ruins.' There were, he suggested, responsibilities that needed to be met in new and imaginative ways:

> I believe that if a body like the National Trust were willing to equip itself to become a landlord on an ampler scale, it would gradually draw into its orbit quite a large number of historic furnished houses. ... At any rate, I venture to put the suggestion before you for your consideration, as one of the steps which might be taken to preserve for posterity in living form a national treasure of beauty and inspiration which is quite unique in the modern world.[15]

With that prophetic idea of the Trust as the guardian of many of the nation's finest country house estates, he concluded.

At the time Lothian spoke at the Trust's Annual General Meeting, he was in something of a political and personal wilderness, partly on account of his relationship with the Astors. He was associated with what Claud Cockburn, writing for *The Week* (and later to contribute to *Private Eye*), called 'the Cliveden set', after the Astors' country house overlooking the Thames in Buckinghamshire, and which was associated with efforts to appease rather than confront Hitler and Nazi Germany. In reality, as Norman Rose has demonstrated, the idea of a conspiratorial 'set' was largely a myth created by Cockburn and sections of the press.[16] Lothian did, however, have a wide circle of German friends, many of whom were former Rhodes scholars, including Adam von Trott, who was to be executed for his part in the plot to assassinate Hitler in 1944.

The emotional hold that Nancy Astor had over Lothian can be explained partly by the kindness he received from her and Waldorf when, as a young man, he was recovering from his nervous breakdown. It was further strengthened by Lothian's emotional and practical support of Nancy when the son of her first marriage, Bobby Shaw, was forced to resign his commission in the Royal Horse Guards and, in July 1931, was sentenced to four months imprisonment for homosexual soliciting. A few days later, the Astors left London with Lothian and George Bernard Shaw for a visit to Russia and an interview with Stalin.

Michael Astor wrote of their relationship that: 'There was an affinity between Philip and my mother: love on his side, and something deeper than friendship and less passionate than love on hers.'[17] Somerset de Chair, a Norfolk MP who became a tenant of Blickling after Lothian's death, believed that the relationship was more than platonic:

> In Lord Lothian's time and mine there was a pair of twin beds in the Chinese Room, and Mrs Skinner, who was an under-housemaid then, always had to tie the legs of the twin beds together when Lady Astor visited Lord Lothian. Mrs Skinner slept in a bedroom in the attic above the Chinese Room, and on one occasion heard a frightful rumpus going on below. She went down to see if she could help, and found Lord Lothian and Lady Astor chasing a bat out of the room.[18]

The conclusion that de Chair intended should be drawn from Mrs Skinner's anecdote is clear enough, but is not necessarily the correct one. He may have found the aura of sanctity that surrounded Lothian's reputation irksome, and his own colourful private life would not have inclined him to give Lothian the benefit of any doubt. Michael Astor's verdict seems more plausible.

In spite of Lothian's despondency at the deteriorating political situation, he kept in constant touch with the National Trust's Chairman over the progress of the Country Houses Scheme and the National Trust Act of 1937. This legislation laid the foundations for the Trust's rapid post-war expansion. It enabled the charity to hold land and investments, free of tax, as endowments for country houses. In future, whole estates could be given to the Trust without incurring tax liabilities. Lothian also advised the Trust's Chairman and Secretary on the terms for future occupation of houses, once they had passed to the organisation. Writing to Matheson, he explained: 'We ought not to give the owners something that they can in fact make a profit on or give them the right for very unsuitable heirs to live in the house… This needs careful thought.'

What Lothian foresaw was the extension of country house visiting from a socially exclusive activity to a form of cultural enrichment that should be available to everyone. 'The core of the whole system is the tourist industry,' he continued; and then prophesied:

> I see no reason why, once prejudice against intrusion into privacy is broken down in this country, a very considerable income should not be made available to the owners of ancient houses… I should imagine that a good many thousand people every year, both foreign and British, would spend part of the summer holidays in visiting houses as they now do in visiting cathedrals and natural beauty spots.[19]

He was looking ahead to a post-war world that he helped to shape; but which he was not to experience. During the relatively brief period that he was responsible for Blickling he encouraged concerts in the Long Gallery, Vaughan Williams lectured there, and in August 1938 *The Masque of Anne Boleyn* – involving scores of local children and attended by Queen Mary – was staged in the forecourt.

That same year Lothian was appointed British ambassador in Washington. During the next two years he subjected himself to a punishing schedule of lecturing across America on the dangers posed to its own interests by a Europe dominated by Nazi Germany. He was, in Churchill's words, 'a deeply-stirred man', whose empathy with Americans played a decisive part in bringing them into the war against Hitler.

At the time that Lothian was ambassador in Washington, his old friend John Buchan, the novelist, was serving as Governor-General in Canada (he had been made Lord Tweedsmuir on his appointment in 1934, against his own better judgement, but at the insistence of the King). Buchan had, as a trustee of the Pilgrim Trust (a charity established in 1930 by the American railway tycoon, Edward Harkness), directed substantial donations to the National Trust. He and Lothian shared common interests and ideals. In October 1939 Buchan had a secret meeting with Lothian in Washington, to discuss American and Canadian reactions to the war in Europe, then in a disastrous phase. Within four months Buchan was dead. Among Lothian's papers there is the tribute that he wrote immediately he received the news, and which describes Buchan as 'the last of the romantics', who was 'passionately attached to the Scottish Borders and its peoples'. He attributed the immense success of Buchan's stories to the way they 'glowed with chivalry… in an age which has almost forgotten what chivalry means'. Lothian concluded:

> But of one thing I am sure, like so many of the characters in his novels, he was glad that he died gallantly in harness, serving Canada, Scotland, and the British Commonwealth to the end.[20]

The tribute could serve as Lothian's own obituary. He died just a few months later, in December 1940, of uraemic poisoning, probably brought on by overwork. The illness was, at the time, untreatable; but as a Christian Scientist, he would anyway have refused conventional medical help. The *New York Times* referred to 'Lothian's earnestness and ability, the confidences he won and the energy he expended tirelessly'.[21] In the House of Commons, two Prime Ministers paid him tribute. Lloyd George referred to his understanding of the American people and his ability to 'talk to them in a language which no other man of British birth could dare'. Churchill described him as 'a man of the very highest character and of far-ranging intellectual scope'.[22] Those visionary qualities were going to transform the National Trust.

The Blickling estate comprised 4,767 acres of Norfolk countryside and over a hundred houses and cottages. Under Lothian's will these came to the Trust as part of the endowment to support the Jacobean hall and its collections, and did so free of tax under the provisions of the National Trust Act of 1937, which he had done so much to draft and promote. The Trust now had the opportunity to bring to reality his idea that great houses should not become 'melancholy museums', but should set 'a standard of beauty, in garden and furniture and decoration, by which later generations can mould their own practice'.[23]

Was this gift simply a matter of Lothian demonstrating by example what he hoped for the future of great houses and the National Trust? The codicil to his will, in which he specified that Blickling should be 'a place from which public or intellectual or artistic practices go forth,' makes clear that it was. But the gift was not as entirely straightforward as that. In the codicil Lothian stipulated that his successor-in-title and honours should be offered the right to live at Blickling, provided he was 'actively interested in public and artistic activities.' In the event of his not being able or wanting to do so, the right of occupation was to be offered to:

> … whichever of the three sons of William Waldorf and Nancy, 2nd Viscount and
> Viscountess Astor,… is in the opinion of the Directors of the National Trust, after
> consultation with their parents, if alive, most likely to use the house wisely….

Neither the 12th Marquess of Lothian nor the Astors chose to take up these opportunities. The provision does, however, imply that Lothian involved the Astors in his plans for Blickling, and the outcome effectively disinherited his Catholic cousins. His decision, consciously or not, may have been influenced by Nancy Astor's anti-Catholic bigotry. She referred to 'Roman candles', forbade her butler Edwin Lee to employ Catholics, and when – as can happen with intolerant parents – her son Jake married an Argentinian Catholic, she refused to attend the wedding.[24]

Lothian's gift of Blickling to the National Trust prevented the gradual dispersal of its collections and the sale of land to meet death duties on the estate, which, if it had continued in private hands, would have been at 50% of its valuation for probate. The arrangements he made for Blickling, Ferniehurst and Newbattle meant that his cousin Peter Kerr, 12th Marquess of Lothian, succeeded to a greatly diminished inheritance, and a correspondingly reduced tax liability. His response was extraordinarily generous. When given the opportunity to take any personal belongings from Blickling, he chose only some engraved wine glasses and a bag of golf clubs. In 1990 he returned to Norfolk for a party to mark the 50th anniversary of the gift of Blickling to the National Trust, and shortly afterwards presented a portrait of Philip Lothian, which he felt should hang in the house, and his visitors' book.

Christopher Hussey served on the Trust's sub-committee charged with following up the proposals put forward by Lothian, and then on most of the committees which dealt with protecting and repairing historic buildings. When he died in 1970, Scotney Castle Garden in Kent passed as a gift to the National Trust. His friend Ralph Dutton, the 8th and last Lord Sherborne, left his house and garden at Hinton Ampner in Hampshire to the Trust in 1986.

The fourteenth-century ruin of the old Scotney Castle in Kent, with the nineteenth-century house designed by Salvin beyond it.

Hussey's wife Betty outlived him by 36 years, during which time the garden at Scotney benefitted from her exceptional knowledge as a plantswoman and her determination to continue her husband's stewardship. She ensured that the Castle went on being an inspiration to visitors, as it had been to their friends, the artists Reynolds Stone and John Piper. Following her death in 2006, the New House at Scotney, designed by Anthony Salvin in the 1830s, was opened to the public by the National Trust.

Hussey and Lothian deserve to be remembered for much more than their gifts to the Trust. Thanks to their work, the owners of many country houses took advantage of the provisions of the National Trust Act of 1937. The Act also made it possible to give furniture, pictures and other chattels, free of tax, to the National Trust, provided they were of 'national or historic or artistic interest', and confirmed that this was for 'the access to and enjoyment of such buildings, places and chattels by the public'. In the 1950s and 1960s only a trickle of visitors – largely members of the Trust – came to see them. But with increased mobility and prosperity, country house visiting became fashionable and popular, as Lothian had predicted. The increase in National Trust membership from 23,000 in 1950 to over three million 50 years later was largely a consequence of the recruiting of members at its country houses. The setting-up of shops and tearooms proved no less successful, and led to the rapid growth of National Trust Enterprises. Countryside properties and gardens would play their part in the development of the Trust's educational activities; but an initiative such as the Young National Trust Theatre was almost entirely country-house based. The growth of the Trust to the point which it now holds in our national life is inconceivable without the acquisitions made possible by the National Trust Act of 1937. At just the moment when it looked as though the lights of a civilised Europe might be snuffed out, Clough Williams-Ellis, Christopher Hussey and Philip Lothian together lit what was to become a chain of beacons.

4

THE DIARIST

James Lees-Milne and The Country Houses Scheme

I N T H E T W E L F T H A N D C O N C L U D I N G volume of his diaries, *The Milk of Paradise*, James Lees-Milne records one of his final services to the National Trust.[1] He had decided, in 1996, to move out of the room in Bath that had once been William Beckford's library. For 22 years it was where Lees-Milne had done most of his writing, involving a journey from his home at Badminton to a place where he could work relatively undisturbed. The image that he presented of himself in the diaries, of a dandified aesthete and society gossip, was also, in his writing, a creature of formidable self-discipline.[2]

The process of packing up his library is described with admirable cheerfulness. Relatives came to take away 'unreadable books relevant to the family'. He appreciated the way John Saumarez Smith quickly made up his mind over what was worth selling in the bookshop he managed, Heywood Hill. Tony Mitchell, formerly the National Trust's Historic Buildings Representative in its Wessex region, came over to help with the removal of furniture. To Lees-Milne's astonishment, the books raised £15,000, most of which he donated to the National Trust, to be used to re-establish libraries in its country houses. His gift was spent on the long-dismantled library at Gunby Hall in Lincolnshire.

The choice of Gunby, by the Trust's Director-General, Martin Drury, was inspired. In March 1943 the owners of this unpretentious early-eighteenth-century house, Field Marshal Sir Archibald and Lady Montgomery-Massingberd, had turned to the National Trust for help in resisting an Air Ministry proposal to build an aerodrome next to the park. There were rumours that the house itself might have to be demolished. The field marshal's letter found its way to Lees-Milne, recently released from the army on health grounds and back in post as the National Trust's Country Houses Secretary, who pointed out as tactfully as he could that the Trust could only be involved if the property was a prospective gift or already in its ownership. The immediate response was that Gunby should be given to the National Trust right away. Lees-Milne lost no time in making his first visit, and the transfer was arranged quickly and with a minimum of fuss. There could be no better example of the way Lees-Milne was able to win the confidence of potential benefactors and reassure them that a gift to the National Trust was the safest way of protecting their inheritance.

The transfer of the contents of Gunby was similarly speedy and trouble-free; indeed the only difficulty was that the field marshal wanted to give minor pictures that he himself had

collected, but which the Trust felt were not integral to its history. Lees-Milne's efficiency, his youthful enthusiasm (he was still in his early thirties) and his empathy with the house and its donors were exactly what was needed to reassure the Montgomery-Massingberds and others like them. The accounts in his diaries of visits to Attingham Park, Charlecote Park, Hanbury Hall, Stourhead and other houses destined to come to the Trust, and the portraits of their donors in his book, *People and Places*, written half a century later, have established the author as the brilliant and heroic promulgator of the National Trust's Country Houses Scheme.

As Lees-Milne himself noted, it was not that he had made extravagant claims for credit. 'I was only a servant of the committee, that's all,'[3] he told a visiting journalist, and on another occasion wrote:

> … it is perhaps true that my having written so much about the National Trust and its efforts to save historic buildings may have drawn undue attention to the small part I played in the process.[4]

He was aware that, as Churchill observed, history is often kind to those who write it.[5] His diffidence fed the adulation of growing numbers of youthful admirers who came to visit him. In Hugh Massingberd's *Daydream Believer: Confessions of a Hero Worshipper*, published in 2001, the chapter on Lees-Milne is entitled 'Saint Jim'.

The admiration is not universal. Two historians who had consulted the Trust's records regarded Lees-Milne differently. David Cannadine's *In Churchill's Shadow* (2002) refers to him as 'a Catholic reactionary', who saw the purpose of the National Trust as safeguarding 'country houses and their occupants against the levelling social tendencies of the time' – a view that Lees-Milne himself might have endorsed. Peter Mandler, in *The Fall and Rise of the Stately Home* (1997), slipped into a footnote a reference to Lees-Milne's 'genius for retrospective self-fashioning'. They had failed to get on when Mandler interviewed him. The criticisms are not groundless. Mandler had found that after Lees-Milne left the National Trust's full-time employment he saw himself as a champion of country house owners against the Government and even the Trust.

Private Eye and its writer on architectural matters, Gavin Stamp, regarded Lees-Milne as a legitimate target. In his lifetime the magazine branded him 'the arch-snob and bore of all time', and after his death, in December 1997, *Private Eye* published its own attempt at 'James Lees-Milne's Heavenly Diary':

> Pass away and go to heaven, much over-rated but not without its modicum of somewhat fanciful charm. The golden gates, written up in such hushed tones by the guide-books, prove a tremendous disappointment.... At last I find myself with an *entrée* to God the Father. His house may indeed have many mansions, but to my eye every one of them is fearfully déclassé. I fear it would have been rather more accurate for the scribe in question to have declared that His villa had many chalets.[6]

Lees-Milne's many admirers may find the caricature less amusing than some of the self-deprecating things he wrote about himself in his diaries, which, even at their most provocative, are seldom boring. He could be malicious and unfair about other people, but relished the opportunity to reflect on some of his own weaknesses and least attractive characteristics. What is not always conveyed is his kindness, particularly to young people. I think he knew that his politics and mine were miles apart, but his encouragement and praise went far beyond what I expected or deserved.

The appointment in 1936 of Lees-Milne to the post of Country Houses Secretary was a stroke of luck for him and for the National Trust. His qualifications were unimpressive, and he only learnt of the job because his friend Vita Sackville-West heard about it from Hilda Matheson, sister of the Trust's Secretary, and suggested he should apply. He arrived at the moment that the Chairman, Lord Zetland, and Lothian were in difficult and detailed discussions with the Government over whether there should be tax provisions to help a loose association of private country house owners (it came to be called Scheme 2), or whether tax benefits should apply only to property given to the National Trust (referred to as Scheme 1 and eventually adopted through the National Trust Act of 1937). The correspondence between Zetland and the Treasury, with Lothian giving careful and detailed advice, shows how effectively the Trust argued its case. The image of a highly professional organisation, steering Government towards new legislation, was, however, misleading.

The Chairman of the Country Houses Committee was the clever, witty and irreverent

[opposite left]
Sir Oswald Birley, *Field Marshal Sir Archibald Montgomery-Massingberd*, 1945, who with his wife gave Gunby Hall in Lincolnshire to the National Trust in 1944, thereby saving the early-eighteenth-century house and its park from an Air Ministry proposal to build an aerodrome on the site.

[opposite right]
Richard Ziegler, *Lady Montgomery-Massingberd*, 1943, who inherited Gunby Hall and the Massingberd estates through her mother's family in 1926.

Oliver, 3rd Viscount Esher. Under his influence the National Trust changed from being the austere, predominantly countryside organisation that Bailey and the historian G.M. Trevelyan had shaped, into one preoccupied with, and burdened by, country houses. The aesthetes, particularly Lees-Milne and his friends, were in the ascendant.

In 1936 the organisation of the National Trust was largely amateur, not remotely bureaucratic, and not always efficient. Lord Esher recalled that, when attending a meeting of the Trust's Finance Committee, he took the seat of a former Chairman and came across a note in the drawer of the table. It had been placed there for inspection before meetings, and read:

> Try to remember that the figures on the left-hand of the page (the page next to the window) represent the assets of the Trust and those on the opposite side the liabilities.[7]

Of the handful of staff, the most important was the Secretary, Donald MacLeod Matheson, whose letters and committee minutes were admirably succinct, but whose attention to detail and worries about his health seem to have confined him largely to London. Christopher Gibbs, who had joined the Trust in 1935, was an energetic and effective Assistant Secretary, then Deputy Chief Agent, and finally a revered Chief Agent. In the 1960s he lived near my childhood home in Surrey, and his daughters were friends of my sister. When I was considering working for the Trust in the late '60s, he kindly agreed to see me. Standing with his back to the fire, eyes twinkling, puffing meditatively on his pipe, and in the tweedy uniform of a traditional Land Agent, he gave exactly the advice I needed: 'Visit lots of Trust properties and make sure that if you are asked at interview which are your favourites, don't say "Longleat".' Gibbs, more than anyone else, gave impetus to the idea – also promoted by G.M. Trevelyan – of the Trust pursuing a campaign to protect the coastline, eventually to be christened Enterprise Neptune. He was benevolent, persistent and a shrewd negotiator, but was not good at writing reports for committees, and was therefore sometimes underestimated. During the war he served as a gunner, which may explain his habit of shouting down the telephone. When discussions on the possible gift of Stourhead to the Trust began in 1936, it was Christopher Gibbs who made the initial contact and then reported back enthusiastically.

Lees-Milne brought to the Trust knowledge and a passion for all the arts, enthusing one moment about a monument in a parish church or a contemporary painting, and the next over the decoration of a great house or a recently written poem or piece of music. He was 28 when first appointed, good-looking but without machismo, an engaging conversationalist, and with literary gifts which he continued to hone throughout his long life. With these attributes he was well equipped to develop a philosophy for looking after country houses that we now tend to take for granted but which, in the 1940s and '50s, involved breaking new ground. He valued historic houses not just as monuments of art or architecture, but as the expression of family, local and national history. Like all good historians he had a real engagement with the past, could empathise with the long-dead in a personal way, and wanted to share that empathy with others. There was, in his response to the people and places he found congenial, a warmth and a feeling for individuality that persisted. Some of his dislikes and prejudices were no less enduring.

One of the first tasks that Lees-Milne was given was to consult the owners of distinguished country houses on whether they would consider handing over their property to the

Trust, so avoiding death duties, in return for a continuing right to live there – the Scheme 1 formulated by Zetland and Lothian – or whether they would prefer to form some sort of association of private owners with a view to securing tax concessions – Scheme 2 – which might or might not involve a co-ordinating role for the Trust.

In what he later referred to as 'the most enjoyable summer of my existence', Lees-Milne embarked in 1936 on a succession of visits to country house owners who had enquired about the scheme. He experienced some outright hostility, some guarded interest in Scheme 1, and virtually none at all in Scheme 2. In January 1937 the Country Houses Committee, chaired by Lord Esher, decided to drop the second scheme altogether. Already the possibility of another World War was looming over what must have seemed a relatively unimportant concern, and there were no meetings of the Committee between July 1936 and March 1941. Lees-Milne joined the Army in 1939. By that date he had done no more than establish useful contacts with a handful of sympathetic owners.

It was only on being invalided out of the Army in 1941 that Lees-Milne was able to help carry forward the scheme that had been so painstakingly formulated before the War. Blickling Hall passed to the Trust in 1940. Dinton Park, Gunby Hall, Hatchlands, Lacock Abbey, Packwood House, Speke Hall and West Wycombe Park all came during the war years, and in most cases Lees-Milne's contribution was important and sometimes crucial. Outstanding urban houses came just after the war, including Osterley Park, in south-west London, which was given by Lord Jersey in 1949 and, because there was insufficient endowment, was leased to the Ministry of Works. A measure of Lees-Milne's success is that these and other great houses adapted relatively smoothly to their new role in the ten years that he was Secretary to what, in 1945, had been renamed the Historic Buildings Committee. He retired from the post in 1951, but continued to work part-time as an adviser until 1966.

The Staircase at West Wycombe Park, Buckinghamshire; the house was given to the National Trust with an endowment by Sir John Dashwood, 10th Bt. in 1943.

One of the intentions of the Country Houses Scheme was that, whenever possible, donor families should continue to live in their ancestral homes. In some cases there were no direct descendants to occupy a house; and then the donor might specify, in a memorandum of wishes, another relative or friend of the family who might be given that option. To Lees-Milne in particular this right of continuing occupation was the key to retaining the vitality of the houses transferred through the scheme, and would prevent them becoming lifeless museums. By remaining family homes, the National Trust was not allowing itself to become the agent of the state in what might otherwise be a socialist takeover. He expressed his views very plainly in *People and Places*, writing:

The Etruscan Dressing Room at Osterley Park, Middlesex. The original Elizabethan house was remodelled in 1760–80 by Robert Adam, and given to the National Trust by George, 9th Earl of Jersey in 1949.

My loyalties were to the houses, the families and the National Trust (which I regarded as the instrument of the others' preservation) in that order; and received criticism from a younger generation for so doing.[8]

The statement that the Trust was an instrument for the preservation of houses and their owners still causes unease. It might seem to imply that gifts of property to the Trust were motivated by expediency and self-interest. In reality there is abundant evidence to show that many owners of country houses made considerable personal sacrifices when giving their homes to the Trust, which they believed to be a reliable guardian of places that could be enriching for everyone. These ideals had been articulated by the Trust's founders, and reaffirmed for a later generation by benefactors like G.M. Trevelyan – who gave land in the Lake District to the Trust – and Lord Lothian. Some of the things Lees-Milne wrote can be misleading about his own idealism and the attributes he brought to his role.

Lees-Milne believed that the finest, and indeed many less-distinguished country houses, were 'our most precious shrines, just as the cathedrals were their sacred counterparts'. He believed this passionately and expressed it, in writing and in conversation, with touching eloquence. As John Cornforth remarked in the 1970s when he was Architectural Editor of *Country Life*, 'there is nothing quite like visiting a country house with Jim.' He never lost the ability to win round a committee, to convince a potential benefactor, or to write a compelling letter to *The Times*.

Harold Nicolson and his wife, Vita Sackville-West, at Sissinghurst Castle, Kent, in 1932. The remains of this Elizabethan moated house, and the famous garden they created, were transferred to the National Trust in lieu of tax in 1967, with their son Nigel Nicolson providing an endowment.

By the standards of the time he was also an established and admired architectural historian. Books such as *Roman Mornings* (1956) and *Earls of Creation* (1962) are still highly readable, if overtaken by later scholarship. The breadth of his architectural interests was always remarkable, and by no means confined to the Baroque and Georgian houses which particularly delighted him. When he visited country house owners who were considering a gift to the Trust, they would be left in no doubt that what was precious to them was appreciated in a way that was genuine and scholarly. He was also the most engaging companion. As Harold Nicolson, one of his enthusiastic admirers, wrote to his wife Vita in 1934:

Jim is such a charming person. He has a passion for poetry and knows masses about it. I like my friends to be well-read and well-bred. Jim is such an aristocrat in mind and culture. You would like him enormously.[9]

Indeed she did. Many years later Nigel Nicolson chose Lees-Milne to write his father's biography, which, when published in 1981, won the Heinemann Award.

Charm can be a lethal attribute, but in Lees-Milne it was combined with a capacity for sustained hard work, a tidy mind and considerable organising skill. If the Country Houses Scheme was a success, it owed a good deal to Lees-Milne's capacity for friendship, and at least as much to straightforward administrative ability. Most donors of properties both liked him and had confidence that he would spare no effort to solve their problems.

In spite of all his achievements and attractive qualities, there was a long period when his reputation within the National Trust was not what it had been when he was working in partnership with Lord Esher, or would become when his canonisation was complete. Both Esher and Lees-Milne enjoyed jokes at the expense of the Trust's committee members and staff, particularly the Land Agents, who were labelled 'mangle-wurzels'. Resentments were stored up. They were exacerbated by what today would be regarded as unacceptable prejudice – his and other people's.

Lees-Milne's circle of friends included those who made no secret of their sexuality, whether homosexual or bisexual. Many were discreet. Harold Nicolson, for example, believed that his homosexual adventures were safe – though a criminal offence – because they were conducted with men of his own class: 'the idea of a gentleman of birth and education sleeping with a guardsman is repugnant to me'. He found this confidence was misplaced when he contracted venereal disease, probably from a male fellow-guest during a stay at Knebworth in 1917, causing much distress to himself and his wife, Vita Sackville-West, and nearly ending their marriage.[10] Years later, in 1957, his wife was to make another disturbing discovery, when she found that her passionate letters to Alvilde Lees-Milne (who had married Jim in 1951) were being tampered with, and she feared blackmail.

Other friends were less constrained. Guy Burgess, remembered as a Soviet spy, and the writer James Pope-Hennessy were certainly reckless in their liaisons, which included gentlemen, guardsmen and a Stalinist Pole. Noel Coward – the subject of a biography Pope-Hennessy was working on when he was murdered in 1974 – particularly enjoyed a story which summed up the often confusing bisexuality of the group. Waking in Pope-Hennessy's bed, his female companion was disconcerted to be asked drowsily, 'Do you want to borrow my razor, or would you rather shave when you get back to the barracks?'[11]

That Lees-Milne had these associations mattered not at all to many in the National Trust. Michael Trinick, initially a Land Agent in Cornwall and then Regional Secretary, always believed that diversity of sexual orientation 'has long played an important part in the work of the National Trust, much to its advantage'. He enjoyed hearing Lees-Milne ('at that time unmarried and – so we thought – never likely to be') and his companions refer to a statue of Neptune, acquired for the upper garden at Cotehele, as having 'delicious and positively callipygian buttocks'.[12]

Others were worried that the National Trust's reputation might be damaged in the eyes of supporters with a more rigid moral outlook. The Chairman, Lord Crawford, was a man of the utmost propriety, who saw the protection of the Trust's reputation as one of his responsibilies. He was genuinely shocked to find, while staying in the same hotel in Paris, that Lees-Milne and a young man on the Trust's historic buildings' staff were sharing a bedroom. 'Ah, doubling up, I see,' he remarked.

Lees-Milne's retirement from full-time work for the Trust in 1951 was greeted with regret in some quarters and relief in others. His published diaries throw little light on exactly what happened. The fourth volume ends in 1949 and the fifth resumes in 1953, with a note in the preface to say that 'a lot I destroyed one day in revulsion'. Both volumes were published after a considerable gap, during which Lees-Milne had been working on other books. The preface to *A Mingled Measure*, the fifth volume, gives a simple explanation for his decision to become a part-time adviser to the Trust. After their marriage in 1951, Alvilde decided to retain her French passport for tax reasons, and lived at Roquebrune in the Alpes Maritimes. Jim would divide his time between France and England, with the result that his position in the National Trust was semi-detached. He was left out of touch and sympathy with changes happening within the organisation.

His voice was heard during the furore of 1966 caused by Commander Conrad Rawnsley's criticisms of the Trust's Chairman and Council, which caused considerable acrimony and led to an Extraordinary General Meeting of members in the Central Hall at Westminster in February 1967. Lees-Milne's letters to *The Times* were forceful, elegant and persuasive. He was no less eloquent when responding to a long article by Roger Scruton in *The Times* of 21 February 1984, entitled 'Out with the Stately, Enter the State', which asserted that the National Trust was the agent of a philistine government and that its 'dead hand' left its houses 'eternally fossilised'. In reply Lees-Milne reminded readers that the alternative to ownership by the Trust was all too often decay or demolition; and for this he received letters of thanks from the Chairman and Director-General. But in private, to friends such as Eardley

Knollys, he was highly critical, writing in 1958 of 'that love-hate for the N.T. which in my case is now more hate than love'.[13]

When *Another Self* appeared in 1970, it produced the mixed reaction which was increasingly to greet Lees-Milne's books. It is a beautifully written memoir, part fact and part fantasy, modelled on Harold Nicolson's widely admired *Some People* of 1927, in which easily recognised friends and acquaintances were given semi-fictional treatment, and which caused considerable offence. The genre allowed Lees-Milne to present his father, with whom he had always had a troubled relationship, as part ogre, part philandering philistine. He was in fact a knowledgeable gardener who loved the vernacular buildings of the Cotswolds; but Lees-Milne gives no hint of that, nor that his father took him as a boy to see Little Moreton Hall in Cheshire, which he steadfastly refused to admire. He chose not to mention that far from coming from a long line of Cotswold squires, his father's money came from the cotton industry. The political views expounded in *Another Self* included the regret that the author had not fought in the Spanish Civil War on the side of Franco, 'who was engaged in a life-and-death struggle with the forces of world disruption and anarchy'. *Another Self* proved to be Lees-Milne's most successful and widely praised book to date. There were some readers, however, who found its politics unsympathetic and its self-deprecating humour a bit too contrived.

Like Harold Nicolson, Lees-Milne always aspired to write novels. Right at the end of his life he had struggled to find a publisher for a ghost story, *Ruthenshaw*, which failed completely. The book which followed *Another Self* prompted a reviewer in *The Times Literary Supplement* to write that Lees-Milne had 'written (or rather overwritten) a quite ghastly novel called *Heretics in Love*, combining that subject with snobbery and with some of the pet hates that

The inner courtyard at Little Moreton Hall, Cheshire, given to the National Trust in 1938 by Bishop C.W.R. Abraham and his son, Rupert Abraham.

made Nancy Mitford dub him "Old Grumpikins".'[14] For his next book, he reverted to non-fiction, or rather partial fiction. The first volume of his diaries, *Ancestral Voices*, was published in 1975, ostensibly to 'record some past encounters with the owners and donors of historic houses during the course of my work with the National Trust'. The introduction makes clear that this was its overriding aim. The later volumes were deliberately much wider in scope and were intended to provide a portrait of an age.

Ancestral Voices caused considerable upset, inside and outside the Trust. Lees-Milne had been a senior member of staff, who had visited country house owners in that capacity. Some of his hosts and hostesses, like Lord Berwick of Attingham Park, were treated as eccentric figures of fun. Others, such as Sir Henry Fairfax-Lucy of Charlecote Park, were disparaged: he was 'obstinate and muddle-headed… His ideas do not coordinate. His lisp is like that of a peevish child eating pap.' Then, when the image has been sealed with phrases such as 'pompous ass', 'strutting', 'peppery' and 'arrogant', Lees-Milne throws in that Sir Henry was 'underneath… a kindly old man… In fact I am rather sorry for him, because I think he is a little odd.' The damage had been done, but the author allows himself a perceptive and tolerant last word.

Far greater scorn was reserved for the lower orders. Following a visit to Polesden Lacey in Surrey, where he had been told that the housemaid was not to be trusted, he noted:

> I never expect gratitude, loyalty, affection, etc., from servants. They don't know the meaning of these qualities. From the uneducated one must expect self-interest, meanness, mendacity and guile. Of such is the kingdom of the proletariat.[15]

When confronted by a journalist, later in his life, who accused him of being a snob, he pondered, 'There are elements of truth in that, I suppose,' but then added, as if having second thoughts, 'Actually, you know, I don't think I am a snob. But I am an elitist.'[16]

The west front of Charlecote Park, Warwickshire, viewed from across the River Avon. The house was given to the National Trust by Sir Montgomerie Fairfax-Lucy, 4th Bt. in 1946.

The Long Gallery at Ham House, Richmond-upon-Thames, Surrey. The house and grounds were given to the National Trust by Sir Lyonel Tollemache, 4th Bt. and his son Cecil Lyonel Tollemache in 1948.

Ancestral Voices did not encourage the assessment that he was not a snob; nor the view that he maintained consistent loyalty to the National Trust.

The second volume of diaries, published two years later under the title *Prophesying Peace*, brought the unease and disapproval into the public domain. Parts were serialised in the press, including a long account of a visit to Shaw's Corner in Hertfordshire, the former home of George Bernard Shaw:

> A young member of the Trust called for me at the office and at 11.30 we set off in the car for Hitchin. He is a nice, earnest black-coated worker, called Teagle, madly keen on archaeological remains, birds and nature. He hikes every weekend in the summer in the Home Counties with his wife, and stays in youth hostels.… we went to an area of land which he has found and wants us to save. We got out and walked for an hour. A small river valley bounded by a straight stretch of the Icknield Way. In this sunswept, windswept landscape our noses ran. He wiped his nose with the back of his hand. I had one handkerchief and debated with myself whether to share it. Decided against.'[17]

The serialisation prompted a dignified letter from Mr Teagle. He had always regarded that visit with Lees-Milne, whom he revered, as one of the most memorable episodes in his life. He was hurt to find himself described in a way that made him seem uncouth.

Another passage describes a visit to Plas Newydd, on the island of Anglesey off the north coast of Wales, with an incomparable view across the Menai Strait to Snowdonia. The house, with its Rex Whistler mural in the dining room and relics of the Waterloo veteran, Henry,

1st Marquess of Anglesey, was to be given to the National Trust in 1976. I happened to be working in the house when *Prophesying Peace* appeared. The present Marquess of Anglesey read extracts before lunch, including the account of his mother, whom Lees-Milne described:

> with very white hair, slight and well made, and well dressed in a tartan skirt, smelling of upper-class scent and cigarettes. She has a little wizened face like a marmoset's, and is extremely attractive.[18]

Lord Anglesey found this description clever but mildly offensive. Then and since I found myself assuring benefactors of the Trust who had been offended by Lees-Milne that I did not keep a diary, still less had I any intention of publishing one.

Years after their publication the extent to which Lees-Milne's diaries rankled would occasionally surface. In 2006 a book launch was held at Lanhydrock in Cornwall, to mark the publication of a memoir of Michael Trinick, the National Trust's Regional Secretary in Devon and Cornwall from 1958 to 1984. One of the speeches was made by John, 4th Lord St Levan, whose father had given St Michael's Mount to the Trust in 1954. In it he alluded to the passage in Jim's diary for 1953, in which he gave what the family regarded as a disparaging description of the 3rd Lord St Levan's appearance:

> He is tall, weak-chinned, distinguished and probably clever in that English way which disconcerts and misleads foreign diplomats. Must have been attractive to women as a young man, with reservation (the chin).[19]

The relationship with Jim was complicated by the fact that he had also written about Lady St Levan in his biography of her brother, Harold Nicolson, in which he had referred to an affair in the 1930s with her sister-in-law, Vita Sackville-West. St Michael's Mount was one of the houses where Lees-Milne was *persona non grata*.

The Tollemaches were another family who felt traduced by the diaries. When Lees-Milne visited Ham House, on the south bank of the Thames at Richmond, in March 1943, the garden was pitted with bomb craters and several windows had been shattered. He went to the back door, which was eventually opened to the accompaniment of 'heavy breathing from within'. The entry continues:

> An elderly man of sixty stood before me. He had red hair and a red face, carrot and port wine. He wore a tail coat and a starched shirt front which had come adrift from the waistcoat. 'The old alcoholic family butler,' I said to myself.

Jim was then led down a dark passage and eventually to a door, where the 'butler' knocked nervously:

> An ancient voice cried, 'Come in!' The seedy butler then said to me, 'Daddy is expecting you,' and left me. I realized that he was the bachelor son of Sir Lyonel Tollemache, aged eighty-nine. As I entered the ancient voice said, 'You can leave us alone, boy!' For a moment I did not understand that Sir Lyonel was addressing his already departed son.[20]

In a novel this account might score high marks for Dickensian pastiche. Jim is amusing himself (and most of his readers) when he writes of the younger Lyonel Tollemache that 'his legs must be webbed for he moved in painful jerks.' But is the description accurate? Or is it a piece of literary indulgence? The Tollemache family do not believe that Lyonel (who succeeded as 5th Baronet in 1952) would ever have referred to his father, the 4th Baronet, as 'Daddy', still less would the elder Sir Lyonel, whom Jim described as 'very courteous', have called his son 'boy' in front of a young official from the National Trust. The truth was that the younger Tollemache was making a great financial sacrifice when he and his father gave Ham House to the Trust in 1948; although it is also true that the responsibilities of looking after the house in wartime had weighed heavily on him.

Sometimes what Lees-Milne wrote acted like slow poison. In his accounts of visits to Bradley Manor in Devon, he described the husband of the donor as 'an ungracious, ugly man', and the house as 'shockingly neglected' and 'swarming with babies'.[21] He also wrote unkindly of the donor herself, whom he gave a cruel nickname. In a letter of 1985, Michael Trinick mentioned 'the serious and justifiable offence' taken by Mrs A.H. Woolner, 'good and worthy woman that she is', at what the 'wicked James Lees-Milne' (whose virtues Michael greatly admired) had written. As far as she, and others lampooned in the diaries, were concerned, the offence was compounded every time they came across a copy of his books in their neighbours' houses.

The later volumes of Jim's diaries were edited by his literary executor, Michael Bloch, who, at the end of the ninth, *Holy Dread*, added a note about Lees-Milne's complex relationship with the National Trust. Bloch recorded how, on 13 October 1983, at a meeting with his publisher, Faber and Faber, Lees-Milne was told that 'the N.T. definitely refused to have my diaries in their shops, considering them shocking and in bad taste'.[22] That the Trust should have continued not to stock what Bloch described as 'the greatest work of literature to emerge from its history'[23] seems to have struck him as incomprehensible and wrong. But in 1983 Mrs Woolner, and many other donors who had been deeply wounded, were very much alive.

After Lees-Milne retired as architectural adviser in 1966, he continued to serve on the National Trust's Architectural Panel and Properties Committee, and then its Arts Panel. In these capacities, he was sometimes asked to visit prospective properties. However, in the eyes of the Chairman, Lord Antrim, and the Director-General, Jack Boles, he had compromised his authority and influence. Nor did he really engage with the issues around whether a property would or would not come to the Trust, however important it might be. One such case was Tabley House in Cheshire, which he and I visited with Eardley Knollys. Jim had known the owner, Colonel John Leicester-Warren at Eton, where he was 'a ridiculous figure with absolutely no chin and a bewildered expression' and was 'cruelly mobbed'. As we walked around the lake there was more schoolboy ridicule:

> Eardley observed the curious, idiosyncratic manner in which Leicester-Warren walks, with a slight lilt of the bottom, a walk of great confidence and quiet authority. He said he has remarked that only men owning more than 5,000 acres walk like that, the squire's gait.[24]

One aspect of a long life is that it holds out the possibility that the wheel of fortune and reputation will turn advantageously. In old age Lees-Milne was lionised, with acolytes flocking to his door and glowing reviews for his later books. When the National Trust celebrated its centenary in 1995, with the lunch at Grosvenor House in London, Lees-Milne was whisked away from the Duke and Duchess of Devonshire, who had given him a lift, and directed to the top table, where the Prince of Wales was the guest of honour. He may not have been given the Companion of Honour, which he coveted – he turned down a CBE in 1992 – but he had come to be regarded, quite rightly, as one of a small band who had had a lasting impact, and for the good, on the National Trust. In 1997 the Director-General, Martin Drury, arranged for him to be presented with the Founders' Medal at a special lunch at Brooks's in St James's Street.

James Lees-Milne wrote his own epilogue. The twelfth volume of his diaries, *The Milk of Paradise*, covering the years 1993 to 1997, appeared in 2005, eight years after his death. Like the earlier volumes, it makes compulsive reading, particularly for those who, like myself, have been enthused, delighted and exasperated by the author. There is plenty in it to infuriate those who find his writing self-indulgent and his opinions distasteful. Some of the passages which might have given most offence were dropped by the editor, when Tony Mitchell warned that they would seriously damage Lees-Milne's reputation, even among those who valued him as a friend. He was sometimes confused about the buildings and pictures he wrote about, as when he visited an exhibition of National Trust paintings at the National Gallery:

> ... am most moved by *Christ and the Woman of Samaria* by Strozzi from Dunham Massey (Cheshire), a house which came to the N.T. just after my time.

In fact, the picture came from Kedleston Hall in Derbyshire, not Dunham Massey, which was bequeathed to the National Trust in 1976.

Lees-Milne can seem ungenerous towards those who had valued his friendship. John Cornforth continued in the 1970s to ask Jim to write for *Country Life* about houses that he thought would particularly appeal to him; but he also encouraged a younger generation of scholars, including Gervase Jackson-Stops, Giles Worsley and Jeremy Musson. Lees-Milne once remarked that his architectural writing had been overtaken by these and others, such as Mark Girouard, who attached more importance to rigorous examination of documentary evidence than to poetic description.

Whatever the reason, Lees-Milne seems to have relished disparaging references to Cornforth. His entry for 12 January 1995 records a conversation at Chatsworth, when Cornforth was dismissed as 'very limited in his interests', and a man who 'gives one a pitying look if one

Bernardo Strozzi, *Christ and the Woman of Samaria*, a painting acquired when Kedleston Hall in Derbyshire was given to the National Trust by Francis, 3rd Viscount Scarsdale in 1987.

tries to change the subject from curtain tassels and Georgian wallpapers to, say, the Bosnia crisis'. The truth was that Cornforth and many others had learnt years ago not to discuss politics with Lees-Milne, because their views were likely to be incompatible. On a visit to Farnborough Hall in Warwickshire, and hearing that Cornforth had preceded him, Lees-Milne was prompted to say: 'You can bet that we shall read in *Country Life* that the ceiling relief work is not stucco but *papier mâché*.'

The picture that the diary paints of Cornforth would mislead those who did not know this generous, dedicated scholar. When he died in 2004, still in his mid-sixties, a wide circle of friends launched an appeal in Cornforth's memory. Immediately, £50,000 was raised to endow a scholarship for the Attingham Summer School, in acknowledgement of the guidance and support he had given to young curators. The fundraising events included a series of lectures at Christie's, at which the Earl of Leicester, the Marquess of Cholmondeley and the Earl of Dalkeith talked about their houses, all of which had benefited from Cornforth's advice. A further £40,000 was donated to reweave silk damask for the state rooms at Kedleston Hall, one of his and Lees-Milne's favourite houses. In May 2006 Sotheby's auctioned some twenty paintings donated by artists whom Cornforth had patronised when they were relatively unknown. Those snide diary references to Cornforth are answered by his magisterial *Early Georgian Interiors*, which was published after his death, and by the determination of his many friends that he should be remembered fittingly. By 2010 the fund in Cornforth's memory had reached over £170,000.

Unfortunately, such disparagements cannot be blamed on posthumous editing, because Lees-Milne himself was quite prepared to include passages in the earlier diaries that he knew would wound. His prejudices had, over time, lapsed into silliness. In one of the final volumes of his diaries he speculates about the sexuality of someone he meets, without caring what they or others might feel when his misplaced supposition appeared in print.

The recreation of the library at Gunby, in Lees-Milne's memory, was devised with great care by Martin Drury, who also took immense pains over the details of Lees-Milne's memorial service, held at the Grosvenor Chapel in South Audley Street in March 1998. The tributes to him from Nigel Nicolson and others were generous, just and full of affection: 'Passionate defender of what was beautiful, inspired and inspiring' – undoubtedly; 'Protector of fine buildings and guardian of much of what was and is best about the National Trust' – certainly.

But 'Saint Jim'?

5

THE AGENTS

Cubby Acland, Michael Trinick and Gull Rock

I N THE YEARS BEFORE Lord Lothian left for Washington in 1939, he corresponded with the National Trust's Chairman, Lord Zetland, and Secretary, Matheson, about progress with the Country Houses Scheme. He rightly predicted that it would transform an organisation which had previously been small and largely amateur. 'If the Trust is to embark upon this venture, as I hope it will,' he wrote to Matheson in November 1935, 'it will have to have a special Land and Land Management Department because I fancy that in time a very considerable amount of property will come into its hands.'[1]

Lothian's prediction was correct. The National Trust's Chief Agent, based in London, held the purse strings, with an accountant to keep the books. Around the country, a new breed of Regional Agents controlled and managed most of the Trust's properties. The agents appointed after the Second World War had usually been in the armed services and were accustomed to giving orders. They were effective, assertive, sometimes abrasive, and were inclined to believe that aesthetes like Lees-Milne were indulging in inessentials. If a choice had to be made between repairing a roof, improving a tenant farmer's buildings, or decorating an historic interior, there was rarely much contest. As the Deputy Chairman of the Trust, Mark Norman, wrote of the Regional Agents:

> They were the frontline troops, aided by a few Historic Buildings representatives. All of them, nearly, were a talented band of rather under-paid over-worked heroes, who did their multifarious jobs more for duty and satisfaction than for pay.[2]

The agents had powerful allies on the Trust's committees, including the Chairman of its Estates Committee, Dr. G.M. Trevelyan, who had learnt a good deal about estate management by observing how his family home at Wallington in Northumberland was run. He was a distinguished historian, but no aesthete. When the Trust marked its jubilee in 1945 with the publication of a collection of essays entitled *The National Trust: A Record Of Fifty Years' Achievement*, Trevelyan wrote in the introduction:

> In the management of its properties the Trust endeavours to avoid the evils of bureaucracy and over-centralization…. In order to prevent centralizing things too much on the London

Michael Trinick, National Trust Land Agent and Regional Director from 1953 to 1984, photographed at Lanhydrock in Cornwall, shortly before his retirement.

George Macaulay Trevelyan, historian, benefactor and supporter of the National Trust, and his brother Sir Charles Trevelyan, 3rd Bt., who gave his house, its contents and the surrounding estate at Wallington, Northumberland, to the Trust in 1941.

office, it is establishing a system of Regional Agents, whole-time servants of the Trust and imbued with its ideals, resident each in his allotted Region … a Regional Agent of the Trust must always be, not merely a business land agent, but also a man endowed with the love of natural beauty and sympathetic with the local spirit and with the point of view of the farmers and other tenants and friends of the Trust in his Region.[3]

In 1936 the Trust's already considerable land holding in the Lake District was put in the hands of Bruce Thompson, a man of absolute integrity and dedication who was liked and respected by everyone except Mrs William Heelis, *née* Beatrix Potter. She told the Trust's secretary that Thompson 'seems to have no understanding about anything; and he is not learning either'. She had a prejudice against the breed: 'The typical agent has the faults of the idle rich, with bumptiousness added.'

If Mrs Heelis's idea of a Land Agent was something of a caricature, several of the Trust's agents seemed determined to conform to the stereotype. Some rode to hounds regularly, most shot with varying degrees of enthusiasm, and others – the younger sons of landed families – managed their own farms. Colin Jones, who had an empire stretching from Bristol to Manchester, was often absent from National Trust activities for much of July and August, because he was harvesting. His area was misleadingly designated the Severn Region. An even more improbable area was devised by the Chief Agent, Hubert Smith, for Sir Dawson Bates, who throughout the 1950s, '60s and '70s was responsible for all Trust properties in an attenuated region which stretched from south Birmingham through Oxfordshire, Berkshire and Hampshire to the Isle of Wight. These geographical aberrations brought one definite benefit. Instead of making flying visits, the Trust's agents would go to properties less frequently than their successors but would be there longer, often staying with tenants or resident staff. They knew their properties extremely well.

Some of the agents may have come from aristocratic families, but chose to work for the National Trust because their background was radical or even socialist. One of the most able Regional Agents, Cuthbert Acland (known as 'Cubby'), saw the Trust as an instrument of social improvement. The energy with which he pursued these ideals was very much in the spirit of the founders of the Trust, who were themselves influenced by the Christian Social-ism of F.D. Maurice and by the ideas of their mentors, John Ruskin and William Morris. In the case of Cubby Acland, there was also a long family history of radicalism and philanthro-py. His grandfather, Arthur Acland, was in Gladstone's fourth Cabinet and was regarded as 'a red-hot social reformer'. His great-uncle, Sir Charles Acland, leased 7,000 acres of his Hol-nicote estate in Somerset to the National Trust in 1917, continuing to receive the income from rents but preventing his successors from profiting from any building development. Then, in 1927, Holnicote passed to Cubby's elder brother, Sir Richard Acland, who was to prove more radical than any of his forebears, and even more generous to the National Trust.

In her book, *A Devon Family*, Anne Acland describes how, in 1944, her husband, Sir Richard:

> … gave all the land in his possession on the Killerton and Holnicote estates to the National Trust; partly as a matter of principle, and partly in order to preserve them intact for future generations.[4]

John Tetley's cartoon of the National Trust's area agents, presented to Christopher Gibbs on his retirement as Chief Agent in 1969.

This explanation glosses over what was for his successors an extremely painful episode in the history of the family, which deprived them of huge estates in Devon and Somerset, amount-

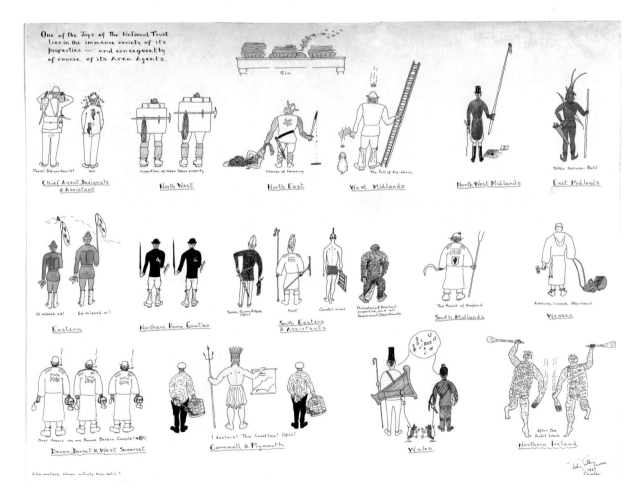

ing to more than 16,000 acres. What in fact had happened was that Sir Richard and J.B. Priestley had set up the Common Wealth Party in 1943, which advocated the common ownership of property and which, during the war years of a national government, enjoyed spectacular success in by-elections. The ideals of his political party did not sit easily with the personal wealth of one of the largest landowners in the west of England; and this Sir Richard resolved by handing over his estates to the National Trust. What he and his wife studiously concealed from both the public and their own children was that a very substantial sum of money – £141,000, now worth around twenty times that amount – was paid by the Trust to Sir Richard. He needed this to pay off some of the debts incurred while establishing the Common Wealth party, to meet death duties, legacy duty and estate duty, and to buy himself a suitable house in Hampstead. He had 'sprung the idea' on his dismayed wife in 1942, 'that the estates are sold and money given to C.W.'[5]

When pressed by his family on what he had done, and why, Sir Richard adopted the style he used whenever challenged: he harangued rather than discussed. Lady Acland went so far as to ensure that the correspondence dealing with the transfer was kept separate from the deposit of the rest of the family papers in the Devon Record Office, was omitted from the archive catalogue, and was stored in a different building. Their contemporaries were not entirely deceived. In a letter of 23 July 1943, Richard described to Anne an exchange in the House of Commons:

> Lady Astor said, 'You're doing pretty well for yourself, young man, anyway,' and it was perfectly clear that all the Tories who heard it were chortling with pleasure that my swindle had been shown up.[6]

The view south-east from Castle Crag to the Stonethwaite valley in the Lake District, Cumbria.

Cubby (Cuthbert) Acland [right], the National Trust's Regional Agent in the Lake District from 1948 to 1973, with one of the Trust's tenant famers at Yew Tree Farm, Cumbria.

The sad fact is that the money Sir Richard received from the National Trust, in exchange for the 'gift' of Holnicote and Killerton, was then poured into Common Wealth and went down a political drain. The party ceased to exist after the Labour landslide of 1945. Members of the Labour Party had come to regard him as 'a bit fraudulent'.[7]

Unlike his brother, Cubby Acland was not involved publicly in politics. Instead he devoted himself single-mindedly to the management of his National Trust demesne, in a style that was radical, progressive and patrician. He wanted the Lake District, where he had become Regional Agent in 1948, to be enjoyed by anyone with a love of the hills. Camping sites were opened in some of the most beautiful valleys where, sometimes years before, trees had been planted to screen them. He was the first agent to make Trust properties available as holiday cottages. The recruitment of National Trust members and the provision of information for visitors were discreetly provided from what became known as 'Cubby Holes'. All of this was benign, but not indulgent. Acland bullied tent manufacturers to use muted earth colours. Static caravans were allowed on National Trust farms only if they too were painted a subdued colour. The very best sites were to be given to those who were prepared to use camouflage nets over their caravans. The 'bothies' provided in the hills were cheap to rent, but often had no electricity or mains water.

The Chairman of the Trust, Lord Crawford, used to refer to Acland as 'The Cock of the North', but the avian analogy is not entirely apt. Cubby was lean and athletic, with longish fair hair and an aquiline nose. He was more like an upland bird of prey: imperious, elegant and lethal when he chose to stoop. A confirmed bachelor, he liked beautiful but unassertive women, fast cars and sailing boats. He built his own ice yacht for the winters when Lake Windermere froze over. Remembering the rhododendrons which grow so abundantly at Killerton, he created a woodland garden at Stagshaw, near Ambleside in Cumbria, which is now open to the public. In a grove of native trees, he planted a moss garden with specimens he had collected and identified.

There were, however, aversions and blind spots. Cubby failed to appreciate that many of the Trust's farms in the Lake District included vernacular buildings of exceptional rarity, historic interest and importance. Alterations were sometimes damaging, with unsuitable materials used and long-term problems stored up. Cubby took pride in rarely, if ever, referring plans to the Trust's Architectural Panel. He also allowed Beatrix Potter's watercolours and book illustrations to languish in damp and unsuitable conditions at Hill Top, the farm she had bequeathed to the Trust, where they would probably have deteriorated irreparably had the Trust's Adviser on Paintings, St John Gore, not insisted that they be properly stored in solander boxes. When he was crossed, particularly by local authority officials, his brother's tendency to lecture asserted itself. His assistant agent, Tony Lord, recalled that at meetings of the Lake District Planning Board he would argue his case, 'and if he couldn't get his own way, he would get up, slam his desk, pick up his books and walk out'.[8] After he had retired, I asked him to produce a report on the park at Shugborough, which was managed on a full repairing lease by Staffordshire County Council. The intention of his report was to encourage more public access, but this did not find favour with the Council's officers. Cubby's parting shot was to tell them that, if they chose to reject his recommendations, a time would come when they would admit to themselves: 'Ah! Acland was right after all.' He was deluding himself.

Much of what Cubby pioneered in the Lake District – the holiday cottages, the encouragement to farm tenants to diversify their income by welcoming visitors, the information and recruitment buildings – became accepted National Trust policy and practice. He was not alone either in such initiatives, or in his attitudes. In the extreme south-west, Michael Trinick was similarly redefining the role of the Trust and, like Cubby, saw himself as a radical in the tradition of the founders of the charity. 'There had always been a left-wing side to the Trust, which is one of the reasons I joined it,' Trinick once volunteered.[9]

Although he usually spoke quietly, in a measured way, Michael Trinick was a large and powerful presence. There were those who saw something of a Cornish pirate about him. For others he was a latter-day Celtic saint. Perhaps he was a bit of both. What is indisputable is that, for over 30 years, he shaped and stood for the Trust's work in the South West.

The sense that history is a common thread that joins together land, buildings and the people that care for them came naturally to Michael, who was proud of his yeoman origins. 'There is something deeply satisfying, and romantic too, in taking one's family name from the place where one's ancestors held land,' he once wrote; and went on, 'I wish that my own forbears, who spelt their name Trennick, had not lost their little manor of Trennick in the parish of St Clement, on the outskirts of Truro.' The manor is more correctly called Trewythenick, but is pronounced 'Trennick'. The family of that name died out in the thirteenth century. Michael's association with it was a romantic notion, and a revealing one. He always felt deeply rooted in Cornwall, and the National Trust gave him a way of furthering that allegiance.

When the Trust first dispatched Michael to Cornwall in 1953, as assistant agent, he was still in his twenties. But like many of the staff recruited shortly after the war, his knowledge and experience went well beyond what he had been taught at Christ's College, Cambridge, and the Royal Agricultural College, Cirencester. Shortly after joining the Royal Engineers early in the war – he had read engineering at Cambridge – Michael contracted meningitis. After his convalescence, he was given the task of researching, largely in the British Library, the northern French ports, in preparation for the Normandy landings. Getting the facts right, based on sound research, was not academic pedantry but a matter of life and death. He lodged at the time with the entomologist and curator Gilbert Bryant, who was an authority on country houses. Thereafter, Michael was as much at ease disputing the identity of a Cornish portrait or the provenance of a piece of furniture as he was discussing the need for a new farm building with a tenant.

Michael's National Trust responsibilities were initially modest. In 1953 the Trust owned just twelve miles of coastline in Cornwall, one country house – Cotehele – and employed less than a dozen staff. Three years after his appointment, the Trust took the first faltering steps to reorganise its regional staff, in due course appointing two Regional Secretaries who were to act as director, agent and curator combined. Michael was made Regional Secretary for Devon and Cornwall in 1965. The considerable influence and authority that this post gave him was enhanced when in the same year a regional committee for Devon and Cornwall was established, with Major General Sir Julian Gascoigne as its first Chairman and Michael as Secretary. They were a formidable combination.

Michael assumed that it was the role of the Trust's head office to listen attentively to his proposals for acquisitions and improvements to properties, to approve them, and then to provide financial support. He quickly established a reputation for being a persistent, eloquent advocate for a sustained campaign of acquisition. He had powerful allies on the committees, among them John Smith, at that stage Chairman of the General Purposes Committee, and later creator of the Landmark Trust, a charity that rescues historic buildings, repairs them and then makes them available to rent for holidays. The Trust's aesthetes were also won over, James Lees-Milne once describing Trinick as 'a wonder of a man, really a treasure to the National Trust'.[10]

Long before Enterprise Neptune was launched in 1965, there had been a plan for coastal acquisitions in Devon and Cornwall. To further its objectives Michael set up his own Cornwall Coastal Committee. By the mid-1960s, the Trust already owned over 100 miles of coast in the two counties, much of it secured during Michael's first ten years as agent. Writing in the National Trust's magazine, shortly after his retirement in 1984, he remembered the freedom of those early years:

> They were swashbuckling days for me in Cornwall, for the present Regional Committees had not then been set up and I was on my own. Every month I would come up to the committee meetings in London with news of generous gifts of land and proposals to spend legacies on further purchases. The string of legacies then, as now, was vital. Somehow they always appeared in the nick of time and successive chairmen of the Trust's committees have always believed in

spending them on what was then available, and not hoarding them in case something better turned up. In those years the Trust never missed the chance of a first-class coastal acquisition for want of money – a record of which the whole membership could be proud.[11]

Fiercely acquisitive though Michael could be, he was acutely aware of the obligation to manage new properties in a way which ensured that they were enhanced and gave public benefit. Such work was often invisible or unobtrusive. It might involve putting overhead wires underground, screening a new car park, building new farm buildings with local materials and locating them with care, or providing discreet signs. The need to protect hinterland, to pursue a policy of 'one farm deep', was also carefully explained to benefactors and to the Trust's committees. His aim was, whenever possible, to secure not only the cliff-top or beach, but also the farmland which lay behind and could serve as a line of defence. Only someone with Michael's combination of tact and complete conviction could have secured the financial support for so ambitious a strategy, as was revealed by one particular incident:

> In 1972 I was asked to go and see an elderly lady in Budleigh Salterton. She explained diffidently that she wanted to give money to the Trust to buy beautiful land but had clearly made the wrong approach, since the local members' centre, with whom she had been put in touch, had told her that the best way was to pay their subscription of 50p. She was thinking in rather different terms. She knew she had not long to live and it was a great pleasure to her to be able to effect a major purchase before she died, of the Great Hangman, where Exmoor sweeps down to the sea on the finest part of the north Devon coast. The good Mrs Lethaby left the Trust £275,000, and she also paid her 50p to the local centre.[12]

The extent to which Michael was prepared to intervene precipitately was demonstrated when he was told in 1957 that St Ives Borough Council was on the point of deciding they could save themselves the expense of creating a new rubbish dump by tipping refuse over the cliffs near Hellesveor Farm, on the West Penwith coast. Michael drove over immediately to see John Husband, the owner of the farm which included the cliff-top, who believed that any resistance to the idea would be futile because the Borough Council would resort to compulsory purchase. Michael's account continues:

> I told him there was a solution. Was he prepared to sell the cliff to the Trust, which, in that event, could refuse to bow to such an order? I went on to say that I was sure that this would be the end of this disgraceful proposal. Good Mr Husband said he would gladly sell. We looked at a map, and we agreed a price of £100 for twenty-four acres of cliff. But since the Borough Council was to meet that very evening, delay would be fatal. It happened that I had in my pocket two fivers, much rarer then than now. So we found a piece of paper. 'In consideration,' I wrote, 'of the sum of £10 hereby paid by the National Trust and received by Mr Husband, he agrees to sell the land to the Trust for £100.' Two hurried signatures and the deed was done.[13]

With the acquisition of ever more coastline came the responsibility of managing the miles of coastal path that came with it. Michael ensured that this was done in a low-key, sensitive

Ruined cottages beside the Old Battery on the west coast of Lundy Island in the Bristol Channel. The island was bought by the National Trust in conjunction with the Landmark Trust in 1969, with money given by Sir Jack Hayward.

way with meticulous attention to detail. Signs were kept to an absolute minimum and way-markers erected only when essential. He believed in the joy of discovery and was initially dismissive of the growing trend to 'interpret' the countryside. 'Anyone with a decent education and an Ordnance Survey map should be able to work it out for themselves' was his intuitive approach which, over time, he reluctantly had to modify. Yet when the editorial team producing the hugely successful *Coast of Cornwall* series of interpretative leaflets turned to him for help and advice, he generously gave it and the authoritative contents owe much to his knowledge and love of the coastline he did so much to save.

Perhaps the most publicised campaign was for Land's End. One of the most successful was for Lundy, an island in the Bristol Channel, which, thanks to the generosity of Jack Hayward and of John Smith, was bought in 1969. There was no such happy ending at Land's End, and indeed at the outset Michael and the Trust had misgivings that the area was already so damaged that Enterprise Neptune funds might be better spent elsewhere. In 1981, however, public opinion and the media seemed to swing behind the Trust; excellent plans for the provision of new, discreet buildings and car parks were devised by Elizabeth Chesterton; and

The Kitchen at Cotehele in Cornwall. Built between 1485 and 1627, Cotehele was the first property to be accepted in part-payment of death duties, in 1947, with the considerable co-operation of Kenelm, 6th Earl of Mount Edgcumbe.

Michael again secured the offer of a major financial contribution from 'Union Jack' Hayward, who was living in the Bahamas, but promised what was needed over the telephone. The Trust put in its bid, held its breath, and then found out that it had been substantially outbid.

Michael was at least as concerned about the future of the historic houses of Devon and Cornwall as he was about their coastline. The first major house with which he was involved was the ancient manor of Cotehele in Cornwall. In 1947 it had been offered by the 6th Earl of Mount Edgcumbe in part-payment of death duties and after every conceivable prevarication it was agreed that the Treasury could be reimbursed from the National Land Fund. Had Lord Mount Edgcumbe not shown such persistence, this important precedent would not have been set. For much of its long history Cotehele had been allowed to slumber, and Michael saw it as his personal responsibility that there should not be a rude awakening. Gradually he helped to reveal its full historical significance. In doing so he provided a model for how such properties can be presented:

> Work was done gradually, year in and year out as money was scratched together or left to the Trust in their wills by splendid benefactors. Forty years later I think it is apparent that this way of doing things, though apparently muddled and financially risky, really is better for an old country house which has run down.[14]

Michael was anxious to show not only the finest rooms in the house, but also more modest ones, and he wanted to devise a route to enable visitors to make their own way round, rather than in a guided party, as was usual. His solution was to use both the granite stairs and the main staircase, which gave access to the kitchen court. To avoid a bottleneck, visitors were then routed through the kitchen, which he arranged 'exactly as it had been in 1890, probably the first kitchen to be shown by the Trust, the first of many'. He also borrowed, from Holker Hall in Lancashire, the idea of giving each visitor a simple leaflet with a brief description of each room and its contents. The guidebook could, he believed, be read subsequently. With his characteristic attention to detail, the leaflets were printed on pale green paper, 'because white paper distracts the eye.'

As visitor numbers to Cotehele increased, Michael was under pressure to limit numbers in the house. His response was to offer more to visitors, including the watermill, the estate workshops, and the quays and warehouses on the River Tamar, which had been the highway for the neighbourhood before the railway came, surprisingly late, in 1907. Michael had pioneered a policy of providing secondary attractions to spread the load of visitors.

The great Cornish houses of Antony, Lanhydrock and St Michael's Mount benefited from Michael's capacity to get on with the families of donors. Negotiations over Lanhydrock began the year that he arrived in Cornwall and were successfully concluded when the house, 441 acres and an endowment were given to the National Trust in 1953. It was not a straightforward acquisition, because much of the house was a Victorian rebuild following a disastrous

The seventeenth-century gatehouse of Lanhydrock in Cornwall, with the house, partially rebuilt after a fire in 1881, in the background. Lanhydrock and much of its estate was given to the National Trust by Gerald, 7th Viscount Clifden in 1953 and his brother, Victor, 8th Viscount Clifden in the 1970s.

Gerald, 7th Viscount Clifden, the donor of Lanhydrock in Cornwall, on a trip to Brussels with his sisters Violet and Everilda in the 1920s.

fire in 1881. There was a strained visit from Lord Esher, Chairman of the Trust's Historic Buildings Committee, whose personal taste was for pure Georgian architecture and whose concluding words were: 'Now, Trinick, when you report to the committees we want to hear about the landscape. The house is incidental.' With this in mind, Michael stressed to the future donor, Gerald, 7th Viscount Clifden, that he particularly admired the cricket ground and the surrounding woodland:

> Because Lord Clifden was deaf, Miss Eva [his sister] stationed herself on one side of him and Miss Violet [another sister] on the other. Anything said by Mr Clemo [the estate steward] or by me was relayed to him. 'Mr Clemo says Mr Trinick likes the Cricket Ground.' 'What's that, Eva? What's that? Of course Mr Trinick likes cricket.' I explained that I felt the Cricket Ground and the woods round it should be included in any gift made to the Trust. It was no good. It was established that I liked cricket and I earned a totally undeserved reputation as a cricketer.[15]

The way Lanhydrock was arranged was very much Michael's invention. After the death of Lord Clifden and his sisters, his brother Victor and his wife took furniture and pictures to their house on Jersey, leaving many of the rooms at Lanhydrock bereft. To fill the gaps, Michael steered collections to the Trust, very much in the spirit that country houses in the past had amassed furniture from all manner of disparate sources. Some came to Lanhydrock as legacies, some as gifts, and some were astute purchases. The same approach was adopted at Dunsland in Devon and at Trerice in Cornwall, both of which came to the Trust virtually empty. 'It was like playing with a doll's house on a large scale,' Michael confessed. Today curatorial eyebrows would be raised at this promiscuous attitude to collecting on the Trust's behalf; but Michael would have been unapologetic.

Some of his acquisitions, such as a roasting spit for the kitchen at Lanhydrock, were brilliantly opportunistic. When a modern electric stove had been installed in the twentieth century, the coal grate, frame and chains for the spits had been disposed of, although the big fan remained in the chimney flue. By happy coincidence, Michael received a note from the historic buildings department at head office to say that one of the city livery companies, the Ironmongers' Company, was reorganising its kitchen and wanted to find a home for a great roasting spit. What delighted Michael was that the whole ensemble was a perfect fit, and he was even able to show that it was supplied by the same firm, Clements Jeakes and Co., and in the same year that the new Lanhydrock kitchen had been equipped:

> In no time at all we had fixed the whole thing up, roasted a side of beef on the spit, baked bread in the ovens and had steam issuing from the jets in the scullery used to clean greasy saucepans.[16]

It was because Michael was responsive to family history that he had such a fruitful relationship with the donors of country houses. The respect was mutual, buttressed by occasional sparring on points of principle, as is evident in his account of the gift of Antony in Cornwall:

Michael Trinick [left] testing the newly-installed roasting spit in the kitchen at Lanhydrock.

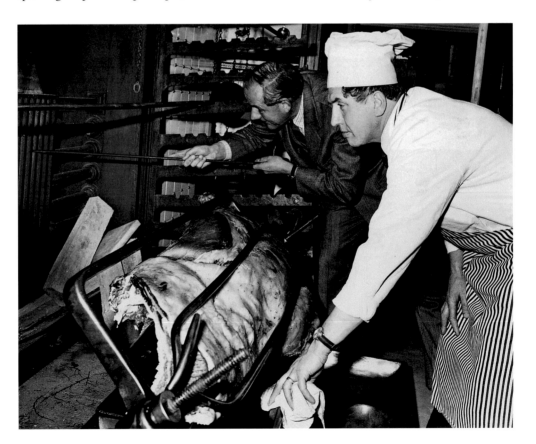

In 1960 Sir John Carew Pole asked me over to discuss a possible gift. He was a leading figure in the county, a substantial landowner, a distinguished soldier, chairman of the County Council and later Lord Lieutenant, living comfortably in his ancestral home with servants inside and out. I wondered why he had come to the Trust. Inflation had not then seriously begun, but the confidence of landowners had been sapped by the socialist government for six years after the war, taxes were high, and the arrangement under which owners of country houses can set up their own charitable trusts to endow them, in return for some public access, did not exist. A great many owners wanted to talk to the man from the National Trust.

Sir John was a delight to deal with. He loved pulling my leg, and everyone else's. Clearly his house was entirely acceptable to the Trust. My job was to work out what it would cost to maintain it, calculate the necessary endowment, and then persuade him to provide this.... 'An excellent report, Trinick. I can only agree with it. In fact, I think you need rather more endowment, to allow for unforeseen contingencies.' My hopes rose, but this was only a leg-pull. 'Of course, you know I'm broke, can't conceivably afford to stay here. Nothing for it but to pull out and give up.' My hopes fell, but I thought I could see a twinkle in his eye. 'I'll see if I can find something, but it won't begin to be enough. Of course, if you could get Alan Lascelles and David Crawford down here, I'm sure they would help. They've got lots of money.' These two were the chairmen respectively of the newly formed Historic Buildings Council and the Pilgrim Trust. I reported to head office, and was told that Lascelles and Crawford would be asked to come but, in the meantime, it was essential to find out what endowment Sir John could be expected to give. I tried again. 'Ah, Trinick, I see they've told you to get tough. That's no good. I shall have to sell up and move. I've got a little cottage down the road.' I knew that he also had thousands of acres of good land, some of it on the outskirts of the nearest town and sure to be developed. I didn't believe in the move to a cottage. We sat facing each other, Sir John chuckling as we sparred. 'All right then, you can have a couple of farms. But when the tenants leave, and you want to sell them, I must be able to buy them back.' And so it was arranged. Sir Alan Lascelles and Lord Crawford, both old friends of Sir John, came and proffered financial help. And years later – when Sir John sold land for development – he honourably provided further endowment.[17]

Not all the negotiations conducted by Michael were concluded successfully. The trustees of the Kitley estate, east of Plymouth at the head of the Yealm estuary, were concerned that the heir, John Bastard, was too fond of gambling on the horses, and that the future of the house was at risk. Michael arranged a visit, and arrived at an agreed time to discuss whether the National Trust might have a role to play. He was greeted on the doorstep by Bastard, who said: 'Who are you?' When Michael reminded his host of the purpose of the meeting, he was told: 'It's no use coming today. I always go to the pictures on Wednesday afternoons, and I'm just off.' They never saw each other again, and in 1987 the contents of Kitley were dispersed in a three-day sale.

There was an equally fruitless meeting with the 9th Earl of St Germans to discuss the future of Port Eliot, to the west of Saltash and up the Lynher estuary from Antony. On this occasion Michael was invited to lunch at the St James's Club in Piccadilly. After an excellent meal they repaired to the coffee room, Lord St Germans declaring, 'And now to business.' But before anything remotely business-like was said, the Earl had nodded off in his chair.

Sir Oswald Birley, *Sir John Carew Pole, 12th Bt.*, 1944. In 1959 Sir John gave his Elizabethan manor house at Shute Barton to the National Trust, followed by a further gift, in 1961, of Antony in Cornwall, with 29 acres and an endowment.

Michael tried kicking his ankle, then prodding him sharply, all to no avail. Aware that fellow members were watching him, Michael concluded that he ought to slip quietly away. His letter of thanks for lunch and their preliminary discussion went unanswered.[18]

What separates Michael's approach from that of today's curators is that he saw himself as entitled to act as the owner of a great house might have done, discarding some things, acquiring others, and interested above all in what would bring its history to life. At that time there was a prevailing view that the Trust's houses were not museums in the countryside, but were to be used and enjoyed, even if that meant occasional damage.

Michael's cavalier attitude to conservation and provenance took an extreme form when he acquired, for Lanhydrock, a painting of a lifeboat to accompany a watercolour of the *Anna Maria*, a ten-oared vessel provided by the Robartes family to assist the many rescues carried out from Polpeor Cove, immediately under the Lizard Point. Michael recorded that he had bought the oil painting in a local saleroom in the early 1970s, his note continuing:

Could it possibly portray the *Anna Maria*? It was surely too much to hope. The painting, very dirty, was cleaned by Mr Robert Morris, the Trust's then tenant at South Bohetherick farmhouse at Cotehele, a man who was always willing to take great trouble to do what his clients wished. And his trouble paid off, for when the painting returned to Lanhydrock, *mirabile dictu*, on the stern, in letters only just decipherable, the name of the boat had appeared, *ANNA MARIA*.[19]

Michael was in fact telling less than the whole truth. Among his papers, he left a copy of a letter to the Rev. Canon G.W. Harmer, who lived in the South Flat at Lanhydrock, and who was a friend: '… to my dismay, you have uncovered a little Trinick leg-pull, only a very little one, I assure you.' He then explained that he had gathered together various pictures and bits and pieces associated with the Robartes family's contributions to the Royal National Lifeboat Institution. They had been generous supporters, and here was an important aspect of local history which visitors might find interesting. Michael then went on to tell the Canon that when he spotted the painting of a lifeboat in a sale, 'I pounced on it, since it is rather good of its sort. Have you looked at the faces of the individual lifeboatmen – hearts of oak, each one of them?' Then came the confession:

The anonymous painting of a lifeboat, bought by Michael Trinick in the 1970s, to accompany a watercolour of the *Anna Maria*, the vessel provided by the Robartes family of Lanhydrock to rescue sailors in the seas off the south Cornish coast.

But sadly it was not the *Anna Maria*. The devil, always alert as you know, tempted me, and with the help of Robert Morris, who then cleaned and tidied up our second-rate pictures, a name was discovered to exist on the port bow. I swore him to secrecy and he did only sketch it in lightly… *Mea maxima culpa*.[20]

Of course, there will be those who are incensed by this willingness to falsify history. It lays the National Trust open to the charge that its houses are heritage concoctions, devised to pull in sentimental and sometimes snobbish tourists, and that they are not treated as serious historical documents. Others may regard the episode as evidence of arrogance and presumption. But in Michael's defence, he did leave a trail of clues leading to a written confession, so that anyone seriously interested could discover the truth. He wanted to be discovered, and to provoke a forgiving smile at what was a sin, but perhaps a venial one.

What is unquestionable is that Michael brought not only considerable knowledge to the houses in his care, but also an open and independent mind. In 1974, when he reported to the Trust's committees on Anthony Drewe's offer of Castle Drogo in Devon, not all were sympathetic to the acquisition of a building only completed in 1930, and by an architect, Sir Edwin Lutyens, whose reputation was only just beginning to be reassessed. Michael was in no doubt of its architectural importance, its significance as a document of social history, and its superb setting on a rocky outcrop high above the wooded gorge of the River Teign on Dartmoor. He was able to articulate the importance of those attributes as an entity, not just assessing them in parts.

What few, if any, of Michael's colleagues would have suspected was the extent of his radicalism or his contacts with one of the more left-wing, if idiosyncratic, ministers in Harold Wilson's government. In a diary entry for September 1967, Richard Crossman, then Lord President of the Council and Leader of the House of Commons, described visiting the Trinick family in the little coastguard look-out near the Dodman, on the south Cornish coast, which they used for holidays. Michael made no secret of his belief that the National Trust had, in the early 1960s, been allowed to get 'into the hands of the ultra-right-wing, politically,' and he was convinced that radical reform was necessary. Crossman's diary notes:

> I had some interesting talk, as I always do, about the National Trust and was very much struck by his disappointment when I told him that I hadn't persuaded the Prime Minister to order an independent enquiry into the National Trust. As a National Trust official he feels it is essential.'[21]

Crossman was strongly opposed to Enterprise Neptune, the Trust's campaign to acquire coastal property, on the basis of his naïve belief that 'socialism and planning would save the coast.' On this Michael must have strongly disagreed. It is not recorded whether Crossman ever sounded him out on his proposal, put to Harold Wilson, that the National Trust should be nationalised. Fortunately, the Prime Minister heeded the advice of his Minister of Health, Kenneth Robinson – later a member of the Trust's Executive Committee – who told him that the suggestion was thoroughly misguided.

Michael had a meticulous eye for detail and would always visit properties with a supply of postcards in his pocket, on which he would note things that had been done particularly well, or which needed immediate attention. At his retirement party in 1984, the Head Gardener of Lanhydrock in Cornwall, Peter Borlase, produced over a hundred of these cards, all carefully retained. The postcards would often be dispatched on Sunday (no doubt after church at Lanhydrock, when Michael had the opportunity to inspect the garden), but would also arrive during the week. They would always be written with the utmost courtesy ('No doubt you already had it in mind…' they might say), but could also be risqué – the reference to the fragrance of Daphne being sometimes left ambiguous, so that it was not entirely clear whether the plant or the Lanhydrock shop manager of that name was being referred to. Occasionally Borlase would receive one in red ink, which meant immediate action.

Michael's position was further strengthened by his knack of being proved right. In the mid-1970s, the National Trust was experiencing what felt at the time like a severe and possibly disastrous financial crisis, brought about by high inflation and the eroding value of the endowments of its major houses. At a meeting of senior staff at Attingham Park in Shropshire, the Chief Finance Officer explained just how precarious the Trust's finances were. The Director-General, Sir Frederick Bishop, was also pessimistic, advising that in such circumstances it was best 'to keep a low profile'.

This was the cue for a carefully prepared address from Michael. 'Trying to keep a low profile does not really suit me,' began the giant from Cornwall. He then listed the ways in which the Trust was failing to maximise its income, by the unduly restrictive opening hours of its country houses, by not serving visitors with locally prepared tea and scones, and by being unprofessional in the way it used its rentable property. 'Organisations that confront financial difficulty by retrenchment run the risk of losing public confidence,' he asserted. 'The National Trust is a great institution and if it needs and deserves more support, let's spread that message.'

When I was working as an assistant to Robin Fedden in London, before dispatch to Shropshire, there was what would now be called an induction. It consisted of spending time with staff who were good at their jobs; and because the organisation was still small, the impo-

The Yorke family bicycles at Erddig in Wales, as arranged by Michael Trinick.

sition occurred relatively infrequently. A stay with Michael Trinick, whom I had never met, was high on the list, and the visit was planned for early in 1971. One evening, a few days before I was due – with a certain amount of nervousness – to go down to Cornwall, the telephone rang at home and Michael introduced himself. He had got hold of my number from friends who had been staying at Lanhydrock, having noticed that their address was close to mine. The call was simply to say that he and Elizabeth were greatly looking forward to my visit. The kindness of this welcome to a young man, whom they did not know but were due to have to stay for several days, was typical of the National Trust at that time, and was the beginning of a much-valued friendship.

Michael took me to Cotehele on a damp, cold winter's day, when it was at its most romantic. On long car journeys, he told me how he had rebuilt the outer breakwater at Boscastle harbour on the north Cornish coast, using the region's building staff and so concealing the true cost, which would never have been authorised by head office. At Arlington Court in Devon I helped him arrange the ship models around the staircase hall. On the Saturday of my visit – it included the weekend – we rearranged some of the display cabinets in the morning room at Lanhydrock. Michael told me that he often kept enjoyable tasks such as this for a Saturday when he was not shooting.

Over the next twenty years, until his death in 1994, Michael was always ready with practical help and guidance. He followed each new acquisition with the closest interest, and he and Elizabeth came to Erddig in Wales and Dunham Massey in Cheshire at the time when plans for how they might be presented were at a formative stage. The display of bicycles at Erddig looks as though they have been left in the coach house by the Yorke family when they were away for a few days. The haphazard arrangement, with some leant casually against walls and others hanging from hooks in the ceiling beams, is in fact Michael's handiwork.

Just a third of a mile off Nare Head, on the south coast of Cornwall, there is a pinnacle of rock hospitable only to seabirds. Gull Rock was given to the National Trust, to mark Michael's year as High Sheriff of Cornwall in 1989. True to character, he did not intend his gift to go unremarked. Having met the Captain of the Royal Navy's brand new and most technologically advanced anti-submarine frigate, HMS *Cornwall*, Michael enlisted his support for a hand-over ceremony that was to be both memorable and good publicity for Enterprise Neptune. The plan involved Royal Marines landing on the rock and planting the National Trust's oak-leaf flag on its craggy summit, while Michael and colleagues embarked on HMS *Cornwall* from Portscatho. His considerable bulk had to be squeezed into a standard-sized immersion suit. Exactly how this was accomplished remains something of a mystery.

The warship then steamed at twenty knots through the narrow passage between the shore and island, while guns were fired and a helicopter flew overhead with the oak leaf and the White Ensign suspended beneath. Michael duly presented the deeds of the rock to the chairman of the Trust's regional committee, standing on the roof of the ship's bridge. A rising gale prevented the party from returning to Portscatho, so the frigate steamed to Plymouth, where the Royal Navy laid on dinner in the ward room. Moved by the occasion, the High Sheriff attempted to stand to propose the Loyal Toast. What would have been a breach of naval etiquette was averted, because Michael's height brought him smartly into contact with the deck-head and returned him unceremoniously to his seat.

With the independence of mind of a Cornishman, Michael was never predictable in his reactions to change in the National Trust. In 1981 he welcomed the first-time appointment of a Regional Director who was not a qualified Land Agent and came from a curatorial background, writing to me: 'I have hoped (and said!) that people other than tweedy old land agents ought to be put in charge of NT regions. It will do the Trust an enormous amount of good.'[22] Some of his agent colleagues strongly disagreed.[23] There was even greater disquiet in 1977 when the Director-General, Jack Boles, announced that a Personnel Officer was to be appointed. Sir Dawson Bates, Regional Director for the Northern Home Counties, wrote to him:

> What is happening to the Trust? Where has it gone from the happy days when people worked for it because they believed in it? Now it is all 9–5 and shop-keepers and accountants and people who don't care. No, not all, but far, far too much.
> What would the old Trust possibly have done with a personnel officer? What is the work of the new Trust if it thinks it needs one?

The long hand-written reply from the Director-General was no less blunt:

> Written in haste, as yours was. Indeed, I can't read any of the 2nd page… You should accept that we must make changes to meet the vastly bigger NT needs in a vastly more complicated world. More professionalism on establishment matters is long overdue… sorry to take a totally different line to yours.[24]

Michael, too, was deeply committed to the belief that the Trust's affairs should be directed by amateurs, whose knowledge derived from personal interest and enthusiasm, not professional obligation. He was concerned at the way:

> … the National Trust has changed its spots from being an organisation run by amateurs to being one run by professionals. For whom? There is the problem. The general public much preferred the amateur approach. I comfort myself by saying we couldn't have gone on for ever.[25]

6

THE 'HEIR OF TAILYIE'

Mrs Dalyell and The House of The Binns

THE GENIUS OF THE SCOTS takes many forms. The gift of song, the building of bridges and lighthouses, philosophy, poetry and the law spring to mind. No less remarkable is the Scots' capacity for destroying their finest buildings, narrowly surpassed by the Irish Republic. Colin McWilliam, who joined the ten-year-old National Monuments of Scotland in 1951, wrote of:

> … a certain Scots pride which tends to embrace disaster, fearful of accepting grants because of the strings attached (in fact these strings are few and feeble), but prepared to accept without question the ill-founded fallacy that a house could not be zero-rated until its roof was taken off.[1]

McWilliam was English and an architect by training, so his strictures, particularly his criticisms of the supine government agencies charged with the protection of Scotland's built heritage, could be dismissed by native Scots. What cannot be denied is the inventory of losses, and their architectural significance, displayed so graphically in the Victoria and Albert Museum's exhibition on *The Destruction of the Country House* in 1974. Ian Gow's book, *Scotland's Lost Houses*, which was published in 2006, is just as compelling and eloquent.

The simple facts are these. Scotland's greatest architect, Robert Adam, and his brother James, who worked with him, were responsible for about a hundred buildings north of the border. Less than half of these survive. The casualties include Balbardie House in West Lothian, a classical building of exceptional refinement built at the end of Adam's career, and demolished in 1955. Schawpark in Clackmannanshire went in 1961, Jerviston House in Lanarkshire in 1966, and Hawkhill House in Edinburgh, by John Adam, in 1970. Many of Adam's lost houses were not minor works, but masterpieces.

The work of other, less familiar, architects fared even worse. *The Destruction of the Country House* exhibition included photographs of outstanding buildings by Joseph Bonomi, James Gillespie Graham, Thomas Harrison, James Playfair and Isaac Ware, as well as James Smith's stupendous Hamilton Palace. In the last hundred years, well over three hundred substantial country houses were demolished in Scotland, most of them of interest and some of outstanding architectural significance. The majority of these were destroyed in the 1950s

The north front of Hamilton Palace, Scotland, photographed in 1919, shortly before the demolition of the house in 1921.

and '60s. Gow refers to 'the uniquely Scottish predilection for dynamiting houses',[2] and relates how McWilliam had:

> a party-piece lecture providing an outline of Scottish architectural history through slides of key representative buildings, only at the end revealing to the audience that they had all been demolished in the recent past.[3]

Seen in this gloomy context, the nature of the gift of the House of The Binns to the National Trust for Scotland in 1946 might seem surprising. It was the first country house to pass to the Scottish Trust, and it made an important and influential statement. The cross-currents of influence that brought the gift about ran deep.

The Binns is one of several historic houses to the west of Edinburgh, the wooded parks of which enrich the gently rolling countryside bordering the Firth of Forth. Unlike the nearby palaces of Hopetoun and Dalmeny, it is a laird's house, less grand but more ancient. In 1826 the owner of The Binns, Sir James Dalyell, 5th Baronet, built a tower on the hill to the east of the house with the proceeds of a wager, so that he could look over his neighbour's new plantations – intended as a screen – and down on his great classical mansion of Hopetoun. The exterior of The Binns, with its corner towers and crenellations, suggests the influence of Abbotsford; and indeed, Sir Walter Scott was a friend of Sir James Dalyell, who encased a much earlier house in the 1820s, to the discreet designs of William Burn. The site – the name 'Binns' means hills in old Scots – had been built on since the fifteenth century or earlier, but the core of the present building is largely seventeenth-century. The later his-

The House of The Binns, Scotland, a seventeenth-century house with mid-eighteenth and early-nineteenth-century additions, and the home of the Dalyell family since 1612.

tory of the Dalyell family was so distinguished and colourful that they saw little need to aggrandise their house.

General Tam Dalyell fought for both Charles I and Charles II in the Civil War, was captured at the Battle of Worcester in 1651 and imprisoned by Cromwell; and was one of the few ever to escape from the Tower of London. He fled abroad, served as a mercenary for Tsar Alexei Mikhailovich, the father of Peter the Great, became a Russian noble and married a Russian wife. Having returned to Scotland after the Restoration, in 1681 he raised the Royal Regiment of Scots Dragoons, which later achieved lasting renown as the Royal Scots Greys. Although both Tam Dalyell and Charles II died in 1685, before the king was able to grant an intended baronetcy, James II conferred the title on the General's son, Thomas, in November of that year, with a special dispensation that, in default of a male heir, it could pass through the female line to 'the heir of tailyie', as has happened on three occasions. Later members of the family to achieve distinction include Captain James Dalyell, who was killed and scalped by Native Americans in 1763, and Sir John Graham Dalyell, 6th Baronet, advocate, scientist, naturalist and teacher of Charles Darwin.

By the end of the First World War, the issue of land reform was simmering, particularly in the Highlands, with the example of Ireland a constant reminder of what could happen in Scotland if grievances were not addressed. Sir James Dalyell, the 9th Baronet – who had inherited The Binns in 1913 from his cousin Elizabeth – had fought in Egypt and at Gallipoli, and was acutely aware of the sacrifices made by the Scots, 128,000 of whom had been killed in the Great War, the highest death toll per capita of any Allied nation. He arranged for parts of the Binns estate to be sold to the Department of Agriculture to provide smallholdings for returning soldiers. On his death in 1935, Sir James left the rest of the estate and the house to his daughter, Eleanor, the 'heir of tailyie'. She had married Lt Col Gordon Loch in 1928, and in 1938 he changed his name to Dalyell. In 1942 Eleanor Dalyell received an unsolicited approach from the National Trust for Scotland, asking whether she would consider involving the organisation, then barely ten years old, in the future preservation of the house.

The founders of the National Trust had intended that its remit would cover the whole of the British Isles; and indeed, the first really substantial building to be acquired, Kanturk Castle in County Cork, is now in the Republic of Ireland. Robert Hunter, the Chairman, dealt with the negotiations himself, in letters written in 1900 from the General Post Office in Dublin, a building which, in the Easter uprising sixteen years later, would become the very symbol of republicanism. A resolution to set up a National Trust in Scotland was seconded by Octavia Hill and passed by the Executive Committee in 1899, but nothing came of the two visits Canon Hardwicke Rawnsley made to Edinburgh to seek support for the idea.

The ceremony, held at the House of The Binns, to mark the union of the Royal Scots Greys and the 3rd Carabiniers to form the Royal Scots Dragoon Guards in 1971. General Tam Dalyell (d.1685) raised the cavalry regiment later known as the 'Scots Greys' in 1681.

This may ultimately have been beneficial, because it left the Scots free to form their own organisation, with no ties to London other than goodwill. The National Trust for Scotland was established in 1931 and incorporated by statute four years later. The purposes of the new body, set out in the National Trust for Scotland Confirmation Act of 1935, were modelled on the National Trust Act of 1907, but included the preservation of chattels – a provision which did not apply south of the border until the National Trust Act of 1937, and which would be relevant to the future of The Binns.

Had the National Trust for Scotland been securely established a few years earlier, perhaps Lord Lothian would have considered putting Newbattle Abbey into its hands, rather than transferring it to the Universities of Scotland in 1931. Certainly the recently formed National Trust for Scotland quickly established its own Country Houses Scheme. A leaflet entitled *Historic Country Houses in Scotland and their Preservation*, based on the one produced by its sister organisation, was distributed to the owners of great houses, to let them know about the potential benefits of the recent legislation. It explained that property transferred to the National Trust for Scotland would then be free of tax; there would be a right of continuing occupation for the family making the gift; and the necessary endowment, in either land or capital, would also be tax-free. One of the leaflets was sent to Colonel and Mrs Dalyell of the House of The Binns, without question one of Scotland's most historic houses. Their son, Tam Dalyell, was eleven years old at the time.

Although he was then at a preparatory school, Harecroft Hall in Cumberland, Tam Dalyell remembers being closely involved by his parents in decisions affecting the future of The Binns, which he would otherwise have expected to inherit.[4] He recalls that the approach from the National Trust for Scotland went further than merely sending the leaflet about the Country Houses Scheme. The Binns was specifically identified as a house which might set useful precedents and initiate the scheme in a secure and reassuring way. For a building with such a long history, it presented remarkably few complications. In spite of wartime constraints, it had been carefully maintained, was in generally sound condition and, by the standards of many of Scotland's great houses, was compact and not unduly large. The style of its Regency, Scotch Baronial exterior was, at that time, heartily despised, particularly north of the border, but it was nevertheless a house of impeccable Scottish credentials, uncontaminated by English or industrial wealth. The succession was also uncomplicated: it had passed to an only child, with an only child. Another branch of the family that might have had a claim to The Binns was American, but the potential beneficiary, Harry S. Truman, had other, rather more pressing responsibilities to contend with. The Dalyell family was represented by a respected and sympathetic legal adviser, Sir Ernest Wedderburn, of the Edinburgh firm of Shepherd and Wedderburn, who was professor of conveyancing in the University of Edinburgh. He was not a socialist, but voted Labour in the general election of 1945 and had a commitment to public service characteristic of many in the professions in Scotland.

There was a web of other influences and connections which would have a bearing. Colonel Dalyell was a senior civil servant, who had worked in India and had served as British principal agent in Bahrain from 1932 to 1937, the equivalent of a British Ambassador today. Eleanor Dalyell spoke fluent Arabic, and they both immersed themselves in the political and cultural life of the region. They assisted the archaeologist Leonard Wooley, then excavating the royal cemetery at Ur, in what is now southern Iraq, and knew the writer and traveller Gertrude Bell well. Stuart Piggott, one of the excavators of the Sutton Hoo treasure in Suffolk and later Professor of Archaeology at Edinburgh, was another friend. Colonel Dalyell's views on Middle Eastern and Southern Asian affairs carried weight in both the Foreign Office and the India Office; and this in turn brought him into contact with those who were shaping the future of

Persian miniatures commissioned by Eleanor Dalyell in 1934, while her husband was serving as the British principal agent in Bahrain.

the National Trust. Viscount Grey of Fallodon (Liberal Foreign Secretary from 1905 to 1916, when Sir Edward Grey) – the driving force behind the National Trust's acquisition of the Farne Islands, off the Northumberland coast, in 1925 – was a personal friend of both the Dalyell and Trevelyan families, and was Eleanor Dalyell's godfather. Wallington in Northumberland had been given to the National Trust by Sir Charles Trevelyan in 1941, and his brother G.M. Trevelyan was still the vice chairman of the Trust's Executive Committee in 1942.

The future of India was an issue which united those who, like Dalyell, believed that self-government had to come. He knew and admired Lord Zetland, who had published *Steps towards Indian Home Rule* in 1935. As chairman of the National Trust, Zetland had helped steer through the legislation which would give an assured future to The Binns. Dalyell also knew Lord Lothian, who was exceptionally well-informed on the problems of India, not just because of his service as Under-Secretary of State for India from 1931 to 1932, but also through his visit there as chairman of the Indian Franchise Committee, which reported to the Government on election issues in 1932. Lothian stayed with Gandhi for three days, living in a mud and wattle hut, eating vegetarian food and talking to the Mahatma, who subsequently wrote a paper for him headed 'For Lord Lothian and responsible statesmen only.' When writing in the winter of 1935 to invite Jawaharlal Nehru to stay at Blickling, Lothian commented that 'friendly and informal personal contacts, though they may lead to no immediate agreement, may make possible understanding later on.'[5] These sentiments applied to his attitude to the future of India; and, much closer to home, coloured his and his associates' efforts to find ways of preserving historic houses and estates.

For the Dalyell family, as for Lothian, their inherited estates had been entrusted to them as a cultural and historical asset, rather than for personal enrichment. It was an attitude that had been eloquently expressed by John Ruskin, who saw himself as not simply the owner of his collections, but as their guardian, who in due course would give them to several carefully chosen museums. The Dalyells believed that they too were custodians and The Binns belonged, in spirit if not legally, to the people of Scotland. The way Colonel and Mrs Dalyell expressed this to their eleven-year-old son was clearly recollected over 50 years later:

> 'We are thinking of giving the house which, in the normal course of events when we die, would belong to you, to an organisation called the National Trust for Scotland,' (which in effect for them was Scotland itself). My parents said they could not know what I would do in life, but they were very clear about the importance of the family in Scottish history.[6]

The gift was to comprise the house, its collections of pictures, furniture and other historic contents, and the park of 200 acres. Colonel Dalyell also provided an endowment of £4,000. Sir Ernest Wedderburn issued a statement saying:

> Mrs Dalyell has been actuated by a desire to ensure, so far as she can do so, that The Binns with its traditions and legends may be preserved for future generations and that her son Thomas Dalyell of The Binns may be able to reside there.[7]

The House of The Binns was legally transferred to the National Trust for Scotland by charter in 1944. Tam Dalyell was asked to add his signature to that of his parents on the trans-

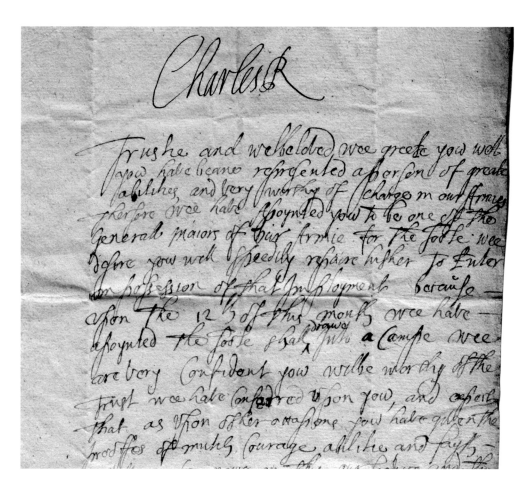

Letter from King Charles II appointing Colonel Tam Dalyell as a Major General in his army.

fer document, which he did in the study of his Harefields headmaster, who allowed him to use his fountain pen. The Charter of Gift begins:

> Considering that I am in sympathy with the purposes and aims of the National Trust for Scotland… and that I am desirous that The Binns with its history and legend and the memory of the family of Dalyell of The Binns shall be preserved for all time coming for the benefit and enjoyment of the Nation…

and then reserves the right to fly the armorial Banner of Dalyell of The Binns 'and to the hidden treasure of The Binns should it be recovered'.

Tam understood the implications of the gift for him personally, and had been convinced by his parents that it was the right thing to do. On 30 April 1946 the Earl of Wemyss and March, chairman of the National Trust for Scotland, received a formal handing-over of stone and soil, or *sasine*, from Mrs Dalyell. In press reports it was recorded that 'the sod was dug from the old garden by the thirteen-year-old Tam Dalyell of the Binns'. The photograph recording the exchange shows Colonel Dalyell standing behind his wife, and between her and the chairman, a kilted Tam, facing the cameraman and staring straight at him. Some gifts of great estates have been carried out with minimum, if any, involvement of the next generation, often leading to lasting resentment. That was not the case with The Binns.

Throughout the negotiations Colonel Dalyell kept well out of the limelight, which he directed to his wife and son. Most of the correspondence about the transfer was, however, dealt with by him, and it shows how the theory of the Country Houses Scheme was, step by step, made to work in Scotland. The Trust was asked to arrange for an 'Inventory of the Furnishings', on the basis that everything of historical and artistic importance would, regardless of financial value, come as a gift with the house. In a letter of 17 March 1944 Colonel Dalyell raised the issue of vandalism, suggesting that 'the English National Trust may have experience of this, for example at Sir Charles Trevelyan's Trust property at Wallington (where, I fancy, the visitors might as here include a rather rough type),' adding that 'flowers and so on in gardens seem to offer strong temptation to some folk.' He proposed that all staff appointed at The Binns should report to his wife and then found a retired police inspector to act as 'Baron Officer of the Binns',

Stanley Cursiter, *Eleanor Dalyell*.

as the custodian was to be called, who was 'much liked in Bo'ness… has the Gaelic… is of good physique and would be able to keep order if need were to arise'. Colonel Dalyell also slipped in a note suggesting that the Trust should make Tam a Life Member, 'causa honoris'; and when this was confirmed, wrote to thank the Secretary, Arthur Russell, saying that Tam 'has taken a great interest in the whole matter and will, I know, very much appreciate the honour the Trust has done him'.

Initially the house was only open to the public on one afternoon a week. The arrangements for showing the main rooms were left to Mrs Dalyell, who, in the early years, generally employed people who had retired from the armed services. Increasingly, however, she liked to involve the young, for the same reasons that Lady Mander preferred to use students as guides at Wightwick Manor. It was an opportunity for them to develop their confidence and speaking skills, with gentle encouragement and guidance. One of her recruits was the son of the local minister. In his autobiography, *Against Goliath: David Steel's Story*, he wrote:

> For two summers I worked as a guide in a National Trust stately home, The Binns, near Linlithgow, the seventeenth-century home of the persecutor of my covenanting ancestors, 'Bloody Tam' Dalyell; by then it was that of a young man just down from Cambridge who was prospective Labour candidate for Roxburgh, Selkirk and Peebles, Tam Dalyell – now MP for Linlithgow. His mother was a wonderful and great eccentric who was very kind to me, though exasperated at my inability to clear up after her prodigious flower-arranging. Tam appeared only occasionally, being busy campaigning in this faraway place – the Borders – of which I knew little.[8]

Relations with the officers of the National Trust for Scotland were and remained distant but cordial. The exception was the Secretary and Treasurer from 1947 to 1949, Jo Grimond, whom the Dalyells thought was using the organisation as a stepping-stone towards a career at Westminster. They were dismayed to learn that, on resigning, he had left a note for his successor, saying that he felt the National Trust for Scotland's finances were so precarious that it was not really viable and should be wound up. The Dalyell family were among those who believed that the young lawyer from Kelso appointed to succeed Grimond should be given a chance. Jamie Stormonth Darling not only helped to put the National Trust for Scotland on a secure footing, but substantially increased its holdings of countryside and historic properties, and gave it an international reputation, before retiring from the post of Director – by then 'Sir James' – in 1983.

Colonel and Mrs Dalyell continued to involve themselves in conservation issues. In 1948 the Chancellor of the Exchequer, Sir Stafford Cripps, appointed a committee to investigate what the government might do to give historic houses greater protection, with Sir Ernest Gowers as its chairman and other distinguished members, including the director of the Courtauld Institute and Surveyor of the King's Pictures, Anthony Blunt. In the summer of 1949 they visited The Binns, where Tam Dalyell was on holiday from Eton. He recalls Sir Ernest as grave and friendly, Blunt questioning his parents, and, as a fifteen-year-old, being interrogated as to what he thought by the formidable Ava, Lady Anderson.[9]

The Gowers Committee report, *Houses of Outstanding Historic or Architectural Interest*, published in 1950, provided the foundations for the government's heritage policy for the next 50 years. The report paid particular attention to the issue of chattels, advocating that these should, whenever possible, be retained *in situ*. It also emphasised the value of family occupation, quoting from the evidence submitted by Christopher Hussey, who had said how important it was that country houses should 'remain a living element in the social fabric of the nation'.[10] The authority of the report was enhanced by the breadth of evidence taken, and by visits such as the one to The Binns, to discuss the position of those grappling with the problem of responsibility for a great house. The outcome was the Historic Buildings and Ancient Monuments Act of 1953, which established the Historic Buildings Councils for England, Wales and Scotland. These bodies could make grants for the repair and maintenance of houses of outstanding architectural or historic importance, and for the conservation of their contents. The Act also, through a late and reluctantly granted amendment, allowed the National Land Fund to be used both for the transfer of historic houses to the two National Trusts, and to provide endowments, although in practice the latter happened only in Scotland and Northern Ireland. The preservation of Kellie Castle in Fife and Craigievar in Aberdeenshire, as well as houses such as Dyrham Park in Gloucestershire and Beningbrough Hall near York, with their collections, was made possible by this legislation.

Because of their first-hand experience, Colonel and Mrs Dalyell were consulted by other families that were considering giving their houses to the National Trust for Scotland. One enquiry came from Charles, 5th Marquess of Ailsa, who was negotiating with the Trust over the possible gift of Culzean Castle, perched on rocks above the Firth of Clyde, with views across to Arran and the Mull of Kintyre. It is a house of exceptional importance and on a very grand scale. Only an architect of Robert Adam's ingenuity could have combined so successfully the Gothic form and silhouette of the exterior of the Castle with one of the most disciplined and elegant of classical interiors.

In 1945, before making the gift, Lord Ailsa had written a prescient letter to the secretary of the National Trust for Scotland, sounding a note of warning:

> One is apt to upset the balance by tampering with old buildings, and using these for a purpose the Designer did not have in mind when he made his creation.[11]

Sadly, the warning went unheeded, and changes were carried out by the Trust which upset the family profoundly. In order to make the park pay its way, a golf course was revived and another planned closer to the sea. Planting in the garden was entrusted to Jim Russell, a nurseryman from Surrey who was a partner of the National Trust's gardens adviser, Graham Stuart Thomas. Many of the plants recommended did not survive the cold, coastal winds, as the family could have warned had they been consulted. The running and presentation of the Castle itself was put in the hands of a local committee, whose chairman, Lady Fergusson of Kilkerran, was determined to restore Culzean 'to its rightful place as conceived by Robert Adam 160 years ago'.[12] As a result, important ethnological collections amassed in the eighteenth century by Archibald, 11th Earl of Cassillis, were thrown out; the pictures were 'blitzed and re-hung' (Lady Fergusson's words); and the 3rd Marquess of Ailsa's taxidermy was banished, including two stuffed monkeys which had previously swung from the chandelier hanging above Adam's oval staircase.[13] When the family remonstrated, Sir James Fergusson told them loftily, 'Allow me to be right.'[14]

Unfortunately for Culzean and the National Trust for Scotland, it was the family who were right. In a letter to Colin McWilliam, who had been asked to write the first guidebook in 1954, the 7th Marquess of Ailsa expressed his belief that much of the decoration attributed to Robert Adam had in fact been carried out long after his death in 1792.[15] Recent research carried out by Ian Gow and Eileen Harris has revealed successive waves of 'Adamisation,' initiated in 1877 and given another layer in 1909. Much of what Lady Fergusson's committee believed to be the authentic eighteenth-century work of Robert Adam was in fact part of the twentieth-century Adam revival. Relations had become so strained that, shortly after inheriting the title in 1957, the 7th Marquess decided to move out of Culzean Castle to another family home, Cassillis House in Ayrshire.

The painful arguments at Culzean, and the departure of the family, are a striking contrast to the recent history of The Binns. It continued to be the home of Tam Dalyell during the years that he was Member of Parliament for Linlithgow and then West Lothian. Much of his writing was done there. His books include accounts of the Falklands War; *Devolution: The End Of Britain?* (1977); *A Science Policy for Britain* (1983); and *Dick Crossman: A Portrait* (1989). He has also served on the All Party Heritage Group, and his wife Kathleen has been chairman of the Royal Commission on the Ancient and Historical Monuments of Scotland.

The house is the only National Trust for Scotland property still lived in by the family whose ancestors built it, as had originally been envisaged under the Country Houses Scheme. Tam and Kathleen Dalyell have continued the cataloguing of the family records, begun by Eleanor's father, Sir James Dalyell, and have set up an archive room where scholars can work. Recent introductions to the house include political cartoons, on topics ranging from Tam's

Paxton House in Scotland, designed by John Adam in 1758, was extended with a Picture Gallery by Robert Reid between 1811 and 1814, which is now hung with paintings on loan from the National Galleries of Scotland.

pursuit in the House of Commons of the Prime Minister Margaret Thatcher, over the sinking of the *Belgrano* in 1982, to his no less persistent harrying of Tony Blair on the 'dodgy dossier' used to justify the invasion of Iraq.

Tam Dalyell's long service as a Labour Member of Parliament might suggest that the gift of The House of The Binns to the National Trust for Scotland was an expression of socialist ideals. This was certainly the motive for the transfer in 1993 of Paxton House, in the Borders, into the hands of a charitable trust. Its former owner, John Home Robertson, Labour MP for East Lothian, described his decision as 'socialism in action.' He moved with his wife and two sons into part of the west wing, which is retained in family ownership, but on the condition that if they leave it has to be sold to the Paxton Trust for £1. Through an agreement with the National Gallery of Scotland, the picture gallery adjoining the original house, which was designed by John Adam in 1758, is used for the display of eighteenth-century paintings which would otherwise be in store in Edinburgh. At the time he made the decision, Home Robertson remarked: 'I can imagine that some people, heirs to estates, would be unhappy about something going into public ownership, but I am fairly comfortable about it all.' He explained that 'it would have broken my heart to see the place flogged off – it was important to me, as well as being important to the local and national heritage… you could say it's the only example of a Labour man setting up a quango over the last fourteen years.'[16]

Unlike Home Robertson, Eleanor Dalyell's gift was motivated not by socialism, but by a highly developed sense of public service. The two may overlap; but the differences are as significant as the similarities. The House of The Binns came to the National Trust for Scotland not as a political statement, but out of a belief in the value of sharing a sense of history.

7

THE PAINTER'S DAUGHTER
AND THE BIOGRAPHER

Lady Berwick and Attingham Park;
Lady Mander and Wightwick Manor

ADY MANDER WAS RARELY SLOW in letting the National Trust know when it was at fault. Her letters, identifiable from her erratic typing, would arrive at the regional office at Attingham Park in Shropshire, and might be warmly appreciative. Often they were waspish and withering. The Trust's failure to acknowledge the timing and significance of the gift by her husband, Sir Geoffrey Mander, of Wightwick Manor, on the edge of Wolverhampton, caused her particular irritation. An article in the *National Trust Magazine* in the autumn of 1987, on 'The Early Years of the Country Houses Scheme', stated that 'the first person to take advantage of the scheme was Lord Lothian… in 1940 bequeathing Blickling Hall in Norfolk to the Trust.' Its author received a sharp reminder that it was Sir Geoffrey Mander who first took up the scheme, giving Wightwick in 1937.[1] To Rosalie Mander the mistake was symptomatic of the Trust's snobbery, disregard for historical accuracy, and ingratitude. She knew that Wightwick was scarcely regarded as a country house: it was built by a Midlands industrialist, and was less than fifty years old at the time it was accepted.

National Trust grandees might also incur her displeasure. When the Chairman of the Mercia region, Gerald, 6th Earl of Bradford, felt obliged to visit Wightwick Manor in the mid-1970s, he thought it sensible to take his wife Mary with him, because she had been responsible for much interior redecoration in the eighteenth-century rooms at their house, Weston Park in Shropshire. His particular interest was forestry, which was not much help at suburban Wightwick. Within a few minutes of their arrival, it became evident that Lady Bradford knew little about William Morris, whose textiles and wallpapers were a feature of the house, and still less about the Pre-Raphaelite painters who were the subject of Rosalie Mander's acclaimed biographies.

Sir Geoffrey and Lady Mander had built up an outstanding collection of Pre-Raphaelite pictures, at a time when they were unfashionable, inexpensive and little studied. One of the most interesting groups of paintings to find its way to Wightwick came through her friendship with the Rossetti family. The daughters of William Michael Rossetti lived in a house in St John's Wood which was bombed during the War. Their pictures were salvaged, were temporarily stored at the Tate and at Lady Mander's suggestion were loaned to Wightwick.

Rosalie Mander's knowledge and enthusiasm were shared with the students she recruit-

ed as guides to Wightwick and with a wide circle of scholars. She corresponded with Arthur Grogan, the tenant of another National Trust house with Pre-Raphaelite associations, Standen, in Sussex. Both were acquiring pictures, furniture and ceramics for their respective houses, to enhance their historical and visual appeal, and they exchanged notes on the Trust's inadequate recognition of their efforts.[2]

[above] Wightwick Manor, near Wolverhampton in the West Midlands, was given to the National Trust by Sir Geoffrey Mander in 1937, acquired under the Trust's new 'Country Houses Scheme'.

If the Bradfords' visit to Wightwick was an ordeal for all concerned, that of the Trust's Chairman, Lord Gibson, shortly afterwards was a pleasure. Lady Gibson had assembled a collection of Pre-Raphaelite paintings and drawings to match that at Wightwick; and Lady Mander could not have been more welcoming when they arrived in the middle of a thunderstorm. Many of her closest friends were academics or curators in art galleries and museums. When she died in 1983 there were scarcely any county figures at her funeral, but her student guides acted as ushers, and the Trust's builders and gardeners were there in force.

The acceptance of Wightwick was made easier by Sir Geoffrey's provision of a substantial endowment in the form of shares in Manders, the Wolverhampton paint manufacturers of which he was chairman. The case for acquisition was supported by G.M. Trevelyan, the chairman of the Trust's Estates Committee, whose family house, Wallington in Northumberland, was also rich in Pre-Raphaelite associations.

The gift of Wightwick to the National Trust may have been intended to resolve a potentially contentious inheritance. Rosalie Glynn Grylls, who became Sir Geoffrey Mander's second wife, had been employed as his secretary: he was

Dante Gabriel Rossetti, *Jane Morris*, completed by Ford Madox Brown; the painting was the first Pre-Raphaelite picture bought by Sir Geoffrey and Lady Mander, and hangs now in the Drawing Room at Wightwick Manor.

[opposite] Detail of William Morris's 'Bird' textile on the sofa in the Great Parlour at Wightwick Manor.

Liberal MP for East Wolverhampton. She came from a long line of Cornish clergymen, was a highly intelligent Oxford graduate and an aspiring writer, whose *Portrait of Rossetti* (1964) was widely praised. The painting of her in academic dress, by Feliks Topolski, conveys just how pretty and vivacious she was, but she disliked it and the picture was hidden on a back staircase at Wightwick. When she was photographed in the library with Sir Geoffrey and her two children – Anthea clutching her panda, John self-consciously holding an arts and crafts jug – she chose to be seated at a small table, her fingers on the keys of a portable typewriter. The gift of Wightwick to the National Trust meant that any disputes with the son of Sir Geoffrey's first marriage over the ownership of the house were avoided.

Sir Geoffrey Mander died in 1962, having set up a fund to enable Lady Mander to go on living at Wightwick. The National Trust's Regional Agent had to provide confirmation annually to the trustees of the fund that she was continuing to reside there. At the time the arrangement was made, it may have suited Rosalie Mander, because she was bringing up her children at Wightwick and the house was relevant to her research. In due course it became a life

Sir Geoffrey Mander with his second wife, Rosalie Glynn Grylls, and their children, John and Anthea, in the Library at Wightwick Manor.

sentence in the suburbs of Wolverhampton, far away from Oxford, which was her intellectual home, and London, where most of her friends lived. When Gerard Noel was the Regional Agent he found the annual residency return an invidious requirement and gave the necessary confirmation without question.

One of the few people in the West Midlands to share her interests was Lady Berwick, whose husband had given Attingham Park to the National Trust in 1947. In one of Rosalie Mander's biographies, *Mrs Browning: The Story of Elizabeth Barrett* (1980), there is an account of the funeral of Robert Browning, which took place in Venice in 1889, and which involved a gondola procession, lit by a setting sun, to San Michele. It came from the previously unpublished diary of Costanza Hulton, a friend of the Brownings, and Lady Berwick's mother.

When Teresa Berwick first came to Attingham in 1919, as the young wife of Thomas, 8th Lord Berwick, one painting in the collection must have been particularly evocative. The picture, possibly after a lost original by Giorgione, is apparently of a concert at the court of Queen Caterina Cornaro. The town in the middle distance, dominated by its castle, can be identified as Asolo, given to the Queen in 1489 by the Venetian Republic in exchange for her dominion of Cyprus, and where she lived until her death in 1510. It was in Asolo that Teresa was born on 6 August 1890 to William and Costanza Hulton.[3]

Costanza's father, Vicenzo Mazini, was Italian and after his death in 1869 her English mother, Linda, lived in Florence. William Hulton, the son of a clergyman, was a serious but struggling painter who found Italy cheap and congenial. After their marriage in 1886 they moved to Venice and bought the two upper floors of the Palazzo Dona, opposite SS. Giovanni e Paolo (known familiarly to the Venetians as 'San Zanipolo') and with Pietro Lombardo's ingenious façade of the Scuola di San Marco immediately across the canal. The Campo San Zanipolo offered William Hulton inexhaustible subject matter. He particularly admired Verrochio's masterpiece, later referred to by the Hulton children, with proprietorial affection, as 'old Colleoni on his horse'.

Their elder daughter, Gioconda, was born in 1887. With Costanza's charm and William's ability as a painter, they quickly made friends with Mr and Mrs Daniel Sargent Curtis, whose cousin, John Singer Sargent, frequently stayed with them at the Palazzo Barbaro. It was there, in 1889, that Costanza attended one of Robert Browning's readings of his own poems. By that time Browning, his son Penini and American daughter-in-law, Fannie (later to be Teresa's godmother), were well-known to the Hultons; in her diary, Costanza notes that they dined together in November 1888, when 'R.B. talked wonderfully about Ezzelino da Romano and the crusade against him.'[4] The Brownings were again their guests in December of that year. Another close friend was the artist Reginald Barratt, who had studied with William Hulton in 1885 and 1886 at Julien's in Paris, and who painted his portrait. The small oil studies Hulton painted during his years in France are among his most attractive work.

In 1887, at one of the Curtises' frequent dinner parties, Costanza re-encountered Henry James – she had first met him in 1880 – who had just returned to Venice from Florence. 'It was a pleasure to meet him again,' she recalled, 'but he incensed me by calling Bellosguardo "a windy snare" and then telling us Venice was "a slimy delusion".'[5]

The Court of Queen Caterina Cornaro at Asolo, Venetian School, now in the Picture Gallery at Attingham Park.

When in May 1890, with Costanza expecting their second child, the Hultons decided to escape the summer heat of Venice, Asolo was a convenient and obvious retreat. The town had become something of an English colony since Robert Browning had lived there, and the surrounding landscape appealed to William Hulton. They took the Casa Bolzon with its large airy rooms and wide views over the plain, and moved in with their servants on 22 May. For most of the early summer, William painted in and around Asolo, particularly the view of the town from the south, the subject of a picture now at Attingham. Then, after the birth of Teresa, the family returned to Venice.

The painter whose friendship meant most to the Hulton family was Walter Sickert. Writing in 1959, seventeen years after his death, Lady Berwick remembered him as 'so cheerful and clever and amusing and good-looking… he often came to our house and we were all fond of him.' Lady Berwick kept a series of his letters to her mother, carefully annotating them. In the earliest, which is undated but apparently written in 1901, he claimed that he had:

> … started to come and see the Asolo picture one Sunday morning, but reflected that Hulton, like all good Englishmen, was probably at church…[6]

When in May 1901 a *festa* was held in the Giardinetto Reale, Costanza wore a dress which particularly appealed to Sickert. She sat for him three times in it for a sketch in black chalk, with a touch of pink in the sash. Later that year Sickert returned to Dieppe. He wrote to Costanza from the Maison Villain, the home of his mistress Titine, saying he was 'sending Miss Gioconda a calle down which she passes, I daresay, nearly every day,' and later: 'I have not forgotten the exchange Gioconda said she would make with me but I cannot quite decide

William Hulton, *Asolo from the South*, 1890, painted from a similar viewpoint to that used in the picture of Queen Caterina Cornaro's Court (see page 105).

on what to do for her, a Dieppe or a Venice drawing.' The exchange Sickert refers to was for one of Gioconda's own drawings. He admired her depictions of saints, and, to help her with her paintings of knights in armour, sent her annotated studies explaining the various joints.

Teresa also had her admirers. Another of William Hulton's friends, Count Rudolf von Wickenburg, a young Austrian who had come to Venice to paint, sketched Teresa in 1903 and gave the drawing to her parents. Sickert wrote to Costanza: 'I saw a very charming sketch of your little Miss Bimbale that Wickenburgh did. I am instilling into him the elements of oil-painting.' Between 1904 and 1928, the Hulton family seem to have lost touch with Sickert. William Hulton found another sympathetic painting companion in John Singer Sargent, and in 1909 the whole family joined his party at Berisal in Switzerland. Costanza found Sargent's painting of a waterfall and his small studies 'very strong and admirable but not very pleasing'.[7] At this time William Hulton was painting modest watercolours of Alpine scenery.

Although the Hulton family continued to use their house in Venice, they spent much of 1905 in Munich, where Teresa took intensive piano lessons with a view to becoming a professional musician. Her life was to take a very different direction, however. After a distressing *affaire de coeur*, which she subsequently preferred not to discuss, she gave up her musical studies entirely. During the First World War, she worked with the British Red Cross at Cervignano, close behind the front line, and narrowly avoided capture after the disaster of Caporetto. In 1919 she received the Croce di Guerra. The same year she married Thomas, 8th Lord Berwick, in the English Church of S. Giorgio, where she had been christened and confirmed. The service combined English liturgy with Venetian elegance. Teresa's long journey to Attingham began in a gondola, a sight which the literary critic Percy Lubbock recalled as the most beautiful he had ever seen.[8]

For somebody brought up in a Venetian palace visited by some of the greatest writers and painters in Europe, adapting to life in Shropshire proved difficult and painful. Her loneliness was compounded by their failure to have children and by a period when she became convinced that she was going blind. She also found it distressing that Lord Berwick was paying an annuity to a Parisian former lover. Most of her neighbours preferred chasing foxes to cultural pursuits. Initially, the Berwicks lived at Cronkhill, Nash's Italianate villa built in 1805 for an agent of the Attingham estate, with its views across the wide meanders of the Severn to the Wrekin, the most easterly of the Shropshire hills. However Lord Berwick quickly found that his young wife had all the knowledge and artistic sense to be the perfect custodian of Attingham itself. The house was in a sad state of depletion and disarray.

Attingham Park was built for Noel, 1st Lord Berwick between 1782 and 1785 in an austere classical style, and was furnished by his son Thomas with great extravagance. Indeed, the 2nd Lord Berwick's life shows how destructive unbridled acquisitiveness can be. His grand tour, which began in 1792, gave him the opportunity to buy feverishly, purchasing antique sculpture for the Outer Library at Attingham and paintings by Angelica Kauffman, Fagan and Hackert. Other pictures, optimistically attributed to Raphael, Leonardo da Vinci and Guercino, were bought for the Picture Gallery, designed by John Nash in 1805 to house Berwick's collection. In 1812 his spending reached a new pitch when, at the age of 42, he married the seventeen-year-old daughter of a Swiss clockmaker, Sophia Dubouchet, who was a courtesan favoured by friends of the Prince of Wales. Her own sister remarked that, 'Sophia, having the command of more guineas than ever she had expected to have had pence, did nothing from morning till night, but throw them away.' To his brother William Noel-Hill, who served as a diplomat in Italy from 1808 to 1832, Thomas confessed that financial problems were accumulating as fast as his collections, from 'not having resolution to abstain from Building and Picture buying'.[9] By 1827 Lord Berwick was bankrupt.

The process of dispersal was even more spectacular than his acquisitions. The entire contents of Attingham Park were auctioned in a sixteen-day sale. Because many of the lots failed to sell, there was a further sale in 1829, lasting seven days, to meet debts which were still unpaid. Some pieces from Attingham, including a marble bust of Augustus Caesar and a cork model of an Etruscan tomb, were bought by Sir John Soane for his own house and museum in Lincoln's Inn Fields.[10] Many more were purchased by William Noel-Hill.

The Drawing Room at Attingham Park, with Italian Empire furniture bought by William, 3rd Lord Berwick, who served as British Ambassador in Naples in the 1820s. The house, its contents, and the surrounding estate were bequeathed to the National Trust by Thomas, 8th Lord Berwick, who died in 1947.

When he succeeded to his brother's title in 1832, his own collections, accumulated while he was an ambassador resident first in Sardinia and then in Naples, combined with the purchases from his brother, made Attingham's interior seem like an Italian palazzo transported to Shropshire. The association with Italy was to be extended in the early twentieth century.

For most of the second half of the nineteenth century, Attingham had been largely shut up or tenanted. The 2nd Lord Berwick's collecting and excessive expenditure had left the estate impoverished. When the author of *Saddle and Sirloin* came to Attingham in the 1860s, he found the deserted stable yard overrun with rats, and only a single light burning faintly in the basement of the main house.[11] The 4th Lord Berwick was a clergyman who chose to live at Berrington, on the Attingham estate.

The sadly neglected house to which Lord and Lady Berwick devoted themselves in the 1920s and 1930s was all the more interesting for having escaped the attentions of late-Victorian and Edwardian decorators. A scholarly interest in Empire and Regency furniture and design was just beginning to be revived by Lord Gerald Wellesley, later 7th Duke of Wellington, at his own houses, 11 Titchfield Street in London and Stratfield Saye in Hampshire; and, in Italy, by Professor Mario Praz.[12] Attingham presented an opportunity that was both exciting and daunting.

Because she was its custodian for so long, there was for many years an assumption that it was Teresa Berwick who initiated the revival of the house.[13] This was fuelled by James Lees-Milne's descriptions of Lord Berwick as 'a shadow' who was 'incapable of attending to any issue or making up his mind on any business which he found awkward or disagreeable.'[14] Scrutiny of the Attingham records by Belinda Cousens and Sarah Kay has shown that he was far from ineffectual over the care of the house, initiating redecoration and acquiring works of art which supplemented the collections of Italian furniture and pictures.

In 1911, eight years before his marriage, and while he was serving in the British Embassy in Paris, Lord Berwick arranged to have silk, which he had acquired with an Empire bed, copied in Lyons. The pattern, he was told, was by Lassalles, one of the finest Lyons textile designers of the mid-eighteenth century, and the rewoven silk was ultimately used for new curtains in the Drawing Room at Attingham. The Paris Embassy also gave Lord Berwick contacts he used to buy an Aubusson carpet, ornamental candlesticks and Empire furniture, which in due course found their way to Attingham.

After their marriage, Lady Berwick joined in the enthusiastic and discerning pursuit of sculpture and paintings with interesting Napoleonic or Neapolitan associations, which would complement the collections of the 3rd Lord Berwick. In 1927 they bought a portrait of Caroline Murat, sister of Napoleon and briefly Queen of Naples, by Louis Ducis, and, the previous year, acquired a life-size version of Canova's *Venus Italica*, both for the Drawing Room. Canova's house and studio at Possagno are just nine kilometres north of Asolo, Lady Berwick's birthplace.

Lady Berwick's re-encounter with Sickert was occasioned by his quest for a portrait of Signor de Rossi, the *padrone* of the Giorgione, his favourite Venetian restaurant. Sickert had presented the portrait to the de Rossi family in 1901, shortly after it was painted. Years later, when he was having the bitter experience of seeing his early work, little of which he owned, being sold for high prices by London dealers, he realised that he might be able to buy back

Sir Gerald Kelly, *Teresa, Lady Berwick*, painted in 1923, and now in the East Ante-room at Attingham Park.

the de Rossi portrait. He needed an agent and must have known that Costanza Hulton was still living in Venice. Contact was made through Clementine Churchill, whom he had met in Dieppe and who had encouraged her husband Winston to take painting lessons from him. In a letter of November 1928, Sickert resumed his correspondence with Costanza after a lapse of over a quarter of a century:

Your house was a valued hearth to me, & I think your dear husband was at the time perhaps the only man in Venice who thought there was any justification at all for my trying to paint! I remember a sort of Festa in the Giardino del Rey, for some charity I think I remember, I did a sketch of you in a dress you wore. I may tell you I want de Rossi's portrait not essentially to make money out of it, but to get it classified at Christie's or at my dealer's among my work. I gave it to him but it is unlikely that a Venetian family would like it as a portrait. Do you think they would take £50 sterling for it?

Costanza was able to purchase the portrait for the equivalent of forty pounds, and it was duly sent to London where Sickert collected it from Lady Berwick. He wrote to Costanza in May 1929 to say that he was delighted to find the child he had known as 'Bim' 'grown to such a superb plant' and 'the first peeress that I tutoyer!' When he learnt that a small Venetian picture he had given Teresa as a child had been stolen, he proposed painting both her portrait and Gioconda's to make good the loss.

Sittings for the portraits were arranged in London in the autumn of 1933. Lady Berwick recounted how Sickert proceeded:

Walter Sickert's *Lady in Blue*, 1933–34, which Lady Berwick called a 'fantasia', rather than a portrait, now hanging in the East Anteroom at Attingham Park.

> We went to his studio in Barnsbury Park & he took some photos. From these he did two large canvasses, three-quarter length, rather over life-size, the one of Gioconda, standing, in grisaille, mine in a figured blue dress, also standing, a hat on a chair nearby. The picture of my sister was later sold – mine is here. No one could call it a portrait, it is a fantasia in a characteristic subdued colour scheme. Both pictures had narrow gilt frames and were signed by Sickert at the Elvaston Place flat on 10 January 1934. We saw a lot of him and his charming second wife Thérèse Lessore then. He was cheerful and amusing as ever, but his health was troubling him.[15]

Lady Berwick was not unduly surprised that Sickert was at that period working largely from photographs. Sir Gerald Kelly had adopted a similar procedure when he painted her portrait in 1923, although he paid three visits to Attingham that year to make studies. But the comparison between Kelly's realism and Sickert's 'fantasia' is a revealing one. In a final letter, dated 22 December 1933, Sickert wrote: 'My dear Bim said her sister's picture had a *kolossalen scheidung* [a great clarity] which pleased me.'

For all the gusto with which he described the success of his exhibitions and the academic distinctions awarded him, Sickert was dogged not only by ill health, but also by money troubles. His attitude to making money was summed up in the epigram by the Roman poet Martial, which he added to his etching of a much put-upon woman contemplating her hopeless, dissolute male companion:

Et delator es, et calumniator;
Et fraudator es, et negotiator;
Et fellator es, et lanista: miror
Quare no habeas, Vacerra, nummos

which can be translated: 'You are an informer and a slanderer; you are a cheat and a pimp; you are a cock-sucker and an agitator: I can't imagine, Vacerra, why you are not rich.'

When his female friends visited Sickert's studio, they would often leave with a present of an etching or drawings thrust into their hands.[16] On one occasion Costanza was given a study for *Ennui*, a version of which is in the Tate.[17] On 14 January 1934 she went with Gioconda to dine with Sickert and his wife, noting in her memoir:

> It was a really delicious dinner & very good claret – amusing talk and reminiscences of Venice – he insisted on giving me an old engraving of SS. Giovanni e Paolo & when we left he kissed me on both cheeks. Poor old dear, he has a hard time of it still, only making just enough to live. His little Anglo-French wife Thérèse Lessore works hard too, painting and not selling much.[18]

Costanza was not alone in appreciating his difficulties. That same year Sir Alec Martin, the chairman of Christie's, confidentially raised over £2,000 from Sickert's friends and admirers to save him from bankruptcy. Lady Berwick was among the contributors; and Kelly was one of the trustees responsible for ensuring that Sickert did not squander the fund.

The political events of the 1930s, particularly in Italy, meant that visits from their Italian friends became less frequent. The invasion of Abyssinia finally forced Gioconda Hulton and Teresa Berwick to the conclusion that their house in Venice was likely to be, at best, a millstone round their necks, at worst, confiscated; and should be sold. William Hulton had died in 1921 and Constanza in 1939. The problem was that the Italian government had by then blocked the export of *lire* so the property was apparently un-saleable. The only way out of this *impasse* was to arrange a deal with Commendatore Tranquillo Sidoli, an Italian living in Shrewsbury.

Sidoli's family came from Bardi, an Apennine village, near Parma. During the First World War, while serving in the Bersaglieri, one of the most distinguished Italian regiments, he had been gassed and his health severely damaged. Partly to receive medical treatment, and partly to join his sister who was living in Blackpool, Sidoli settled in England and began to build, out of what had been an ice-cream business, a chain of highly successful confectionary shops, one of which was in Shrewsbury. To be able to buy superb Italian-style cakes there was a delight for Lady Berwick; and tea with the Sidoli family gave her one of the few opportunities she had in Shropshire for informal conversation in Italian.

In 1939 both Sidoli's property in Shrewsbury and the Hultons' house in Venice were threatened with confiscation by their respective governments. The solution was to swap the Palazzo Dona for Sidoli's premises on Wyle Cop in Shrewsbury. No money was to pass hands. To achieve an exchange of title deeds that was legally binding in both countries involved frantic telegrams to Venice, Florence and London, and relentless pressure from Lady Berwick on all those acting for her. It is a measure of her determination that the deal was concluded successfully. After the war the Palazzo Dona was sold by the Sidoli family to their tenant, a Venetian doctor.

The Boudoir at Attingham Park.

The Berwicks, who had no close relatives wishing to inherit the house, concluded that the preservation of Attingham could best be achieved by giving it to the National Trust. Contact was made with James Lees-Milne, who visited it in August 1936, arriving on his bicycle which had travelled with him on the train from London to Shrewsbury. He fell in love with the house, and came to regard Lady Berwick as 'a sort of Grecian goddess whom I held in respectful homage'.[19] On one of his wartime visits, Lady Berwick told him that the Shropshire Education Committee was considering taking a lease of the house, once the war was over, for use as an adult education college. As tenants they would be preferable to the Van Bergens – a Canadian family with a fortune made from margarine – who had leased Attingham between 1913 and 1920 and who had, in Lady Berwick's words, 'made it hideous and covered up all the nice furniture'.[20]

During the Second World War, a hospital was built in the park to serve a nearby airfield. The house was requisitioned, and Lord and Lady Berwick retreated to the rooms on its east side. Lord Berwick's health was failing, and he adopted the exquisite boudoir on the ground floor as his bedroom. The boudoir is circular, with a domed ceiling and walls decorated with painted swags, roundels and flowers of the 1780s, almost certainly executed by Guinand and Girard, who carried out similar work for the 5th Duke of Argyll at Inveraray Castle on Loch

Fyne. Lord Berwick brought in the Empire bed he had purchased in Paris and a set of early-nineteenth-century Italian painted chairs. From his bed he could look past a group of cedars of Lebanon, over the placid River Tern to the Wrekin, a view shaped by Humphry Repton when he worked at Attingham in 1797.

Knowledge of his illness encouraged friends to write to him with advice about what to do with the house. In 1943 the chairman of a local charity, the Walker Trust, urged him to sell Attingham to them for use as an adult college, rather than involving the National Trust in its future, on the grounds that 'very socialistic [sic], Communist ideas and actions may be ahead of England and the world in the distant, or even near, future.' Lord Berwick's agent, Gordon Miller, wrote 'out of a sense of duty' in August 1946 strongly advocating a sale, with a lease to an adult college as a far less satisfactory alternative. Lord Berwick's reply could not have made his decision plainer. He feared the college 'would have complete power to alter it to suit their requirements, this regardless of my wish to maintain the house for preservation by the National Trust.' He concluded: 'I have no confidence whatsoever in the taste of the body which controls, or is likely to be represented by the Education Authorities. They do not appear to be even masters in their own house, but to be state-controlled. I say definitely 'no' to this suggestion, having some pride in this house and having been owner of the Attingham estate since Nov 1897, nearly 50 years.' The letter refutes Lees-Milne's assertion that it was inconceivable 'this delightful man had ever come to any decision in his life'. Lord Berwick was prepared to accept the adult college as tenants of part of the house, but ownership of Attingham would pass to the National Trust on his death.

Having already retrenched because of the war, the Berwicks were disrupted less by the arrival of the Shropshire Adult Education College in 1946 than might be expected. Most of the rooms on the west and north sides of the house were given over to accommodation for the college. When Lord Berwick died in 1947, Attingham became the property of the National Trust under the terms of his will. Lady Berwick had at one time thought of returning to Cronkhill, barely a mile from Attingham, where her father's Italian pictures and the furniture from Palazzo Dona would have complemented its Claudean colonnades and views of gentle, wooded hills. She had also considered sharing a house with Gioconda, but the idea was dashed by her sister's death in a road accident in 1940. She decided instead to stay on in the rooms on the east side of Attingham. A great deal of furniture had already been sold to clear rooms for the Adult Education College. She may have concluded that, if she vacated her side of the house, it might in due course be included in the lease to the college, which was likely to expand under the direction of its energetic warden.

There were tensions, not least because the first warden was George Trevelyan, the son of Sir Charles Trevelyan, who had given Wallington to the National Trust in 1941. George was a casualty of his father's peculiarly self-indulgent form of generosity. In 1937 Sir Charles Trevelyan delivered a public broadcast from Newcastle stating that, because of his socialist beliefs, Wallington was to pass to the National Trust. But this was not to be in his own lifetime: the deed of settlement which he signed in 1941 stipulated that the estate should pass to the Trust only on his death.[21] Until then he went on living there and exercised absolute authority over every decision affecting the estate, including the leasing of about 3,000 acres to the Forestry Commission for conifer planting, without consulting the National Trust. His brother, Professor G.M. Trevelyan, had been prominent in the Trust's campaign to prevent the planting of conifers in the Lake District, and was embarrassed. Professor Trevelyan also remonstrated with Sir Charles over his relationships with tenants on the estate, which included fathering a child when in his seventies.[22] Sir Charles accepted and exercised the post of Lord Lieutenant of Northumberland but, with his notorious meanness, refused to buy its uniform. His exhibitionism took various forms, from painting a hammer and sickle on the gate piers of Wallington, to walking its moors completely naked. For his son, but scarcely heir, he was not an easy parent.

Writing in April 1941, Professor Trevelyan expressed his unease at his brother's attitude:

> I confess I think George has been hardly treated in not being more consulted and not being given a more definite place in the arrangements. But in the old days he showed no interest in Wallington, and his father is absolutely determined (in theory) not to treat him as an 'eldest son'.[23]

As a young man, George Trevelyan had hoped that Wallington might be used as a college for adult education. His appointment to the post of warden at Attingham gave him the opportunity to fulfil his ambition in another National Trust house, where his Trevelyan talents could be given free rein. Sir George (the baronetcy passed to him on his father's death in 1958) had trained as a cabinet-maker under Peter Wahls, whose workshop at Chalford in Gloucestershire kept alive the ideals of William Morris. At Gordonstoun he had taught history, literature, woodwork, and outdoor pursuits. As an intrepid pot-holer and fell-runner, the ethos of the school suited him. To those interests were added a love of music: the Amadeus String Quartet came to play in what had been the Dining Room at Attingham, but which became a lecture room. With Trevelyan's encouragement, the serious study of industrial history was pioneered by the Adult College. The term 'industrial archaeology' was first adopted in lectures given by Barrie Trinder at Attingham, and applied to research at nearby Ironbridge, long before it became a museum.

Sir George's dynamism might well have overwhelmed Attingham and its own artistic significance. He promoted classes in mosaic-making, which involved producing large versions of the coats of arms of both the Berwick and Trevelyan families, for display in the house. Lady Berwick tolerated such tactlessness. She had found her husband's preoccupations with the supernatural irritating, and now experienced her home being used for George's courses on 'Frontiers of Reality', 'Finding the Inner Teacher' and 'Spiritual Awakening'. These attracted hugely enthusiastic audiences, as did his talks on country houses. The Attingham Summer School was launched in 1953 for students of the decorative arts from America and many other countries.

I remember sitting on the steps of Attingham, beneath its towering, attenuated portico, listening to George expounding on the glories of the English country house. This was in 1971, when he was 65, and although crippled with arthritis, still a powerful physical presence, with abundant white hair and moustache. He seemed part-Old Testament prophet, part-New Age guru, and would fix his piercing eyes on the adoring faithful. What he was saying seemed to me a rambling stream of consciousness, drawn from innumerable, vaguely related lectures. When he finished, with a final oratorical flourish, his arms flung wide, the

Sir George Trevelyan, 4th Bt., lecturing in the Dining Room at Attingham Park, alongside a mosaic produced by his students.

delightful American student sitting next to me whispered: 'That was just the most inspiring talk I have *ever* heard.'

In contrast, Lady Berwick was self-effacing. She welcomed visitors to Attingham on the days it was open to the public, but many of them never realised who she was: she was always elegantly dressed, often with a large grey or blue hat at a slight angle, and they may have been confused by the trace of an Italian accent. She remained absorbed in the history of the house, but grew impatient with the National Trust's reattribution of some of the paintings, offering to lend visitors an early edition of the guide with the artists' names as she preferred them. Although considerably more than half of the house was given over to college use, she ensured that precious fragments of wallpaper, drawings, early-nineteenth-century fringes and tassles, and documents throwing light on the history of the house were carefully labelled and preserved. In recent years, this archive has proved invaluable.

Lady Berwick also encouraged and befriended the National Trust staff working in the regional office, which occupied the west wing, including the Outer Library. The Trust's agents, first John Cripwell and then Gerard Noel, would always give priority to repair work on her side of the house, and did all they could to make her comfortable there. She particularly enjoyed helping the Trust's honorary Historic Buildings Representative, Colonel Charles Brocklehurst, over curatorial decisions (he was to become one of her executors), and when his successor, Christopher Wall, was appointed, was delighted to find that his wife Francesca knew Italy well and spoke Italian. One of the frustrations of those living in National Trust houses is that the staff come and go, and Lady Berwick was sad that Christopher was moved to work in the home counties. When Robin Fedden sent out a note saying that Wall's replacement was a young man still in his early twenties, Lady Mander wrote to Lady Berwick saying:

> The more I think of it, the more I laugh to wonder what use a degree in Roman Baroque will be for us when we want the curtains cleaned or daily help found – not that they do much of that anyway.[24]

Lady Mander became a much-valued source of advice on what should be done with Lady Berwick's own Italian pictures and drawings. Those with Pre-Raphaelite associations, including the portrait of Gioconda Hulton by Lisa Stillman and that of Costanza by Marie Spartali, went to Wightwick Manor. Sickert's black and coloured chalk drawing of Costanza, wearing the *festa* dress in 1901, with an affectionate inscription by the artist, was given to the Ashmolean Museum. Dr Kenneth Garlick and Ian Lowe of the museum's Print Room were well known to Lady Mander, and indicated that they would welcome any further gifts of papers describing the Hultons' life in Venice. In the summer of 1972, I drove Lady Berwick to Oxford, where she presented the Ashmolean Museum with drawings given to her mother by Sickert, the considerable correspondence between the two friends, and Costanza's journal.

When Lord and Lady Berwick first arrived at Attingham, they gave Christmas parties in the Steward's Room for the tenants' children. Lady Berwick continued the tradition until the autumn of 1972, when she let it be known that, because of failing health – she was in fact terminally ill – the party for the sons and daughters of Attingham tenants held that year in the Sultana Room would be her last. She was still the most welcoming, considerate hostess. After the party she left to have dinner with a very old friend, Mrs 'Goody' Burton, whose family lived at Longnor, the neighbouring estate. As they were crossing the road at the gates of Attingham, they were hit by another car and both died, Lady Berwick never regaining consciousness. The novelist L.P. Hartley, who had known her when she was a child, wrote:

> In a way she was a prisoner of her station and its duties, an outward honour for an inward toil. But how little would she have liked this to be said or thought about her, who could remember the brave, gay days in Venice, when Teresa Berwick (née Hulton) was at the centre of a care-free social life.[25]

At the time of her death, none of the staff of the National Trust could have predicted what would happen at Attingham. Nevertheless, I shall always rebuke myself for allowing Lady Berwick's personal collections to be dispersed. In 1972 the future of the Adult Education College looked secure. Sir George Trevelyan had retired the previous year, leaving his farewell party at Attingham in a hot-air balloon. He was succeeded as Warden by his former deputy, Geoffrey Toms, just as the County Council began to withdraw funding from the college. By 1976 it was no longer financially viable and had to close. When the rooms vacated by the college were being cleaned and redecorated, a pair of scarlet knickers was found on top of the bookcases in the Inner Library. I regret that these were removed: what a discovery they would have made for some future archaeologist or social historian.

The National Trust was, for the first time, in a position to show all the main rooms with their surviving historic furniture reinstated. Under the terms of Lord Berwick's will, the Trust had been given most of the contents of the Picture Gallery, the Drawing Room and the Sultana Room. There was an immensely important further gift made by Lady Berwick on her death. This included much of the Empire furniture collected by her husband before their marriage, a carefully selected group of her father's pictures, and Sickert's *Lady in Blue*. The rest of her possessions were left to Hulton relatives living in Canada. Her executors were duly instructed to sell the exquisite group of early-twentieth-century pictures, which Lady Berwick had hung in her small dining room, adjoining the Boudoir. Among these were a flower picture by Vuillard, a harbour scene by Marquet and Orpen's *Fair at Neuilly: Man versus Beast*, which shows a bear being taunted in a ring. Lady Berwick, who was very fond of animals, had been touched by the depiction of the dignified animal being persecuted for the amusement of a degenerate audience.[26]

The National Trust had very limited funds in the 1970s for the acquisition of paintings, and little expectation that there might one day be suitable space at Attingham for exhibiting Lady Berwick's collections. The better pieces were sold at Christie's in London, while others went to the local auctioneer in Shrewsbury.

Hanging by my writing desk is an honourable discharge, in a contemporary frame, for Sous-Lieutenant Vierre-Louis Prétôt, lately of Bonaparte's Régiment de Dromedaires. It is

The Sultana Room at Attingham Park, with the sofa or 'sultane' in the alcove.

signed by, amongst others, the commander of the regiment, is dated 1801, and is surmounted by an engraving showing a column of soldiers mounted on dromedaries, with palm trees and pyramids in the background. It was once in the Collection Brouwet and speaks of Thomas and Teresa Berwick's historical imagination, their engagement with Napoleon's Mediterranean adventures – and of her kindness. It was a wedding present from her.

Lady Mander was also generous to those she regarded as helpful to Wightwick and genuinely interested in its significance. Rather like James Lees-Milne – who was a friend and who presented a version of Rossetti's death mask to Wightwick – she had come to dislike the National Trust as an institution, while remaining close to many of those who worked for it. She was devoted to the Trust's custodian of Wightwick, Monty Smith, who had previously been a designer for the firm of Manders, was a brilliant draughtsman and had the knack of getting on with everyone, whatever their allegiances. In 1989, in her will, she left bequests to members of the Trust's staff who had greatly valued her friendship and encouragement. To the National Trust she left one shilling.

THE PLANTSMEN

Henry, 2nd Lord Aberconway and Bodnant;
Graham Stuart Thomas

WHEN GRAHAM STUART THOMAS, the National Trust's Gardens Adviser from 1955 to 1974, was referred to as 'a good plantsman', it was not necessarily meant as a compliment. For much of his time with the Trust there was a feeling among some of its aesthetes that, while Graham Thomas's knowledge of plants was indisputable, his 'taste' was somehow suspect. The implied criticism is revealing of a time when the strong colours and elaborate bedding schemes of the Victorians were deplored and 'good taste' was associated with pale pinks and greys. Thomas was sensitive to criticism, but was unashamed that he had started his professional career in the potting shed as a nurseryman.

At the age of eight Thomas decided that he wanted to be a gardener. After a two-year apprenticeship at the Cambridge Botanic Gardens, which allowed him to attend university lectures on botany, he worked for a nursery in Hertfordshire and then, from 1931, for T. Hilling and Company, the Woking nurserymen. Surrey became his home, and was where he began building collections of the plants that appealed to him, particularly old roses. At that time the possibility of a career advising the National Trust would never have occurred to him. It was only after the war, and largely due to the McLaren family, that the Trust began to acquire great gardens. Even then, it was a tragic accident that led Graham Thomas to apply for the vacancy of Horticultural Adviser.

As well as being sometimes tainted with snobbery, the use of the word 'plantsman' is dated and to some people inapposite, because so many of the twentieth century's greatest gardeners were in fact women. A list of them might start with Gertrude Jekyll, followed by Vita Sackville-West and Norah Lindsay, and could then be expanded to the many women working today as horticulturalists and garden historians. One of the most influential gardeners of the last hundred years, although least acknowledged, was Laura McLaren. As Lady Aberconway (her husband was knighted in 1902 and raised to the peerage in 1911), she played a major part in the creation of the great garden at Bodnant, near Colwyn Bay in North Wales. She had many other attributes.

Laura McLaren's grandfather was a yeoman farmer in Leicestershire, and her father, Henry Davis Pochin, was an industrial chemist. Pochin was largely self-made and self-educated, and – like many other pioneering Manchester industrialists – was a Unitarian. One of his two sons was killed in action in 1917, and there was a rift with the other. As was not uncommon among the industrial elite of the Midlands, but would have offended many established landed families, Pochin attached more importance to the effective management of his business interests than he did to primogeniture.[1] Laura became heir to her father's industrial empire, which included the manufacture of alum cake for papermaking and, a related concern, the mining of china clay, as well as involvement in the iron, steel, coal and engineering industries. He also left her the Bodnant estate, which he had bought in 1874, and where he had begun to plant a riverside garden, had created the spectacular laburnum arch and planted specimen conifers in the Dell.

From her father Laura inherited business drive and acumen; and from her mother Agnes a commitment to radical politics and women's rights. When Laura married Charles Benjamin Bright McLaren in 1877, one of the witnesses was his uncle John Bright, opponent of the Corn Laws and the Crimean War, and one of the most eloquent orators of his time. When still a child she had heard Agnes Pochin speak at the first public women's suffrage meeting. Laura's belief that women should be the political and legal equals of men never faltered. Shortly after her marriage she joined the finance committee of the London National Society of Women's Suffrage and became its treasurer in 1885.

James Jacques Tissot, *Laura, Lady Aberconway*, who inherited the Bodnant estate from her father, Henry Pochin, and continued to develop the garden he had begun in 1874.

For Laura McLaren, as for later generations of her family, gardening was not simply a welcome escape from political and business responsibilities. It was to be pursued with the same energy, creativity, intelligence and professionalism as the McLarens' business concerns. She brought to the gardens at Bodnant an artist's eye (she was a talented painter), a formidable knowledge of plants (particularly roses and peonies), and an understanding of propagation that ensured the nursery was run on almost industrial lines. When she died in 1933 she was described in an obituary in *The Times* as one of Europe's foremost horticulturalists.

Her son Henry, 2nd Lord Aberconway, shared many of her interests and abilities, working closely with her on the development of the garden. He was responsible for the construction of the terraces at Bodnant, including the relocation of the Pin Mill, an early-eighteenth-century building, which he moved in 1938 from Gloucestershire to form an eye-catcher at the end of an ornamental canal. It is a brilliant *coup de théâtre*, combining the formality of the great seventeenth-century continental gardens with the mountains of Snowdonia as a backdrop. As plants were collected avidly, so the garden was enlarged in carefully planned stages. The 2nd Lord Aberconway sponsored expeditions led by George Forrest, Kingdon Ward and others, whose finds were grown on and hybridised at Bodnant. Rhododendrons were a particular passion of his, and Bodnant hybrids can now be found in many of the world's finest gardens.

The Canal Terrace
and the Pin Mill at
Bodnant Garden in
Conwy, North Wales.

Henry Aberconway served as the President of the Royal Horticultural Society from 1931 until his death in 1953. It was on his initiative that an alliance between the Society and the National Trust was forged in 1947, to find ways of protecting gardens of national importance, many of which had been neglected during the war years. As the Trust's *Annual Report* for 1948 put it, the intention was to extend 'its protection to yet another of our national heritages, the English garden'.

During its first half-century, the National Trust was relatively little involved with gardens. This was surprising, because Octavia Hill believed that gardens could provide pleasure and benefit to the urban poor. Indeed, it was her efforts in 1884 to find a secure future for John Evelyn's garden at Sayes Court in Deptford that prompted her legal adviser, Robert Hunter, to propose an organisation which he suggested might be called 'The National Trust'. It was only when the Trust began to acquire the historic gardens attached to country houses that it found itself, almost unwittingly, drawn into horticulture on a large scale.

The property which helped to define the Trust's responsibilities was Montacute in Somerset, acquired in 1937, and with gardens enclosed by balustrades, raised walks and summer houses which are integral to the design of the late-sixteenth-century house. In 1946, while arranging pictures and furniture loaned to Montacute, James Lees-Milne was depressed by the 'sad state' of the garden.[2] The Trust's solution was to recruit an advisory committee which included Christopher Hussey, Henry Aberconway, and later Vita Sackville-West, who planned a rose border. One of the first decisions of the committee was to sack the local gardening firm supposedly responsible for Montacute, and to employ its own garden staff. With these faltering steps the National Trust set out to become one of the nation's great gardeners.

Henry Aberconway was not, however, an ambler by nature. He saw that the statutory powers given to the Trust in its original Act of Parliament, extended in 1937, could make it the instrument for a national strategy for the conservation of great gardens, which he and the Royal Horticultural Society would drive forward. He believed that, faced with post-war levels of taxation, the owners of distinguished gardens might be attracted to the idea of a gift to the National Trust, which as a charity was exempt from tax.

Aberconway was a persuasive, powerful ally. The Trust's senior staff were invited to stay at Bodnant, and found him a genial and generous host. The Chief Agent, Hubert Smith, got on particularly well with him, not least because he was himself a good and knowledgeable gardener. However, the Trust's solicitor, Anthony Martineau, and the Secretary, Admiral Bevir, were worried. They were concerned that the management of gardens by a joint committee of the National Trust and the Royal Horticultural Society would ultimately lead to friction; and apprehensive that departure from the policy of insisting on endowments for each property, to ensure that they were self-supporting, would set a dangerous precedent.

Their concerns were justified. Inside Aberconway's velvet glove was the hand of the Victorian ironmaster. His son Charles, who succeeded him in 1953 as the 3rd Lord Aberconway, acknowledged that his father could be autocratic and difficult to approach.[3] When he conducted visitors around the John Brown shipyards in Glasgow, some were disconcerted to observe that he never addressed or acknowledged any of his workers. He had shown his attitude to them when a steelworker fell into a vat of molten metal and had died instantly. His colleagues had asked if they might stop work for the rest of the day, as a mark of respect. They were told to go back to work immediately.

In the late 1930s Aberconway, with many others, advocated an accommodation with Germany. In August 1939 his son Charles McLaren, then aged 26, was part of a delegation of young industrialists encouraged by the Foreign Secretary, who favoured a negotiated settlement with the Nazis, to hold a secret meeting with the head of the *Luftwaffe*, Hermann Goering, on the Baltic island of Sylt. For over 60 years McLaren never spoke publicly about the meeting. It was only in 2000 that it became public knowledge, prompting the headline in the *Sydney Morning Herald*, 'Floral Lord kept Goering talks secret'. McLaren maintained that the delegation had intended to convey to Goering that Britain would stand by Poland. That was not the message the German took away, believing that the British response to an invasion of Poland would be another Munich-style agreement.[4] The *blitzkreig* on Poland was launched by Goering three weeks later.

In 1940 Henry Aberconway still believed that making peace with Germany would be advantageous. Travelling back from London to north Wales, he found himself in a carriage with a neighbouring landowner, whose son was shortly to join the army. 'I expect we shall find we get on all right with the Germans,' remarked Aberconway. His neighbour went white, and not another word was exchanged until the train reached Bangor.

As so often, James Lees-Milne's assessment of the man was a perceptive one. In February 1948 he dined with the Aberconways (Anthony Blunt and the Husseys were also guests), noting in his diary:

Lady Aberconway, with her milk complexion, wants to appear a pretty goose, but is as clever and calculating as a monkey. He affability and big business. He holds up a hand as a dog holds a paw to be taken. But one is not disposed to stroke him.[5]

Nervously, the National Trust accepted the proffered paw. In March 1948 Aberconway outlined his proposed scheme at the Annual General Meeting of the Royal Horticultural Society. The Trust and the Society should seek to acquire gardens 'of great beauty, gardens of outstanding design, or historic interest', as well as those having 'collections of plants or trees of value to the nation either botanically, horticulturally or scientifically'. The two organisations would manage these gardens through a joint committee, and should raise money for them jointly.

The appeals for funds had limited success. There was a radio broadcast in 1948 by Vita Sackville-West, whose garden at Sissinghurst Castle in Kent came to the National Trust on her death in 1962. She was also instrumental in setting up what became the National Gardens Scheme, by which some of the money raised from the opening of private gardens would be donated to the Trust's Gardens Fund. Originally the openings had been organised by the Queen's Institute for District Nurses; but when the National Health Service absorbed the Institute, there was a case for allowing other charities to benefit. The Institute's Gardens Committee chairman, Ruby Fleischmann, was unconvinced by the approaches from Henry Aberconway and Vita Sackville-West, Admiral Bevir writing:

To be quite candid I have been trying to put the brake on Aberconway a little bit, because I feel we shall get the best result by agreement and not by trying to bully the District Nurses' Committee.[6]

View from the Tower at Sissinghurst Castle in Kent, showing the South Cottage and part of the Rose Garden with the rondel.

Thanks in part to discreet diplomacy from Michael, 6th Earl of Rosse, who sat on the Trust's General Purposes Committee, agreement was reached. Contributions from the scheme continue to be of importance to the Trust. No less valuable has been a joint training scheme for young gardeners intending to pursue a career in horticulture, many of whom gain experience at Trust properties.

The fruits of the joint scheme ripened fast. In 1948 Lawrence Johnston agreed to give the National Trust the magnificent garden he had created at Hidcote in Gloucestershire. He was not in a position to endow the garden, which the Trust was consequently only able to accept because the Joint Gardens Scheme, agreed with the Royal Horticultural Society, held out the promise of financial support. Aberconway, who had now been invited to join the Trust's Executive Committee, had been keen that the first garden to be acquired under the scheme should not be one with which he was associated. With that hurdle crossed, he was now able to offer Bodnant to the Trust with a substantial endowment, which his son Charles supplemented in 1974 with an additional £131,000 and with further contributions in later years. Single-minded he may have been in achieving his objectives, but in his gift of Bodnant, Henry Aberconway was a lasting force for good. He was motivated principally by his pride in Bodnant and his wish to see it constantly improved. By giving it to the National Trust it would be exempt from the punitive post-war levels of taxation, as would the financial provisions he made for it, though its endownment. The hundreds of thousands of visitors to that and other National Trust gardens have reason to be grateful for his drive, his horticultural expertise, and his generosity.

The arrangements for the management of Bodnant were, characteristically, carefully tailored to achieve what Aberconway thought was best for the garden and his family. The National Trust became owners of the garden, and its staff were, strictly speaking, employed by the Trust. The McLaren family retained the estate of over 2,000 acres and the house,

The Red Borders and Pavilions at Hidcote Manor in Gloucestershire, the first garden to be accepted by the National Trust on its own merit, when it was presented by Lawrence Johnston in 1948.

The Middle Lake at Sheffield Park Garden, East Sussex, in early autumn; the gardens, extending to just over 200 acres, were bought between 1954 and 1991 with bequests, local authority grants, subscriptions obtained from a public appeal, and an anonymous donation.

designed in 1881 by W.J. Green in what Mark Girouard, the authority on Victorian architecture, described as ' dim and grim Old English'. They also continued to be responsible for all enterprises, including plant sales and the nursery. First Henry Aberconway, and then Charles, acted as garden manager, with the Head Gardener reporting to him. When Frederick Puddle retired from the post of Head Gardener in 1947, he was succeeded by his son, Charles Puddle, who was in turn succeeded in 1982 by his son, Martin Puddle. Every aspect of maintaining Bodnant continued to be directed by the McLaren family, from the replanting and enrichment of the garden to the running of the car park and tearoom. The arrangement could be justified by the steady enhancements and the long list of rhododendrons and other plants raised at Bodnant that received awards from the Royal Horticultural Society.

The gift of Bodnant established that the National Trust, guided by the Royal Horticultural Society, was now equipped to look after the very finest gardens in the country, if their future upkeep was in doubt. This was borne out by the ensuing acquisitions: Winkworth Arboretum in Surrey came as a gift from Dr Wilfrid Fox in 1952; and Nymans in Sussex was given by Lord Rosse's father-in-law, Lieutenant Colonel L.C.R. Messel, in 1954. The same year, Sheffield Park Garden, also in Sussex – planned by 'Capability' Brown in the 1770s and enriched by Humphry Repton – was saved from dismemberment and development thanks to a bequest, grants from local authorities and a public appeal.

Graham Stuart Thomas, Gardens Adviser to the National Trust from 1955 to 1974, with the honeysuckle *Lonicera periclymenum* named after him.

In theory the care of these and the Trust's other gardens was the responsibility of the Gardens Committee. In practice it rapidly became evident that management by committee was ineffective. The Trust needed an experienced horticulturalist, who could instruct its gardeners, working through the Regional Agents. In June 1954 Miss Ellen Field was appointed Horticultural Adviser, and immediately produced sound practical proposals for Stourhead in Wiltshire and other properties. Then, after a few promising months of working for the Trust she was fatally injured in a car crash when returning on a November night from a visit to Cotehele in Cornwall. As a consequence of this tragedy, the National Trust recruited Graham Stuart Thomas. By the time he retired in 1974, after eighteen years as the Trust's Horticultural Adviser (later Gardens Adviser), Graham Thomas had not only improved, shaped and enriched gardens that are now among the most cherished in the country, but had also helped to establish the art of historic garden conservation.

Initially Thomas was responsible for only six gardens: Blickling Hall (Norfolk), Glendurgan (Cornwall), Hidcote (Gloucestershire), Killerton (Devon), Sheffield Park (Sussex) and Stourhead (Wiltshire). He was to devote nine months of the year to advising the National Trust, on a salary of £400, while continuing to work for Hilling's and at Sunningdale Nursery. Only someone of an ascetic temperament, with dedication and rigorous self-discipline, could have made a success of the arrangement. It may also have helped that he was a bachelor, with no constraints on being away from home except the upkeep of his own small garden, which was full of choice and unusual plants. When I first visited him in 1970, he was able to show me plants that were flowering in the depths of winter. His house, like the man, was modest. In his suburban bungalow in Surrey, he had just enough space for his library, for writing during the winter months, for two grand pianos which filled a room, and for drawing and painting the illustrations in his twenty books.

Graham Thomas was, like his watercolours, meticulous. When he visited gardens he usually wore a flower in his buttonhole, often but not invariably a rose. Head Gardeners were expected to identify what variety it was, the Historic Buildings Representative would be allowed to comment favourably in more general terms, and if those he was meeting seemed to be oblivious of the flower, Graham would draw his own conclusions. Pinned behind his lapel was a silver phial, with water to ensure that it remained fresh all day.[7] He disliked sloppiness, in dress or in gardening, and could be fiercely critical of any gardeners, however competent, whom he suspected of laziness. When visiting Beningbrough Hall, a seriously under-endowed and under-staffed house and garden near York, he discussed with the Regional Agent, Ben Proud, what needed to be done; and that evening the two of them put on boots, gathered up tools, and set about digging the borders themselves.

Watercolour of *Gentiana Asclepiaedea 'Knightshayes'* by Graham Stuart Thomas.

The pattern of visits that Graham adopted quickly became established and has been followed by his successors. Early in the year a programme would be agreed, so there could be no excuse for the Head Gardener, agent or representative not to be present. He would arrive promptly, and usually inspected the garden in the same order as on the previous visit, so that his notes were easy to cross-reference. Sometimes he would propose that special attention should be given to an area that he believed was below standard or where there was the potential for improvement, perhaps the removal of an overgrown shrubbery or scope for a new design to a tired herbaceous border. Lengthy debate was not encouraged: changes would either be settled on the spot or the principle would be agreed, with an assurance that detailed plans would follow in due course. When redesigning the herbaceous borders on the terraces at Powis Castle – now regarded as one of his outstanding achievements and among the best of their period – he worked on immaculately prepared plans during the winter months, to be implemented the following year.

Graham's reports were almost always written up the same day, in his elegant, legible handwriting (he never learnt to type) using duplicate paper. When invited to stay by a member of the Trust's staff, he would usually decline, on the grounds that he valued the time at a quiet hotel or guesthouse, for writing his notes and preparing for forthcoming visits. He did, however, enjoy staying with staff who were enthusiastic gardeners; and could also be tempted by the prospect of a good tea and a carefully prepared evening meal. Other hosts recall how he would teach their children card games, and would join in musical evenings, playing the piano and singing.

When he knew that a Head Gardener was musical, there might be an interlude in an otherwise intensely business-like visit. Richard Ayres, who in 1974 succeeded his father Noel as Head Gardener at Anglesey Abbey in Cambridgeshire, remembers being sent off to fetch a tool and returning to find Graham and Noel singing a round in the Coronation Avenue. On other occasions they would sing parts of Gilbert and Sullivan operas together.[8] Like most of the Trust's Head Gardeners, Richard and his father had great professional respect for Graham and, behind a mask of formality, considerable personal affection.

At Anglesey Abbey the relationship was complicated by the fact that the donor of the property, Huttleston Broughton, 1st Lord Fairhaven, had a continuing regard for the garden designer Lanning Roper. He and Graham had different attributes. Lanning created gardens for wealthy clients, was an extremely successful gardening journalist, and had been commissioned to write a book, *The Gardens of Anglesey Abbey*, which was published by *Country Life* in 1964. He had immense charm and enjoyed staying as a guest at the Abbey, not least because he could describe the unusual experience to other patrons and friends. Lord Fairhaven had begun his education in the United States, and had used part of his fortune from mining and railways to enlarge and furnish Anglesey Abbey with considerable opulence. Lanning would be invited by the butler to join his host for drinks in the Library before dinner. He was amused when the butler added: 'Please do not appear before 6.30, because the carpet is brushed in the late-afternoon, and when his Lordship comes to the Library, he dislikes seeing the footsteps of guests preceding his own.'[9] Unlike Lanning Roper, when Graham Thomas was visiting Anglesey Abbey, he stayed with a relative in Cambridge.

Because Lanning Roper was so admired and liked by influential figures in the National Trust, including Lord Rosse, he would occasionally be brought in to advise on a particular scheme or to resolve an impasse. At Anglesey Abbey he devised an elegant solution for the planting around the statue of *Narcissus*, when earlier proposals proved contentious. At Tatton Park in Cheshire, disagreements over the garden led to Lanning taking over as adviser from Graham. When the estate was transferred to the National Trust in 1960 through National Land Fund procedures, the endowment was insufficient and the property could only be accepted because Cheshire County Council agreed to manage it, on a full repairing lease. The Head Gardener, who was employed by the Council, was not inclined to carry out the work recommended by the Trust's adviser; and for his part, Graham made no secret of his belief that the gardens at Tatton were becoming municipalised. Eventually there was a complete breakdown in relations. The solution was for Rosse to ask Lanning for his help at Tatton. Within a couple of visits, Lanning had the garden staff and the property manager, Brigadier Chestnutt, eating out of his hand.

No such problems arose at Lyme Park, also in Cheshire. This most romantic of estates, perched high on the edge of the Peak District, had been given to the National Trust in 1947 by Richard, 3rd Lord Newton, without an endowment. The local authority, the metropoli-

The Dutch Garden at Lyme Park in Cheshire. The original Elizabethan house, altered by Giacomo Leoni in 1726 and Lewis Wyatt in 1817, was given to the National Trust by Richard, 3rd Lord Newton, in 1947, with over 1,300 acres of surrounding park and moorland.

tan borough of Stockport, undertook to fund and manage the property largely because it served as a public park on the outskirts of Manchester. The house itself included parts of the original Elizabethan building, a magnificent south front by Giacomo Leoni added in 1726, and impressive nineteenth-century rooms by Lewis Wyatt. The grounds were on a similarly grand scale, with a Dutch garden of formal beds and a fountain set well below the house and with tall retaining walls on two sides. In the immediate post-war years the long decline of the property continued, with councillors regarding Lyme as very low on their scale of priorities. Their interest did not extend much beyond ordering, after local elections, that the bedding plants in the Dutch garden parterre should be changed, depending on which political party had the majority: red plants for Labour; blue for Conservative. The staff were aimless and demoralised.

Credit for beginning the revival of Lyme belongs principally to two of those involved there in the 1970s. John Fowler advised on the redecoration of the Entrance Hall, staircase and other rooms, bringing more light and colour back into the building, and opening the eyes of those working there to its beauty and importance. In the garden Graham Thomas achieved a similar transformation. He produced a particularly imaginative planting scheme for an area known as 'Killtime', where a stream cascades down a steep ravine, the banks of which he had planted with moisture-loving primulas, irises, hostas and ferns, combined with azaleas and other flowering shrubs. What had been dank, derelict and forbidding became a delight. More than that, it inspired the head of the borough's gardens and parks, Geoff Burrows, to divert funds and resources to Lyme. He and his staff read Graham's books, including *Perennial Garden Plants* (1976), as they appeared, regarded him with awe, and looked forward to his visits with palpable enthusiasm. The scheme for 'Killtime' and the pond into which the stream flowed achieved almost mystical status in a way Graham could never have foreseen. It was here that Colin Firth, playing Mr Darcy in the 1995 television film of *Pride*

and Prejudice, dived into the pool and emerged in a clinging white shirt. The delectable Miss Bennett was not the only admirer of this spectacle. A National Trust benefactor, Mrs Leffman, was so moved that she made special provision of £100,000 for Lyme Park in her will.

Throughout his career Graham Thomas educated himself assiduously. When still a teenager he had borrowed a copy of Gertrude Jekyll's *Colour Schemes for the Flower Garden* (1914), which, he later wrote, 'fired my enthusiasm for graded colours in herbaceous borders.'[10] His move to Woking in Surrey put him within cycling distance of her garden at Munstead Wood, and in the autumn of 1931 he arranged to visit her. Writing about it 70 years later he remembered the plants that excited him, naming and describing them vividly. He also recalled exactly what they had for tea, although he confessed to not remembering what preserve was offered with the thin white bread and butter. From her he learnt the importance of plants that 'made *effect* in gardens',[11] and which could be more useful than botanical rarities.

It would scarcely be an exaggeration to say that Thomas first taught himself garden history and then instructed others through his books and by example. In the 1960s there was very little interest in changes in taste and design in historic gardens over succeeding centuries. In Holland the reinstatement of the seventeenth-century garden design at Het Loo preceded comparable schemes at the English historic royal palaces by over twenty years. Thomas learnt much from the books of Miles Hadfield – including *Gardening in Britain* (1960) and *A History of British Gardening* (1969) – and it was to him he turned when asked by Christopher Wall, the National Trust's representative in the West Midlands, to produce plans for the garden at Moseley Old Hall in Staffordshire. The property, on the edge of Wolverhampton, had been in open country when Charles II fled there after his defeat at the Battle of Worcester in 1651. By the 1960s it was threatened by road proposals and encroaching suburbia. There was much agonising over whether the house should be accepted at all by the National Trust, when offered as a gift in 1962, because in the nineteenth century the timber-framed exterior had been encased in unattractive blue and red bricks. Robin Fedden used to say that the deciding factor was James Lees-Milne's identification, as a convert, with its seventeenth-century Catholic associations. At Moseley the future king met Father John Huddleston, who 34 years later, as Charles lay dying, was to receive him into the Catholic church.

In 1962 the garden was no more than an abandoned smallholding. In Graham's words:

> Apart from a few wind-bitten yews, a few old fruit trees, a variegated holly and an old pear growing up the south wall, there was nothing. Nothing, that is, except the old surrounding wall, some pigsties, hen-coops and broken glass cloches.[12]

What might have dismayed many gardeners was seized on as an opportunity for radical transformation. Using the design of a knot garden devised in 1640 by the Reverend Walter Stonehouse and recorded in a manuscript now in the library of Magdalen College in Oxford, Graham's scheme used clipped box and different coloured gravels to achieve the strict formality that the fugitive Charles might have seen as he apprehensively looked out over the garden from an upstairs window.

Admiration for the knot garden at Moseley gave the National Trust the confidence to recreate gardens at other properties, where there was sufficient evidence for a strictly historical approach. When the garden of Westbury Court in Gloucestershire was acquired in 1967 there were excellent photographs showing how its Dutch-inspired design had survived well into the twentieth century. It too was in the final stages of dereliction. For some years after the restoration, the rebuilt pavilion, dredged canals and yew hedges looked raw and unconvincing. Twenty years on and the continuities had been reasserted: it is as though the original garden has survived without disruption.

By the early 1970s the Trust had embarked on the restoration of the garden – originally designed by Sir John Vanbrugh, William Kent and Charles Bridgeman in the early eighteenth century – at Claremont in Surrey. The success of these and other schemes prepared the ground for the recreation of the garden at Erddig, planned by Graham's successor, John Sales, and for the restoration, on a huge scale, of the landscape at Stowe.

One National Trust property that Graham knew only as a member of the visiting public was Bodnant. The 3rd Lord Aberconway made clear that the suggestions of the Trust's Gardens Adviser were neither needed nor welcome. The same applied after Graham had retired. 'Mar-

[opposite] The water garden, pavilion and statue of Neptune at Westbury Court, Gloucestershire, photographed by *Country Life* in 1908. The property was given to the National Trust in 1967 by Gloucestershire County Council, and subsequently restored and endowed with public donations, an anonymous gift, and a grant from the Historic Buildings Council.

[opposite] The mid-seventeenth-century statue of Neptune in the T-Canal at Westbury Court in Gloucestershire, following the National Trust's restoration of the garden.

Henry, 2nd Lord Aberconway, President of the Royal Horticultural Society from 1931 to 1953, with Her Majesty The Queen at the Chelsea Flower Show in 1952.

tin Puddle does a very good job, responsible to me and not to any other employer or amorphous body,' Aberconway would explain. 'We never receive the Gardens Adviser John Sales. He may come here to walk around. He never makes a suggestion.'[13] Aberconway applied the same imperious approach to his responsibilities as President of the Royal Horticultural Society from 1961 to 1984, and in particular to the planning of the Chelsea Flower Show. As at Bodnant the results were impressive and justly admired. He could be an astute, galvanising chairman of a committee; his knowledge of plants sometimes disconcerted professional horticulturalists; he had a sharp eye for detail; and he was an extremely effective administrator. But his domineering style became increasingly out of tune with the times. He strongly resisted representations to admit guide dogs. Suggestions that more women should be included on the Society's Council were generally resisted. The prejudice seems strange in someone whose grandmother had done so much to improve the position of women; but then Aberconway denied his family's roots in radical politics.[14]

His sister's response to her intellectual inheritance could not have been more different. A brilliant zoologist, Dame Anne McLaren published highly influential books on germ cells, sex determination, genetic imprinting and the X chromosome. She made major contributions to medical ethics, became a member of the Royal Society in 1975, and received its Gold Medal in 1990. A member of the Communist Party for much of the Cold War, she was a socialist who readily joined anti-war demonstrations.[15] Her second Christian name was Laura, and like her grandmother, she was passionately committed to social justice.

Lord Aberconway was particularly dismissive of the needs of those in wheelchairs, whether at Chelsea Flower Show or Bodnant. When it was put to him that lavatories for the disabled were desirable at Bodnant, he told the lady making the case, from her wheelchair, that 'such provisions would be completely inappropriate: this is a private garden, not a public park.' Others present were shocked at his lack of sympathy. His attitude may have mellowed when, as an old man, he found that he needed to conduct his tours of the garden from a wheelchair. Meetings with those he felt it necessary to overawe were usually conducted in a room at Bodnant with a strong morning light. A heavily built man, he would sit, his back to the window, as often as not wearing green tweed plus-fours, with orange-ribboned garters above his long stockings, as though he had just returned from an Edwardian shooting party. The person being interviewed would be invited to sit on a low chair, looking up at the silhouette of this formidable interrogator. If it was National Trust affairs that were being discussed, there would be a reminder that the Director-General was not only a friend but, in the case of Sir Frederick Bishop, had been brought onto the board of English China Clays, of which Aberconway was chairman.

Bodnant continued to be run as though it was a private domain; but it was very far from being a paradise. There were periods of unhappiness in the family. John McLaren, Charles's brother and the second son of Henry Aberconway, gassed himself in the garages of his house at Old Bodnod. At the time relationships within the family were so distant that none of them returned home to be with their parents until the day of the funeral. The arrangement that involved the Head Gardener and staff being employed by the National Trust, but taking all their instructions from Lord Aberconway, led to tensions and misunderstanding. Eventually Martin Puddle became so over-stretched that responsibility for the plant centre was taken away from him. There were also problems of bullying among the garden staff, which he found difficult to deal with. One morning in 2005 he was found drowned in one of the pools in the garden. He was 54.

There are contradictions in the character and achievements of Charles Aberconway. Like several generations of his family, he had immense ability. His knowledge as a plantsman and the encouragement he gave to the art of gardening are rightly celebrated. His autocratic behaviour and tendency to disregard the feelings of others may partly have been learnt from his father. It may also have been the consequence of his own disappointments, including the failure of his first marriage, followed by an exceptionally acrimonious divorce; and though his eldest son was to inherit the title, he was excluded from the family interest in the Bodnant estate. Under Charles's chairmanship the John Brown Group of Clydeside shipbuilders dwindled and died. Eventually he had to be eased aside from the presidency of the Royal Horticultural Society: he had become too abrasive, too reactionary.

The powerful patron of the arts is a familiar historical figure, and Henry and Charles Aberconway bring to mind Yeats's *Ancestral Houses*, of 1928:

> Surely among a rich man's flowering lawns
> Amid the rustle of his planted hills,
> Life overflows without ambitious pains…

The Medici in Florence or, closer to home, Elizabethan statesmen and the builders of palatial country houses and great gardens are remembered at least as much for their enlightened patronage as for their other attributes. The Aberconways are of such distinguished company. What will most endure is the beauty they created and which – on their own rather partial terms – they were prepared to share with others:

... What if those things the greatest of mankind
Consider most to magnify, or to bless,
But take our greatness with our bitterness.[16]

When considering the achievements of those two outstanding gardeners, Henry Aberconway and Graham Stuart Thomas, another poet comes to mind. Thomas Hardy's *Architectural Masks* describes reactions to an old and beautiful house and a modern villa in 'blazing brick':

The philosophic passers say,
'See that old mansion mossed and fair,
Poetic souls therein are they:
And O that gaudy box! Away,
You vulgar people there.'[17]

Hardy reveals that it is in fact the occupants of the gleaming villa that, 'with book and pencil, viol and bow, / lead inner lives of dreams.' So too did Graham, in his bungalow in Woking. He was unfailingly generous with gifts of his books – 'I thought you might like to have a copy… it comes with my best wishes & also my best thanks for your help'; of the beautifully produced prints made from his botanical drawings; and, most abundantly, of plants. When he arrived to advise at Cliveden in Buckinghamshire, he would be 'at the wheel of his estate car completely surrounded by clumps of plants'.[18] The former Head Gardener at Wallington in Northumberland, Geoffrey Moon, recalled:

At my home in Cambo in a little border at the front door I have a fern which was given me by Graham Thomas. I see it every day and remember him with great affection and count myself incredibly lucky to have had such a wonderful mentor and good friend.[19]

Gifts of flowers may be impermanent, but that quality has appealed to poets and artists. Such presents may be less fleeting than the donor or recipients imagine. When he was terminally ill Lanning Roper delighted in telling those who came to see him in hospital that the enormous arrangement of flowers had been cut by the Countess of Rosse from shrubs at Nymans in West Sussex. He confided that they had particularly impressed another visitor, the politician Michael Heseltine, whose garden Lanning had helped to create, and who had asked whether he might take a few cuttings from the bedside vase.

Graham's most munificent gift of flowers was to Mottisfont Abbey in Hampshire. The National Trust had for some years thought about establishing a collection of old shrub roses, encouraged by Vita Sackville-West, Ralph Dutton and Michael Rosse. In 1971 the former tenant of the walled kitchen garden at Mottisfont decided to leave. Graham confirmed that the site was ideal and that many of the roses could be provided by the Royal National Rose Society at St Albans. He would also donate the collection that he had steadily built up while he was writing *The Old Shrub Roses* (1957) and *Climbing Roses Old and New* (1965), both published in association with the Royal Horticultural Society. The latter is by far the more attractive of the two books, for being illustrated with Graham's paintings and drawings of the varieties he most admired.

The Mottisfont proposal caught the imagination of the Winchester Centre of the National Trust, which raised the funds for the purchase of plants and for suitable seats. Under Graham's direction virtually all the known old European roses were established, including the early hybrids of the China Rose, the Gallicas and Damasks, and the Noisettes. By the time of the exceptionally hot summer of 1976 the plants at Mottisfont were growing so vigorously that Graham was able to record that two roses he particularly admired, 'Maréchal Niel' and 'Climbing Devoniensis', were producing blooms five inches across.

The rose garden at Mottisfont is Graham's crowning achievement. Writing of it some years after its creation, he said that he hoped:

> … the rose's pomp will be displayed far into the future at Mottisfont, where my work of some thirty years collecting varieties together from France, Germany, and the United States, and numerous gardens and nurseries in the British Isles, will not be set at nought.[20]

He need not have worried. Not only is the future of the rose garden as secure as any collection of plants can be, but its importance and value to other gardens becomes clearer year by year. Graham was, like most of us, anxious not to see his favourite child unduly changed by others. The Head Gardener at Mottisfont, David Stone, once experimented by introducing alliums, of the onion family, among the roses. They looked attractive, but there were worries about how Graham would react on his annual visit. He walked past the border without a word, and it was only as he was leaving that he said: 'By the way, David, there's just one thing … we are a rose garden and not an onion patch.' Stone added: 'It was said quietly to me and never appeared in the garden report.'[21]

In early October 2001 I received a letter from Briar Cottage, Woking, in Graham's instantly recognisable, clear, but now rather shaky, handwriting. It began:

> I hope you and yours are well. I am not too bad for 92, & to keep myself out of mischief have started writing another book! They are such good companions…

The book was about great gardeners of the twentieth century. He had known almost all of them, beginning with Gertrude Jekyll, and he described what he had learnt from their gardens with admiration and affection. Many were his friends. He had largely completed it by the time he died two years later, and it was published the same year with a foreword by John Sales, recalling his predecessor in a particularly sympathetic and perceptive way. All his life Graham Thomas had loved music, painting and poetry that captured the beauty of plants and gardens. He prefaced his final book with some verses by Robert Southey, which, as a very old man, Graham may have felt described his life's work:

> My hopes are with the Dead, anon
> My place with them will be,
> And I with them shall travel on
> Through all Futurity;
> Yet leaving here a name, I trust,
> That will not perish in dust.

9

THE BANKERS

The Rothschilds at Wicken Fen and Waddesdon;
Sir John Smith

ONE WAY IN WHICH FINANCE DIRECTORS can assert their authority is by predicting either huge profits or imminent bankruptcy. Dire warnings of the financial disaster facing the National Trust were regularly sounded in its early years, and usually associated with the continual drain on funds caused by the acquisition in 1907 of its first major country house, Barrington Court in Somerset. In the 1970s the Chief Finance Officer, Jimmy Wheeler, cheerfully confided that he thought the Trust was rather like a great sailing ship, but overloaded, with a shifting cargo and shortly to sink more or less gracefully. The pessimists have been proved wrong.

Why has the National Trust not gone bust? Two of its founders, Octavia Hill and Robert Hunter, had considerable experience of the need to temper idealism with sound business management. Hill had suffered the consequences of her father's ambitious schemes for rural housing and social improvement, which ended with bankruptcy in 1840 and disaster for his family. Her work for John Ruskin was another lesson in how ideas for reordering society needed to be rooted in financial realism. In Hunter she found not only a source of sound legal advice, but a man who had acquired immense experience of efficient administration as chief solicitor to the Post Office, to which he was appointed in 1882. Although she valued donations from working-class supporters more than those from the 'big-moneyed people', she did not hesitate to enlist some of the wealthiest families in the country in her work to protect open spaces in and around London. In 1875, while trying unsuccessfully to raise money to protect the Swiss Cottage Fields west of Hampstead, she received donations of £100 from the Duke of Westminster and Lady (Emma) Rothschild. Their contributions, she wrote, 'won't do to go on'.[1] Twenty years later, and in spite of this disappointment, both families were to give vital support to the newly formed National Trust.

Nathan, 1st Lord Rothschild, Emma's husband, was the head of the family bank, adviser to (and critic of) successive prime ministers, including Disraeli, Gladstone, Rosebery, Balfour and Asquith, and a philanthropist on a scale which involved a whole department of his business devoting itself to support for charitable causes. Much of this activity was anonymous, as advocated by Jewish teaching, and suggests that he also observed the practice of devoting a tithe of both his and the bank's income to charity. The causes he supported ranged from housing schemes in impoverished parts of London and organising soup kitchens for

the unemployed, to helping to establish the Rhodes scholarships in 1902. During the Egyptian campaign of 1901 he badgered the Government to improve supplies for the troops, while he himself sent food and cigars.

Rothschild's second son, Charles, was expected to devote much of his life to the bank and to public service. He did both, but his real passion was natural history. By the time he died in 1923, at the age of 46, he had begun to transform attitudes to nature conservation in Britain. His influence is still powerfully beneficial. Charles Rothschild's brilliance as a naturalist owed little to his schooling at Harrow, which he loathed. His fellow pupils taught him about anti-semitism and philistinism.[2] The ability to set butterflies and mount mammal skins was learnt from the curators of the Rothschild Zoological Museum at Tring in Hertfordshire, created by his brother Walter and opened to the public in 1902. Charles's housemaster noted that he was 'rather below… average' in most subjects, and seems not to have thought it remarkable that a schoolboy of eighteen should be co-author of the two-volume *Harrow Butterflies and Moths*, published in 1895. Throughout his early life his most formative teacher was Walter, nearly ten years his senior and a zoologist whose collecting of specimens has been unrivalled before or since.

Charles Rothschild's parents gave him what his daughter Miriam called 'a crushing overdose of the sense of responsibility and over-concern and over-sensitivity for the ills to which human flesh is heir'.[3] Most of those who met him would have been unaware of this oppressive inheritance: he travelled widely in remote and sometimes dangerous places to collect insects, was an engaging conversationalist, and had that combination of imperiousness and modesty that seems to be a trait in some Rothschilds. He thought nothing of pulling the emergency cord on a railway train travelling through Hungary, because he had seen a rare butterfly and needed to run back down the line to catch it. His future wife, a strikingly beau-

tiful Hungarian called Rozsika von Wertheimstein, he met while on holiday in the Carpathian mountains in 1906, where he was trapping mice in order to study their fleas.

By the time of his marriage in 1907, Rothschild was a world authority on fleas. He had made the connection between the spread of plague and the distribution of the rat flea, *Xenopsylla cheopsis*, which he had discovered in Egypt. In India he advised the plague commission; and he continued to sponsor collecting expeditions in the Far East. At home he worked conscientiously for the family bank. Politically he was well to the left of most of his family, saying he was 'glad if socialism gained ground, but aware that individualism must have its place'.[4]

Among the charities supported by Charles Rothschild was the National Trust. In 1899 he bought thirty acres of Wicken Fen, near Cambridge, by then one of the most celebrated haunts of lepidopterists. In the 1820s Charles Darwin had collected beetles there. Rothschild had known it as an undergraduate studying natural history, and understood both its importance and its fragility. In 1912 he was the anonymous benefactor who enabled the Trust to buy another site of scientific importance, Blakeney Point, on the north Norfolk coast. By then he had joined the Trust's Council and was also serving on its Wicken Fen local management committee. The National Trust Act of 1907, which gave it the statutory powers to manage properties 'for the preservation (so far as practicable) of their natural aspect, features and animal and plant life', encouraged Rothschild to think that it could be the guardian of a growing number of nature reserves, which would ensure the preservation of flora and fauna otherwise threatened with extinction.

However, generous support for the National Trust gradually turned to disenchantment. The charity's annual income was not keeping pace with its steady acquisition of new properties, most of which required active conservation and management. This was particularly true of its nature reserves, which Rothschild thought were being neglected. His response in 1912

was to found – and fund – an organisation entirely devoted to the protection of wildlife, the Society for the Promotion of Nature Reserves, which he intended should acquire reserves that would ultimately be handed over to the National Trust. In practice he had sown the seeds of the County Wildlife Trusts, which were to develop independently.

Rothschild's work was cut short by chronic illness. His depressive tendencies had been exacerbated by the need to take on his brother's responsibilities at the bank after their father's death in 1915, and to sort out Walter's troubled personal and financial affairs, which had been compounded by the fact that the latter had been blackmailed for many years by a former mistress. In 1916 Charles was sent to Switzerland to recuperate from severe depression. While he was convalescing there he was visited by the explorer Sandy Wollaston, who had travelled with him on collecting expeditions to the Sudan. Rothschild was one of the few people who had learnt how to respond to Wollaston's often prickly behaviour. On his return home he informed Wollaston that he was making him a gift of £25,000. When this was refused, Charles responded by saying that the money would be left in his will, but he preferred that his friend did not have to wait for it. The lives of both men were to be cut short. Charles Rothschild took his own life in 1923. He had become a victim of the encephalitis lethargica form of influenza that swept through Europe after the First World War, and which considerably worsened his already acute depression. Sandy Wollaston was shot dead in 1930 by a crazed undergraduate in his rooms at King's in Cambridge, where he was college tutor.

Charles Rothschild's frustration at the failure of the National Trust, despite his financial support, to use its statutory powers to acquire nature reserves around the country was also experienced by Miriam Rothschild, whose achievements as a naturalist and zoologist matched those of her father. Her fame exceeded his, partly because she lived to the age of 96, serving on numerous conservation bodies, and partly because she enjoyed feeding the popular press with revelations not expected from a Rothschild. She once explained that she kept her fleas 'in plastic bags in my bedroom so that the children won't disturb them'.[5] But most of her work was at a microscope and out of the public eye. Her *Illustrated Catalogue of the Rothschild Collection of Fleas, Siphonaptera, in the British Museum* runs to six volumes, published between 1953 and 1983. She was the author of books that combined impeccable science with an extraordinary range of allusions, written in a style that was as much literary as academic, and she contributed to over three hundred scientific papers.

When the Society for the Promotion of Nature Reserves was reconstituted in 1981 as the Royal Society for Nature Conservation and then in 2004 as the Royal Society of Wildlife Trusts, Miriam Rothschild served as vice-president of both in succession. She attributed to her father the realisation that effective nature conservation implied much more than the protection of rare species. 'Sound conservation policy could only be based on adequate surveys, not only of the flora and fauna of a potential reserve, but [of] the habitat in relation to the environment as a whole,' she wrote of her father's pioneering and far-sighted aims.[6] It was the National Trust's failure to meet this aspiration, at Wicken Fen and elsewhere, which attracted the justifiable criticism of Miriam Rothschild and other naturalists.

The Trust's response to concerns that it was not living up to its responsibilities for nature conservation was similar to that adopted for archaeology: it set up a committee composed of some of the most distinguished authorities on the subject. In 1938 Sir Edward Salisbury, director of the Royal Botanic Gardens at Kew, was asked to chair an advisory committee on natural history, on which Miriam Rothschild served. Although it considered issues such as species reintroduction and vermin control, it had very little influence on the standard of management on the Trust's nature reserves. There were two intractable problems. The Trust's regions were largely staffed by Land Agents, who understood about farming, but knew less about unusual and vulnerable habitats. Even if the importance of a site was acknowledged, the charity could not afford the staff and equipment to manage it effectively. When, after twenty years, the advisory committee was wound up, on the grounds that it was ineffectual, Miriam Rothschild was dismayed. Her allegiance and support subsequently shifted increasingly to the County Naturalist Trusts.

Rothschild believed that one of the consequences of her father's death was that 'nature conservation in the UK was virtually brought to a halt and for the next twenty-five years marked time.'[7] She may have overstated the setback, but the loss to the National Trust was certainly immense. Better than anyone her father understood that nature reserves need constant monitoring and energetic control of invasive species, and time and again he had demonstrated a willingness to back his convictions generously. Once his support for reserves such as Wicken Fen ceased, the effectiveness of their species protection tended to decline rapidly.

Avid collecting was not, in other members of the Rothschild family, confined to specimens from the natural world. In 1950 Anthony de Rothschild and his wife Yvonne gave their house, Ascott in Buckinghamshire, to the National Trust, with the greater part of its outstanding collections of English and French furniture, oriental porcelain, and paintings – including works by Cuyp, del Sarto, Gainsborough, Stubbs and Tiepolo. The gardens were largely created in the late nineteenth century, with advice from the horticulturalist and nurseryman Sir Harry Veitch. The Rothschild preoccupation with collections is evident in the group of Dutch pictures, in the accumulation of three-colour late-Ming porcelain, and in the work of eighteenth-century French *ébénistes*. The quality is exceptional, the taste continental rather than English. In the garden the planting relies for impact more on single rare specimens than on broad sweeps and cumulative effect. The house itself expanded to accommodate its burgeoning collections, with late-nineteenth-century additions to the original building of 1606, and a further extension in 1938. Its seventeenth-century, timber-framed vernacular structure was transformed into a rambling picturesque composition that has all but forgotten its minor gentry origins.

When Baron Ferdinand de Rothschild bought the Waddesdon estate in Buckinghamshire in 1874, part of its attraction was that it came with no great house. He was not interested in aligning himself with local landowners; and there is something breathtakingly brazen about the creation of a house which deliberately evokes the châteaux of the Loire, with furniture that belonged to the kings of France and came from the palace at Versailles and from Marie Antoinette's Petit Trianon. Far from using architecture and decoration which rejects French absolutism, Waddesdon embraces it. The grandson of Salomon Rothschild, the founder of the Austrian branch of the dynasty, Baron Ferdinand wanted none of the narrow political and artistic allegiances of Whig Palladianism. His collecting was driven by an uncomplicated pursuit of excellence: the best porcelain came from the Sèvres factory; the finest carpets were Savonnerie; and the furniture he acquired included examples of the top eighteenth-century French cabinet-makers. The French architect of the house, Gabriel-Hippolyte Destailleur, had the confidence and skill to create rooms which, like their contents, are unashamed expressions of *ancien régime* extravagance.

Andrea del Sarto, *The Madonna and Child with St John*, *c*.1521, acquired by the National Trust as part of Mr and Mrs Anthony de Rothschild's gift of Ascott in Buckinghamshire, in 1950, with its outstanding collections of pictures, furniture and porcelain.

When Baron Ferdinand died in 1898 Waddesdon passed to his sister Alice Rothschild, who left it in 1922 – rather to his surprise – to her second cousin, James de Rothschild, of the French branch of the family. In the 1920s and '30s he and his wife Dorothy entertained at Waddesdon with apparently undiminished splendour, but both were aware that European politics were moving in a sinister and threatening direction. Anthony and James de Rothschild were active in arranging protection for German Jews in the 1930s. By 1938 James and Dorothy had concluded that Waddesdon should become a hospital. However, their plans were frustrated, Dorothy describing how they learnt that '*boiserie*, even if covered up, would be a first-class harbourer of germs.'[8] Instead the house became the wartime home for a hundred London schoolchildren under five. James de Rothschild was Liberal MP for the Isle of

Ely from 1929 to 1945, but served in Churchill's government as Under-Secretary to the Ministry of Supply from late 1944. While addressing the House of Commons that year, he thanked the British people for their treatment of German Jewish refugees. In response his fellow members 'all rose to their feet in mute expression of their sympathy'.[9]

When the cots and miniature chairs of the evacuated children were cleared away after the war, and the Rothschild treasures reinstated, James and Dorothy de Rothschild began to plan for the future of the house, in a world that was utterly changed, socially, politically and fiscally. They had no children of their own to inherit, and there was the prospect of very substan-

Waddesdon Manor in Buckinghamshire, bequeathed to the National Trust in 1957 with its magnificent collections and an endowment by James de Rothschild.

Evacuee children and staff at Waddesdon Manor, Buckinghamshire, during the Second World War.

tial death duties being levied on Waddesdon. James was a trustee of the Wallace Collection, and both he and his wife appreciated that much of the significance of Waddesdon lay in its completeness, as an expression of Rothschild taste at a moment when the influence of the family crossed every European frontier. 'The solution of the National Trust began to germinate in my husband's mind,' Dorothy wrote, 'and I cannot say how thankful I am that it did.'[10]

Fulfilling their wishes involved patience and stamina. As an experienced racehorse owner, James knew about both attributes, and the obstacles were gradually surmounted. First the Trust's misgivings had to be overcome. Lord Esher let it be known that he hated French furniture. The house itself was regarded by many as an aberration: a pastiche in the worst possible taste, redeemed only by some decent eighteenth-century portraits by Gainsborough and Reynolds of sitters unrelated to the Rothschilds. Fortunately the Chairman of the National Trust, Lord Crawford, had ultimate authority over artistic matters, not least because he was also chairman of the National Art Collections Fund and a trustee of the British Museum, National Gallery and National Portrait Gallery. He largely took control of the negotiations (the property is not mentioned in James Lees-Milne's diaries for this period), and encouraged a solution unique to Waddesdon.

If the National Trust was initially unenthusiastic, the Inland Revenue was characteristically obdurate. James de Rothschild, who died in 1957, had proposed an endowment for Waddesdon which went far beyond the provisions for most houses being accepted by the Trust at that time. The Treasury concluded that it was unnecessarily large and would therefore be taxable. Their officials may not have seen beyond Mrs James de Rothschild's courteous and formal manner. She set about overcoming their assessment. 'If it be true that the best way of keeping grief under control is to be forced to be very busy,' she wrote, 'the Estate Duty Office of the Inland Revenue must indeed be the widow's best friend.'[11] Her persistence prevailed and the Waddesdon endowment was ultimately untaxed.

Within twenty years it was clear that the original settlement was insufficient for the staffing and conservation needs of the house and its collections. The Trust's Finance Committee gave the Chairman, Lord Gibson, and Treasurer, Nicholas Baring, the delicate task of talking to Dorothy de Rothschild, then well into her eighties, about the possible need to supplement her husband's original provisions for the estate. By the time they called on her for tea at her London house, she had ascertained the purpose of the visit and elegantly steered the conversation away from any mention of Waddesdon's future finances. Eventually, without a glimmer of an opening and having elicited nothing, the deputation realised that the discussion was over. As they rose to leave, Gibson and Baring were encouraged to pause for a moment: 'You don't need to worry,' their hostess told them, 'there is a safety net.'[12] That was the extent of the reassurance they were able to take back to the Finance Committee.

Indeed the Trust ought not to have worried. The Rothschild family had no intention of allowing funding from the National Trust to compromise the property's independence, preferring instead to supplement the endowment income from the Waddesdon Trust with infusions from other family sources. Crawford had encouraged this spirit of autonomy, by arranging for the endowment to be put into the hands of a board of trustees, whose membership was made up of the donor's widow, two other members nominated by the family, three by the National Trust and with a neutral chairman. The family reports on the running of the property at the six-monthly meetings of trustees and is responsible for appointing the administrative, curatorial and conservation staff necessary to maintain standards which the National Trust could not begin to match at most of its other properties.

Between the gift of the property in 1957 and her death in 1988, Dorothy de Rothschild personally supervised much of the work in the house, relying particularly on the Trust's Paintings Adviser, Bobby Gore, and on John Fowler for decoration. She was much less interested in the garden, and there the standard of planting and maintenance began to attract criticism. Eventually the Trust's Gardens Panel was deputed to write a report, which was highly critical. Rather than letting Mrs de Rothschild see a paper which was bound to cause offence, the Trust decided that a carefully edited version should be sent to its benefactor. Through some dreadful muddle, the unexpurgated copy was sent to Waddesdon. Predictably enough, the response was rapid and icy. It was only after a considerable interlude that there could be any thought of repairing the damage. Two members of the panel, George Clive and Mary Keen, were invited to lunch at Waddesdon. The signal that the Trust had been forgiven came when Clive was asked for his view on the wine. 'What year do you think it might be?' asked Dorothy de Rothschild. Wisely, Clive responded: 'Well, it's pre-war.' His hostess countered: 'Yes, but which war?' It was a Château Lafite of 1914; and a gesture of renewed friendliness.[13]

The way in which the National Trust managed its finances did not keep pace with the rapid acquisition of great houses and estates after the war and during the 1950s and '60s. When Mark Norman joined the Finance Committee in 1953 he found a 'haphazard, happy, hilarious' head office, occupying an elegant but decrepit Georgian building at 42 Queen Anne's Gate in Westminster.[14] His uncle had been Governor of the Bank of England and his father, Ronald Norman, a revered Chairman of the Trust's Finance and General Purposes Committee from 1923 to 1935, and Vice-Chairman from 1924 to 1948. In an unpublished memoir written in 1984, Mark Norman noted his dismay on joining the Trust's committees at finding that the accountant 'did not know what *had* happened (financially), let alone what was likely to happen in the next weeks or months.' His assessment was that 'the NT's finances were rather like the "corner shop" – let's look and see what's in the till.'[15] Norman believed that the contents of the till would not be sufficient to maintain the growing number of under-endowed country houses now owned by the Trust.

A similar conclusion had been reached by John Smith, who had joined the Trust's committees in 1952, a year before Norman. Temperamentally they were very different. Both came from distinguished banking families. Smith's father Eric had been chairman of the National Provincial Bank, and in 1950 John became a director of Coutts, which had absorbed the Smith family's banking businesses. Norman noted as 'nearly all true' Smith's assessment of himself as 'the only rich, intelligent eccentric left in England'.[16] As well as an ingenious and resourceful financial mind, Smith was a man of originality and immense creative energy, which he applied to the things which fascinated him, from canals and industrial archaeology to small buildings and historic ships. He believed that these interests would be shared by a new generation of Trust supporters and, if vigorously pursued, would lead to a hugely increased membership. That in turn would help to generate the income which the charity urgently needed.

Norman's solution was less glamorous and a good deal more cautious. He wanted to see the Trust's properties managed more professionally and prudently. In order to recruit the calibre of staff needed to look after its growing responsibilities, salaries needed to be comparable to those paid by the civil service and museums. Like Smith, Norman was witty, had a penetrating mind, and could be formidable one moment and genial the next. Under his chairmanship the Finance Committee was the most exacting but also the most entertaining of the Trust's governing bodies. At a distance of 50 years, both men can be seen to have contributed in their different ways to a resurgence of the National Trust, which in turn put it on a far more secure financial footing.

Of all the activities that John Smith wanted to see pursued by the Trust, the most ambitious was the campaign, reactivated after the war by the Chief Agent Christopher Gibbs, to protect the coastline. For Smith this meant much more than preserving beautiful beaches and cliffs. It involved the industrial archaeology of the Cornish tin mines, the conservation of lighthouses and historic harbours such as Boscastle in Cornwall, and the protection of coastal defences that had been constructed, adapted and abandoned over centuries.

To support conservation on such a wide front, Smith set about using his financial acumen to create his own charitable trusts. His most substantial source of income came from buying property, much of it in Belgravia, shortly before long leases expired. Frequently it was under-valued because of fears of the landlords' claims for dilapidations. Using his knowledge of historic buildings, Smith selected carefully, avoiding properties that were unsound and choosing those which could be re-let to businessmen and diplomats. He channelled all his profits into the Manifold Trust, set up in 1962 with charitable status and thus free of tax, initially offering the idea to the National Trust. Although the offer was not taken up, the National Trust became his chosen instrument for pursuing many of his conservation aims: it was the Manifold Trust that paid for a section of the Stratford-upon-Avon canal running through the park of Charlecote, which was then passed to the Trust. But increasingly he liked to go his own way, without recourse to the National Trust and its committees, or to the statutory bodies whose offers of grants might constrain his often radical treatment of historic buildings.

In 1965 Smith founded the Landmark Trust, principally to preserve minor but quirky and interesting historic buildings which, once restored, could be let for holidays. 'A stay in a Landmark is meant to offer not just a holiday,' he wrote, 'but an experience of a mildly elevating kind, a fresh window on life, to be looked through or not, as you please.'[17] In its early years the Landmark Trust championed humble buildings, 'once so ordinary as to be taken for granted.'[18] In due course its success led it to acquire properties abroad, including Palladio's Villa Saraceno in the Italian Veneto. When the National Trust acquired the island of Lundy off the north Devon coast in 1969, with twenty-three houses and cottages, a castle and a lighthouse, the whole property was leased to the Landmark Trust, which bore all the costs of repair and management. By then Smith's relationship with the National Trust had been complicated and damaged; but that did not prevent him coming to its aid when a project or potential acquisition particularly excited him.

Tensions between Smith and the Trust's staff had been simmering for some time, and well before the eruptions of 1966. The root of the problem was his dissatisfaction with the Secretary of the Trust, Jack Rathbone, whom he found effete and over-cautious in his response to the initiatives that came in droves. Smith began to involve himself directly in disputes at properties in a way that undermined Rathbone. A particularly contentious issue arose at Bodnant, over Lord Aberconway's proposal to charge the National Trust for plants propagated in what was then called the 'retained garden', and which was managed by the family as a separate enterprise. Rathbone not unreasonably questioned whether it was right for Aberconway to sell plants with his commercial hand and buy on behalf of the Bodnant Trust with the other, in his capacity as manager of a garden that belonged to the National Trust, which was a charity. When this developed into what Aberconway called 'a monumental row',[19] Smith became involved and let it be known that he thought Rathbone's attitude absurd. Eventually a compromise arrangement was agreed, which involved channelling funds for the purchase of plants through a specially constituted trust, of which both Aberconway and his wife were trustees.

In his account of the episode, Aberconway noted that 'Rathbone shortly afterwards had a breakdown and left the Trust. John Smith told me it was largely due to this issue.'[20] The altercation may have contributed to Rathbone's collapse, but it was not the principal cause. What forced him out of the National Trust was the appointment in 1963 of Commander Conrad Rawnsley as appeals director of Enterprise Neptune, in spite of warnings from both Gibbs and Rathbone that he was likely to prove troublesome. They were right to be concerned. As the grandson of Canon Hardwicke Rawnsley, one of the Trust's founders, Rawnsley believed that he had been appointed to reshape the organisation in ways which he and Smith felt would capture the public's imagination. Much of what Rawnsley proposed had already been advocated by Smith, was enlightened and overdue. It was the manner in which he set about promoting his plans for Enterprise Neptune that was calculated to cause a rift within the Trust.

Rawnsley appointed and sacked his staff without reference to the Secretary or others. Some were paid far more than those working in the regions; and at Christmas one of his recruits was given a bonus of £500, which was more than the annual salary of some property staff. Enterprise Neptune was successfully raising substantial sums of money, but the Finance Committee was concerned that the expenses of the appeal were disproportionate. Among the evidence of extravagance was the report that Rawnsley had taken a taxi from London to Manchester to give a talk on Enterprise Neptune. Staff, members of the Neptune committee and supporters were all so incensed by his behaviour that it became clear he had to leave. The Chairman of the National Trust, Lord Antrim, began discreet discussions over terms for Rawnsley's departure, which was to be with a testimonial praising, quite justifiably, his 'originality and intensity of purpose'.[21]

Characteristically, Rawnsley opted for a pre-emptive strike. In October 1966 he used a press conference in Plymouth to accuse the National Trust of 'moral bankruptcy', issuing a written statement detailing the ways in which the ideals of the founders were being betrayed. Immediately afterwards he was sacked. He and his supporters then embarked on a sustained attack on the Trust, to which Rawnsley devoted his considerable oratorical and organising abilities. It culminated in an Extraordinary General Meeting, held at Central Hall, Westminster, in February 1967. For those who valued what the Trust had achieved, it was an agonising occasion. Although the membership remained overwhelmingly loyal to the governing Council, a motion calling for a review into how the Trust could widen its support and appeal was approved.

Out of the whole sorry affair came the Benson Report, the recommendations of which paved the way for the Trust's extraordinary growth in the years since. In 1967 the National Trust had barely 160,000 members. By 1975 membership stood at 539,000; and by 2000 it was over

HMS *Warrior*, Britain's first ironclad battleship, which was restored by Sir John Smith's Manifold Trust in the late 1980s.

3 million. During the same period the acreage owned by the charity more than doubled.

Another consequence of the upheaval was that, two years before the Extraordinary General Meeting, John Smith, who had been involved in the appointment of Rawnsley, stood down from the chairmanship of the General Purposes Committee. He moved from a central role in the Trust's affairs, to being a source of occasional support, usually through the Landmark Trust. At Canons Ashby in Northamptonshire, Gibside in County Durham, Stowe in Buckinghamshire and other properties, it was the Landmark Trust's adoption of part of the house or a key park building that provided the first step towards repair and acquisition by the National Trust.

In 1980 the Chairman, Lord Gibson, persuaded Smith to accept the post of Deputy Chairman, which he held until 1995. Smith's ability to swing an argument was demonstrated at the Extraordinary General Meeting held in 1982. It had been called because of the outrage felt by many members at the Trust's decision, in the face of a likely compulsory purchase order, to lease land at Bradenham in Buckinghamshire to the Ministry of Defence for use as a command centre. The Council of the Trust had decided that it was better to negotiate a lease stipulating remedial work than to risk losing all control of the site. Members were unconvinced; and even as experienced a chairman as Gibson was unable to prevent the mood of the EGM turning ugly. Then John Smith intervened. 'I suppose you are aware that if the motion critical of the Council is carried, Lord Gibson will have to resign?' he said. There was a moment of uncertainty about what Smith would say next. 'If that happens,' he went on, 'you would have me as Chairman.' Another pause. 'You might want to think very carefully about that.' For the first time during the meeting laughter swept through the hall. The motions deploring the Council's decisions were decisively defeated.

Smith's contribution to conservation went far beyond what he did for the National Trust and the Landmark Trust. By 1987 the Manifold Trust had given over £41.5 million to 813 different charities, contributing to the rescue of a whole range of buildings and artefacts that caught Smith's imagination. The assurance and style with which these projects were brought to completion are exemplified by the resurrection of HMS *Warrior*, Britain's first ironclad battleship, the hull of which survived as a floating jetty near Milford Haven. Smith had it transported to Hartlepool for complete restoration, down to the last detail of its rigging. When the ship made her triumphant return to Portsmouth in March 1988, there was a lunch on board for HRH The Duke of Edinburgh and all those involved with the Warrior Preservation Trust. Among the characteristic touches was a covering note to the invitation:

> The ship has been restored <u>exactly</u> as she was in 1860 – accordingly the ladders, though having broad treads, are quite steep, and have ropes instead of handrails. Stiletto heels therefore, besides damaging the decks, may kill you.

Sir John Smith (left) and HRH The Duke of Edinburgh at the lunch held on board HMS *Warrior* in March 1988, to celebrate the ship's restoration and triumphant return to Portsmouth.

Smith commissioned a train to bring all those who had worked on the ship in Hartlepool down to Portsmouth to share in the celebrations.

John Smith was knighted that year; and in 1994 he was made a Companion of Honour. Such recognition of his achievements, far from calming his restless self-criticism, seemed to fuel it. His response was to say that he was '*mystified* to be made a CH… I am already over-rewarded. I put it down to teething troubles with Mr Major's new classless honours system.'[22] In other people this might have been indulging in habitual English self-deprecation. Smith, however, seemed to be oblivious to praise, but hyper-sensitive to criticism, having, as his wife Christian acknowledged, 'such a low opinion of himself'.[23] This found expression in ways which were sometimes amusing, and sometimes faintly absurd. He might one moment be telling friends about a recent trip to the Falklands to examine the abandoned tall ships laid up there; or of a visit to one of Scott's huts in Antarctica; or to St Helena where he gave £25,000 to support the museum. He would then add with genuine anxiety, 'I mustn't *bore* you,' before plunging on. He always contrived to be his own man, even on the ski-slopes, where he wore silk gloves – the benefits of which he had learnt while flying in a Swordfish squadron of the Fleet Air Arm during the war – and a bulky Balaclava knitted by Christian.

When Smith felt he had been in any way slighted, the break would be irrevocable. Among the files in the Landmark Trust office at Shottesbrooke Park, his home in Berkshire, were those in which he kept notes and correspondence – from former Landmark directors, people who had once helped his trusts, and his own sons – which he felt implied criticism or were evidence of perceived disloyalty. By the time of his death he had cut himself off from many of his friends and admirers.

He was particularly upset by what was written about him in the three histories of the National Trust published for its centenary in 1995. In spite of extended appreciations of what he had achieved, he took offence at the accounts of his resignation from the chairmanship of the General Purposes Committee in 1964, and to a passage in Jennifer Jenkins's book about his deteriorating relationship with Rathbone, in which she quoted a letter from Crawford to Rosse, saying: 'They are both rather neurotic and both work themselves into a frenzy of nerves and overwork.'[24] Smith had agreed to review the three books for the *Spectator*, and having read them in succession felt that taken together they 'reveal me as such a loony monster that I'm too embarrassed ever to appear at the Trust again – have told them so.'[25] Nothing that anyone could do would persuade him that he continued to be regarded with huge admiration and affection by those in the Trust with whom he had worked.[26] It is hard to reconcile two different images of him: the soaked and lonely figure deliberately standing on his own in torrential rain at the very end of the platform at Truro railway station after Michael Trinick's memorial service in 1994, while his National Trust friends waited under a canopy for the London train; or the witty, welcoming host on the deck of HMS *Warrior*, receiving royalty and unqualified praise for one of his many triumphs.

A measure of John Smith's achievement is that most of the things that he was advocating in the 1960s have, over time, been embraced by the National Trust. They have contributed to a level of support that would have been unimaginable when it was in the introverted, impoverished condition in which he found it. Credit is also due to Sir Henry Benson, Len Clark, Patrick Gibson and Sir William Hayter, who produced the Benson Report. Essentially, however, it was the revolution that Smith helped to bring about that led to the review. The role of the Finance Committee, under Mark Norman's chairmanship, was also crucial, demanding and securing far more disciplined financial management. Without the new formula devised in 1976 by Lord Chorley for calculating the endowments required for new acquisitions, Norman's fears that its country houses would ultimately bankrupt the Trust might well have proved justified.

***

A reformed and more outward-looking National Trust was well placed to take advantage of the grants that became available following the formation of the National Heritage Memorial Fund (NHMF) in 1980 and the Heritage Lottery Fund (HLF) in 1995. Not only did the Trust receive substantial help towards the acquisition and repair of many of the properties described in later chapters, but there was now the possibility of funding to enhance and extend sites where financial problems had resulted in years of neglect. This was particularly true of some of the Trust's nature reserves, including Wicken Fen.

When the idea of a national lottery was proposed by John Major's government, it was on the understanding that among the good causes to benefit would be the arts and heritage, including natural and man-made landscapes. There were discussions both inside and outside Whitehall about whether a distributing body should be specially created, or whether an existing one might take on this role. English Heritage was keen to add the distribution of HLF grants to its other responsibilities, but had the obvious disadvantage that it was perceived to be a government body. Sir Hayden Phillips, the permanent secretary at the Department of National Heritage, believed that the NHMF, with a record of acting at arms-length from government and with trustees who were knowledgeable and decisive, would be a more appropriate distributor. Phillips had the opportunity to sound out their chairman, Jacob, 4th Lord Rothschild, when they happened to meet at a point-to-point; and the response was positive.

The announcement that the trustees of the NHMF were also to be responsible for distributing lottery funds was not universally welcomed, because they – and particularly the chairman – were thought to be biased in favour of architecture and the visual arts. Jacob Rothschild had been chairman of the trustees of the National Gallery from 1985 to 1991, at the time the Sainsbury Wing was built. Not only had there been impressive additions to the collections, but, with Neil MacGregor as director, the appearance of the gallery itself had dramatically improved. The previous director, Sir Michael Levey, was an outstanding scholar and a brilliant lecturer. He successfully nurtured the talents of his staff, encouraging them to re-hang and decorate some of the galleries with relatively little supervision and with mixed results. Levey believed that the qualities of fine paintings could be enjoyed regardless of their setting, and that the gallery was simply a box for displaying them. MacGregor and Rothschild, on the other hand, believed that the building itself was a great work of art. The culmination of its redecoration was the restoration of the great hall at the top of the entrance steps, where the benefactor responsible is recorded in the frieze:

IACOBI. ROTHSCHILD. MUNIFICENTIA. IN. INTEGRUM. RESTITUTA

Rothschild was also responsible for the no-less splendid restoration of Spencer House and of parts of Waddesdon.

Those who perceived in Rothschild a bias towards the arts may have overlooked the part that nature conservation played in his upbringing. He was close to his aunt Miriam, and revered the memory of Charles Rothschild, the grandfather he never knew. The director of the HLF, Anthea Case, who was conscious of her role as accounting officer for the Department of Culture, Media and Sport, had to discourage her chairman from giving grants to the wildlife trusts his grandfather had initiated, simply to help towards their general running costs. Instead they, and the National Trust, were encouraged to apply for funding towards specific schemes of acquisition, improvement or consolidation.

Some of the HLF's unexpected but highly successful initiatives came from Rothschild himself. The programme of grants to restore Britain's urban parks was very much his idea. Their revival demonstrated a commitment to preserving a peculiarly British achievement, which also provided continuing public and social benefit, often in cities struggling to recover from industrial decline.

Jacob, 4th Lord Rothschild, photographed by Hugh Palmer.

With the HLF giving itself such a broad remit, Rothschild wanted to bring those with specialist knowledge and experience onto its staff. In the summer of 1996, when I was with the Attingham Summer School at Waddesdon, he asked: 'Will you come and help us?' The invitation was irresistible and, after a formal interview, I joined the HLF, on a year's secondment from the National Trust, as the policy adviser on built heritage and historic sites. There was the opportunity to make good the years of neglect and under-funding that had done so much damage to nature conservation, museums and great buildings.

One of the fascinations of working for the HLF was seeing its chairman and trustees in action. Of course, proper procedures were followed in meetings, but often those trustees whose views on a grant application were particularly respected had been carefully consulted beforehand. With major schemes, such as the restoration of Somerset House, Rothschild involved himself in every stage of the negotiations to persuade the Inland Revenue to release parts of the building, so that the courtyard could once again be one of London's great public spaces. Anthea Case believed that only Jacob Rothschild could have secured the Gilbert Collection of silver for display there. When the National Trust for Scotland was exploring the possibility of acquiring the Mar Lodge estate in the Cairngorms, it was Rothschild who undertook to talk to its American owner about gifting the property to the nation to mark Her Majesty Queen Elizabeth II's Golden Jubilee, or of selling the property on favourable terms. 'I was warned I might get a haircut when you came to see me,' the owner confessed, 'but I wasn't expecting a shave.'[27]

With grants from the HLF, the prospects for Wicken Fen have been transformed, in ways which would have delighted its early benefactor, Charles Rothschild. During the 1990s research had shown that it was drying out, so putting its many rare species at risk. Under a particularly far-sighted chairman, Norman Moore, the Wicken Fen committee and the National Trust set about inserting a waterproof membrane along the banks, which helped to maintain a high water table. This was a necessary first step towards an ambitious plan to extend the area of protection to create a 15,000-acre reserve for wildlife and public enjoyment, extending ten miles to Cambridge.

This could only be done piece-by-piece. In 1992 Priory Farm, an area of intensely farmed arable land, came on the market and was bought by the National Trust. The water levels have been raised and it is now grazed with Konik ponies, which can cope with the rough, wet conditions, and help to achieve a mosaic of Wicken's varied plant communities. With grants from the HLF the Trust has been able to make a succession of further acquisitions. Echoing what Charles Rothschild had advocated a century earlier, Moore explained the need for ambitious, landscape-scale action, adding that 'it's always been a perfectly logical, sensible way of conserving wildlife in the UK.'[28] In 2009 Miriam Rothschild's centre for the study of dragonflies was given a permanent home at Wicken Fen.

The last twenty years have also seen major work at Waddesdon, with Lord Rothschild continuing to take the lead when there are opportunities for appropriate accessions. In 2008 Chardin's *Boy Building a House of Cards* was bought with money from the Rothschilds' family trusts. Other acquisitions included two paintings by Panini of the celebrations in Rome to mark the birth in 1751 of a new heir to the French throne, further strengthening the French associations of the collections. These are purchases which the National Trust could not have contemplated, and which consciously affect the relationship between the two parties. By providing for Waddesdon through substantial donations to the endowment and by funding acquisitions using family trusts, Rothschild can feel justified in taking a leading role in the way the property is presented and run. The objectives are shared ones, and were clearly understood when Waddesdon was given to the National Trust in 1957.

Baron Ferdinand believed that, at a time when royalty and the church were no longer major patrons of the arts, he was able to provide a worthy alternative at Waddesdon, which would be 'a new centre of attraction'. [29] His successors were charged with responsibility for not allowing it to decay; and that obligation was met by its gift to the Trust. Mrs James de Rothschild concluded that:

> … the very evident pleasure of our visitors seems to confirm his judgement: pleasure gives pleasure and to me it is an exceptional privilege and delight to witness it at Waddesdon year after year.[30]

THE MILL OWNER
AND THE WOODLANDER
Alec Greg and Styal; John Workman and Ebworth

Is it John Ward's illustration of Uncle Charlie, in *Cider with Rosie*, as much as Laurie Lee's description that makes him unforgettable? Ward's sinewy line shows him broad-shouldered, with big boxing hands, breeches pulled high by braces stretched over a huge chest, and gaitered legs. Lee tells us that Uncle Charlie survived the Boer War, the mud and carnage of Flanders, and the stews of Johannesburg to become one of the best woodsmen in the Cotswolds. Some of the most beautiful and enduring woods that he planted enclose the valley around Sheepscombe and Ebworth in Gloucestershire.

A note at the beginning of *Cider with Rosie* mentions that 'The book is a recollection of early boyhood, and some of the facts may be distorted by time.' But Charlie Light was real enough. He was employed by Ernest Workman, the owner of the Ebworth estate, was paid an agricultural labourer's wage of 35 shillings a week, and in the 1920s and 1930s was joined in the woods by his son, another Charlie, who was called Maurice to avoid confusion.

The Workman family were not Gloucestershire squires, but successful timber merchants, with a six-storey mill in Woodchester, south of Stroud, where they also lived until 1960. Henry Workman bought the Ebworth estate in 1901, to guarantee supplies of timber for his factory. For the billiard cues, cotton reels and yo-yos made in its turnery, Workman needed fine quality hardwoods, particularly ash. Beech was also in demand for furniture. Cotswold land prices had fallen to such low levels in the early twentieth century that Workman was able to buy the whole estate for the value of its timber. Less than a quarter of his land at Ebworth was wooded in the nineteenth century, but the decline in the profitability of both the wool trade and sheep farming meant that Henry Workman had no hesitation in planting former pasture with beech and larch. Much of what was woodland had been coppiced to provide small-diameter timber for the colony of charcoal burners who lived in the woods in conical huts, close to their kilns; but with the arrival of cheap coal by rail, charcoal burning rapidly declined. What Henry Workman needed was beech, ash and larch, grown to maturity, and he planted accordingly.

The Ebworth estate produced excellent timber, but the existing roads were few and extraction was difficult, even with skilfully managed heavy horses. The solution was to build new roads, using gangs of unemployed men from Stroud, a specially constructed light railway, tip wagons, and in some places dynamite. The forest road constructed in this way between 1932

John Workman, appointed Forestry Adviser to the National Trust in 1953, in Workmans Wood at Ebworth, in Gloucestershire. In 1989 he donated this 288-acre beech wood to the Trust.

and 1936 provided an extraction route for horse-drawn wagons at a gradient of 1 in 37, rather than the 1 in 4 gradients of the roads out of the Sheepscombe valley. A private railway line linked the factory and mill at Woodchester with the Nailsworth branch line.

After Henry Workman's death in 1924, the family business passed to his nephew, Ernest Workman. Although the sawmill and factory closed in 1953, he continued to supervise the management of the woods until his death in 1962. By then the talents of his son, John, had been put to use elsewhere.

Father and son never really got on. There is a photograph of John aged about four, on his father's knee. In it Ernest Workman has an Elgarian moustache, the authority of the successful mill owner, and looks straight at the camera. John looks away from both. The father was stern, authoritarian and very conscious of his social position. The son was to prove quick-witted, open-minded and radical.

Unsurprisingly in someone with a family background in business and industry, John studied electronics at Clare College, Cambridge. A two-year spell of working on farms convinced him that his real interests lay in the countryside, and he transferred to Oxford to read forestry. This was followed by six months in Sweden studying arboriculture, then by an unhappy period working for his father in Gloucestershire on an agricultural wage of £2 a week. As an old man, John would say: 'I am not my father's son.' He needed to escape and it was the National Trust that provided him with a way of doing so.

In 1950 the Royal Forestry Society awarded its Gold Medal to Ernest Workman for Pope's Wood. Its president, Lord Bolton, had been head of the Government's Timber Control Commission, owned large estates in Yorkshire, and was also an honorary adviser on forestry to the

The Workman family's saw mills at Woodchester in Gloucestershire, close to the Ebworth estate bought in 1901 to supply timber for their factory.

National Trust. He knew Ernest Workman well, having worked with him on the implementation of the Forestry Act of 1948, and found that his son John was a well-qualified forester who in 1946, while still a student, had become a life member of the Trust at the cost of £20. He could be useful.

Bolton proposed that John should assist with surveys of National Trust woodland, working on a voluntary basis. There was a further interview with the Trust's Chief Agent, Hubert Smith, and then the years of travelling to Trust properties in all corners of the country began. His association with the Trust, as Forestry and Conservation Adviser, committee member, volunteer and benefactor, was to extend over 60 years.

The early annual reports of the National Trust list gifts of small areas of woodland throughout the country. Many had previously been open common or heath, but as grazing declined had become first scrub and then woods. Some had curious historical associations. Maggoty's Wood in Cheshire, which amounts to only two and a half acres, was given in 1935, not so much for the beauty of its trees, but because it contains the grave of Maggoty Johnson, a poet and dramatist who in the eighteenth century was employed as a dancing-master at near-by Gawsworth Hall. His tombstone of 1773 records that he chose to be buried in unconsecrated ground:

Quarry Bank Mill on the banks of the River Bollin in Cheshire: the eighteenth-century cotton mill and the village of Styal, an early example of an industrial settlement, were given to the National Trust by Alec Greg in 1939.

Stay, thou whom Chance directs or ease persuades,
To seek the Quiet of these Sylvan shades,
Here, undisturbed and hid from Vulgar Eyes,
A Wit, Musician, Poet, Player, lies.
A Dancing Master too in Grace he shone,
And all the arts of Opera were his own…
Averse to Strife how oft he'd gravely say,
These peaceful Groves should shade his breathless Clay,
That when he rose again, laid here alone,
No friend and he should quarrel for a Bone,
Thinking that were some old lame Gossip nigh,
She possibly might take his Leg or Thigh.

Alongside is a pious Victorian inscription of 1851, warning of the perils of such frivolity:

… Boast not of silly art or wit or fame,
Be thou ambitious of a Christian's name,
Seek not thy body's rest in peaceful grove,
Pray that thy soul may rest in Jesus' love,
O speak not lightly of that dreadful day,
When all must rise in joy or in dismay…
Look on that stone and this, and ponder well,
Then choose twixt Life and Death, Heaven and Hell.

In the case of other properties, an area of surrounding woodland might tip the scales towards acceptance. When Alec Greg offered the National Trust the eighteenth-century Quarry Bank Mill at Styal in Cheshire in 1939, he included in the proposed gift 250 acres of beech woods on either side of the River Bollin. The Trust correctly saw that these woods would not only be valued and enjoyed by local people, but would help to contain the relentless spread of suburban housing on the southern edge of Manchester. What could not have been foreseen was that they would also restrict the expansion of Manchester airport at Styal.

Greg realised that the woods at Styal were, at the time of the gift, its chief asset. For over 30 years after their transfer, the Trust regarded the cotton mill as an industrial building which could be rented out for commercial uses. The mill was built by Samuel Greg in 1784. Like

the mill, Greg's model village and Apprentice House, constructed as accommodation for his workforce, were used by the Trust as property to rent. It was not until 1978 that, thanks to the drive and imagination of the Regional Agent, Gerard Noel, Quarry Bank Mill was first opened to the public as a museum of the cotton industry, with portraits, sketchbooks and photograph albums lent by the Greg family. By 1993 it was attracting over 200,000 visitors a year, most of whom were scarcely aware of the extent of the surrounding woodland.

Like many successful Manchester businessmen, the Gregs believed in philanthropy because it helped to ensure that their workforce was healthy, placid and disinclined to join radical movements such as Chartism or trade unionism.[1] Indeed, it was exactly the combination of paternalism, manipulation and self-interested philanthropy which prompted Friedrich Engels to write critically of Quarry Bank Mill in *The Condition of the Working Class in England*, first published in 1845, which in turn provided Karl Marx with material for *Das Kapital*.[2] However complex the Gregs' motives, the benefits for their workers were very real: in the early 1800s the apprentices working at Styal were well fed, clothed and housed, and had skilled medical care from the mill doctor, Mr Holland. Through the Chapel, they were given regular teaching, informal lectures and the opportunity to join the village choir. In return they were expected to work hard and to conform.

The Gregs were Unitarians, meaning theologically that they believed in God as one person, and not in the Trinity. Unitarianism also involved social and political freedom of belief.

[above left] John Workman as a child, with his father Ernest Workman, c.1925.

[above right] Alec Greg, donor of Quarry Bank Mill and Styal Village to the National Trust in 1939.

Octavia Hill's mother Caroline was a Unitarian, as were many supporters of the National Trust in its early years.

The gift of Quarry Bank Mill by Alec Greg was consistent with the philanthropy of his great-grandfather, Richard Hyde Greg. The National Trust was a charity and, once weaving at Styal was no longer viable, a future for the mill, the village, and the surrounding countryside, which involved considerable community benefit, clearly appealed to him. Family tragedy also played a part. Both of Alec Greg's elder brothers were killed in the First World War.

When Quarry Bank Mill was established as a museum to the cotton industry, Alec Greg was a founder trustee. He attended meetings regularly, was extremely helpful to those researching the history of his family and their business interests, and gave short shrift to those on the museum board who were tiresome or obstructive. At such moments the assertiveness of his pioneering forbears was briefly evident. Greg saw, rather more clearly than some of those working for the Trust, that the mill and its related buildings were of exceptional historical importance; and he also appreciated the value and beauty of the Styal beech woods.

John Workman's involvement with the National Trust's woods came at a turning point. Up until the Second World War, the Trust employed only a handful of professional staff, and most of its properties, including woodlands, were managed by local committees. There were honorary advisers and, until 1953, a Forestry Sub-Committee. What constituted good woodland management was a matter of fierce and at times even ferocious debate.

The controversies went back to the Trust's earliest years, and particularly to the opposition of walkers and climbers to the insensitive planting of huge areas of conifers in the Lake District. The Fell and Rock Climbing Club strongly objected to the Forestry Commission's plantations which, between the wars, did so much damage to areas such as Ennerdale; and several of the club's members were also involved with the National Trust. Rows about the desecration of the Lake District by the Forestry Commission inflamed passions nationally and were the subject of heated debate in Parliament. In the postwar period, the issue again became politically fraught, with blankets of Sitka spruce in the uplands somehow symbolising the spread of the socialist state.

These disputes were in some ways useful to both the Council for the Preservation (later Protection) of Rural England and the National Trust, because they encouraged

WOODMAN, SPARE THAT TREE.

Canon Rawnsley has protested strongly against the action of the Manchester Corporation in cutting down the oak wood on the shores of Thirlmere.

support and the recruitment of members. The Trust was seen to have a role, not only in protecting the coastline from invading lines of bungalows, but also in not allowing the hills of the Lake District, Wales and the Peak District to be suffocated by softwoods. This it could do by acquiring property at risk from afforestation. However the Trust had to be seen to manage its woodlands sensitively, both as a valuable resource and as a public amenity. It was fortunate to recruit, as its first honorary adviser, Major H.M. Heyder, who had previously worked for the Indian Forest Service. His reports for the Trust on the Ashridge Estate in Hertfordshire had exactly the pragmatism then sought by the Chairman of the Estates Committee – and a major benefactor himself – G.M. Trevelyan. Heyder then applied the same practical, thoroughly professional approach to the plans for other Trust woodlands, so providing the models that were to be developed and extended by John Workman.

After two years of working as a volunteer, John had made himself sufficiently useful to be brought onto the staff, working alternate weeks. He reported to the Trust's Chief Agent, but was largely left to organise his work unsupervised. This involved liaising with the local

Autumnal trees at Ashridge in Hertfordshire, an estate of over 4,000 acres of woods, heath, down and farmland, acquired by the National Trust between 1921 and 1991 with bequests, grants, subscriptions to public appeals, and donations from both individuals and national organisations.

committees, running many of the Trust's open spaces, and writing reports for the half-dozen Area Agents. While responsibility for the Trust's woods took John to much beautiful countryside, the peripatetic life would only have suited a bachelor with few family ties. The strain was considerable and ultimately unsustainable.

Half a century later, the memory still lingered of just how cold and miserable those journeys could be. John travelled by motorbike, and the distances from, say, Gloucestershire to Norfolk seemed greater then than they do now. His maps, gumboots and a suit travelled with him. Eventually he got a van, into which equipment and a suitcase could be thrown, and that too was remembered without affection:

> I never slept in it – I decided I didn't want to be a gypsy, so I stayed in modest hotels or local staff put me up. But for twenty-five years I never put my suitcase away, not for a day. After twenty-five years I was absolutely worn out.... I did go potty in the end. When I finally broke down, the Trust realised that they had to let me take things more slowly. It took me a year to perk up again.[3]

John's nervous breakdown prompted him to wonder what would have happened had he got on with his father, or if he had inherited sooner. He concluded that he might never have worked professionally for the Trust, or his involvement might have been limited to serving on a local committee. It is a measure of how valuable to the Trust he had proved to be, and how much he was respected by the Land Agents and foresters, that he was encouraged to return only when he was well enough.

Part of his value was that, after 25 years, John knew the Trust's woods better than any other staff. 'You could parachute me blindfold into any forest in England and I'd know exactly where I was,' he would say. Because there were so few other staff, John was free to make his own recommendations, which were usually implemented quickly and with little questioning. 'Now it's difficult to get a decision,' he observed in retirement: 'it might sometimes have been the wrong decision, but I often wonder if a non-decision is almost as wrong.'

Another of John's strengths was that he was in neither the Land Agents' nor the aesthetes' camp. He would tease the Trust's Land Agents that the less they had to do with the woods, the better managed they were. Certainly few, if any of them, had his feel for the special qualities of a particular wood, or indeed an individual tree. I remember being taken to see a stand of trees on the Lower Brockhampton estate in Herefordshire, which for two centuries had somehow escaped the attention of Land Agents or timber merchants anxious to extract profit from the woods. They were like the soaring columns of a cathedral. In the woods at Attingham Park in Shropshire, he led me to one specimen of oak that would have been ideal timber for ship or house building, but had been overlooked. It too had survived to tower over its neighbours, which had been left alone precisely because they were twisted and crooked.

Woodland plans were not the only fruits of John's visits. He made it his responsibility to guide and encourage the Trust's woodlands staff. On his own initiative he arranged the first training course for foresters – Land Agents were not invited – using the Ebworth woods for teaching. He would demonstrate how, at Ebworth, it was possible to mix hardwoods with softwoods, which could then be harvested much earlier and would make a wood financially viable. There were some areas which had once been coppiced, and where the nature conser-

vation benefits of cropping in rotation were evident. He also saw the value of woodland felled immediately after the Second World War, which could be seen to have regenerated natural-ly. In other parts of the estate there was a mix of planting of different ages, giving variety and making it possible to get a financial return in stages and not only when the woodland was clear-felled.

In the 1960s the practice of selective felling and uneven-aged planting was, under John's guidance, introduced on the National Trust's Wallington estate in Northumberland, prompt-ing accusations of vandalism from the Trust's Secretary, Jack Rathbone. Time proved John Workman right, and Wallington is the better for having varied, rather than uniformly geri-atric woods.

Wallington was just one of the many great estates that came to the National Trust in the early years of the Country Houses Scheme. Such properties were usually accepted because James Lees-Milne and Lord Esher admired the principal house. Scant attention was paid to the park and woods until John Workman visited, and it was really only then that the scale of his task became evident. Killerton in Devon, Holnicote in Somerset, Clumber in Notting-hamshire, Dolaucothi and Ysbyty in Wales, and Blickling in Norfolk were just a few of the wave of acquisitions in the 1940s and 1950s, all with major woodlands needing attention. John was also one of the National Trust's main links with the Forestry Commission and with the Ministry of Agriculture, and as he recalled: 'Half the time I was in gumboots and the other half I was in a suit in London, battering away at Ministry doors.'[4]

A cork oak tree in the woodland garden at Killerton in Devon, one of the many large estates with extensive woodlands acquired by the National Trust in the mid-twentieth century. The property was partly given by, and bought from, Sir Richard Acland, 15th Bt., in 1944.

John was a man of apparent contradictions: practical but also – with a small 'p' – political; a landowner but radical in reaction to his father's conservatism. Most of his own staff and the National Trust's foresters were friends, but he was equally at ease among the rich and influential:

> They know I don't ride, shoot, gamble, dance, have grandchildren, and am difficult and argumentative and always in the thick of things.… I am still amazed how generous they are.[5]

Although successive Chief Agents of the National Trust were aware of the increasing demands being made of him, his responsibilities were widened still further when he was re-designated Adviser for Conservation and Woodlands. That his remit was extended so considerably is a measure of the confidence there was in his ability to absorb new thinking; and also of how limited funds were for any new appointments in the 1970s. It was not until the mid-1980s that the Trust appointed a Chief Nature Conservation Adviser, employing an academic biologist, Dr John Harvey, who had been secretary of the Wicken Fen committee and so knew the organisation well.

For years John Workman had urged the Trust's agents to look at its woods not just with the eyes of a commercial forester. He believed that woodlands should give visual delight to those who walked in them. One of his first decisions after he inherited the Ebworth estate, on his father's death in 1962, was to open up a network of footpaths for the enjoyment of local people (something his father would never have countenanced). Later in his career he began to feel that the pendulum had swung too far away from the aim of growing fine timber, and he enjoyed telling his critics that he was 'a wicked forester'. He would point out, with his teasing mischievous twinkle, that 'dead trees are now almost more important than live ones'. His successors favoured a far less interventionist approach, leaving what he called 'oak trees with a lot of other things, wonky oak trees, dead oak trees and rotten oak trees'. He continued:

> That's a perfectly valid opinion, but I'm interested in the Trust making money. I'd rather make money out of woods than the pressured shopping they have now. I think it's sad that people should be pushed through a shop before they get to a house.… I'm trying to provide them, in the Trust's countryside, with beautiful free space; and then they go to a house and it's just like going to Tescos.[6]

John also found himself out of step with some of the Trust's new generation of landscape historians and archaeologists. He was sceptical of the value of restoring 'Capability' Brown's much eroded and damaged landscape at Croome Park in Worcestershire: 'We've got plenty of Brown's things that are still there. What's the point of restoring one that isn't?'

Even more contentious was the gradual collapse of Ebworth House. Nikolaus Pevsner, writing in the Gloucestershire volume of *The Buildings of England*, describes the house as 'Tudor, but greatly enlarged in 1722. L-shaped, with two big façades of three storeys and seven bays flanked by pilasters. The mansion is remote, and was derelict in 1966.' When I was first taken round the Ebworth woods on a sparkling morning in the late 1970s, the variety and beauty of the different plantations – each explained by John with the intimate knowledge of

John Workman in Workmans Wood, Gloucestershire, in February 1994.

a man who had tended them for 50 years – was a revelation. At one point the pediment of Ebworth House, its warm Cotswold stone bathed in sunshine, was clearly visible through the trees. My enquiries did not elicit much of a response. By then it was a shell and had been largely engulfed by twentieth-century planting.

The sale particulars of 1899 show Ebworth House on a largely open Cotswold escarpment, with scattered clumps of trees planted to give the effect of picturesque parkland. Photographs of a hundred years later, taken from the same spot, show the valley filled with almost continuous woodland. The house had never been a Workman family home, and John himself lived in a modest cottage at Far End, Sheepscombe. He did not want Ebworth House occupied by someone who might set themselves up as a quasi-squire in the heart of the estate. During the final stages of its collapse, John allowed the building to be used for practice exercises by the local fire brigade, which enflamed the feelings of local architectural historians. When the shell was finally demolished the base of the walls was capped. The stone stables and outbuildings are now used by the wardens working at Ebworth and neighbouring properties, with Natural England occupying a small office there.

The purpose of my first visit had been to discuss with John what ought to be done to ensure the safekeeping of the National Trust's archives. There was a misguided idea among some senior staff that the Trust existed to look after its properties and that the organisation was, in Lees-Milne's words, only 'an instrument'. With his strong historical sense, John realised that the Trust was itself of great cultural significance and that it ought to be preserving its records with care, for the benefit of future scholars. He was consequently appalled when he heard that the 1930s *Minute Book* of Ferguson's Gang had been mislaid, and it was only after his storm of protest that it was eventually tracked down. A letter which he had seen from Octavia Hill, one of the Trust's founders, had also been lost and, in that case, was never recovered. Thanks to John and the support of the Director of Finance, Ian Bollom, an archivist was eventually appointed in the 1980s to look after the Trust's own records.

In 1989 John decided that he wished to transfer what was now called Workman's Wood, 288 acres of beech woodland at Sheepscombe, to the National Trust in his own lifetime. At the same time he and his sister, Mrs D.D. Walmsley, gave the nearby Overtown Farm of 608 acres. John had always been struck by the way the Trust's work could expand, thanks to the legacies that came every year. The *Annual Report* for 1991 showed that the charity had received £27 million in legacies, prompting him to say:

> If you analysed it, I think a huge proportion would be from single people, who have come to love the Trust as much as their relations. That's rather my position. I like my relations too, but the Trust meant more to me.[7]

During the summer of 2006 there was a party at Ebworth. John's invitation was to 'a happy informal event with those I knew best between the years 1950 to 1980,' all of whom were encouraged to bring spouses or partners. Well over a hundred people came, on a hot and cloudless July day. At one time or another, most had experienced his encouragement, his gentle instruction and his criticism, usually articulated with startling clarity, a glance of extreme seriousness, and then a smile. As he conducted his old friends on a tour of the woods, he could not resist the occasional sally, pointing out a field which he said had been carpeted with orchids when he had managed it:

> Now English Nature are responsible and it is a National Nature Reserve, there are fewer orchids. But then their staff are not prepared to go down on their hands and knees to remove the weeds, as I used to.[8]

In the last verse of his poem 'Woods', W.H. Auden warned that 'A culture is no better than its woods,' and went on to suggest that 'This great society is going smash.' But in the penultimate verse he strikes a less pessimistic note:

> A well-kempt forest begs Our Lady's grace;
> Someone is not disgusted, or at least
> Is laying bets upon the human race
> Retaining enough decency to last;
> The trees encountered on a country stroll
> Reveal a lot about a country's soul.[9]

The woods at Ebworth had been 'well-kempt' for over half a century by the time John Workman gave them to the National Trust.

11

THE MILITARY HISTORIAN
The Marquess of Anglesey and Plas Newydd

THE AWARDING OF HONOURS was relatively straightforward when knights were dubbed on the field of battle by a grateful sovereign. In recent times that has scarcely been practicable. After the Battle of Waterloo, however, the Prince Regent was quick off the mark: Henry, 2nd Earl of Uxbridge, who had commanded the Allied cavalry and had lost a leg in the closing moments of the battle, was promptly made Marquess of Anglesey. Not far behind were the people of the Isle of Anglesey, who as a tribute raised a Doric column a hundred feet high, overlooking the Menai Strait and the estate of the Marquess, Plas Newydd. The tributes were not without complications.

When Uxbridge was offered the Order of the Bath in January 1815, six months before the battle, he wrote to his brother: 'The short view of the thing is this. If I deserve it at all & *ought* to have it at all (all things considered), I ought to have had it a long while ago.'[1] Shortly after Waterloo, he offended the Prince Regent by using a letter of condolence to remind him that he had been promised the Garter. Disfavour was short-lived, and the Garter was granted in February 1818.

The biographer of the 1st Marquess, his descendant, Henry, 7th Marquess of Anglesey, fought in Italy when in his early twenties. Some of the drawings made to relieve boredom hang in one of the bedrooms at Plas Newydd: a sketch of Casoli made in June 1944, and others of a monastery and hill town from the month before. His painting had been encouraged by the artist Rex Whistler, when he was working at Plas Newydd on the mural in the dining room. Both Henry's grandmother and his mother, who learnt from John Singer Sargent, produced portrait drawings of professional quality. However, after the war he decided to devote himself not to art, but to military history and architectural conservation.

In the course of a long life, the 7th Marquess has not lacked recognition. He is a Fellow of the Society of Antiquaries, the Royal Historical Society, the Royal Society of Literature, and an Honorary Fellow of the Royal Institute of British Architects, the latter in recognition of his role as chairman of the Historic Buildings Council for Wales, and for stopping what had been the relentless destruction of Welsh country houses. The award which gave him the most pleasure was the Chesney Gold Medal of the Royal United Services Institute, for an outstanding contribution to military history. When stacked up, the

R.I. Bott, *Henry, 1st Marquess of Anglesey*, 1839.

eight volumes of *A History of the British Cavalry, 1819–1919* almost rival the Anglesey column, and are a prodigious feat of sustained scholarship. The Chesney Gold Medal is only awarded from time to time – the intervals have been for as much as eight years – and former recipients have included Professor Sir Michael Howard and Sir Winston Churchill.

Tucked inside my copies of the *History* are some very typical postcards. One is of the State Bed from Beaudesert (the house of his Paget ancestors in Staffordshire) and now at Plas Newydd. 'Yet another volume of "my life's work",' the postcard reads. 'It is the shortest yet, so it'll not take up too much room in your library.' On another he writes: 'I'm slowly sloughing off the incubus of the bloomin' British cavalry, thank God. Here's vol. 5 of "my life's work"… it is monumentally boring. Don't read it. It'll look nice in your bookcase.' Another card, of Conwy Castle, has a P.S.: 'Come over to this neck o' t' woods next year and visit your old haunts. See and drive through the Conwy tunnel, & bless yours truly that it is there.' More of that particular battle later.

My first encounter with Lord Anglesey was in 1971, during the tortuous negotiations over Erddig, a derelict house near Wrexham which is the subject of the succeeding chapter. The National Trust's Committee for Wales was visiting the property, which Anglesey – the vice chairman – had been to twenty years before at the suggestion of Ralph Edwards, author of *The Dictionary of English Furniture*, in which Erddig features prominently. Much of the committee's attention was directed to the contents of the house and, discreetly, to the perilous condition of just about everything in it. Anglesey was also conducting a campaign of encouragement and flattery, intended to persuade the owner, Philip Yorke, to put the whole estate into the hands of the National Trust. The knowledge and concern shown by Anglesey were palpably genuine, and there was the beginning of a sense of shared endeavour. There was also a shared sense of theatricality, Yorke displaying undue modesty about the wonders of Erddig, Anglesey exclaiming: 'My God, what quality! What rarity!' It became a masterly double act, which was continued in an almost daily correspondence over the next five years. Whenever tensions between Yorke and the Trust reached breaking point, there would be a letter from Anglesey loaded with what he called 'spadefuls of flattery' to shore things up.

During that first encounter at Erddig, Anglesey also wanted to know about the research which the National Trust's Architectural Adviser, Gervase Jackson-Stops, and I were engaged on, and how it might be translated into plans for showing the house. Anglesey gradually won the confidence of Philip Yorke and he won ours too. There was never – there never could be – any suggestion that we would not ultimately succeed in rescuing the house: like any good general he instilled belief that we would ultimately prevail. This may sound as though his assumed role was an overbearing one, but it could not have been less so. He immediately insisted that I use his Christian name, Henry, as did his wife, Shirley. It was the beginning of exchanges that were continued by letters and postcards, sometimes several at a time, illuminated with puns and sketches. They still come, 35 years later, and more elaborate than ever.

The responsibilities at Erddig were, in spite of this encouragement, daunting. There was also the prospect of work and reorganisation at other National Trust properties: at Lyme Park near Stockport there were major repairs; and there were tricky relationships with the local authorities running Tatton Park in Cheshire and Shugborough in Staffordshire. So when Henry asked whether I would make an informal assessment of whether Plas Newydd was of a quality that might make it acceptable to the National Trust, I was alarmed, not least at the thought that I might have to explain that the house was scarcely up to scratch. The intention was that the Trust's agent for north Wales, John Tetley, his wife Vyvyan, and Imogen – we were married in 1971 – and I would come over for dinner, stay the night, and see everything the next morning.

In the early 1970s the drive from our home near Shrewsbury to Plas Newydd took one through the heart of Snowdonia, over Thomas Telford's Menai Bridge, and then to a castellated lodge. The long entrance drive passes through woodland, before arriving at the main entrance, which is at the back of the house, leaving its east front to look down sloping lawns to the Menai Strait, with the mountains beyond. The setting of the house and the views from it are unsurpassed. The building itself is curiously hybrid, with Gothic windows of the 1790s by James Wyatt, but with the façades recast in the early-twentieth century, when a plain parapet replaced castellations and Tudor-style caps were added to the octagonal turrets on the east front. Would the National Trust's committees conclude that the house had been so extensively remodelled in the relatively recent past that it would not rank as being of 'outstanding national importance'?

All I really remember of dinner on that first evening was the incident of the dog. The Tetleys had warned they would be bringing a labrador and that it was perfectly used to spending the night in the car. Henry's sisters had had two French bulldogs and a pug, who found their way into Rex Whistler's mural in the dining room, where their behaviour had been

The east front of Plas Newydd on the Isle of Anglesey, viewed from across the Menai Strait in North Wales. The house, with its important military relics and surrounding gardens, was given to the National Trust by Henry, 7th Marquess of Anglesey in 1976.

exemplary. The same could not be said for the Tetleys' labrador. Before dinner Henry repeatedly interjected that he could 'not bear to think of that dog left out in the car'. Eventually John relented and the dog was brought into the drawing room. Instead of settling down in front of the fire, it bounded round the room and then lifted its leg on the Chinese embroidered shawl draped over the grand piano. There was an audible groan from Shirley Anglesey, and Henry rushed to get a soda siphon.

It would be a dull soul who was not entranced, first thing in the morning, by the views from the bedroom windows, with the sun rising behind Snowdon and turning the Menai Strait into a sheet of agitated silver. The building itself had been so altered that it could be argued that restrictive covenants in favour of the National Trust – preventing alterations or additions to the house and garden, but falling short of outright ownership – would be sufficient to protect the landscape. But that would not solve Lord Anglesey's problems and fell far short of his intentions. At the time I failed to appreciate how agonising Henry's position was. This was partly a personal failure of imagination. But also, in the early 1970s, there was nothing unusual or surprising in the possibility that another round of death duties would have to be met by sales of much of what remained of the estate, including probably Plas Newydd itself and at least some of its most valuable contents. It was happening at scores of important country houses, at least as significant as Plas Newydd. Thereafter what happened to this much-altered house would not greatly matter: perhaps conversion to a hotel, sympathetically done if handled by the likes of Clough Williams-Ellis, but in all probability not. The garden and park would attract the owners of caravan sites, for which there was an insatiable demand on Anglesey. Since the Second World War, many Welsh country houses had been treated in this way or had simply been demolished. Why should Plas Newydd be regarded differently?

Long before Henry approached the National Trust he had concluded that continuing family ownership would ultimately mean the break-up of the house and estate. On his father's death in 1947, death duties had been charged at 75% on the value of his estates. After the Second World War, he had tried to increase estate income by setting up a garden centre and by letting much of the north wing, the stables and many of the outbuildings to H.M.S. *Conway* Training School and subsequently to Cheshire County Council. Part of the deal, discussed over a good dinner and excellent claret with the chief executive, was that the council would provide central heating to the parts of the house still occupied by the family. This bought time, not a secure long-term solution.

In the early 1970s Henry wrote a paper, at his own initiative, for his trustees, saying why he believed that a gift to the National Trust was the only way that Plas Newydd could be preserved. He had discussed the situation with his son, Alexander, then in his twenties, who had made it clear that he did not want his father's burdensome inheritance and was unlikely to live at Plas Newydd. The decision was in many ways harder for Shirley Anglesey, who had less confidence about what might be in the best interests of their children. She was, however, well aware of the benefits, as well as the pitfalls, of a gift to the Trust.

At that time, the Marchioness of Anglesey was playing a part in the cultural life of Wales, comparable to that of the Marquess in the field of conservation. She was chairman of the Welsh Arts Council, of the National Federation of Women's Institutes, of the Broadcasting Complaints Commission and of the Royal Commission on Pollution. Like her father, the novelist, playwright and essayist, Charles Morgan, and her mother, the novelist, Hilda Vaughan, she is Welsh, with strong European allegiances and a particular interest in Russian literature. One of Morgan's early novels, *The Fountain*, of 1932, was a bestseller on the continent and *Sparkenbroke*, of 1936, was set partly in Italy and won acclaim there. Lady Berwick was a family friend.

A connection with the National Trust of greater significance was through Nigel Nicolson and Sissinghurst Castle. In his memoirs, *Long Life*, Nicolson relates how, as a young man, he was deeply in love with Shirley; how he proposed beneath what became known as 'Shirley's tree' in the woods at Sissinghurst; how he was given the unmistakeable message that she could not accept; and how some of his pain was assuaged by his mother's decision to have dinner in a corner of the White Garden, where a barn owl flew across the rising full moon. They remained close friends and Nigel became godfather to Henry and Shirley's youngest daughter, Amelia.

Although Nigel's mother, Vita Sackville-West, had served on its Gardens Committee, she was against the idea of giving Sissinghurst to the National Trust, writing in her diary: 'Not that hard little metal plate at my door.'[2] Nigel, however, was entirely clear that Sissinghurst deserved and needed the Trust's protection. There were major obstacles to be overcome – the director of the Botanic Garden at Kew and chairman of the Trust's Gardens Committee, Sir George Taylor, was against acceptance, and agreeing on a figure for the necessary endowment was difficult – but eventually the arguments of Alvilde Lees-Milne and others prevailed.

What was significant for Plas Newydd about the transfer of Sissinghurst was that Nigel Nicolson remained absolutely resolute over the rightness of his decision and his loyalty to the National Trust. Whenever there were articles critical of the way the Trust treated its houses and donor families, as happened over Sudbury Hall and Kedleston Hall, Nigel was ready to respond with an elegant, generous letter to *The Times* or other papers. Thirty years after Sissinghurst was accepted by the Treasury in part-payment of death duties and then passed to the Trust, Nigel was able to write: 'Those who claim that the Trust's ownership is the kiss of death should visit Sissinghurst to witness its vitality.'

By example, Nigel reassured Henry and Shirley that the relationship with the Trust could be made to work. More than that, he demonstrated how relief from the day-to-day responsibilities for the direction and conservation of the property freed time for other things, including research and writing. Henry's years on the Trust's Committee for Wales had given him experience of one side of the partnership. Friendship with Lady Berwick, with Sir Felix and Lady Brunner, who gave Greys Court in Oxfordshire to the Trust in 1969, and with Nigel Nicolson meant that the donor's role was also familiar.

None of this background was evident to me on that initial visit. What was expected in the first instance was a personal assessment of whether the National Trust would want to accept the offer. If not, Henry preferred to be told with a minimum of fuss.

The importance of the setting was indisputable, and much of the furniture and pictures of far higher quality than Henry sometimes implied. When Ralph Edwards came to assess them, it was immediately after visiting Vaynol, on the opposite side of the Menai Strait, where Sir Michael Duff had drawn his attention to various pieces which he believed to be extremely important, only to have them cursorily dismissed. At Plas Newydd Henry had told him that there would be little to interest him, and was consequently rewarded with the identification of several pieces, including side tables with lion masks from Ingestre in Staffordshire, which were judged to be of outstanding quality.

Nor could anyone dispute the historical importance of the relics of the 1st Marquess, which at that time were kept in display cases in the cellars and were seen by occasional parties of visitors. The *pièce de résistance* was the 'Anglesey leg', designed by James Potts of Northumberland and the world's first articulated wooden leg. When lecturing about his ancestor, the 7th Marquess would give a graphic account of Waterloo and its aftermath, and reaching below the lectern produce the 'Anglesey leg'. The effect on his audiences was not unlike that induced in a Catholic congregation by the parading of a religious relic. Uxbridge's trousers were another object of veneration. Around the holes where grapeshot had torn into his leg were marks that might have been mistaken for evidence of a serious attack of moth but were in fact – they had been scientifically tested, the audience was told – bloodstains.

The 'Anglesey Leg', the world's first articulated wooden leg, in the Cavalry Museum at Plas Newydd. The 1st Marquess of Anglesey, who lost his right leg at the Battle of Waterloo in 1815, used this artificial limb.

What was not at all clear was what the Trust's committees would feel about the major interventions in the house during the 1930s, carried out to the designs of the architect Harry Goodhart-Rendel. It was a profoundly unfashionable period. In 1979 the Royal Institute of British Architects mounted an exhibition on the 1930s, which prompted an article in *The Times* by the doyen of architectural historians, Sir John Summerson, who wrote:

> Now that I look calmly at the architecture of the 1930s, how does the decade strike me? I am afraid to say that it strikes me very much as it did then… ; as a decade lacking in vigour of invention or refinement of style. Indeed it had no style.

One of the few architects of the period taken seriously by Summerson was Goodhart-Rendel, whom he described as 'one of the most prominent and interesting figures in the profession'. This Summerson attributed less to his buildings – although these were 'vigorous and original' – than to 'his personality, his scholarship, his wit, and his willingness to devote himself assiduously and sympathetically to professional affairs'.

Goodhart-Rendel's talents were so varied that he might well have become a professional musician. But he mistakenly became a pupil of the ardent Brahmsian, Sir Donald Tovey, who had no time for the French light opera which Goodhart-Rendel loved. As he wrote later: 'It was Tovey's efforts to make me a good musician that determined me to become an architect instead'.[3] Nevertheless he continued to compose and was a brilliant sight-reader of music. Has anyone else been president of the Architectural Association and the Royal Institute of

British Architects, and vice president of the Royal Academy of Music? Goodhart-Rendel's transformation of Plas Newydd was not to be dismissed out of hand.

In his choice of architect, the 6th Marquess of Anglesey was acting entirely in character. He wanted competence and skill, but he expected intelligence, scholarship and wit as well. Nor did he seek stock solutions: 'every bathroom must have a bedroom,' he insisted. Sometimes this perversity was misguided, as when he planted shrubs and trees not in the usually favoured clumps of three, but in groups of two or four. The involvement of Goodhart-Rendel deprived Plas Newydd of its Gothic pinnacles and decaying crenellations, but at the Marquess' insistence left much of Wyatt's work intact, and made the house easy and comfortable to live in. Goodhart-Rendel would have sympathised with the 7th Marquess's worries about the future of Plas Newydd. In 1945, after tortuous negotiations and much uncertainty, he gave his own house, Hatchlands in Surrey, partly decorated by Robert Adam, to the National Trust.[4]

View from the gallery of the Gothick Hall at Plas Newydd, designed by James Wyatt and his assistant, Joseph Potter of Lichfield, in the late eighteenth century.

As the importance of Plas Newydd was assessed by the Trust, it became increasingly evident that the transformation carried out in the 1930s, far from detracting from the property, might be of great interest to future generations. John Cornforth, deputed by the Properties Committee to advise on its significance, reported that the work organised by the wife of the 6th Marquess, Lady Marjorie Manners, with advice from Lady Colefax, was among the best country house decoration of its time, and that the textiles and wallpaper in Lady Anglesey's bedroom, for instance, would be regarded as valuable documents in the history of taste. Above all, what made this period in the history of Plas Newydd so exceptionally rewarding and enjoyable to scholars and the visiting public alike was Rex Whistler's work in the dining room.

One reason why his huge mural of an Italianate seaport never palls is that with its gaiety, brilliance and sheer panache are the gathering clouds of tragedy. On one of his visits to help with the permanent exhibition at Plas Newydd on the work of Rex Whistler, his brother Laurence – poet, glass engraver and best man at Henry's marriage to Shirley – remarked that it had been the work which had brought Rex the greatest pleasure, and that the equally ambitious mural at Mottisfont Abbey in Hampshire had been misery. The Angleseys were generous clients and, as Rex wrote in a letter of thanks in April 1936, he could not 'ever hope to repay for all those lovely days of fun & bathing & sunshine & moonlight & luxurious nights and enormous delicious meals'.[5]

During the day, Henry would be encouraged to assist with the painting. He would then disappear off to bed, and the next morning his efforts would be miraculously and brilliantly transformed. Henry was the model for the small boys, one relieving himself up a back street, another stealing apples from a butt. But like the music of Mozart or Schubert, there is a heart-stopping interruption, in a minor key, to all this laughter. Rex was in love with Lady Caroline Paget, Henry's sister, and his paintings of her at Plas Newydd tend to be unresolved, incomplete. On one of the end walls, Rex, in the guise of a gardener holding a broom, is sweeping up fallen rose petals – symbols of lost love – and putting them in a basket. The darting swallows are about to depart. In 1940 he was still writing to the 6th Marquess promising to come down to Plas Newydd 'to dot the anchors and cross the masts'. Four years later he was dead, killed during the tank battles in Normandy.

It was not until late in 1974 that the National Trust was finally able to confirm that it would accept the gift of Plas Newydd. The size of the endowment was modest compared with what would be expected a few years later under what became known as the 'Chorley formula', which was used to calculate how the costs of repair and conservation could be met over a 50-year period. But to raise the required capital Henry had to sell some of the most valuable silver and family miniatures, which he steered to the National Museum of Wales. Solicitors were instructed and the Trust's staff were told by Henry that the house was to be ready for opening to the public in July 1976. Thereafter he wanted to be able to return to his *History of the British Cavalry*.

It is tempting to remember that year of work at Plas Newydd as one of decisions made quickly by Henry, by the Trust's Regional Agent, Ian Kennaway, and by myself, and then implemented without pause; of builders, painters and craftsmen scampering around under the constant eye of the Marquess; and of summer evenings spent playing tennis with Henry and his daughter, Amelia, before supper with the family. I came to know why Rex Whistler

A detail of Rex Whistler's mural in the dining room at Plas Newydd, commissioned by Charles, 6th Marquess of Anglesey, in 1936.

loved working there. The open invitation to stay the night whenever it suited helped greatly, because the journey from Shrewsbury was a round trip of five hours. But other properties, not least Erddig, were clamouring for attention. The National Trust employed no conservation staff at that time, and its Historic Buildings Representatives were single-handed. If many of the pictures at Plas Newydd needed to be re-hung, and furniture moved, that was a job for myself and the admirable house carpenter, Mr Cartwright.

The plan for the reordering of the house was simple: most activities would move upstairs. The military relics would be brought up from the basement to the old service rooms at ground level. The ground floor and first floor would be given over to public viewing. On the second floor the Angleseys would have their drawing room, dining room, kitchen and bedrooms. Lord Anglesey's study near the front door would not be disturbed, and when he was working there visitors in the entrance hall might be aware of a faint but distinct smell of cigars, as was the case at Chartwell in Kent for several years after Sir Winston Churchill's death. There was one significant advantage in the migration of the family. The floor plans of the rooms at the top of the house were mostly the same as those on the ground floor, and although the ceilings were lower, the views across the Menai Strait were even more spectacularly beautiful.

Since early in the twentieth century the billiard room, which adjoined the dining room, had been divided to provide a kitchen and pantry. There was some debate over whether this arrangement should be preserved, to be consistent with the presentation of the house at a high point in the early twentieth century. The prevailing argument was that Rex Whistler's dining room was of the first importance, and it would greatly add to the enjoyment of visitors if there could be an exhibition about his work in the preceding room. But all these dis-

Henry, 7th Marquess of Anglesey, in his study at Plas Newydd.

cussions nearly became academic, when the room in question and Plas Newydd itself very nearly burnt down.

On an evening when members of the family had gone out and Henry was alone, writing in his study, the fire alarms went off, and then the lights went out. Henry went to investigate and quickly discovered the kitchen was ablaze. A chip pan, full of oil, had been left on the lighted cooker and had become a sheet of flame. The nearest fire-extinguisher was in the passage outside, but Henry was unable to detach it from its bracket. With what he said later was the strength of desperation, he wrenched both bracket and extinguisher from the wall and put out the fire. Minutes later smoke damage would have wrecked Rex's painting or, at worst, the house would have been lost.

If there had been any qualms about transforming the kitchen into a Whistler museum, the fire dispelled them. Laurence Whistler made several visits and agreed to loan most of his collection of Rex's work as a book illustrator, stage designer and amateur architect. To these could be added the paintings of the Paget family that Rex had left behind at Plas Newydd, including several pictures of Caroline, and his illustrated letters to the 6th Marquess and to Henry. With Laurence's guidance, a central display case was designed by Christopher Hobbs, who also made two urns to fill a pair of niches in the room, modelled on those supplied by Rex for Samuel Courtauld's house in London. The exhibition is the single largest collection of Rex Whistler's work, is changed regularly, and provides an effective prelude to the dining room.

Rex Whistler, *The Family of the 6th Marquess of Anglesey in the Music Room at Plas Newydd*, begun in 1938 but never completed; Lady Caroline Paget stands in the doorway, and the future 7th Marquess is at his easel.

Decisions about what should or should not be given to the National Trust were far from straightforward. Henry had assured the Trust that most of the historic contents of Plas Newydd would come as part of the gift, but of course what was historic was open to different interpretations. Naturally Shirley wanted the paintings of their children and several favourite pictures in their flat on the top floor. The Welsh artist Kyffin Williams lived on the estate and was a close friend. His watercolours of Venice, which Henry adored, would obviously stay with the family. But there was argument over the topographical views of Plas Newydd, with Shirley saying: 'Don't you think, Henry, that Alex might like some paintings of his ancestral home, if he is not going to live here?' 'That's exactly why I am giving everything to the National Trust – so they can't be taken away,' Henry countered. The house, paintings, furniture, garden and 169 acres of surrounding woodland and foreshore were an outright gift. There were no offers in lieu of tax and no grants.

Alexander, the present Earl of Uxbridge, has himself been generous to the National Trust. His godfather, the 7th Duke of Wellington, had given him a painting depicting a meeting – which never actually took place – between their respective ancestors, shortly after the amputation of Anglesey's right leg. The picture has been presented to the Trust for display in the Cavalry Museum. He has made another important contribution to the house. In the 1990s he painted a cycle of pictures of Plas Newydd as he remembered it as a child, which were exhibited at the National Theatre in London and widely admired. The National Trust's Foundation for Art was able to buy some of these, and they now provide an evocative record of family life at Plas Newydd shortly before it was given to the Trust.

One of the most impressive pictures in the house is a huge painting by Denis Dighton of the Battle of Waterloo. This particularly fascinated Henry because of the accuracy of its

Denis Dighton, *The Battle of Waterloo*, 1816, (detail), now hanging in the Cavalry Museum at Plas Newydd.

[From left to right] Peter Chance, Chairman of the National Trust's Properties Committee; Lady Anglesey; Sir Clough Williams-Ellis; Robin Herbert, chairman of the Trust's Committee for Wales; Lord Anglesey (standing); and Lady Williams-Ellis, at the opening ceremony of Plas Newydd in July 1976.

depiction of the uniforms, down to the oilskin protective covers on the shakos and sabre-taches, still in place because of rain the night before the battle. The picture was in poor condition, had been removed from its stretcher, and was rolled up. Few conservators would have had room for it in their studios, and there was precious little time for the considerable amount of work required. Fortunately the Area Museum Service came to the rescue, and it was returned to Plas Newydd a few days before the house was due to open.

The official opening took place during one of the hottest Julys of the last century. The main speaker, Sir Clough Williams-Ellis, had declined an invitation from the Royal Institute of British Architects to hold a dinner in London in his honour and to celebrate Portmeirion's golden jubilee, explaining that the heat in the metropolis might not suit a 93-year-old. No such excuses were made for Plas Newydd, and he delivered one of the three speeches he had prepared for the occasion with his usual passion. In it he postulated that but for the gallantry of Wellington and Uxbridge at Waterloo, the battle might well have gone the other way, 'and I should now be addressing you in bastard French and the victorious Emperor would be watching us from atop that column there instead of our host's great ancestor'. Everyone was in shirtsleeves and the garden was brown and parched. Only Henry and Shirley knew that we had still been hanging pictures and putting the finishing touches to the Cavalry Museum the evening before.

Within a couple of days I received one of Henry's characteristically generous letters. It ends:

> You always kept (a) calm and (b) faith; & the result is <u>good</u>. The strain of this forced effort superimposed on your already formidable work-load must have been far from inconsiderable, but the whole thing was certainly worthwhile. Now for <u>Chirk</u>!!

Chirk Castle in Wales – the home of the Myddelton family and the subject of protracted negotiations with the Welsh Office – did indeed pass to the National Trust, but not until 1981. And the solicitors completed the legal transfer of Plas Newydd some months after the official opening. Thereafter Henry described his position on the second floor of the house as 'living in the howdah on top of a white elephant which somebody else feeds'.

In 2003 the National Trust presented Henry with its Octavia Hill medal, given to those whom the Chairman and the Director-General wish to honour for exceptional service. At the time there had been only nine recipients of the award. In his thanks Henry suggested that it should not have been given principally for the gift of Plas Newydd and his continuing involvement in the care of the house and garden. He believed that the contribution he had made to the National Trust through the National Heritage Memorial Fund was at least as significant. The assertion was made with good reason.

Hugh Dalton, the Chancellor of the Exchequer, had established the National Land Fund in 1946, as a memorial to those who had fallen in two World Wars. The Fund had promised much but had gradually been strangled with Treasury red tape and small-mindedness. The needless and deplorable dispersal of the contents of Mentmore in Buckinghamshire in 1977 led to furious articles in the press, to debates in the House of Commons, and ultimately, in 1980, to the formation of the National Heritage Memorial Fund (NHMF). Unlike the National Land Fund, it was to be controlled not by the Treasury, but by independent trustees, under the chairmanship of Lord Charteris of Amisfield, formerly Private Secretary to the Queen and, as it happened, Henry's cousin.

One of the first things Lord Charteris did on becoming chairman was to contact Henry with a simple message: 'I don't know about great historic buildings. I need your help.' Because the point of the NHMF was that it should be independent of government, there was to be minimal interference from the Treasury and other Whitehall departments. But this was a two-edged sword, leaving the trustees to define their role and how it was to be carried out. Its future depended on satisfying Parliament and the press that the use of the Fund was meeting expectations and that the £15 million allocated to it was being put to good use.

In the NHMF's first *Annual Report* of 1980–81, there was discussion on the question of how the national heritage could be defined:

> We decided that it was ananswerable; we could no more define, say, beauty or art... so we decided to let the national heritage define itself. We awaited requests for assistance from those who believed they had a part of the national heritage worth saving....[6]

There was such general goodwill towards the NHMF at its inception, and Lord Charteris used his candour and charm so skilfully, that his attitude seemed sensible and undoctrinaire. But critics such as Robert Hewitson were waiting in the wings, and it was not long before he was writing scornfully that when Lord Charteris said that the heritage meant 'anything you want', what he in fact was saying was that 'it means everything and it means nothing'.[7]

Lord Anglesey was one of the trustees who had absolute conviction about what was worth saving, and after his years as chairman of the Historic Buildings Council for Wales, no shadow of doubt that the protection of great houses and unspoilt landscape should be a priority for the Fund. Those convictions helped to shape the work of the NHMF and to build its reputation for being a powerful force for good.

Nevertheless, the NHMF got off to a shaky start when it promised the National Trust a grant for the purchase of ivory-veneered Indian furniture – collected by Lord Curzon, when Viceroy of India from 1899 to 1905, for his house, Kedleston in Derbyshire – in the hope that it could be returned there, only to find that different conservation bodies were bidding against each other. What was needed was a cause that really captured the public's imagination, in which something that was clearly precious was about to be lost, and where the NHMF could gallop to the rescue. It was, after all, the example of Mentmore that had led to its creation. In 1980 the NHMF had a notable success with the last-ditch rescue of Canons Ashby in Northamptonshire. The prelude there to the NHMF providing a grant of £1 million was a visit that Henry made with Gervase Jackson-Stops and myself in the summer of 1980. As so often, his belief that a solution had to be found never faltered.

In Calke Abbey the NHMF found not a maiden in distress, but a single family who, over 150 years, had thrown scarcely anything away. Their house, near Derby, was of no great archi-

The bedroom of Sir Vauncey Harpur Crewe, 10th Bt. (1846–1924), at Calke Abbey, in Derbyshire.

tectural distinction, but as a document of social history, it was curious, melancholy and of great appeal to anyone with historical imagination. The bachelor owner of Calke, Henry Harpur-Crewe, had inherited an estate worth some £14 million in 1981, on which liability for Capital Transfer Tax amounted to nearly £10 million. He was quite prepared to offer the whole of the estate in lieu of tax, so that it could pass to the National Trust, but as so often in the past the Treasury managed to erect apparently insuperable obstacles. The most likely outcome, as the interest on the amount owed in tax mounted by £1,300 a day, seemed to be another Mentmore-like dispersal. Some of those consulted about Calke's merits were luke-warm, largely because they were unimpressed by its architecture and decoration. But Marcus Binney of SAVE Britain's Heritage, a highly effective propaganda organisation established in 1975, Gervase Jackson-Stops and *Country Life* were powerful advocates for its preservation. As Lord Charteris was himself unsure of his ground, he rang his trustees to discuss it; and again it was Henry's conviction that won the day. Thereafter the NHMF took the initiative, bringing together all the parties, including the Department of the Environment, the National Trust, the Historic Buildings and Monuments Commission, the relevant local authorities and the Harpur-Crewe trustees. Eventually, it took a supplementary grant, expressly for Calke, of £2 million, announced in the Chancellor of the Exchequer Nigel Lawson's budget statement of 1984, to achieve the transfer of the property to the National Trust so fervently desired by Henry Harpur-Crewe and the thousands who responded to the Calke Abbey Appeal.

Canons Ashby and Calke were valuable precedents for the NHMF. Another was the grant offered in 1981 for the purchase of Bernardo Bellotto's *View of Verona from the Ponte Nuovo*. This supremely beautiful picture was painted between 1745 and 1747, when Bellotto was beginning to break free from the influence of his maternal uncle, Canaletto, and was tack-ling seven-feet canvases with increasing assurance. It had been owned by the 1st Lord Clive, had hung in his London house in Berkeley Square, and had then been transferred to Powis Castle in Wales, which in 1952 became the property of the National Trust. The Bellotto was retained by the family, and in 1981 they decided to offer it for sale.

What was controversial was not the quality of the picture, nor the size of the grant. It was that both the National Gallery in London and the National Museum of Wales wanted it on their walls. Henry had been president of the National Museum of Wales from 1962 to 1968, and a trustee of the National Portrait Gallery. He was, however, determined that the Bellotto should not be lost from Powis Castle. For 80 years it had hung in the Oak Drawing Room, where the architect G.F. Bodley had designed an oak-panelled niche expressly for it. It was, Henry asserted, an integral part of one of the greatest buildings in Wales, and was seen there by thousands of visitors every year. A major benefactor, Simon Sainsbury, supported this view and offered to help. Their arguments prevailed, and thereafter the NHMF preferred, whenever possible, that great collections should be preserved *in situ* and not dispersed to museums. In the case of the Bellotto ownership is now shared by the Trust and the Nation-al Museum of Wales.

On a recent visit to Plas Newydd I came, as Henry advised, on the road that runs along the north Wales coast between Chester and Bangor. I asked him to tell me how it was that he had managed to get the highway authority and the Welsh Office to agree that, rather than building a bridge for the dual carriageway close to Edward I's castle at Conwy, they would instead put the road in a tunnel, at an increased cost of £107 million. Henry confirmed that

The Conwy
Suspension Bridge,
completed by
Thomas Telford in
1826, leading to King
Edward I's thirteenth-
century Conwy Castle.
The bridge was trans-
ferred to the National
Trust by Conwy Bor-
ough Council in 1965.

the chief civil servants had been adamantly opposed to the tunnel, but they had underestimated its advocates. Conwy is a World Heritage Site, and the issue became one of not just
Welsh but European significance. Although the extra cost of the tunnel was considerable, its
supporters were able to show that this represented less than 1% of the total cost of the road.
Henry attended every day of the public enquiry in person. The final decision rested with the
Secretary of State for Wales, Nicholas Edwards (the son of his old friend, the furniture
historian Ralph Edwards). Henry insisted that they went together into the fields to the south
of Conwy to judge the impact on the castle of the towers of a new bridge. They agreed the
bridge would be sacrilege; and the tunnel was built.

During a visit in September 2006 I asked Henry about the gift of Plas Newydd and its contents to the National Trust, and how he regarded his decision 30 years on. He replied that
beautiful things had always mattered to him at least as much as people, although the two
were indivisible, because human beings are enriched by beauty, whether in landscape, paintings or buildings. Before Plas Newydd was transferred to the Trust, he had been obsessed by
his duty to posterity. Afterwards he was no longer 'in a perpetual state of despair about its
future'. The house had been re-roofed. He had helped to plan the replanting of the Terrace
Garden, for which Lord Charteris – an accomplished sculptor – had made a tiger's mouth
spout for an ornamental jet of water. Drawings and paintings by Rex Whistler had been
bought by the Trust and added to the displays of his work.

Lord Anglesey's whole life changed following the handover. There were, it is true, moments
of exasperation at the Trust's sometimes tardy, sometimes insensitive behaviour, but by giving
Plas Newydd away, its future had been assured. That overriding objective had been achieved.

12

THE ACTOR

Philip Yorke and Erddig

ACCOUNTS OF AMATEUR THEATRICALS began to appear in the correspondence of the Yorke family in the 1770s.[1] The more ambitious productions were put on at Sir Watkin Williams Wynn's house, Wynnstay, a few miles south of the Yorkes' home, Erddig, near Wrexham, in what used to be Denbighshire. In 1778 Philip Yorke – an antiquarian and writer of humorous verse – played Antonio in *The Merchant of Venice* at Wynnstay. Sir Watkin, would invite the great actor David Garrick down from London to attend his productions. When *Henry V* was performed at Erddig in January 1786, Philip's nine-year-old son Brownlow Yorke was given a specially written prologue to recite. In it Philip made references to their cook, Mary Rice, to John their gardener, and to a housemaid, Betty Jones. The prologue marks the beginning of the Yorkes' highly unusual tradition of recording their staff in verse, soon to be incorporated into painted portraits. Brownlow began:

> To please you all, from Eton, have I run,
> Through mire and dirt, to kick-up Christmas fun:
> To be the Prologue to my Brother's play,
> And make you, as the season asks, be gay.
> You cook for me, and shall not I again,
> Give Mary Rice, some pleasure for her pain;
> Her pies indeed, are excellent, and good,
> And I will pay her in dramatic food.
> To Gard'ner John, I own but little less,
> I prog his peaches, and his apple dress;
> His fairest apricots, I pull, and plunder;
> That boys love fruit, pray where the mighty wonder?
> To Betty Jones, I am as much in debt,
> I daub her hearths, and give her many a sweat;
> Thro' me, her stairs, require successive scrubbing,
> And all her floors, reiterated rubbing:
> For so much mischief, you must charge my years,
> And I in time, will pay you all arrears.

Philip Yorke (1905–1978), who gave Erddig, near Wrexham in North Wales, to the National Trust in 1973, riding his penny-farthing bicycle in his early seventies.

Clearly the staff of Erddig were in the audience and were expected to enjoy this banter, no doubt smiling at the boy whom they indulged, and who had the run of the house and estate. Successive Yorkes continued to have an affectionate regard for most of their servants until, in the mid-twentieth century, they could no longer afford any resident staff. The oil paintings and photographs of blacksmiths, gardeners, housekeepers, joiners, woodmen and a 'spider-brusher', which line the Servants' Hall and the basement passage walls at Erddig, begin in the 1790s and continued to be commissioned until just before the First World War. Initially Philip Yorke (1743–1804), then Simon Yorke (1771–1834), and finally the second Philip (1849–1922) added the verse inscriptions to the pictures, so making it easier to engage with them than with many of the subjects of the portraits above stairs.

When the third Philip Yorke (1905–1978), the last squire of Erddig, began discussions with the National Trust in the 1960s about the possible gift of the house and estate, the rarity and interest of the portraits of servants was an important consideration. So too was the survival of much of the silvered and gilded furniture, supplied for the house by the very finest London cabinet-makers in the 1720s. The house itself combined a straightforward, early-eighteenth-century elevation of mellow brick on the garden side, which was pleasant but undistinguished, with a rather grim late-eighteenth-century re-facing by James Wyatt on the entrance side, which looked across parkland to Bersham colliery. It was coalmining that for a time provided the estate with much-needed income and, after nationalisation, came close to wrecking its buildings through subsidence. The damage, which continued during the early stages of discussions with the Trust, was one reason why the negotiations took so long to conclude. Another was Philip Yorke's unpredictability.

Philip had inherited Erddig in 1966 on the death of his bachelor brother Simon. By then the whole estate was in an advanced state of dereliction. The house had been racked by subsidence, which had resulted in the northern end dropping five feet and the southern half three feet six inches. Simon Yorke was a recluse, whose response to the post-war difficulties of running a country house estate besieged by coalmining was to cut himself off from the outside world. Tenants on the estate were strongly discouraged from installing a telephone, in case messages might be relayed to the squire. Wheeled vehicles, including perambulators, were banned from the park. When the postman complained of being bitten by a dog, he was told that in future he should deliver only to the lodge at the entrance to the estate. The Wynnstay Hunt met at Erddig occasionally, and would be greeted with extreme formality at the entrance steps by Simon Yorke, who would raise his hat to the master with such an extravagant gesture that several horses shied. Any ladies wishing to use a lavatory were directed to the bushes.[2] Philip inherited by default: his brother never made a will.

Simon and Philip's parents were married in 1902, when their father was 53. His first wife had left him, using the milk-float to make her escape very early one morning in 1877, and he was only free to marry again when she died 22 years later.[3] Simon was the longed-for heir: but was earnest, awkward, and notably unsuccessful at school and then at Cambridge, where he had to sit the entrance exam six times.[4] During war service he was made responsible for a steamroller, which disappeared. Having injured an eye chopping wood, he was invalided out of the army, and returned to Erddig to preside over its gradual disintegration.

Except that he was also a bachelor, Philip Yorke could not have been more different. At Corpus Christi College he was secretary of the Boat Club, rowed in the Cambridge University trial eights, graduated in 1927, and then went on to Ridley Hall to read theology, in preparation for ordination. There his unorthodox views and behaviour began to raise doubts.

The garden front of Erddig, near Wrexham, in north Wales, with the restored nineteenth-century parterres and topiary.

A future bishop of Ely, Ted Roberts, recalled a sermon about the apostle Peter which upset Philip's congregation because of its Romish tendencies.[5] But Philip's interpretations of the Scriptures were more theologically extreme than mere sectarianism. Solomon, he proposed, was 'one of the most brainless men in all history; so conscious of his stupidity was he that he admitted himself that he did not know how to go in or come out.'[6] In the Ridley College photograph of prospective ordinands, Philip is at the end of the row, emulating the solemn faces of those around him. Perched on his right hand is a stuffed pigeon. In 1928 the Principal agreed with his decision to postpone ordination, certainly until he felt ready to tackle Greek. By the following year his vocation had transmigrated from the church to the theatre.

At the Northampton Repertory Theatre Company, which he joined in 1930, Philip made friends with people who, 40 years later, would appear unexpectedly at Erddig, stay in considerable discomfort for a night or two, and then move on. He was remembered with affection, rather than admiration, for his acting ability: 'It was a sort of "presence" we hadn't had ever before and couldn't have again,' a fellow-actor wrote to Philip's mother, Louisa Yorke, 'He is so kind, so funny, so entertaining.'[7] Already he was moving in the direction of theatre management, embarking in 1932 on a tour with his own London and Country Theatre Players. He would sometimes take leading parts 'with panache unchecked by much consideration for textual accuracy,' as the actor Frank Thornton recalled.[8] Philip kept a review from the *Bexhill-on-Sea Observer*, which noted:

> He was not always word-perfect on Fridays, let alone on Mondays, a circumstance that tended to keep the rest of the company on the hop. But the swish of the waves under the Pavilion floor was good cover for his prompter.[9]

The outbreak of the Second World War imposed a right incline rather than an about-turn. Some inspired recruiting officer decided that Philip could best serve his country as a Sergeant-Instructor in the Army Education Corps, posting him to Northern Ireland. As an actress friend Diana Carroll put it, following a visit to Erddig in February 1945, Philip 'thinks a little constructive work he can do is occasionally to put a non-left point of view over in talks and discussions.'[10] In 1945 this meant being out on a limb, and that was where he continued to feel most comfortable. He would also entertain the troops on his musical saw – a conventional joiner's saw, which he held between his legs and which produced plaintive versions of ballads such as *Home Sweet Home* when he drew a violin bow along its un-serrated edge, bending it to vary the note. His discharge certificate described him as 'a very fine type of senior NCO who could easily have taken a commission – an excellent teacher and exemplar.' His tendency to wear his army beret in a 'totally distinctive and peculiar way' was overlooked or forgotten.[11]

Philip's peacetime activities included a return to the stage; serving as a merchant seaman; applying to become a Conservative Party candidate; a stint as a master at a preparatory school in Dorset; and groundsman at another school in Ascot, where he confessed that he had:

> … attacked my grass with more vigour than skill, & the whole place has turned brown like the desert portions of Spain. I am told to leave large portions alone for a fortnight, or the whole place may have to be returfed.[12]

His life was like one of the more erratic Erddig gramophones, inclined to jump from groove to groove at the slightest reverberation.

The nearest he came to any settled activity was conducting his own tours to Spain in an ancient dormobile. When he found himself overtaken by the package holiday business, he joined Horizon Holidays as a courier. What he really yearned for was a post on the Spanish broadcasting service, 'telling England what a good boy Franco is'.[13] But ultimately it was Erddig which lured him back. The first 60 years of his life were, it could be said, aimless and frivolous – although spreading a little frivolity in a grim post-war world was not without its value. During the final twelve years, until his death in 1978, he became a player on a national stage, winning admiration for the single-minded, heroic and ultimately triumphant way he battled to save Erddig, and entertaining audiences with his performances on television. He created his own part, as the last squire of Erddig, in a drama of his own making.

When Philip first approached the National Trust in 1966, Erddig seemed a hopeless case. Today it may seem inconceivable that the house should not have been saved. After all, in a recent poll it was found to be second in popularity only to Chatsworth in Derbyshire. But the outcome was by no means inevitable. The chances of the house being burgled shortly after Philip inherited were extremely high. Its mirrors and pier-tables were illustrated in *The Dictionary of English Furniture* as among the finest of their period; the eighteenth-century porcelain was outstanding; and there were pictures attributed to many celebrated artists, including Kneller and Gainsborough. Fire was an even greater hazard, because without electricity guests were dependent on candles.

Philip's security precautions may have been improvised and theatrical, but they were effective. Last thing at night a small table piled high with Carnation milk tins was attached by a length of string to the door in the entrance passage. Anyone opening the door would overturn the table, and with it the tins. Philip's dog Trixie would then go wild with excitement. A homemade alarm, using a torch battery and sheets of foil, was placed under the carpet on the stairs. Visitors were shown that Philip kept an ancient rifle by the bed he used in a corner of the drawing room, with ammunition to hand; but they could not have known that the gun had no firing pin. The local police were given the use of a field for a football pitch, and were encouraged to call in for tea in the servants' hall, which they frequently did, leaving their panda cars by the front entrance.

The usual advice that unpredictability was the best defence against burglary was scarcely necessary at Erddig. One of Philip's actor friends, Bertram Heyhoe, came to stay for months on end, and preferred to move from bedroom to bedroom, perhaps remembering his touring days. 'Hooha', as Philip called him, rarely retired to bed before 3 a.m., and during the morning unsuspecting visitors would be disconcerted to find that they had blundered into a room with the bed occupied.

Negotiations with the National Trust gave Philip years of worry and frustration, as he longed to hand everything over and go on an extended holiday to Spain. The Trust's need for assurances that mining beneath the house had ceased, that subsidence would not be reactivated by geological faults, and that the structure of the building was not irreparably damaged, all involved investigation by specialists. Initially the Trust was also far from convinced that repairs to a house which was so badly damaged could be carried out in a way that still preserved its character and sense of historical continuity.

The truth was that the condition of the house called for drastic intervention. With all the falls of the roof gutters altered by subsidence, water poured not away from the parapets, but into the principal bedrooms. The ceiling in the State Bedroom had partially collapsed and was supported by what looked like improvised pit-props. Dry rot would have been more prevalent if there had been heating in the building. Panelling groaned at times, and then would occasionally crack with a sound like a pistol-shot. Much of the eighteenth-century glass in the windows was broken. In a bedroom cupboard some of the servants' suits of livery were still hanging; but had been so consumed by moth that only the shoulders and collars remained on the hangers, while the rest of the heavy wool coats lay in heaps of dust and fragments on the floor. When I was staying in the house in February 1973 to work on the archives with the Trust's Architectural Adviser, Gervase Jackson-Stops, snow blew through and round the windows of the Blue Bedroom, and in the morning carpeted the floor at my bedside.

The more Erddig's exceptionally rich documentation was explored and transcribed, the more convinced Gervase and I became that the house itself could be shown to visitors in a way which revealed its full, rich and complex historical significance. This would need to involve not just an understanding of its architectural and decorative importance. It also implied an obligation to make sense of the social and domestic history of Erddig, particularly the remarkable relationship between the Yorke family and their servants.

Guidance on how to approach the redecoration of the house and the arrangement of its rooms came from an authority normally associated with grand châtelaines, smart interiors, and extravagant budgets. Erddig had none of those; but that did not deter John Fowler from

The State Bedroom at Erddig in 1973, with improvised pit-props holding up the ceiling.

becoming its passionate advocate. For years John had longed to examine the Erddig furniture and textiles, and early in 1971 I took him to see the house. At that time there was still scepticism in the Trust's historic buildings department that it could be restored convincingly; and as I might be responsible for its restoration, the idea that the task might prove an impossible one was unappealing. The properties committee wanted to call off negotiations altogether: the acting chairman opening discussions of one report on Erddig with the comment, 'Well, we've got to get out of this one, haven't we?' But John was adamant: it could and must be saved. Just before he caught a train to return to London, he told me to park the car in front of Shrewsbury station and take down letters to Lord Rosse, the Deputy Chairman of the Trust, and to Robin Fedden. The latter began:

> Never since I first saw Uppark in 1930 have I been more moved by so much atmosphere. Of course the quantity and quality of the extraordinarily varied sets of gesso and lacquer furniture in particular dazzle one… If the Trust could feel sure of the stability of the fabric, I am convinced one could create out of the sad chaos of neglect and discouragement something of the rarest beauty. Its resurrection would, I am sure you would agree, have to be handled most sensitively and an emphasis on unapparent restoration, both of furniture, surfaces and fabrics, should be the aim. I do hope, dear Robin, you and your committee will make a supreme effort to do everything possible to save Erddig.[14]

Not only was John's advocacy crucial. He convinced the Trust, and its inexperienced, apprehensive Historic Buildings Representative, that the repair of Erddig and the conservation of its collections were practicable. He proposed the names of those who would assist: Graham Carr to piece together the torn and stained Chinese wallpapers; Mattei Radev to work on the late-seventeenth-century Boulle dressing-table, which had originally been in the best bedchamber; and many more of the conservators whose skills he had nurtured over many years. What Bobby Gore, the Adviser on Paintings, had suggested would have to be a crusade to save the house began to seem less quixotic, less daunting.

Luck also played a part. Although the costs of restoration would be high, there seemed to be the possibility of raising substantial funds. Philip and his advisers began negotiating for compensation from the Coal Board for the damage caused by mining. The effects of subsidence were all too evident, and figures of £95,000 for the repair of the structure of the main house and £30,000 for the roof were proposed. Philip was also prepared to give the National Trust land on the edge of Wrexham, which would be sold for building new houses. Between 1966 and 1972 development land prices in the area increased from £1,000 an acre to £9,000. The restoration of Erddig was largely paid for by the sale of land on the boundary of the park, at what turned out to be the peak of a property boom. By the late 1970s the bubble had burst. The timing was extraordinarily fortunate.

Philip's interest in material wealth was minimal. For 44 years he was unaware that his parents had left him three-quarters of the contents of Erddig, having never troubled to read their wills. When deciding how to divide their inheritance, his mother and father must have been acutely aware of just how unlike the two brothers were. Simon was feckless, uninterested in the history of the house and only showed much engagement with the furniture when he broke the glass top of an early-eighteenth-century pier table with a hammer. He allowed the house and its treasures to decay around him, apparently oblivious to its disintegration. Philip, on the other hand, was never much interested in the monetary value of the contents of Erddig. But he would surprise visitors by telling them when certain pieces were acquired; where they were originally positioned; who the portraits were of, and how they fitted into the story of the house. In his 'Old Furniture' Thomas Hardy could have been writing about Philip Yorke:

Philip Yorke in the drawing room in 1973, reading by candles and gas lighting, reflected in eighteenth-century silver salvers.

I know not how it may be with others
Who sit amid relics of householdry
That date from the days of their mother's mother,
But well I know how it is with me
Continually.

I see the hands of the generations
That owned each shiny familiar thing
In play on its knobs and indentations,
And with its ancient fashioning
Still dallying:

Hands behind hands, growing paler and paler,
As in a mirror a candle-flame
Shows images of itself, each frailer
As it recedes, though the eye may frame
Its shape the same.

Philip's life belied the pessimism of Hardy's conclusion:

Well, well. It is best to be up and doing,
The world has no use for one today
Who eyes things thus – no aim pursuing!
He should not continue in this stay,
But sink away.[15]

The contents of Erddig were regarded by Philip as part family correspondence, part theatrical props, rather than as evidence of his own status or personal wealth. 'This is the State Bedroom', he would tell visitors taken aback by the collapsing ceiling and the water dripping into buckets; and after a pause add, ' because it is in such a state.' As they sighed at the rusty, lop-sided Rover in one of the carriage sheds, Philip would appear oblivious to its condition: 'It's a 1907 model, which we bought in the 1920s from the chimney sweep. I'm afraid the second gear is giving a little trouble.'

Scattered around the estate were his own cars, which were even more derelict than the house. The passenger seats were usually removed for the benefit of his dog. Doors were held on with string, and, in the case of the Robin Reliant, the clutch was operated with a piece of wire passed through the dashboard. His suits were bought second-hand from a store in

Liverpool. He was, however, lavish in his generosity to others, giving money to former staff at Erddig, and to actors who turned to him for help. The Erddig estate, the house with all its contents, and the development land which came with it, were all to be outright gifts to the National Trust.

Given the scale of his proposed generosity, it is not surprising that he became frrustrated at the time it took the Trust to decide whether or not to accept Erddig. One of the ways he tried to expedite the transfer was to threaten damage to the National Trust's reputation. He told the Trust that he was changing his mind, and the whole estate was to be left to the Welsh Nationalists. He also proposed to enlist the press, principally the *Wrexham Leader*. Philip was a frequent contributor to the *Daily Telegraph* and several local papers, on subjects ranging from the case for selling arms to South Africa and frigates to Franco's Spain, to a cure at Lourdes of a painful mouth ulcer. No doubt it was these literary excursions which led to him being called 'probably the best-loved fascist in modern British history'.[16]

In April 1970 he sent the National Trust a draft of a letter to the *Wrexham Leader*, saying that the charity had, over four years, been unable to make up its mind about his offer, and that he was publicly setting a deadline for completion by the following June, in eight weeks' time. When the draft landed on the Solicitor's desk, Robert Latham scribbled 'Help!' on the top and passed it to Robin Fedden. With some difficulty Philip was persuaded not to send the letter, which had served its purpose. Although at the time there was still coal-mining beneath the house, the likely consequences of which were part of the reason for delays, minds were concentrated wonderfully.

A Deed of Gift was finally ready to be signed in February 1973. Now it was Philip's turn to prevaricate. The Trust's solicitor returned to London, and there was a growing sense that the opportunity might slip once and for all. Gervase and I decided to stay on in the house, transcribing documents relevant to its ultimate presentation, in the hope that this would help to convince Philip of the Trust's continuing commitment. He would go backwards and forwards to Wrexham to collect Chinese and Indian takeaways, which catered for his vegetarianism. Elaborate electric lights were rigged up, fed by a generator which was as erratic as his motor cars. On Sunday he proposed going to a morning service at one of the many local churches he attended. Among his favourites was Penylan (it was where he died in 1978, just as a service was about to begin), which was unheated. In winter Philip would attend in a large overcoat, beneath which he concealed a portable paraffin stove, which would sometimes smoke alarmingly.[17]

Trips to the Wrexham cinema were arranged and, at Philip's suggestion, Gervase and I went with him to see Stanley Kubrick's notorious *A Clockwork Orange*. Philip had a reputation for falling asleep in films, but not on this occasion. During the stylised scene of gang rape, accompanied by one of Rossini's extended crescendos, Philip was audibly disturbed, making little grunting noises. When we returned to Erddig he was asked whether he had enjoyed the film. 'Oh yes,' he replied, 'it was a marvellous film – but perfectly horrible.' The very next evening, perhaps still in a state of shock, he signed the Deed of Gift, which is dated 14 March 1973.

Erddig had been thought of as a connoisseurs' house, its plain panelled rooms filled with furniture and textiles of great rarity. What caught the public's imagination, however, was not the grand, but the domestic. In this respect it represented a decisive shift in attitudes inside

the Trust and more widely. The National Trust's previous approach was summed up by Harold Nicolson, who in 1948 wrote disparagingly of museums of social history, and then made a telling comparison:

> It is no such kitchen, scullery or bathroom vestiges which the National Trust is out to protect. Their aim is to save works of beauty rather than to collect quaint articles of past convenience.[18]

The way Erddig was ultimately shown rejected these assumptions and encouraged visitors to appreciate its social history first of all, then to regard its art history as an element – a very important one – in the story of the Yorke family and their servants. The presentation of Erddig was influenced by Michael Trinick's pioneering work in Cornwall, but took his ideas a good deal further. The approach was closer to the showing of historic houses in Scandinavia and the United States, but was unfamiliar in the United Kingdom.

Influence from abroad was no accident. In the early 1970s there was a growing awareness that visitors to national parks and historic sites in North America were treated very differently from those in Britain, and that there were lessons to learn. This view was held strongly by the Countryside Commission and its director, Reg Hookway. With funding from the Commission, staff from the United States National Parks Service, including their head of interpretation, Marc Sagan, visited Tatton Park in Cheshire to write a report on how its presentation could be improved. When Tatton was given to the National Trust in 1960, there was no endowment and so it was leased to Cheshire County Council. As the Trust's representative on the Council's management committee, I got to know the National Parks Service team well.

When the Chairman of the National Trust's committee for Wales, Robin Herbert (who was also a Countryside Commissioner), heard that Marc had invited me to visit the United States to see their historic properties, he suggested that the Commission might fund the trip, provided that I wrote a report on my conclusions, to be shared with other National Trust staff. What I observed in the summer of 1975, at sites such as the Eleutherian Mills at Hagley, Delaware; George Washington's home, Mount Vernon; Colonial Williamsburg; Thomas Jefferson's Monticello; and Hubble's Trading Post in Arizona, was helpful in practical ways, and suggested a much broader approach to communication, based on scholarly research and going well beyond worthy but staid guidebooks.

One consequence of this visit was the realisation that Erddig provided an opportunity to re-order the way the National Trust showed its houses. Instead of arriving at the front door, visitors were to make their way through a succession of outbuildings, encountering carpenters working in the joiners' shop, a blacksmith, a baker in the bakehouse, and horses in the stable yard. The house was entered via the basement passage and the servants' hall.

In many ways this was like mounting a complicated theatrical performance. At John Cornforth's prompting, the perfect stage manager was found in Elisabeth Beazley, who was a member of the National Trust's architectural panel, and whose two books, *Designed for Recreation* (1969) and *The Countryside on View* (1971), were models of clarity and good sense. Elisabeth brought all her attention to detail and ability to find solutions to logistical problems, to what might otherwise have been a confusion of vague ideas. After 30 years the innovation is still popular with today's visitors, but quite rightly has rarely been adopted elsewhere, because no other house can match Erddig's records of its servants over two centuries.

Philip warmly supported the way the public was to be introduced to Erddig. He invited former staff, such as Edith Haycock and Bessie Gittins, both housemaids whom he had known as a boy, to come to the house and be interviewed, so that their recollections could help with the arrangement of the domestic quarters. However, he was fiercely critical, sometimes justifiably, of some other National Trust decisions, particularly the reduction in size of the playroom (a pavilion adjoining the parterre in the garden); and he complained that the eighteenth-century wrought-iron gates, from Stansty, near Wrexham, had been set too low when positioned as an eye-catcher at the far end of the canal. One day a letter might arrive castigating 'The National Distrust'. The next he would appear unexpectedly at our house near Shrewsbury to discuss something that was worrying him; and when he found we had friends to supper, nip back to the car to get his electric razor, and then stay the night. At considerable trouble and expense he tracked down second-hand copies of the two volumes of Albinia Lucy Cust's *Chronicles of Erthig on the Dyke*, published in 1914 and now very rare, so that I had easy access to them at home. He inscribed them, and then with a touch of irony added, after my name: 'Who knows so much more about all this than I do.' That was nonsense.

Writing about John Meller – the wealthy but childless uncle of Simon Yorke, who bequeathed him the house and its sumptuous collections in 1733 – Albinia Cust wrote:

> A man's immortality is in the seed of his loins. Great possessions, broad acres, a beautiful home, are as dust and ashes where there is no son to step into the inheritance. Life must have been dreary for Master Meller when mirrored walls threw back his lonely reflection, and time hung heavy on his once busy head and hands.[19]

The author was mistaken. Meller may have died without a son and heir, but his furniture is now admired by the thousands who visit Erddig each year. His neighbour Elihu Yale also

The State Bedroom at Erddig after restoration, with the Chinese lacquered screen given by Elihu Yale to Joshua Edisbury, the builder of Erddig in the late seventeenth century, who went bankrupt and sold the unfinished house to John Meller.

died without a male heir; and he too achieved a form of immortality. Yale amassed a vast fortune in India, much of it in dubious circumstances, and in acknowledgement of a relatively small donation to a struggling college in Connecticut, had it named after him. A Chinese lacquered screen, now in the State Bedroom at Erddig, was a gift from Elihu Yale, so ensuring that he is remembered there, as well as in the United States.

After a career in the East India Company that was rumoured to have involved embezzlement and even murder, Yale retired to his old family home of Plas Grono, near Ruabon, now demolished and absorbed into the Erddig estate. Yale's original gift to the college was made in 1718, three years before his death. It comprised a collection of religious books, a portrait of King George I by Kneller, now in the university art gallery, and £200 sterling. In the exchange of correspondence with the college, its representative, Cotton Mather, proposed that it should be named after him, and that this 'would be better than a name of sons and daughters.' The language of university philanthropy seems scarcely to have changed. Mather assured his colleagues that, 'What he now does is very little in proportion to what he will do.'[20] These expectations were never realised. Yale's will was contested and the intended legacy of £500 to 'Connecticut College' never materialised. But his immortality was assured.

Erddig will always be Philip Yorke's memorial. There may also be a lasting place for him in twentieth-century literature. Philip would draw visitors' attention to the use of Erddig made by Nigel Dennis in his book, *Cards of Identity*, a copy of which was left on the table in the entrance hall. The novel was highly praised by W.H. Auden and others when it appeared in 1955. Although the author deliberately altered and transformed the country house in which it is set, there are features which derive from Erddig and, prophetically, the closing chapters reveal that the estate is to be bequeathed to the National Trust.[21] The book ends with a bizarre production of a Shakespearian play, very different in spirit to those performed at Erddig when the first Philip Yorke was squire.

The last Philip Yorke is the subject of *Lantern Lecture* by Adam Mars-Jones, which won the Somerset Maugham Award in 1982. His father, Sir William Mars-Jones, was a high court judge, and the family would occasionally go to tea at Erddig. The book is what is sometimes called 'faction'. Although it reads like a novel, the narrative is not chronological, but more like a jumble of snapshots, or lantern-slides, which have been left in chaotic disorder, and from which a series of pictures of Erddig emerge. The people described are real, named and immediately recognisable, including the National Trust's staff. The depiction of Philip Yorke is assembled rather like a Cubist portrait.

Are the portrayals in the story truthful? Does it matter if they are not? When *Lantern Lecture* was first published, I was miffed by Mars-Jones's reference to the National Trust's representatives as 'pompous go-getters to a man'.[22] The judgement, in my case, may have been deserved. But it was that 'to a man' which was unjust. The senior member of staff involved in the Erddig negotiations was John Tetley, the Trust's Regional Agent for North Wales. Much of his professional life was spent looking after the 36,000-acre Penrhyn and Ysbyty estate in Snowdonia, transferred to the National Trust in 1951, where he was much loved for his efforts to support the traditional Welsh hill-farmers, the upland villages, and particularly their schools. He was much less concerned about instructions sent from the Trust's head office: 'Wouldn't work up here,' he would scribble across the top, before sending them back. When a high-powered committee, under the chairmanship of Sir Henry Benson, reported on the Trust's outdated working practices in 1968, Tetley penned one of his widely circulated poems, which ended:

Now was the fellow just a jerk
Or have I got the thing awry?
And does Efficiency imply
An ever-growing paper crop
That ultimately brings a stop
To all that childish wasteful fun
Of really getting something <u>done</u>?

On my copy he added: 'Just to keep up the morale – John.'[23] Was this a 'go-getter'?

A more serious concern about *Lantern Lecture* is that it presents a portrait of Philip Yorke which is clever in a technical literary sense, but which is curiously misleading. As was observed when the book first appeared, the Philip Yorke described by Mars-Jones becomes 'in his innocence, slightly sinister'.[24] The effect on the reader is similar to that of the author's most recent fiction, which one reviewer found gives off 'a certain chill' and is 'curiously uncongenial'.[25] The Philip Yorke that his friends, visitors to Erddig, and those who met him at local fêtes (on a penny farthing bicycle, or playing the euphonium, or dressed as a chinaman) remember was anything but sinister. He was needlessly generous, funny, gregarious and full of spontaneous kindnesses. What was usually regarded as eccentricity may, it is true, sometimes have crossed over into egocentricity. But his need to perform seems to have been inherited, and was a trait of the two earlier Philip Yorkes.

In the space of four years Erddig was transformed from a pathetic wreck to the most talked-about house in Britain. It was the subject of three television programmes, was opened in 1977 by the Prince of Wales, to a blaze of national publicity, and in 1978 won the Museum of the Year Award, the first country house to do so. Philip became as much a national celebrity as the house itself, perhaps more so. This only fed his sense of the dramatic. He told me and others that because the Prince had asked to ride one of the Erddig penny-farthing bicycles, and had fallen off, perhaps – as his host – he should 'do the right thing' and take his own life as an act of contrition and loyalty. Philip was with difficulty persuaded that this was unnecessary, and instead presented the bicycle to the Prince of Wales as a gift.

HRH The Prince of Wales at the opening ceremony, to mark the completion of the restoration of Erddig, in 1977.

Towards the end of one of the films, Philip turned to the camera and said, in his rich, unmistakably theatrical voice, 'Oh, I've always thought Erddig was the best place in the world.' It was exactly what the director wanted: Philip was playing the part of last squire of Erddig to perfection. But of course the truth was not quite so simple. On one car journey to a terraced house of his in Ruabon, I remember him saying, as we skirted the colliery, that he used to dread coming home to Erddig. There were all the problems of the estate, and his elderly parents' anxiety about what they referred to as Simon's 'desultory and slack ways'.[26] His touring theatre company and the dormobile trips to Spain had been a welcome escape. Then Erddig gave him his last and best part, brought about by his own generosity. 'It's probably what my father would have liked,' he concluded, 'the old place restored to its former glory.'

What had been restored were not just the bricks and mortar, the peeling wallpapers, and the pleached limes. Using the National Trust as an ally, Philip had revived a community of gardeners, joiners, cooks and conservators. The connections with the past were sometimes tenuous and sometimes remarkably close. Perhaps the most unexpected contact was made in a letter from Mrs Beryl Jones, the great-great-granddaughter of Thomas Rogers, the carpenter whose portrait of 1830 hangs in the servants' hall. She had kept his tools, which were loaned back to Erddig for the opening. Partly influenced by the family involvement with Erddig, her son Kevin Jones trained as a cabinet-maker and restorer at West Dean College in Sussex, and has become one of the National Trust's most valued conservators. In 1990 Beryl Jones wrote to say that Kevin had been desperately busy with work for the Trust. 'The restoration of Erddig changed our lives.' She added, 'I daresay quite a few people say that.'[27]

13

THE SQUIRE,
THE SCHOOLMASTER AND
SPECIAL INTELLIGENCE

Wyndham Ketton-Cremer and Felbrigg Hall;
Mildred Cordeaux, Bill Smith and Sheringham Park

THE ESSAY ON 'Humphry Repton in Norfolk' by R.W. Ketton-Cremer is a minor masterpiece, painstakingly researched and with all the elegance of a perfectly constructed short story. The same is true of the other chapters in his book, *A Norfolk Gallery* (1948). Ketton-Cremer was a distinguished scholar, whose books on Thomas Gray and Horace Walpole are among the best biographies of the mid-twentieth century. What makes Ketton-Cremer's books about Norfolk history so rewarding is that he had spent a lifetime immersed in the records not only of his own estate at Felbrigg, but also in those of other country houses that he knew intimately, and which he was then able to write about with humanity and understanding. It is as though he is describing neighbours he knows personally, whatever the period. Ketton-Cremer was the last squire of Felbrigg Hall, one of the last scholar-squires, and was revered in his native county.

Of the 200 or more major landscape and garden commissions undertaken by Repton, it was the house and park at Sheringham in Norfolk which he himself singled out as 'my most

Allan Gwynne-Jones, *Robert Wyndham Ketton-Cremer*, who bequeathed Felbrigg Hall, in Norfolk, to the National Trust on his death in 1969.

John Adey Repton, *The south front of Sheringham Park, Norfolk*, 1812, from his father Humphry's *Red Book*. The house and its park were acquired by the National Trust in 1987 with major grants from national and regional organisations, bequests and donations from private individuals, and a public appeal.

favourite work'. It lies on the north side of the road between Holt and Cromer, and runs down to sandy cliffs that are continually crumbling and collapsing into the North Sea or, as it was known in Repton's time, the German Ocean – a name no longer acceptable in the twentieth century. On the other side of the road is the Felbrigg estate, and it too extended to the coast. Of Sheringham, Ketton-Cremer wrote:

> There is nothing more beautiful in Norfolk, at any season of the year, than the wide amphitheatre of parkland with its varying backgrounds of woodland and sea. It is loveliest of all, perhaps, on one of those magical days in May when every tree, each individual oak and beech, sycamore and chestnut and lime, displays its own particular shade of green against the blue of an unruffled sea and an unclouded sky.[1]

[below] Barthélémy du Pan, *William Windham II (1717–1761)*, a pastel probably painted in Geneva, where Windham lived from 1738 to 1742.

Sheringham has the most skilfully contrived parkland in Norfolk. The park at Felbrigg is more spacious and the trees were planted over a far longer period. It is the sense of continuity, of the changing aspirations and tastes of the Windham family over successive generations that makes Felbrigg such a fascinating and satisfying house. The south front is an early-seventeenth-century paraphrase of Blickling Hall and is almost certainly by the same architect, Robert Lyminge; the west front, with its immaculate brickwork, is of the 1670s; there is also an early-eighteenth-century orangery and a nineteenth-century stable block.

This tranquil place came perilously close to disaster on several occasions. One of the most attractive of its owners, William Windham II, as well as collecting avidly while travelling on the Continent, also had a passion for fireworks. On 27 December 1755 there was a great explosion, which blew the roof off his firework shop and over the top of the granary. It was

found still blazing in the coal-yard. Many windows were broken, but fortunately the damage was confined to the service wing.

Potentially even more catastrophic was the case of William Frederick Windham or 'Mad Windham', as he became known in the 1860s. The full story of this inadequate, exploited and pathetic man is told by Ketton-Cremer in *Felbrigg: The Story of a House*. One of the objects of the book was to record the mundane, the less attractive, and ultimately the tragic aspects of the unfolding tale. It is as though the house and its collections become, through Ketton-Cremer's pen, a great work of literature. The book is also the product of an historian immersed in sources that he handled with scrupulous objectivity.

Ketton-Cremer was not inhibited by any family loyalties, because he was not a Windham. After William Frederick Windham had bankrupted the Felbrigg estate, it was bought in 1863 by John Ketton, a Norwich merchant. On his death in 1872, he left it to his younger son Robert, who passed it on to his nephew, Wyndham Cremer, on condition that he changed his name to Wyndham Ketton-Cremer. He in turn had two sons, Robert Wyndham Ketton-Cremer, who was born in 1906 and became the scholar-squire, and Richard Ketton-Cremer, born in 1909.

Both boys went to Harrow and for both it was an unhappy experience. Robert suffered so badly from rheumatic fever that he had to be sent home on three occasions by ambulance. As he wrote in *Felbrigg: The Story of a House*: 'If I cannot sing *Forty Years On* with much conviction, it is because I am rather less "rheumatic of shoulder" than I was forty years ago.' 'Richard never found much enjoyment there,' wrote his brother; and although good at cricket and other games, 'he had none of my bookish precocity, my knack of passing examinations.'

As well as enjoying academic success, Ketton-Cremer won the Harrow School poetry prize and, once at Balliol, published poems in the *Oxford Poetry* volumes of 1925, 1926 and 1927. A reviewer singled his contributions out for special praise, and considered them to be superior to the poems by Louis MacNeice which were published in the same volumes. Ketton-Cremer continued to write and publish poetry throughout his life, although in later years in privately printed books which were inscribed and presented to close friends. Some of his poems are on the same subjects that he wrote about in his histories: the graves of his favourite authors, Norfolk churches, beech trees, and Beeston Hall, where the Ketton-Cremers lived before moving to Felbrigg.[2] At some stage he decided to devote himself not to poetry, but to Norfolk history and topography. His life of Thomas Gray remains, 50 years after it was published, unsurpassed, and won the James Tait Black Memorial Prize and the W.H. Heinemann Foundation award. *Felbrigg: the Story of a House* avoids the most common pitfall of the country house biography, in that it gently mocks social pretension and is as concerned with failure and disappointment as with accomplishment and success.

His own experience of miserable schooldays makes Ketton-Cremer's account of William Frederick Windham's time at Eton particularly sympathetic. Windham was a physically unattractive boy, with a malformation of the mouth that caused uncontrollable dribbling. He was prone to laugh and yell incessantly, and apparently rarely washed. The tutor sent with him to Eton in 1854, Reverend H.J. Cheales, recorded that:

> … he had never had a boy so low mentally, or so odd in his habits… he was looked upon by the boys as a buffoon, and he was generally called by them 'Mad Windham'.[3]

Ketton-Cremer researched his life with care and told his story with scrupulous impartiality. He related how 'Mad Windham' was virtually abandoned by his parents (his mother, Lady Sophia Hervey, absconded with an Italian opera singer), how he married a prostitute named Agnes Willoughby who was intent on ruining the estate, and how his uncle attempted to prove in court that he was insane. If successful his own sons would have inherited Felbrigg. The testimony of the 140 witnesses called was sometimes touchingly loyal, but often distasteful. Ketton-Cremer described it in *Felbrigg: The Story of a House* as 'extremely detailed and often quite revolting'.

He then set out the evidence of those prepared to enter the witness box to assert that Windham was simple and misguided, but not mad. Here the historian in Ketton-Cremer was also the squire, and was clearly moved by the willingness of those on the estate, such as the wife of the bailiff and an aged carpenter, to testify on Windham's behalf. One of the most effective witnesses was a neighbour, Ketton-Cremer's grandfather, Thomas Wyndham Cremer, whose moderate and balanced statement he quoted at length, concluding:

> I have been told that he was in the habit of acting as a guard on railways: but I think it perfectly consistent with sanity in a gentleman of rank and property, after coming of age, to dress himself up as a guard and perform the duties of a guard on a railway. Pointing the attention of ladies to mules while staling is not gentlemanly conduct, but I cannot accept it as a proof of insanity. Windham was generally boisterous in his manner. When I was at Felbrigg in August last Windham did not tell me that he was about to marry Agnes Willoughby; if he had, I would have advised him not to marry such a person. I attribute Mr Windham's boisterousness to high spirits, and not to unsoundness of mind.[4]

That, in fact, was what the jury concluded. The evidence presented at the trial and set out by Ketton-Cremer is sufficient for a doctor today to make a reasonably confident assessment. Windham's condition would now be described as disinhibited, with mild learning disability. He would be investigated further for what is called 'attention deficit hyperactivity disorder' and Tourette's Syndrome, which is often linked with an inability to stop swearing and impulsive behaviour. Many of his problems would be attributed to a failure of parental support and affection. There would be no question of treating him as insane. The jury's decision was the right one.

The outcome of the case may even have been right for Felbrigg. 'Mad Windham' was the last of his family to live there and it was sold. After John Ketton bought the estate in 1863 there were very few disposals. It remained an entity, to be studied and cherished by Ketton-Cremer and then by the National Trust.

Ultimately the story of 'Mad Windham' is interesting not so much for what it tells of William Frederick, but for what it reveals of the author of *Felbrigg: The Story of a House*. Ketton-Cremer was for many years a Justice of the Peace, and so was familiar with the distortions and misrepresentations of a legal process that can end in an injustice. He also served as High Sheriff of Norfolk in 1951–52, and was distressed to have to attend two hangings. He told his neighbour, Lady Harrod, that one of the men to be executed 'was very brave'; and although the experience affected him deeply, it was regarded as a duty of service to the county.

Another duty was to find a secure future for Felbrigg, following the death of his brother Richard. Wyndham Ketton-Cremer himself was medically unfit for war service. Dick joined the Royal Air Force Volunteer Reserve intending to fly, but when his eyesight was found to be defective, he was made equipment officer. He was posted to the Middle East, to Cairo, the Western Desert and on to Crete. In May 1941 he was stationed at the airfield of Maleme when it was bombed by the Germans and then assaulted by their parachute and glider troops. Dick was last seen some two miles from the airfield, bleeding from a stomach wound. Writing in 1961, Ketton-Cremer said that he could still hardly bear to read his brother's final letters, full of 'comfort and reassurance'. The penultimate chapter of *Felbrigg: The Story of a House* ends:

> No one will ever know how many hours Dick had lain, and had still to lie, in agony and loneliness on that Cretan hillside.[5]

Although both brothers were bachelors, Ketton-Cremer seems to have felt that Dick, who was 32 when reported missing, was likely to marry, whereas he was not. After a year of waiting agonisingly for news, Ketton-Cremer prepared a will which left Felbrigg to the National Trust. He acknowledged that 'he loved every acre of its modest woods and fields'; but most of his childhood had been spent at nearby Beeston, which he thought of as 'the home of my ancestors, in a sense that Felbrigg can never be'.

On Friday, 1 May 1942, James Lees-Milne visited Felbrigg, to find the house had not been requisitioned, partly because it was lit only with oil lamps, with a single stove in the Great Hall for heating. He noted of Ketton-Cremer:

> He is donnish, extremely cultivated and an urbane and polished writer. He is a trifle ill at ease rather than shy, yet punctilious, methodical and determined. If one let fall ill-considered opinions, he would not leave them unpicked-over, I feel sure. Toryish, if not prejudiced in his views of conduct. Yet open-minded and friendly in a cautious way.'[6]

On the Sunday, Ketton-Cremer took Lees-Milne for a walk around the park, most of which had been ploughed up for wartime food production. They then returned to the Great Hall, where Ketton-Cremer read his will from beginning to end, occasionally pausing for an interrogative glance. With the warmth of the stove after his walk and the interminable legal niceties of the will, Lees-Milne kept falling asleep. When Ketton-Cremer paused, Lees-Milne would say, without much conviction, 'that sounds perfectly satisfactory'; and then nod off again.

Rather characteristically, Ketton-Cremer kept his intentions for Felbrigg to himself. Those who enquired about its future were told it was to be left to a cats' home. He seems to have considered making arrangements for one of the Petworth Wyndhams to have the opportunity to live at Felbrigg, an arrangement he could have agreed with the National Trust through a Memorandum of Wishes specifying the terms of the occupation after the Trust assumed ownership. He may even have thought about making a new will in favour of Lord Egremont's younger son. But these possibilities were extinguished after an exploratory visit to Petworth House, ostensibly to attend a concert. Ketton-Cremer had brought a watercolour by J.M.W. Turner to show his host. Lord Egremont was neither welcoming nor interested. He seemed to imply that there was no reason why he should be, when the walls of Petworth were crammed with Turner masterpieces. Ketton-Cremer left with his mind made up.[7]

During the last twenty years of his life, Ketton-Cremer involved himself more and more with the affairs of the Trust. Many of its advisers became personal friends and went to stay at Felbrigg. Among them was the art historian Brinsley Ford, who described Ketton-Cremer on one of their walks as:

> …a portly figure made even more shapeless by an old mackintosh, his grey hair straggling onto his collar beneath a green pork-pie hat, his slightly gouty step supported by a walking stick.[8]

Over dinner Ketton-Cremer entertained his guests with accounts of his experiences as chairman of the Cromer Bench from 1948 to 1966. The oddest of these concerned a man 'whose strange perverted sexual mania took the harmless though trying form of what Wyndham described as "raping ladies' bicycles"'. Brinsley Ford noted in his journal that:

The Library at
Felbrigg Hall.

… before the man's arrest, many an elderly spinster or carefree schoolgirl had been informed
by the police that their bicycles had been found rudely assaulted and buckled in a ditch.[9]

Much of the pleasure of such stories was that they were delivered 'in the same rounded periods and well-turned phrases in which he might have narrated some stirring episode in the
Civil War in Norfolk'.

For someone intrigued by human nature there was no clear distinction between what was
to be learnt from the Bench one day and from historical records the next. Ketton-Cremer was
an authoritative chairman of the Norwich Diocesan Advisory Committee – Lady Harrod was
one of the few people who could rival his knowledge of Norfolk churches – and he was an
influential supporter of the proposal to have a University of East Anglia based in Norwich.
Many of his own personal books were donated to its library. In the 1950s he assisted the
National Trust's Honorary Regional Representative, Alec Penrose, for example helping with
the choice of colours for the Orangery at Blickling. He also served on the National Trust's
Regional Committee for East Anglia in its early years.

By the time he was in his sixties, the cold of Felbrigg's main room was getting too much for
Ketton-Cremer. The Norwich architect Donovan Purcell, who had supervised repairs to the

house, was commissioned to make a comfortable flat out of rooms in the service courtyard at the back of the house. Friends thought the change to small, centrally-heated rooms was too abrupt. Ketton-Cremer died in December 1969. His intentions were met: the house, furniture, pictures, the estate and woods he loved have been preserved as an entity by the National Trust.

The transfer of Felbrigg to the Trust came at the time when Thomas Upcher and his trustees were considering what should happen to Sheringham Park. He was unmarried and thought that the best way to protect the estate might be to leave it to the National Trust in his will. In May 1970 he invited representatives of the Trust to visit the house and park.

Sadly, discussions got off on entirely the wrong foot. The intention was that Robin Fedden and the Regional Chairman, the Earl of Euston – shortly to become the 11th Duke of Grafton – should meet Upcher; but their over-full diaries conspired to delay the visit until December. The preparation of a financial report also took far longer than it should have done, partly because the staff concerned were struggling to come to terms with the acquisition of Felbrigg and, not long before it, Anglesey Abbey in Cambridgeshire. Immediately after the visit Fedden drafted a long letter, to be sent by the Duke, which explained various ways in which the estate might be protected, including restrictive covenants. The letter, in an amended and unappreciative form, was delayed first by Christmas and then by a postal strike, so that Upcher did not receive a full reply from the National Trust until March. His enthusiasm seemed, understandably, to have cooled. The response to Upcher's intended generosity had been dilatory and unimaginative. In April the Trust's solicitor was informed that the offer was withdrawn. To reactivate an agreement of any sort with the Trust was to prove difficult and expensive.

Why was Upcher's offer not treated with a greater sense of urgency? Part of the explanation was expressed in a note sent to the Duke and Fedden by the Assistant Agent, which concluded:

> Is this important property sufficiently *in danger* to warrant our ownership? I feel that an owner would readily be found for this fine small house. Most of the land could well be protected by covenants. The majority of the woods are already managed by the Forestry Commission. Only the park would appear to be endangered if we do not acquire.[10]

As Humphry Repton's park was what made Sheringham outstanding, the note suggests that the Trust rather missed the point.

The exceptional significance of Sheringham had not been lost on Christopher Hussey when he wrote two articles about it in 1957 for *Country Life*. He recounted how, in 1812, the young Abbot and Charlotte Upcher – when still in their twenties – gave Repton the opportunity to transform a piece of beautiful countryside on the north Norfolk coast into parkland, and to build a new house on a site of their choosing. The relationship between the 60-year-old landscape gardener, with a lifetime of experience to draw on, and the young couple who trusted him to build a comfortable home for their young family, was touching and affectionate. The result was, in Hussey's words, a 'little masterpiece in the synthesis of architecture and landscape'.

Driving through the park in mid-December, the Trust's representatives may not have appreciated just how skilful Repton had been. The approach to the house, beautifully illustrated in his *Red Book*, was entirely Repton's creation, exploiting a sharp bend in the new drive, 'from whence the house will burst at once upon the sight, like some enchanted palace of a fairy tale,' as he wrote enthusiastically. The views to distant Weybourne and out to sea were reshaped and framed by clumps of trees on the encircling ridges. The house itself, largely designed by his son, John Adey Repton, is understated, practical and a model of late-Regency elegance. Repton was in no doubt of Sheringham's place in his *oeuvre*, or indeed in the history of landscape design. He told Abbot Upcher that it represented 'such a specimen of my Art, as I never before had an opportunity of displaying,' and continued:

> After having passed nearly half a century in the study of Natural Scenery, & having been professionally consulted in the improvement of many hundred places in different parts of England, I can with truth pronounce, that Sheringham possesses more natural beauty and local advantages than any place I have ever seen.[11]

In the early 1970s the history of landscape gardening was little studied, in spite of the pioneering work of Christopher Hussey and of Dorothy Stroud, who wrote biographies of both 'Capability' Brown and Repton. In 1949 the National Trust had acquired Claremont

Landscape Garden in Surrey, but its eighteenth-century features were largely left submerged beneath a sea of *Rhododendron ponticum*. Generally, the assumption was that parks were significant as the setting of a great house, but would rarely have been considered sufficiently important on their own merit to warrant the Trust's involvement in their protection.

Another factor in the Trust's lukewarm reaction to Sheringham was that Tom Upcher's household was, by the standards of the time, unconventional. His father, Sir Henry Upcher, was a sportsman, farmer and chairman of the Norfolk Agricultural Executive Committee. Tom Upcher was a talented gardener, an aesthete, and a collector of grand Empire furniture and exotic cars. The pride of the collection, his 'Metallurgique', was powered with a Zeppelin engine and was maintained by a former Panzer-tank mechanic called Gerry Majewski, who came to Norfolk in 1952 following incarceration in a Russian prisoner of war camp. During a period of uncertainty and change at Sheringham, Majewski became its guardian, and was admired and respected by everyone for his complete reliability.

Tom Upcher entrusted much of the care of the grounds to his companion, Douglas Fitzpatrick, a former Irish racing driver and aviator. Unfortunately, he did not restrict himself to looking after the garden, but extended it in ways that conflicted with Repton's intentions. Instead of maintaining open parkland to the east of the house, Fitzpatrick enlarged a small cattle pond into something approximating to a lake, and in the process nearly killed himself when a tractor he was using for excavation overturned. At other times, Fitzpatrick's behaviour was eccentric rather than reckless. He was known to greet guests with a Muscovy duck perched on his head. The Upcher *ménage* was completed by Tony Johnson, who was considerably younger than the others, and who became responsible for much of the running of the house. There is little doubt that the Duke of Grafton would have felt more comfortable dealing with Sir Henry Upcher than with his son.

For the next twelve years there was no further contact between Thomas Upcher, the trustees of the Sheringham estate and the National Trust. Although Upcher continued to believe that the estate would, after his death, be safest in the hands of the Trust, he felt he had been cold-shouldered. Nothing was done to amend the terms of the Sheringham Settlement Deed, which defined the obligations of his trustees, to make involvement by the Trust possible. As Upcher's health deteriorated, it looked increasingly likely that the house, its contents and the estate would have to be sold on the open market, to benefit his nephew.

Realising that this drift towards a country-house sale was not really what Upcher wanted, his friend and neighbour Lady Harrod, who was a member of the National Trust's Regional Committee, contacted Tony Johnson and suggested that it might be sensible to meet to discuss the future of the estate. Billa Harrod, as she was widely known, was the founder of the Norfolk Churches Trust and author of *The Shell Guide to Norfolk*; she was also small in stature though not in energy, and in most things unstoppable. In May 1983, she and Johnson met in my office at Blickling Hall and agreed that the *impasse* might best be overcome if the Trust's Director-General, Jack Boles, wrote to Maurice Hatch, the chairman of the Thomas Upcher Settlement trustees. His letter explained that the problem of providing an endowment, which had been one of the obstacles encountered in the earlier exchanges, might be eased now that there was the possibility of a grant from the newly formed National Heritage Memorial Fund (NHMF). The letter was referred to a meeting of the Sheringham trustees in July, but when there was no response, Boles wrote again.

The reply this time was short and to the point:

> Unfortunately there seems to be absolutely no way in which this property can be made over to the National Trust. The Trustees hold [it] under the terms of a Settlement Deed and the beneficiaries do not include the National Trust or in fact 'Charity' in its widest sense. It therefore seems that there is very little that we can do.[12]

In most circumstances, this letter would have ended the matter; but not as far as Billa Harrod was concerned. She encouraged the Regional Chairman, by then Jonathan Peel, to write to Mildred Cordeaux, who was a friend and co-trustee. She was to prove an outstandingly generous and stalwart ally.

Mildred Cordeaux was a first cousin of Thomas Upcher. As a small girl, when Sheringham was being used as a convalescent hospital during and after the First World War, she accompanied injured soldiers to the top of the gazebo, perched on the summit of what Repton called Spy Hill, up behind the house. From there, they looked along the coast to Blakeney in one direction, towards Cromer in the other, and had Repton's park laid out around them. She never lost her deep affection for those views, nor her conviction that they should be shared with others.

During the Second World War, Cordeaux worked with MI5 and then – she was fluent in Swedish – transferred to MI6. She and Lady Harrod were a formidable combination. If the terms of the Sheringham Settlement now made a gift impossible, then the means had to be found for the National Trust to purchase the estate.

The timing was unhelpful. There had just been a national campaign to preserve Belton House in Lincolnshire as an entity, and with very substantial grants from the NHMF it had been accepted by the National Trust. The NHMF coffers were nearly empty, and Angus Stirling, who had taken over as Director-General from Boles (now Sir Jack), was anxious not to appear greedy. On a visit to the East Anglia region, the Director of Finance, Gordon Lawrence, warned that the sums required for Sheringham amounted to more than an annual allocation to one of the smaller regions and simply were not available. His pessimism was understandable but unjustified.

In November 1985 Thomas Upcher died. There was now at least a recognition that the National Trust should be allowed to buy the Sheringham estate, and might need to raise between two and three million pounds. At just the moment that it was gazing into an empty begging bowl, the news came that Mr E.L. Elliot of Braintree in Essex had died, and had left a substantial sum to the National Trust which was available to be spent on Sheringham. Before a report was submitted to the Finance Committee, Mildred Cordeaux asked Lady Harrod to add the following statement:

> A member of the Upcher family and a close relation of Mr Thomas Upcher, has promised £150,000 on death, with expectations of the residue of her estate.[13]

There was also the promise of another legacy to benefit Sheringham, from Bill and Mollie Smith, but less certainty that their intentions would be realised.

At about the time that the future of Sheringham was hanging in the balance, the

National Trust's solicitor, Bob Latham, introduced me to the Smiths, who had consulted him about leaving a substantial amount of money to the Trust. Bill was a teacher, who had begun his career in London schools and progressed to being a headmaster in Shropshire. He was a good linguist, a fine pianist and photographer, a lover of mountains, and a collector of antique clocks. To these highly civilised attributes he added a talent, unusual in school-masters, for playing the stock exchange. Accomplished he certainly was, but also compli-cated, with strong views on matters such as blood sports, and implacable once offended. In a letter of January 1994 he acknowledged that he 'would win no prizes for tact'; but with those he trusted he was painstaking, patient and prepared to share the dry humour which went with his often bleak view of the world. Mollie was a violinist, who had been employed to 'play in' newly made instruments to ensure they had acquired tone before they were sold. She was the kindest, gentlest person, interested in all aspects of nature conservation, and she particularly valued what she referred to in a letter as 'the friendly atmosphere which surrounds anything to do with the Trust'. They were devoted to each other and had made the decision, at a particularly distressing moment of the Second World War, that they would not have children. As I got to know them better, I wondered whether this was really what Mollie would have chosen for herself.

Our first encounter was at Blickling, and we talked about conservation on the north Nor-folk coast, about an area of the Norfolk Broads – Heigham Holmes – which the Trust was negotiating to purchase, and of course about Sheringham. A telephone call was made to Tony Johnson, and it was agreed that they would be free to explore the park and woods, then at the very moment of spring perfection described by Ketton-Cremer. They were bowled over, and returned to Blickling to say that they wanted to help provide an endowment. In a letter a few days later Bill wrote: 'This place simply must go to the Trust if at all possible, it is as near Paradise as one is likely to attain this side of the Divide.... We should feel happy and humble if we thought that any gift of ours could be the means by which the Estate could be acquired by the Trust for the enjoyment of all for all time.' On subsequent visits to Norfolk – their home was on the Isle of Man – they always included visits to Sheringham.

Even with these substantial contributions, there was a gap which could only be met by the National Heritage Memorial Fund. An application was made more or less jointly with Heigham Holmes. The director, Brian Lang, and his deputy came on a mid-summer day of hot sunshine. Sheringham was looking idyllic. At Heigham Holmes a marsh harrier soared lazily overhead, and there was much talk of swallowtail butterflies. After a leisurely picnic on the edge of the reed beds, it did not seem to matter whether we had seen or imagined them. It was the moment to venture the question: 'Well, what do you feel about the two proper-ties?' The NHMF was at that time still in its infancy, was left alone by Government, and was ready to trust its own judgement. 'Both are stunning,' replied Lang, and turning to his deputy, 'Have we brought the credit card?'

In the space of a few months, a position that had seemed to be financially hopeless was beginning to look much more positive. What finally tipped the scales for the Sheringham trustees was that Maurice Hatch and Michael Verity, of the National Trust's legal department, found that liabilities for Capital Gains Tax and Capital Transfer Tax payable on the estate would be much reduced if a deal could be struck. Taking these figures into account, a sale price to the Trust of one million pounds was proposed. The Finance Committee agreed that

part of the Elliot bequest should be used, as well as legacies from Miss H. Ridler, Miss D.E. Swiffen and Miss Alice M. Weeks. Sheringham was also to be the pretext for an East Anglia Coast and Countryside Appeal, which was given a target of £100,000. On cue the grant from the NHMF was confirmed. The sale was completed early in 1987.

The task of the appeal would, it was felt, be easier with a royal patron. The first member of the royal family to visit after acquisition by the National Trust was Princess Margaret, and her reaction was not encouraging. She had been staying for the weekend at Bayfield, near Holt, and an excursion to Sheringham was proposed after Sunday lunch. The house seemed to bore her. When shown the dining room – then stripped of its furniture, and decorated by Tom Upcher in a strong, Regency yellow – her verdict was, 'It's the most disgusting room I've ever seen.'

The response of the Prince of Wales to Sheringham could not have been in more marked contrast. He readily agreed to become Patron of the appeal, and the ideal occasion for a visit presented itself. He would officially open the gazebo, once it had been rebuilt.

Nearly two years before Sheringham finally passed to the National Trust, Mildred Cordeaux had written to Billa Harrod:

Sheringham is never far from my thoughts. Worries abound. Today, while doing my chores, I just wondered if you &/or the National Trust know about the gazebo that was in the wood behind the Hall…. In the 'old days' it was a great thrill to me as a small child, but due to neglect it became totally unsafe. Some years ago the Trustees offered to rebuild it, as we had just turned down, as not very possible, Tom's idea of rebuilding Repton's orangery. Eventually Tom decided his legs were too bad for him ever to be able to get to or enjoy the gazebo and instead asked us to build the Temple.[14]

There were only the vaguest of recollections of the gazebo locally, with some mention of it being damaged by arson. Its original position was easy to identify in Repton's *Red Book*: it pre-dated the creation of the park and had been erected in 1803 to warn of invasion, at a time when Napoleon's barges were massed at Boulogne. What made locating it difficult was that *Rhododendron ponticum* had created an almost impenetrable jungle among the oaks on Spy Hill. A winter visit by the Secretary of the Trust, David Beeton, to see Sheringham provided an opportunity to explore the hill top. Together we pushed and scrambled through the undergrowth, until we were abruptly confronted by its skeletal remains. It had indeed been damaged by fire, and sections of the steps were missing. A nervous ascent to just under the oak canopy confirmed that the views were just as remarkable as Cordeaux remembered them. As soon as news of its partial survival reached her, she offered to pay for its reinstatement.

Even in the salt-laden winds off the North Sea, the oaks had, during the last half-century, grown above the viewing platform of the original gazebo. It was also of too slight a construction to take the numbers of visitors envisaged at Sheringham. The task of designing its replacement was given to the Trust's Regional Building Manager, Chris Appleton. His solution was to have a steel frame to which steps of English oak would be bolted. Work started in the autumn of 1987. On 20 October – four days after the Great Storm that had brought havoc to so many Norfolk woodlands – an RAF Sea King helicopter flew in perfect weather across the park, with the steel frame dangling beneath, and then lowered it, with inches to spare on either side, through the trees at the top of Spy Hill. All was on course for the Prince of Wales to inspect the gazebo the following year. Then, unexpectedly, a date for the visit was proposed. The Prince would be at Sandringham in January and would like to open the gazebo on the 20th of that month.

The timing was tight, but not impossible. There is nothing like a royal visit to galvanise builders, even over the Christmas period. What the National Trust had not bargained for was a heavy fall of snow in December, and then a prolonged freeze. Transporting building materials through the oak woods to the top of Spy Hill was difficult and hazardous, but was somehow accomplished. On 20 January 1988, Mildred Cordeaux was able to welcome the Prince of Wales to Sheringham, and he broke a flag at the top of the gazebo.

Mildred Cordeaux was true to her word, and on her death the National Trust received well over a million pounds towards the endowment of Sheringham. Her generosity has made it possible to repair the farm buildings, which are an attractive feature in the park, and to continue the task of replanting the woods.

The legacy from Bill and Mollie Smith turned out to be as generous. Many years before, Mollie had been left £200,000 by her sister. Rather than spend the money on themselves, they decided that Bill would treat it as an investment which would ultimately benefit the

National Trust. His management of their portfolio of shares gradually increased its value to more than a million pounds. Their motivation was summarised in a note of 1990, in which they explained that 'it is our gratitude to the Trust for the enrichment of our lives, particularly during the terrible years of the pre-war Depression, which leads us to attempt to repay our debt'. Before it came to the Trust, there were periods of uncertainty and a moment of almost complete breakdown.

The relationship with the Trust weakened when Bob Latham retired. His successor was understandably disconcerted to find that some of the conditions attached to the proposed bequest, particularly a requirement that there should be no hunting or shooting at Sheringham, might be contrary to National Trust policies. In reality the level of public visiting expected at Sheringham meant that field sports would be unacceptably dangerous and were never envisaged. Unfortunately, while these issues were being clarified, a letter from Bill Smith went unanswered for too long. The Trust was informed that the Smiths had decided to redirect their legacy to the Royal National Lifeboat Institution (RNLI).

Over a long period there was a cautious re-building of bridges. Bob Latham agreed to resume responsibility for dealing with their legal worries. A visit was made to the Isle of Man to discuss their other concerns. The will was eventually amended to reinstate the National Trust as principal beneficiary, with a new stipulation that if the Sheringham endowment reached levels that were more than the property was likely to need, part of the bequest could be diverted to Felbrigg. Because Bill Smith would not countenance any use of the legacy where field sports were practised, it could only benefit the Felbrigg walled garden, which was labour intensive and expensive to maintain. There were, however, sections of the will that recognised the need for shooting to control vermin. On the small nature reserve that Bill and Mollie had created on land adjoining their home on the Isle of Man, this was found to be essential, and Bill himself used a shotgun occasionally. They were both as relieved as the Trust that their wish to make a major contribution towards Sheringham, and now Felbrigg as well, was going to be realised.

Through the regular exchange of letters between the National Trust office at Blickling and the Isle of Man, it became apparent that Mollie's health was deteriorating. Then, in June 1996, during a meeting of senior staff at Blickling, I received a message that Bill Smith needed to speak to me urgently. His call was returned immediately, and in great distress he told me that Mollie had just died. I promised to speak again soon and offered to come over to the island, if that was what he wanted. It was our last conversation. Shortly afterwards, I received a call from the Isle of Man police to say that they had found my number among the Smiths' papers. Bill had been found in their nature reserve, where he had shot himself.

Bill and Mollie Smith's generosity to the National Trust went beyond their legacy of £1.3 million, which ensured that, with the addition of Mildred Cordeaux's bequest, Sheringham was now handsomely endowed and the finances of Felbrigg much improved. Bill's collection of antique clocks was distributed to where they were most needed: one is in the dining room at Wimpole Hall in Cambridgeshire; another in the steward's room at Felbrigg. Their garden machinery was also accepted enthusiastically by the Felbrigg head gardener. In the converted barn near the entrance to Sheringham, now serving as a ticket office, there is an exhibition about the Upchers. The part played by Mildred Cordeaux in securing the future of the estate and the generosity of the Smiths are also explained.

Because the National Trust holds properties such as Felbrigg and Sheringham in perpetuity, it is sometimes possible to achieve some sort of resolution to issues that have caused sadness or regret over many years. Just such an opportunity arose in 1986, when the National Maritime Museum purchased an outstanding example of one of the several paintings of the Battle of the Texel by Willem van de Velde the Younger. Another two examples

William van de Velde the Elder and Younger, *The Battle of the Texel*, 1673, now hanging in the drawing room at Felbrigg Hall.

The Drawing Room at Felbrigg Hall.

of the same subject had been acquired by William Windham II, probably when he was passing through Holland in 1742, at the end of his Grand Tour. They were hung by Windham on either side of a door in the drawing room at Felbrigg, where both remained until 1934.

Wyndham Ketton-Cremer had inherited Felbrigg from his father the year before, and repairs were urgently needed. Very reluctantly, he agreed to sell one of the pictures of the Battle of the Texel to the National Maritime Museum. It was the only major painting to leave the house during his tenure. Fifty years later, the Museum agreed that as long as their more recent acquisition was on display, the other version was better not in store, but back at Felbrigg.

Ketton-Cremer would have been still more delighted that Sheringham had been given a secure future. He might have attached significance to the vital contribution from the National Heritage Memorial Fund. When the Fund was set up in 1980, the inclusion of the word 'Memorial' in its title was questioned at the committee stage, but it was retained because Hugh Dalton's creation of its predecessor, the National Land Fund, had expressly been to commemorate those who had given their lives in the Second World War. As Ketton-Cremer wrote in *Felbrigg: The Story of a House*, 'My brother's grave in Crete will be for ever unmarked and unknown.' Sheringham Park and Felbrigg have become his memorial.

14

THE TRAITORS, THE COUNTESS AND MR BOND

Nancy, Countess of Enniskillen and Florence Court;
Walter MacGeough Bond and The Argory

English School, *Florence Bourchier Wrey, c.*1705–15, who married John Cole in 1707, and after whom he named his new house, Florence Court, in Co. Fermanagh, Northern Ireland.

THE URGE TO OBLITERATE THE RELICS of the past will, given the opportunity, surface and resurface. The iconoclasm of the sixteenth century may seem comfortably remote. So too does the wrecking inspired by the French Revolution. The combination of ideological fervour and a frenzy of destruction and looting is not, however, confined to previous centuries. Our government is complicit in the ransacking of the national museum in Baghdad and the smashing by tanks of much of the ancient city of Babylon. The destruction is of our own time and, frequently, of our own place.

This perennial need to destroy calls for an effort at understanding, as does the indifference to the past which can ultimately be almost as destructive. The assumption that historic buildings and artefacts are somehow a sacred inheritance, never to be lost, is a denial of one of the great repeat performances of history. Iconoclasm, it seems, is more instinctive than veneration or conservation. In the twentieth century, when destruction was globalised, the antiquarian was the eccentric, the odd man out.

Few countries can match the zeal with which the Republic of Ireland has got rid of so many of its finest monuments and buildings. Some of Ireland's medieval monuments have been hemmed in with suburban developments which have compromised them permanently. The Hill of Tara in County Meath, the coronation site for hundreds of years of the High Kings of Ireland, is threatened with the noise of a proposed motorway interchange. Perhaps the nearest motorway service station will stock souvenir recordings of Thomas Moore's song, *The Harp that Once Through Tara's Halls*. Ireland's country houses have largely been destroyed and their contents dispersed in a campaign begun during the war of independence between 1919 and 1921, accelerated during the Civil War, and since then sustained by the Irish Government.

What cannot be denied is the extent to which Anglo-Irish landowners brought the destruction of their houses and the break-up of their estates on themselves. Many were absentee landlords, who regarded their Irish property as places for recreation and who, in varying degrees, treated their tenantry with indifference and sometimes appalling lack of humanity. The nannies, governesses and tutors recruited to the big houses of Ireland were usually from England or Scotland.[1] Sons were expected to be educated at Eton or other English public schools, before being dispatched to Oxford, Cambridge or Sandhurst. Sympathetic engagement with their own staff was often limited, and with local communities unusual. Mutual incomprehension could readily turn to resentment and hostility.

The efforts to stem the slide towards open conflict were sincere and the response sometimes generous. One of the most significant provisions was the Wyndham Land Act of 1903, which established funds to enable landlords to sell parts of their estates to their Irish tenants. Inevitably there were landowners who were reluctant to sell, believing that the terms and conditions of sale might improve; but many more were ready to accept payments that cleared debts which had accumulated throughout the nineteenth century.[2] Others, such as the 9th Earl of Dysart, agreed to sell, but more out of a sense of moral responsibility and public duty than because of financial need.[3] George Wyndham deserves to be remembered as a Chief Secretary for Ireland who brought imagination and idealism to its problems, even if he was over-optimistic about what could be achieved from Westminster.[4]

The response of the British government to the Easter Rising of 1916 made a peaceful transition to an independent Ireland impossible and sealed the fate of most of its big houses. In the early stages of the war of independence, historic houses were sometimes burnt on the grounds that they were being used as barracks by the Royal Irish Constabulary.[5] By 1921 the spiral of reprisals carried out by the Black and Tans (the soldiers used by the British government) on one side and the Irish Republican Army on the other made the big house an obvious and easy target. The thirst for revenge was compounded by centuries-old bitterness and by the cruder desire for loot and land. Between April 1920 and July 1921 72 big houses were destroyed, one third of them because the IRA claimed that they were being used for military purposes. On 30 June 1921 *The Irish Times* referred to 'house burning mania' sweeping the country.

The ending of the war of independence on 6 December 1921 and the establishment of the Irish Free State might be thought to have reprieved surviving country houses. Their cultural significance was articulated clearly enough by W.B. Yeats, who wrote:

> … to kill a house
> where great men grew up, married, died,
> I here declare a capital offence.

At a time of civil war, such views counted for very little. The rate at which country houses were burnt increased by three times, with an estimated 199 destroyed in the 26 counties between January 1922 and April 1923.[6] Those in the IRA who were opposed to the Anglo-Irish Treaty of 1921 were given orders to burn the houses of landowners appointed to the Senate. In August 1922 an editorial in *The Irish Times* observed that 'everyone is puzzled to find out what purpose the mutineers can serve, even from their own crazy point of view, by destroying these stately mansions.' But the burnings continued. Of the estimated 4,000 big houses in Ireland in 1860, more than half were destroyed, and of those that survived less than ten per cent are now in the hands of the families that owned them a century ago.

The government of Ireland has, until very recently, been indifferent to the future of the dwindling number of country houses with their historic collections intact. In the case of Shanbally Castle in County Tipperary, it was a government department that decided on demolition, in circumstances which are complex and revealing. Shanbally Castle belonged

Shanbally Castle, in Co. Tipperary, designed by John Nash in 1906 for the descendant of an old Irish family, Cornelius O'Callaghan, but demolished by the Land Commission in 1957.

not to Anglo-Irish absentee landlords, but to one of Tipperary's ancient families, the O'Callaghans. The most recent castle was built in 1806 to the designs of John Nash, perhaps because Cornelius O'Callaghan thought the choice of the Prince Regent's architect might attract attention at court, or even a royal visit. The date of the house and its associations may not have helped the case for preservation, but it was one of Nash's finest picturesque compositions, with an array of square, circular and hexagonal castellated towers, linking balustrades, and a gothic cloister. In 1954 it was acquired, in good condition, by the Land Commission, and in 1957 the department decided it should be demolished. The Cork Advisory Group of the Arts Council objected, appealing to the Minister of Lands, Erskine Childers. The official reason for his apparent indifference was that he was away on holiday when the appeal was made. By the time he returned, demolition had already begun. No effort was made to intervene. Eventually dynamite had to be used to level the fine stonework.[7]

That Erskine Hamilton Childers should have been drawn into the controversy surrounding Shanbally is a reminder of the tragedies and cruelties of Ireland. He had been educated at a comparatively enlightened and liberal English public school, Gresham's in Norfolk, and it was there, in November 1922, that his headmaster, Ronald Earles, had to tell him that his father, the author of *The Riddle of the Sands*, had been arrested for unlawful possession of a firearm, given to him by Michael Collins.[8] Shortly before Robert Erskine Childers was executed by firing squad as a traitor, he urged his son, visiting him in prison, to work for reconciliation between the English and Irish. Appeals for a reprieve were ignored.

Prompted by the destruction of Shanbally, *The Cork Examiner* observed:

> Unless the present trends of the Department of Lands are stayed, there will be nothing left in fifty years to link the age of the Norman castle tower as a habitation, and the latest concrete semi-detached council house.[9]

Government attitudes had changed little by 2002, when there were appeals to keep Lissadell complete as an entity. It was a house which had played a prominent part in the forging of modern Ireland, culturally and politically. Lissadell, overlooking Sligo Bay in the north-west of Ireland, was built in 1834 for Sir Robert Gore-Booth. His architect, Francis Goodwin, was a master of the Grecian style, with a feeling for fine materials, which at Lissadell included Ballysodare limestone and the Kilkenny marble used in the huge columnar gallery. Over the chimneypiece in the dining room there used to hang a painting by Sarah Purser of the young grand-daughters of the builder of the house, Constance and Eva Gore-Booth, both of whom have a prominent place in twentieth-century Irish politics and literature. Constance was married to Count Casimir Markievicz, a painter who decorated the pilasters in the dining room with strangely attenuated, suited male figures.

In 1916 Constance was one of the leaders of the Easter Rising, was condemned to death, and later reprieved. She was the first woman to be elected to the Dail Eireann, serving as Minister of Labour. Her sister was a poet and leading suffragette; and both were friends of Yeats, who stayed at Lissadell in 1893 and 1894. 'In Memory of Eva Gore-Booth and Con Markiewicz' was written in 1927, the year of Constance's death, and begins:

> The light of evening, Lissadell,
> Great windows open to the south,
> Two girls in silk kimonos, both
> Beautiful, one a gazelle...

Lissadell House, overlooking Sligo Bay in north-west Ireland, restored since 2004 and now opened to the public by Edward Walsh and his wife Constance Cassidy, following the dispersal of its original contents in 2003.

The dining room at Lissadell House, with the decorated pilasters by Count Casimir Markievicz, whose wife Constance Gore-Booth can be seen, with her sister Eva, in Sarah Purser's portrait above the fireplace, photographed in 2003.

The poem ponders their dreams of 'some vague Utopia' and how such politics can seem 'withered old and skeleton-gaunt,' like the old woman Eva became:

> The innocent and the beautiful
> Have no enemy but time…

It concludes:

> We the great gazebo built,
> They convicted us of guilt;
> Bid me strike a match and blow.[10]

Fire did not destroy Lissadell. But the Irish Government chose not to intervene and the sale of its contents went ahead.[11]

It could be argued that the poetry of Yeats and Eva Gore-Booth needs no mausoleum, that he was always ambivalent about being the poet of Irish nationalism, as his tribute to Constance and Eva demonstrates. What is regrettable about the dispersal of the contents of Lissadell – Purser's portrait of the two sisters now hangs in a Dublin hotel – is that Yeats and the house itself spoke of the complexities and contradictions of the new Ireland. The failure to preserve it as an entity was as much a failure to understand the uses and value of history, as it was indicative of a peculiarly Irish attitude to the role of government. It is consistent with the willingness to allow so many accessible vantage points in south-west Ireland to be adorned with hacienda-style bungalows, transforming what was once among the most beautiful landscapes in the world. The equivalent organisation to the National Trust, An Taisce, struggles with the government's extremely selective view of what is, and is not, part of the Republic's cultural heritage.

North of the border, the National Trust had acquired properties which range from the Giant's Causeway in County Antrim to Patterson's Spade Mill near Belfast. Although the buildings of Northern Ireland have not been immune to the urge to dismantle or destroy, there was a long period, between the Anglo-Irish truce of 1921 and the resurfacing of 'the Troubles' in the 1950s, when the protection of the coast and the conservation of historic houses continued apace, given impetus by the Northern Ireland Civil Service and by the adroit use of the Ulster Land Fund. A succession of outstanding buildings, including Castle Coole, Derrymore House, Florence Court, Hezlett House, Mount Stewart and Springhill, benefited from the Fund, which was modelled on Hugh Dalton's initiative of 1946 and established by the Ulster Land Fund Act of 1949. In fact it was an enlightened civil servant, Dick Rogers, who drafted the parliamentary question asking whether Ulster might have its own Land Fund, and then convinced the Finance Minister, Major Maynard Sinclair, not only that the idea was worth supporting, but that the remit of the Fund should be wider than its English counterpart, in that it could be used 'for the repair and maintenance of buildings and their contents'. Rogers worked in the Northern Ireland Civil Service from 1926 until 1972, and, in an extremely fruitful coincidence, was also on the National Trust's committee for Northern Ireland from 1943 to 1983.

When Derrymore House in County Armagh was given to the National Trust in 1953 and restored with the aid of the Ulster Land Fund, little if any thought was given to its political significance.[12] The builder of this small thatched manor house, Isaac Corry, had a hand in the Act of Union of 1801 between England and Ireland, which was reputedly drafted in what became known as the Treaty Room at Derrymore. Blissfully unaware of potential sensitivities, the National Trust treated it rather like a colonial outpost, employing an English architect, David Nye, to supervise repairs, and importing Norfolk reed – which failed – to re-thatch the roof.

Between 1972 and 1979 republican terrorists bombed Derrymore House six times. It survived because of the quiet courage of the Trust's caretaker, Edmund Baillie, and his two sisters. When a bomb was planted against the house and they were ordered to leave, Teddy Baillie picked up the device and carried it out into the garden. The Baillie family seemed to be more disconcerted by the Trust's Regional Chairman, who visited the following day: they were worried that they did not have sufficient cups to give their visitors tea. When the Director-General, Martin Drury, met Teddy Baillie at the house and asked about the various bombings, he took from his wallet a very worn piece of paper on which the details of every one was listed.[13]

In 1976 the National Trust's office in Belfast was also bombed. Malone House was not owned by the Trust, but was leased from Belfast Corporation. On the morning of 11 November, when members of the Ulster Tourist Development Association were arriving for a meeting, two young men and a woman slipped past security officers, held up the staff

Detail of the cast-iron balustrade and mahogany handrail inlaid with ebony, created by the Irish craftsman John Ferguson for Mount Stewart in Co. Down. The house was given to the National Trust by Lady Mairi Bury in 1976 with an endowment, supplemented by the Ulster Land Fund.

at gunpoint, and planted one bomb on the ground floor and another upstairs. After the explosions, fire raged through the building. A fire engine arrived and its crew watched the blaze, but did not attempt to contain it because parts of the Fire Service were involved in an industrial dispute. The Ulster Museum's costumes and its unrivalled collection of Irish linen were lost.[14] So too were most of the National Trust's records, photographs and maps. The next day the work of the office resumed at Rowallane House, the home of the Regional Secretary, John Lewis-Crosby, who retained just two rooms for himself, his wife and their dogs.

'The troubles' also came to the Argory in County Armagh. Greek revival houses were once common enough in Ireland, and the Argory, built between 1820 and 1824 to the designs of Arthur and John Williamson of Dublin, might have ranked as a competent but not outstanding example of the genre. Given rarity value by the losses in the Republic, it is now a precious record of the life of the Anglo-Irish gentry, and of the subtle shifts of taste that shaped its unspectacular rooms. The visitor to the Argory approaches past the fold yard, the laundry yard and the poultry yard, glimpses the twin pavilions of the garden, and then enters a house which appears to have been untroubled for a hundred years. But the impression of tranquil timelessness is misleading.[15]

The builder of the house, Walter McGeough Bond, graduated from Trinity College Dublin in 1811 and became a successful barrister.[16] His grandson, Walter Adrian MacGeough Bond, pursued a legal career abroad, receiving a knighthood for services as Vice President of the Court of Appeal in Cairo. Sir Walter's own son, Walter Albert Nevill MacGeough Bond – addressed as 'Mr Bond' by the dwindling staff at the Argory – described himself as a country gentleman. He was born in 1908, educated at Eton, won a scholarship to King's College Cambridge where he developed a love of music and contemporary art, served as High Sheriff of County Armagh in 1952, and was appointed Deputy Lieutenant in 1960. When the former Lord Lieutenant was murdered by the IRA, there was a possibility that Mr Bond would succeed him; but he preferred an increasingly reclusive life at the Argory, accumulating a large collection of paintings and sculpture by contemporary Ulster artists. His bronze portrait bust by Duncan Johnston captures a slightly anxious, melancholy face, with swept-back hair and a prominent moustache. He was unmarried and a hypochondriac, who adored his mother but was regarded by his father as a disappointment.

During the Second World War, the Argory estate was occupied by American forces, with the house largely shut up and the furniture stacked away in the drawing room. Sir Walter MacGeough Bond died in 1945, and over the next 30 years the house was only partially reassembled. The dining room was tidied up for occasional tea parties, and Mr Bond lived in the study and two bedrooms. The rest of the house remained under dust sheets.

Mr Bond's closest relative was a cousin living in England, who had no interest in returning to Northern Ireland. The initial very tentative discussions about the future of the Argory were with the Chairman of the National Trust's Northern Ireland Committee, John, 6th Earl of Clanwilliam. These progressed in a somewhat desultory way over ten years or more, because Mr Bond was not in a position to offer an endowment for the house. Then, in 1979, funding unexpectedly became available. There was an under-spend that year in the Northern Ireland Department of Finance, and the £1,084,650 needed for repairs and an endowment could be made available – the money would otherwise have had to be returned to the Treasury – provided the transfer of the Argory could be completed before the end of the Government's financial year on 31 March.

There were three sets of solicitors involved: the National Trust's in London, Mr Bond's London solicitors and another firm acting for him in Dungannon. The papers were finally signed by the Trust in London a matter of hours before the deadline. The Assistant Solicitor, Suzanne Foye, then rushed to the airport, only to find that it was fogbound and there were no planes for Belfast. In desperation she took a train to the ferry, and then a taxi from Dublin to the Argory. The National Trust took possession of the property on 1 April 1979. A month later the IRA struck.

Mr Bond used to spend most days at the Argory, but because the house was without electricity – apart from a generator for the organ – and had only open fires, he usually retreated in the evening to the Seagoe Hotel in Portadown, which was warm and comfortable. While in his study at the Argory, where there was a coal fire, Mr Bond wore an overcoat, putting on a second overcoat, a hat and a scarf whenever he went to other parts of the house.

In 1979 the only member of staff was Eric Lutton, who acted as chauffeur, lit the study fire, and operated the small generator in one of the outbuildings whenever Mr Bond wanted to play the cabinet barrel organ. The instrument had been commissioned in 1822, adapted after a fire in 1898, and later had an electric air pump installed. Mr Bond would open the window of the organ lobby when he was ready to play and signal to Lutton by waving his hat. Having finished playing, Mr Bond's hat would again be waved out of the window and Lutton would shut down the generator. The rest of his day was as regular as Mr Bond's, and as predictable.

On 1 May 1979 Mr Bond made the journey as usual from the Seagoe Hotel, with Lutton driving him. On the return journey, when they were just inside the entrance gates to the Argory and where the rhododendrons were dense and overgrown, a gunman leapt out and shot Lutton, with Mr Bond in the seat beside him. As so often in Ireland, Lutton was not himself involved in any sectarian organisation. His murder was a reprisal, because the IRA's preferred victim, Lutton's brother, could not be targeted while he was in prison.

The National Trust took possession of a near-derelict house, with a garden so overgrown that it was an impenetrable jungle, and where the only member of staff was murdered within weeks of the transfer. Before 1979 no curatorial staff were employed in Northern Ireland. Deci-

Duncan Johnston, *Walter Albert Nevill MacGeough Bond*, who gave The Argory in Co. Armagh and all its contents to the National Trust in 1979.

sions about the care and decoration of its houses were taken by Lord Clanwilliam and occasionally by staff, principally Robin Fedden, who came over from London. Fortunately the Trust made an unlikely but enlightened appointment: in October 1978 it recruited Peter Marlow – a former American museum director with a wife from Northern Ireland – to be its Historic Buildings Representative in the province. After a brief spell helping to prepare Dunham Massey, in Cheshire, for opening to the public, Marlow took up responsibility for the conservation and presentation of the Argory.

Marlow spent much of the month of May 1979 at the Argory preparing an inventory, getting to know the house, and sleeping most nights at Ardress House, a National Trust property nearby. It rained incessantly and was extremely bleak, lonely and frightening. But he came

The Organ Lobby at The Argory, with the cabinet barrel organ, commissioned in 1822, re-adapted in 1898, and later installed with an electric air pump.

to know the house in a way that occasional visits would never have allowed. Once structural repairs had been carried out, electricity and wiring discreetly installed behind the shutters, and the furniture and pictures brought out of storage, Marlow and Mr Bond set about recreating the house as the latter had known it as a child, immediately after the First World War.

Experimental picture arrangements were difficult, because on the staircase in particular there were stacks of prints to be hung from a high rail. The solution adopted by Marlow was to mark out the dimensions of the wall under consideration, using masking tape, on the floor of an adjoining room. Any niches or window spaces were also marked. Marlow would then lay out the pictures and summon Mr Bond. He would appear in his two overcoats and perch on a tall stool, which he found more comfortable than a chair because one of his hips was giving pain. Marlow was addressed sombrely and precisely: 'I think that one should be about two inches to the left, don't *you*?' The pictures were moved around until Mr Bond was satisfied, and then the hang was transferred to the walls. A few days later he would pass judgement, usually favourably.

The Argory is one of the relatively few National Trust properties where the hand of its restorers and decorators has been so entirely subordinated to the character and atmosphere of the house as to be virtually invisible. This is because of Mr Bond's continuing involvement and Marlow's patient, painstaking respect for his wish to reinstate the arrangement of the house as he remembered it, made possible because he had given the National Trust the entire contents of all the rooms to be opened to the public.

For a period after the opening of the house on 1 July 1981, relations between Mr Bond and the Trust remained good; but then, as often happens, they began to sour. This may have been partly because the Trust decided against converting an outbuilding into a gallery for his collection of contemporary Ulster art, on the grounds that the work was not outstanding. The decision now seems regrettable, and with the considerable increase in visitor numbers since peace returned to Northern Ireland, Mr Bond's pictures might have proved to be of unusual interest. Most were sold by his executors on his death in 1986. Recently, however, the National Trust was able to acquire, through the National Art Collections Fund, an important bronze figure called *The Woman of Belfast* by F.E. McWilliam which is now in the front hall.

Unlike the Argory, the contents of Florence Court, in County Fermanagh, were removed from the house in 1973 and left Ireland. Far from being an unusual occurrence in an Irish country house, this was following an all too familiar pattern. Florence Court was given to the National Trust in 1954 by Michael, Viscount Cole, son of John, 5th Earl of Enniskillen, with the Ministry of Finance providing £45,000 for repairs and the Ulster Land Fund a further £35,000 for an endowment. Less than a year after the official opening, an accidental fire tore through the centre of the house and destroyed much of the roof. Thanks to the rapid erection of a temporary covering, damage to the house was reparable. A sympathetic restoration was guided by Sir Albert Richardson – who had been responsible for repairs to Melford Hall in Suffolk after a wartime fire and for the rebuilding of the Assembly Rooms in Bath after bombing – and the house was able to re-open in 1959. After this disastrous beginning to Trust ownership, matters at Florence Court lurched from crisis to crisis.

When the donor of the property, Viscount Cole, died in 1956, seven years before his

The West Hall and Staircase at The Argory, Co. Armagh. The house dates from 1820 and remains substantially unchanged since the end of the nineteenth century.

father, the contents of Florence Court and the estate passed to his first cousin, David Lowry Cole, who in 1963 became the 6th Earl of Enniskillen. Like many younger sons or relations of the titled aristocracy, Captain David Cole had been dispatched to the colonies, in his case to Africa, where he had become one of the largest private landowners in Kenya. Much of his vast estate there was without irrigation and unproductive. Cole sunk wells, built dams, and erected hundreds of miles of fencing to make his cattle and sheep farm profitable. During the Mau Mau rebellion, from 1950 to 1955, he served as Commandant in the Kenya Police Reserve, for which he was awarded the MBE. He was also active politically, being elected to the legislative council as the member for the constituency of North Kenya, with an unprecedented 90 percent of the vote, in the national election just before independence. Working with the last British Governor and with the future Prime Minister, Jomo Kenyatta, he helped to draft the new Kenyan constitution.

Cole's first wife, the 5th Earl's step-daughter Sonia Syers, whom he married in 1940, was an archaeologist, and they had two children. After several years of separation, they were divorced in 1955, and the same year he married Miss Nancy MacLennan of Bridgeport, Connecticut, formerly a Washington and United Nations correspondent of the *New York Times* and a vice consul and assistant attaché of the U.S. Foreign Service Reserve. In their wedding photograph, she appears glamorous, with a smile which does not disguise that she could be more than a touch formidable.

The east front of Florence Court, in Co. Fermanagh, given to the National Trust by Viscount Cole, son of the 5th Earl of Enniskillen, in 1954, and endowed by the Ulster Land Fund.

On unexpectedly inheriting the title in 1963, the 6th Earl left Kenya and returned to Florence Court. The division of ownership of the land around the house was a prescription for conflict. The National Trust was responsible for the house and for fourteen acres surrounding it. The lawn in front of the house and its parkland were the property of the 6th Earl. Almost immediately there were disagreements over how Florence Court was shown to the public and how its collections, most of which still belonged to Lord Enniskillen, were arranged.

Every year or so, Robin Fedden would visit Florence Court, meet Lady Enniskillen, and attempt to rearrange the furniture and pictures to improve the presentation of the house. Within a few days of his departure, Lady Enniskillen would ring up the Trust's Regional Secretary for Northern Ireland, John Lewis-Crosby, and say: 'You know, Mr Crosby, I had it all back again just as soon as he left the house.' When this was reported to Fedden, his initial response was: 'Oh G-G-God!' and then, after a pause, 'Well, if that's how she wants it, she's the lady of the house, let her have it that way.'[17]

The relationship deteriorated steadily, as did the condition of the house. It did not help that Lord Enniskillen had served in the Irish Guards during the Second World War, and had on one occasion been disciplined by his commanding officer, who happened to be John Lewis-Crosby. Their re-encounter was bound to be uncomfortable: it was made clear to Lewis-Crosby that he was not welcome at Florence Court.[18] When there was a serious outbreak of dry rot, the Trust was refused access to deal with it. The Trust's Chairman, Lord

David, 6th Earl of Enniskillen, with his second wife, Nancy MacLennan, following their marriage on 7 May 1955.

Antrim, who was Northern Irish, was liked and respected by almost everyone, and was a most amusing guest, tried to build bridges. He arranged to visit Florence Court with the Chairman of the Committee for Northern Ireland, Lord Clanwilliam, hoping that, in dealing with the Enniskillens, 'two Earls are better than one'. After an initial discussion, Lord Enniskillen withdrew to have his lunch, leaving Antrim and Clanwilliam to eat sandwiches in the hall.[19] Finally, in 1973, the National Trust and Lord Enniskillen agreed that the situation had become intolerable. Initially Lord and Lady Enniskillen left Northern Ireland to return to Kenya, but found the political situation disturbing. They then lived briefly in Connecticut, before settling at Kinloch House near Dunkeld, in Perthshire.

Their departure from Florence Court solved some problems but created others, principally because they took most of the contents of the house with them. Legally they may have been entitled to do this, but the implications would have an impact on succeeding generations of the Cole family. At the time of the original gift of Florence Court, Viscount Cole had agreed a memorandum of wishes with the Trust in August 1954, which made provision for the future occupation of the house, rent-free, by his successors. This was partly in recognition of the generosity of the gift of the property, but also because the memorandum dealing with its contents, stated:

> I am prepared to allow the National Trust to have on permanent loan… such of the furniture
> and chattels as they may consider suitable for furnishing the rooms open to the public.

The removal of the contents disregarded an important part of the memorandum of wishes, and consequently negated the moral obligations of both parties to respect its provisions, including the right of occupation.

To make the near-empty house presentable, the Trust's staff set about furnishing it with loans and gifts of furniture and pictures, some from generous benefactors, some made available by other National Trust properties. Although Florence Court was made to look less melancholy and abandoned, every introduction, however welcome, tended to misrepresent and so falsify the history of the property. The pictures and furniture which might have given it life were exiled to Scotland. Their custodians had, over twenty years, become increasingly conscious of just how sad this was. Both Lord and Lady Enniskillen loved Florence Court. Her affection for the house, and knowledge of the family history, was poured into her book, *Florence Court: My Irish Home*. But for twenty years there was no communication with the National Trust. In 1989 the 6th Earl died.

In early January 1997, Professor Ronald Buchanan, Chairman of the Trust's Northern Ireland Committee, received a letter in a strong, clear, but unfamiliar hand, a copy of which had also been sent to the National Trust's Chairman, Charles Nunneley.[20] On the first of 21 full-size, handwritten sheets, the sender introduced herself as the widow of Captain David Lowry Cole, MBE, the 6th Earl of Enniskillen. 'The reason I write concerns the National Trust brochure,' which was 'designed, printed and illustrated all so beautifully.' The letter continues:

> I congratulate all who were concerned in the production of this charming guide for the
> National Trust. Particularly I congratulate those persons who researched, who compiled, and
> who wrote it.

> No one, in any way, is to blame, nor would I ever dream of criticising, in the least, anyone, for certain statements in it which to me are unfortunate.

There follows a list of 21 mistakes, or misrepresentations, with suggestions for how they might be rectified. Some were trivial and little more than matters of taste. The guide quoted Sir Richard Colt Hoare, writing in 1806, as saying that Florence Court had 'a superfluity of windows, bearing more the resemblance of a *manufactory* than a comfortable dwelling house'. This Lady Cole found 'most unfortunate'. Yet the truth is that the early-eighteenth-century classicism of Florence Court is architecturally bucolic.[21]

The most serious mistake in the guide was the statement that Florence Court had been given to the National Trust by the 5th Earl of Enniskillen, when in fact it was the gift of his son, Viscount Cole. The letter seemed to be written more in sorrow than in anger, was scrupulously polite, and included an offer to pay for a new edition of the guide:

> Such faults really can cause – and do cause – profound sadness to someone like myself – who happens to be the present-day, still-living, Dowager Countess of Enniskillen – for the sake of my late husband, the sixth Earl of Enniskillen, for the sake of the Cole/Enniskillen family, for the sake of its honour, its history, and for the sake of truth.'

As Regional Chairman, Buchanan was greatly respected for his tact, his friendly, engaging manner, and his integrity. He wrote back promptly:

> I am concerned about the inaccuracies you have found in the current edition of the guide to Florence Court. As an academic I expect accuracy in publications, and I am disappointed to learn that the Trust has not maintained its normally high standards in this booklet.

He went on to say that a new edition of the guide was being prepared, and Lady Enniskillen would be sent a copy of the proofs. Buchanan concluded by mentioning that he would be visiting his son in Edinburgh during February, and if she felt it would be helpful, would be pleased to meet her. The response was immediate. Buchanan was invited to an informal lunch for just the two of them on 21 February.

Lady Enniskillen's house in Perthshire was relatively small, rather gloomy, and surrounded by woodland. Nothing would have suggested that it was packed with paintings, furniture and books from Florence Court. Buchanan was greeted warmly by his hostess, whom he found bright, shrewd and deliberate. She was initially wary; but his academic background clearly reassured her, and a bond was established when they found that they had both been at Cornell University, Buchanan as a visiting professor. The meeting went well. Lady Enniskillen subsequently wrote to say what 'a pleasure and satisfaction' it had been to be able to discuss the guide, and she enclosed several pages of corrections to the proofs she had been sent for a new edition.

In April she wrote again:

> In a few weeks I hope to be able to write to you – or contact you in person – re an idea/suggestion close to my heart; but presently, relatively controversial… It is impossible to

describe my relief and pleasure in the actions you have taken – are taking – together with
your friendly understanding.

She ended her letter by saying a cheque for £1,000 was enclosed, to help pay for the new
edition of the guide. In a further letter she explained both her intentions and her sense of
urgency, writing on 24 May 1997:

> My doctors have given me – statistically speaking – at the outside, five months. I hope of
> course to be an exception and live a little longer (to finish my work for my late husband,
> Lord Enniskillen: his papers, his archives, etcetera, etcetera).

Attached to the letter was an extract from her will and a list of 250 items which 'are of historic interest concerning Ireland, my dear husband, Captain David Lowry Cole MBE, the
sixth Earl of Enniskillen, his family and their seat of Florence Court.' Her letter concluded:

> It has occurred to me that for expediency and for the security of the items of the bequest
> itself – and also for the help to the National Trust (sic) and for the pleasure and peace of
> mind it would give me, if the National Trust were to accept my bequest, and under the
> provisoes [sic] inherent in it, I should give these things now, while I am still alive...

A fortnight later, Buchanan and the Trust's Regional Director for Northern Ireland, Ian
McQuiston, visited Lady Enniskillen at Kinloch House. Her gift was, she explained, subject
to three conditions: it was for the full list of 250 items; all of them would be displayed at Florence Court; and the National Trust would acknowledge the gift as being in accordance with
the wishes of the 6th Earl of Enniskillen. These stipulations were readily agreed to by the
Chairman of the Trust, Charles Nunneley. McQuiston also confirmed that he intended to
have the collection on display at Florence Court by 10 September 1997, the date of the 6th
Earl's birthday. The credit for this extraordinary *rapprochement* was largely due to Lady
Enniskillen, whose initiative it was. Rarely has the acceptance of an olive branch been so
prompt and appreciative.

How and why did this change of heart come about? Unquestionably, Lady Enniskillen's
overriding concern was to honour the memory of her husband, whose wish it was that most
of the family collections should ultimately return to Florence Court. Her own affection for
the house was profound, and she had conscientiously and thoroughly researched its history.
She had also found that the National Trust had changed in the years since she had last had
dealings with it, into a more responsive, open and appreciative organisation, exemplified by
Buchanan's handwritten replies to her letters. Probably she herself had changed, perhaps influenced by the knowledge that she was terminally ill.

There was another consideration. In 1991 her step-son, the 7th Earl of Enniskillen, had
asked the National Trust whether, following the death of his father, he could return to Florence Court, taking over the role of administrator and citing the memorandum of wishes of
1954. When he was told by the Trust that the memorandum had been negated by the
removal of the contents, his response was to say that the clearance of the furniture and pictures by his father was in effect theft, and that the Trust should have recourse in law to get

them back from his stepmother. This was legally incorrect; and it upset the Dowager Countess considerably. The Florence Court collections were indisputably her property, and she was free either to give them to the National Trust or to sell them. Her decision to arrange for their return may have been in part a recognition that their removal had disregarded the moral obligations implicit in the memorandum of wishes. It was certainly not intended to be helpful to her stepson. In one of her last letters to Buchanan, she referred to the correspondence, which she believed 'targeted, *inter alia*, my furnishings' and said she consequently wished to 'disassociate myself completely from the writer of this letter in its allegations and ideas.' She told the Trust:

> Speaking from my own experience and the nature of Florence Court, I believe the family no longer should live in Florence Court… To me, there is a quintessential conflict of interest between family life and public viewing in this case. The house, belying its appearance and despite its wings, is, in fact, too small to resolve that conflict, in my opinion. On the other hand, as the last two decades without the family in the house has shown, the Trust has had a freedom to develop fêtes, programs [sic] and increasing access for the public; and has done so. This has helped the Trust, the property and the Florence Court community itself.
>
> I myself like to think that in coming years more and more of the rooms of the house will be opened to public view – hopefully the <u>entire</u> first floor.

An eighteenth-century watercolour of *The Colosseum*, painted by Abraham Louis Rodolphe Ducros, one of many pictures returned to Florence Court by Lady Enniskillen before her death in 1998.

Nancy Enniskillen had no compunction about closing the Florence Court door to future generations of the family who might want to live there. Her gift to the National Trust of the paintings and furniture from the house, bequeathed to her by her husband, meant that, once returned, they could never again be removed from Florence Court. There was to be no question of her stepson, the 7th Earl, having any claim to a collection which might have continuing importance to his family and their successors; or which could become assets to be sold and dispersed. Florence Court and the National Trust were to benefit from a family rift going back many years.

Lady Enniskillen was personally involved in the packing and dispatch of her gift, which was supervised by Peter Marlow, whom Lady Enniskillen noted with pleasure was 'a fellow New Englander'. They were able to send her photographs of the collection on display at Florence Court by the end of August. On 2 September she wrote back:

I think you have done an excellent job of placing and hanging all these items; notably, of course, the pictures. I am deeply pleased you have placed my late husband, the sixth Earl's portrait by Wraith, in the Florence Court drawing room. And I am charmed by your decision to place Florence Wray – for whom the house was named – over the fireplace in the grand hall.

As well as family portraits, three large paintings of the countryside around Enniskillen – of great interest to landscape historians - a fine collection of miniatures, and two large cannons returned to Florence Court. It was as though the house had rediscovered its identity.

In September 1997 Buchanan wrote to Lady Enniskillen to say that the National Trust hoped to have a small party at Florence Court, to celebrate the return of such a significant part of its collections, and that all concerned very much hoped that she might be able to attend. He also mentioned that he had discussed with Ian MacQuiston how 'we might acknowledge and commemorate your gift to Florence Court on behalf of your late husband.' This prompted Lady Enniskillen to reply that one of the stipulations of the gift was that it should be recorded in the guide to the house that it had been to comply with the 6th Earl's wishes: 'There is, for me, no greater acknowledgement nor commemoration that you could do, than this.' She hoped to return to Florence Court, if her deteriorating health allowed.

Lady Enniskillen died on 2 February 1998 and was buried beside her husband in the family burial ground adjoining St John's Church, Florencecourt. Having already completed her gift to the National Trust, the principal beneficiary of her will was now Cambridge University. Five hundred of the Earls of Enniskillens' early books were retained by the University, but most of the rest of her chattels were to be sold through Christie's. Once the National Trust had made its interest clear, Christie's was able to agree a private treaty sale of 85 items, so securing an exemption from tax of fifty percent of their value. The remainder were sold in London and Glasgow during the autumn and winter of 1999. Using legacies and gifts given to the Trust specifically for the acquisition of chattels, several paintings of historical importance to Florence Court were bought, as well as books and outstanding furniture. There were grants from the National Art Collections Fund towards the purchase of three Italian views by Louis Ducros, and a special allocation of £52,000 from the Department of the Environment for Northern Ireland.

The return of so many original contents to Florence Court, and the securing of funds for a campaign of acquisition, had all been prompted by Lady Enniskillen's decision to make such a major gift in her lifetime. In July 1997 she had been able to write to Buchanan:

With family portraits again in the house and with the return of some of its historic Irish memorabilia, I believe that the public and the family and our friends will take no little joy and pride in the existence per se of the National Trust's Florence Court. Florence Court belongs to everyone. Whatever family and historic spirit shines from the house is lit by the Trust's ever-enhancing maintenance and showing of it. I applaud this truth and give you and all concerned my hearty congratulations.

So often in Ireland a place name, a dilapidated entrance lodge or a stand of ornamental trees by a walled garden holds the promise of an important or interesting building; and all

The Crown Liquor Saloon in Belfast, built in 1826, embellished with Italian tiling, glass and woodwork in 1898, and acquired by the National Trust, with the cooperation of Bass Ireland, in 1978.

too often an apprehensive exploration up a pot-holed entrance drive ends with the sight of a bungalow in a large area of cleared ground, or sometimes just a ploughed field. There have, of course, been some heartening rescues in the Republic. Ballyfin in County Leix is now in excellent order. Although stripped of its indigenous contents, Lissadell has found energetic and enthusiastic new owners. Will these and other houses rescued in recent years be valued partly because of the new identity they have been given, in a new Ireland?

Thanks to the dogged determination of the Irish Georgian Society, the Irish government has never been allowed to forget completely that many of these houses were designed by Irish architects and built by Irish craftsmen. The value of the big house as an historical document has also been forcefully articulated by Dr Terence Dooley, the director of the Centre for the Study of Historic Irish Houses and Estates at the National University of Ireland, Maynooth. Will the signs of a change in the attitude of the government, and more widely, be sustained?

If anyone doubts the value of such efforts, let them visit Derrymore and other National Trust properties in Northern Ireland. When I first sought it out in 1980, there was evidence of the repeated bomb attacks and a sense of menace in the surrounding countryside. In 1985 the original donor, John S.W. Richardson, bequeathed a further 70 acres to the National Trust; and with the coming of peace the walks around the estate are now much used and enjoyed. Florence Court has been revived, thanks largely to Nancy, Countess of Enniskillen. The Crown Liquor Saloon in Belfast – acquired by the Trust in 1978 – has survived the persistent bombing of the Europa Hotel opposite. Perhaps a celebratory glass can be raised after all.

15

THE GROCER

Simon Sainsbury and the Monument Trust

OST OF THE GREAT NINETEENTH-CENTURY philanthropists wanted their generosity to be acknowledged. Concert halls, university buildings, hospitals, and museums were frequently named after them. The reluctance of the Sainsbury family to parade their generosity is in marked contrast, and can be traced back to the founder of the grocery firm, John James Sainsbury (1844–1928). Another family trait is an active involvement in the visual arts, and perhaps that owes something to John Sainsbury (1808–1863), who was an ornament- and picture-frame maker.

The naming of the Sainsbury Wing of the National Gallery in London was, therefore, out of character. But by 1991, when it was completed, Simon Sainsbury – who, with his brothers John and Timothy, largely masterminded and funded the extension – had bowed to the inevitable, and no longer attempted to conceal his identity behind the Monument Trust, the public vehicle that he had created for his generosity. On his death in 2006, the scale of his contribution to both the National Gallery and Tate became evident, with a bequest of paintings which transformed both galleries' holdings, including pictures by Balthus, Bonnard, Degas, Gauguin and Monet.

The paintings destined for Tate included a Lucian Freud, *Boy Smoking*, of disturbing intensity; Francis Bacon's *Study for a Portrait* of 1952; an early Gainsborough double-portrait of *Mr and Mrs Carter*; and a Balthus, *Still Life with a Figure*, of a girl contemplating a loaf of bread pierced by a kitchen knife, in which nothing is as straightforward as it seems. Pierre Bonnard's *Nude in the Bath* of 1925 is one of the artist's most intimate and beautiful paintings. The same is true of *After the Bath* by Edgar Degas, which was left to the National Gallery, with a collection which raised the status of its early-twentieth-century French collections at a stroke. Monet was so attached to his *Water-Lilies, Setting Sun*, painted in about 1907, that he could not bring himself to part with it until 1923, and even begged to be allowed to keep it for a little longer, while he was recovering from a cataract operation.

Simon Sainsbury was the great-grandson of the founder of the grocery empire. His brother, Sir Timothy, became Conservative Trade Minister, and was a major benefactor through his Headley Trust of 2 Willow Road in Hampstead, which was designed by the Modernist architect Ernö Goldfinger in 1938, and acquired by the National Trust in 1993. Another brother, John, Lord Sainsbury of Candover, set up the Linbury Trust, which supports the

2 Willow Road, Hampstead, in London, built as his own home by the Modernist architect Ernö Goldfinger in 1938, and acquired by the National Trust in 1994, partly with the assistance of Sir Timothy Sainsbury's Headley Trust.

performing arts. The brothers together directed the huge expansion of Sainsburys in the 1970s, and then took the decision to float the company on the Stock Exchange. Simon had trained as an accountant, and as a director assumed responsibility for finance and personnel, managing the change from family business to public company with astonishing success.

For many years Simon had been an enthusiastic collector, and a generous benefactor of museums and the National Trust. Thanks to the flotation of the family firm, his Monument Trust now had the funds for generosity on a munificent scale. His early life had equipped him to direct his interventions with rare discernment. At Eton Simon was remembered as a firm disciplinarian (throughout his life he disciplined himself rigorously), as an assured president of Pop, the Eton society, and for scoring the winning runs in the fiercely contested Eton and Harrow cricket match of 1947 at Lord's. Having experienced as a schoolboy what it was like to have the star part, he changed roles. Thereafter Simon Sainsbury was the most discreet of anonymous benefactors.

When his gifts to the nation first went on public exhibition, the former director of the National Gallery, Neil MacGregor, wrote about Simon as a collector-patron.[1] He revealed how at moments relationships between the architect of the new wing at the National Gallery, Robert Venturi, and the client – a collective of trustees, the director and curators, and the three Sainsbury brothers – became fraught. Whenever breakdown threatened, it was Simon who found a way forward that was acceptable to all involved. On one of his plans Venturi scribbled a note for future architectural historians: 'Thank God for Simon.'[2]

During the twenty years that Simon Sainsbury was chairman of the trustees of the Wallace Collection, from 1977 to 1997, the museum was transformed. In his dealings with the director, Rosalind Savill, he was rarely quiescent. Her recruitment of a senior curator was questioned; he was adamant that the franchising of the restaurant should not be dealt with by an eminent – and expensive – firm of accountants; and when she proposed in 1992 that the courtyard should be glazed over to create a public space for meeting and eating, his response was 'over my dead body'.[3] His scepticism could be intimidating.

The outcomes, however, are revealing. Over a period of more than ten years the Monument Trust and the Wolfson Foundation provided for the re-planning, re-hanging and redecoration of one major room after another. Simon himself went through all the figures for the catering franchise, with far more attention to detail and specialist knowledge than any accountancy firm could muster. With the glazing of the courtyard, he allowed himself to be persuaded, and then paid for a trusted architect, Rick Mather, to produce a feasibility study. When the executed scheme was found to have serious acoustic failings, he commissioned Ove Arup's engineers to devise a solution which largely resolved the difficulties without compromising the architecture.

Simon's association with the National Trust became increasingly significant after he took the lease of The Monument in 1965. This Gothick eyecatcher, on the edge of Petworth Park in West Sussex, was picturesque but dilapidated. For its repair, Simon turned to Philip Jebb, an architect admired by the staff of the National Trust for his sensitivity and understatement. The Monument gave Simon an apprenticeship in the management of architectural and decorative projects. Working with Jebb was instructive, and the results were restrained and elegant. Simon also fell under the spell of Petworth House itself: the building, its unsurpassed collections, and the paintings by J.M.W. Turner of its 'Capability' Brown park.

Petworth meant more than frequent exposure to a great composite work of art, although that was formative. Simon became increasingly responsive to the context of furniture and

The Carved Room at Petworth House, West Sussex. The extensive conservation of Grinling Gibbons' carvings and the re-hanging of Turner's four landscapes below the ancestral portraits, as the 3rd Earl of Egremont had first displayed them in the 1820s and 1830s, was paid for by Simon Sainsbury.

The Grand Staircase at Petworth House, with Louis Laguerre's mural *The Triumph of the Duchess of Somerset* and a bronze copy of the Roman statue *Silenus Nursing the Infant Bacchus*.

Thomas Phillips, *George, 3rd Earl of Egremont (1751–1837)*, Turner's great patron, painted posthumously, amid his collections of pictures and statuary in the North Gallery at Petworth.

pictures, and fascinated by the historical associations and connections which can make a great country house so rewarding visually. His visits there brought him into contact with the Wyndham family and with the National Trust's staff. In 1972 Max Wyndham succeeded his father as 2nd Lord Egremont and 7th Lord Leconfield. He had previously shared a flat in London with Gervase Jackson-Stops, a friend from his Oxford University days who had become the Trust's Architectural Historian, and had written articles on Petworth House for *Country Life* in 1973 and 1975. The Trust's Furniture Adviser, Martin Drury, acted as Historic Buildings Representative with responsibility for Petworth; and Bobby St John Gore, the Trust's Historic Buildings Secretary since 1973, was an authority on its pictures. Petworth was once again a meeting-place for those dedicated to the arts, as it had been when George, 3rd Earl of Egremont, Turner's patron, entertained artists there in the early decades of the nineteenth century. What cemented these ties was not the indulgence of shared tastes, but a threat to Petworth which could have damaged it irrevocably.

When Petworth House was rebuilt by Charles, 6th Duke of Somerset, between 1688 and 1702, he chose not to relocate but instead retained much of the fabric of the earlier Percy house of his wife's ancestors behind a new and magnificent west façade, which looks out over expansive parkland. As a result the house turns its back on the town of Petworth, but distances itself from it by only 50 yards. By the 1970s the town was clamouring for a bypass. The proposed route favoured by the National Trust would have been to the east of the town, running through an unspoilt river valley much used by the town's residents. Unsurprisingly this met with fierce public opposition. At the time access to Petworth House and Park was restricted. John Wyndham, who had succeeded to the estates in 1952 (and was created 1st Lord Egremont in 1963), was private secretary to Harold Macmillan, and when not working in London would often accompany the Prime Minister on official visits abroad. One consequence of his demanding position was that he had little time to cultivate good relations with the townspeople of Petworth. Nor at that time did the National Trust's regional staff include anyone with responsibility for public relations. The result was that most local people were determined to protect the countryside east of the town, even if that meant sacrificing Petworth Park.

The extent to which the National Trust had lost the initiative became clear in 1976 when the West Sussex County Council published its preferred route. A new road was proposed that would pass through the Pleasure Ground and would then enter a tunnel immediately to the west of the house, before emerging into a cutting through the park to the south. The scheme would be far more damaging to Petworth House than the Plymouth bypass was to Saltram in Devon. There the National Trust had resisted the proposed road in 1968, had appealed to Parliament on the grounds that the land required was held inalienably, and had lost. At

Petworth the County Council and an articulate majority of local people were ranged against it. The Trust's committee members and regional staff realised that the relationship between the house and the landscape that had inspired several of Turner's greatest pictures would be wrecked forever. But at the public meeting called to discuss the issues the Trust's representatives were hesitant and unconvincing. The mood became increasingly antagonistic.

For Simon Sainsbury the lease of the Monument was to give him privacy and an escape from confrontation. Petworth Park also meant a great deal to him: he had paid for extensive replanting in 1966 and 1967 to perpetuate the 'Capability' Brown landscape. The normally reserved and scrupulously polite Simon now changed mode. He spoke with eloquence and passion, in what his friends would later describe as 'Simon's bypass voice'. 'Taking the road through the park at Petworth was,' he said, 'like slashing a painting in the National Gallery.'[4]

The National Trust found another advocate in the artist and designer David Gentleman, who produced a series of posters, in which giant tyre-tracks and road markings cut across the Elysian landscape painted by Turner.[5] Aware that emotion alone would not win a public enquiry, Simon paid for Professor Colin Buchanan, the most respected planner of his generation, to produce an independent report, demonstrating that there were viable alternatives. What today seems unthinkable was only narrowly averted.

Simon saw advantages in being a tenant of the National Trust. He could enrich a building without aggrandising himself. This he did when, in 1974, he moved to a sleeping-beauty of a house, Woolbeding, in Sussex, where again Philip Jebb advised on repairs and remodelling, and where he created an exceptionally beautiful garden. For a brief period Simon had served on the Trust's Properties Committee, but he was never really a committee man, and the tenancy of Woolbeding gave him the excuse to withdraw on the grounds of a potential conflict of interest. Instead, he acted increasingly as an *éminence grise*, who could be turned to in moments of need. When he was asked whether he might like to come and see Canons Ashby in Northamptonshire, or Uppark in Sussex, he knew it was a coded cry for help. In 1985 the future of Belton in Lincolnshire was in doubt, prompting Martin Drury to visit Simon at Woolbeding, to ask whether he might contribute to the purchase of the contents. His response was to set up a special fund for use in a crisis. He made over shares to what was called the Monument '85 Fund, the income of which was to be available to acquire works of art associated with the Trust's properties. Although the National Trust was responsible for administering the Monument '85 Fund, it was never to be used without Simon's consent. He would question the Trust's curatorial staff about the provenance of a picture or the condition of an item of furniture, would test the conviction of those presenting the case, and once satisfied would share in the enjoyment of the chase.

Other gifts continued to be in the name of the Monument Trust. He wanted none of the trappings and distractions of celebrity philanthropy and his name was never allowed to appear on appeal notepaper, because he argued that his wealth might act as a disincentive to other donors. He could do more, on his own terms and to his own priorities, if his generosity was an exercise in stealth.

At Canons Ashby Simon's involvement was so discreet as to be conspiratorial.[6] The sale of the contents of this decayed and forlorn Northamptonshire house took place in 1980 before the gift of the property to the National Trust had been completed. There was an understand-

[below right] An embroidered, walnut chair of 1714, in the Tapestry Room at Canons Ashby, Northamptonshire. Much of the furniture of the house was purchased anonymously by Simon Sainsbury, prior to the National Trust's successful acquisition of the house, so that it could remain *in situ*.

ing that Simon would buy the furniture, but if the complex negotiations to secure the house and garden failed or if grants for repair were not forthcoming, he would be free to resell or retain them as he chose. That never proved necessary. With grants from the National Heritage Memorial Fund, the Department of the Environment and the Victoria and Albert Museum, assistance from the Landmark Trust, and a public appeal which raised £100,000, the whole property was secured.

Before the National Trust became accustomed to turning to Simon for help, it would probably have regarded the sale from Powis Castle of Bernardo Bellotto's *View of Verona from the Ponte Nuovo* as a lost cause. Certainly ten years earlier it might have left the castle forever with scarcely a murmur. But by 1981, when the Herbert family offered it for sale, the National Heritage Memorial Fund was prepared to make a substantial grant, with Simon Sainsbury making a major contribution.

Simon acquired furniture for Uppark in West Sussex, and Claydon House in Buckinghamshire. The redecoration of the Bath Assembly Rooms was made possible because of his generosity; as was the conservation and re-hanging of the Carved Room at Petworth. He supported the Trust's efforts to prevent the depletion of the collections at Chirk Castle in Wales, which were put up for sale in 2004. The restoration of the buildings at Stowe Landscape Gardens – like Canons Ashby, a project initiated by Gervase Jackson-Stops – received his enthusiastic help. Arts education also engaged him and he funded Attingham Summer School scholarships over many years.

At the same time, Simon was gradually, painstakingly building up his own collections of paintings, furniture, ceramics and carpets. As well as buying antiquities, he patronised living artists, including Francis Bacon, John Craxton, Lucian Freud and Victor Pasmore. The first

Bernardo Bellotto, *View of Verona from the Ponte Nuovo*, bought by the National Heritage Memorial Fund in 1981, with a major contribution from Simon Sainsbury, to ensure it stayed at Powis Castle in Wales.

The Ballroom at the Bath Assembly Rooms, redecorated as a result of Simon Sainsbury's generosity in the 1990s.

Bacon to hang on his walls was loaned to him by his uncle, Robert Sainsbury, who with his wife Lisa established the Sainsbury Centre for the Visual Arts at the University of East Anglia. Simon's own Bacon, *Study for a Portrait* of 1952, one of a series of screaming heads inspired by Velázquez's *Portrait of Pope Innocent X*, in the Galleria Doria Pamphilj in Rome, was bought in 1995. The work of Lucian Freud particularly fascinated him, and he owned outstanding examples from all stages of the artist's life. Freud's portrait of Simon, *Red-Haired Man with Glasses*, was painted in 1987–88, and called for lengthy sittings during which artist and patron talked about horse-racing as much as painting.[7] The portrait is psychologically revealing, but shows Simon looking crumpled, his features immediately identifiable, but perhaps coarsened by the sheer physicality of the painting. Freud looks beyond the fastidiousness with which, even at his most informal, Simon usually presented himself.

It was only when the National Trust tried to give more overt acknowledgement to his generosity and the significance of his gifts that Simon was gently discouraging. It was known that he had declined honours and refused to be included in *Who's Who*. When I was Historic Properties Director, there was a plan to arrange a visit to Sudbury Hall in Derbyshire. An eighteenth-century gilt mirror, sold from the house years before, had reappeared in the sale-rooms and with Simon's help was to return home. A picnic was planned, at which Simon would be presented with the Octavia Hill Medal for exceptional services to the National Trust. Perhaps Simon sensed what was afoot. The picnic and presentation never happened; but the mirror is now safely back at Sudbury.

Since Simon's death in 2006 his partner of 40 years, Stewart Grimshaw, and his fellow trustees continue to ensure that the Monument Trust is used as was intended. It did so spectacularly in 2007 with the rescue of the Dumfries House estate, near Cumnock in Ayrshire, to the south of Glasgow. The house was designed by Robert, James and John Adam in 1754, just as they were consolidating the family's reputation – initially shaped by their father, William Adam – as Scotland's leading architects. The Scottish credentials of Dumfries House were enhanced when furniture was supplied by its leading cabinet-makers, Francis Brodie, William Mathie and Alexander Peter. Much of the rest of the furniture is the work of the young Thomas Chippendale.

The owner, John, 7th Marquess of Bute, wanted to be free of the costs of maintaining Dumfries House and intended to put the proceeds of the sale into the maintenance of his spectacular Victorian Gothic house, Mount Stewart, on the Isle of Bute. His preference was for a private treaty sale to the National Trust for Scotland. The negotiations dragged on for two years and then broke down completely. Both parties agree that the decisive factor was failure to agree what constituted 'fixtures': that is, items which could not legally be removed from a listed building and were therefore unsaleable except as part of the fabric of the house, so making them virtually valueless.

There was a long list of items which might fall into this category, ranging from obelisks in the forecourt to lanterns, fire-grates, hall chairs, pier tables, Chippendale bookcases, carpets, and paintings in carved frames which were part of the architectural decoration of the main rooms. Because the issue was so contentious, and the value of the items so considerable once removed, the National Trust for Scotland commissioned a report from the architectural historian, John Martin Robinson, known as 'Mentmore' by his friends for his strident protests at the break-up in 1977 of the collections at the great Paxton house of that name in Buckinghamshire. Robinson's report was uncompromising. He put the disputed items into three categories: (i) clear-cut cases for 'fixture' status; (ii) intermediate; and (iii) little precedent but which, in the unique circumstances of Dumfries House, should be considered as possible fixtures. The majority he put into the first category.

As a starting point for discussion the report might have been reasonable, but it was not interpreted in that way. Two crucial factors seem to have been overlooked. One was that the legislation covering fixtures in a Scottish category A-listed building made the planning department of the local authority responsible for enforcement. In the case of Dumfries House, the local council showed little appetite for confrontation. The other was that Lord Bute was under no obligation to sell to the National Trust for Scotland if his advisers – in this case Christie's – told him to hold his ground over the disputed prices. When the National Trust for Scotland appeared to be uncompromising, Lord Bute lost patience. The sale was fixed for July 2007.

Securing funding on the scale required by the National Trust for Scotland – the cost would have been over £40 million – would only have been possible if driven by single-minded conviction that purchase by a conservation body was the only satisfactory outcome. Perhaps the Trust's heart was never really in it. The charity was facing major financial problems and the Chief Executive was about to leave. Rescuing Dumfries House seemed a lost cause, given that it was a matter of weeks between the breakdown of negotiations and the date fixed for the sales.

In May a seminar was called by the Prince of Wales – who in Scotland uses the title the Duke of Rothesay – at Holyrood Palace, to discuss the future of conservation in Scotland. Representatives from most of the public and private bodies involved were present. The subject of Dumfries House inevitably came up. The Duke was dismayed to learn that the only hope for the house was a last-minute effort by Marcus Binney, of SAVE Britain's Heritage, to piece together funding for purchase, with the idea that the house and estate could then pass to a specially formed trust.

In the space of four weeks, Binney persuaded the National Heritage Memorial Fund to contribute £7 million; Historic Scotland reversed an earlier decision and, with the support of the new First Minister, Alex Salmond, £5 million was approved by the Scottish Executive; and there were generous contributions from the Garfield Weston Foundation, Sir Siegmund Warburg's Voluntary Settlement and the Dunard Fund. But there was still a chasm to bridge if the £45 million was to be found. That gap was met by a loan of £20 million from the Prince

Thomas Chippendale's mahogany bed, designed in 1759 for William, 5th Earl of Dumfries. In 2007 Simon Sainsbury's Monument Trust helped a consortium led by HRH The Prince of Wales, Duke of Rothesay, to preserve Dumfries House in Scotland.

of Wales's Charities Foundation, on the basis that an outlying area of the estate would be developed, so providing a model for regeneration in a very deprived area of Scotland. The other main contributor was the Monument Trust, which had originally offered £4 million, and then increased the figure to £9 million as the deadline approached. The general public also played a part. The actual purchaser was the Art Fund, acting as a vehicle for all the other contributors, and providing its largest-ever grant of £2.5 million. And £1,250 was raised in street collections from the residents of Cumnock, one of the poorest communities in Scotland.

Quite properly with a rescue on this scale, there are many people whose contribution could be regarded as crucial. The potential for redeveloping remoter parts of the estate was first spotted by Kit Martin of the Prince's Regeneration Trust. The case for preservation was put with great eloquence in Scotland by James Knox of *The Art Newspaper*. As many others will feel their contribution was indispensable, perhaps I should reveal my own role. Repeatedly during the last week in May, Marcus Binney tried to contact me for advice on how to approach the National Heritage Memorial Fund, and on how to deal with various claims on the assets if the project failed. During those crucial few days, I was walking on the remoter hills of northern Scotland, was out of all telephone contact, and so was completely useless. Eventually communication was resumed, and on 26 June Binney rang me to say, 'Our offer has been accepted. The removal vans have been turned back on the motorway between Glasgow and London.' The use of the Monument Trust was exactly as Simon Sainsbury would have wished.

When planning his bequest of pictures to the National Gallery and Tate, Simon asked the two directors not to place a financial value on the gift. Predictably, at the time the bequest was announced, the press persistently asked what the paintings were worth. Thoughtlessly, and to the dismay of Stewart Grimshaw, a figure was mentioned and widely reported. For Simon Sainsbury much of the attraction of giving to the National Gallery, Tate, the Wallace Collection and the two National Trusts was that works of art of pre-eminent importance were removed forever from the market place. What was supremely valuable became valueless.

16

THE SHELLFISH MERCHANT

Cyril Southerland and the Isabel Deborah

IN OCTOBER 1996 I RECEIVED one of those letters that arouses curiosity precisely because it says so little. It was from John Snelling, proprietor of a boatyard at Brancaster Staithe on the north Norfolk coast, between King's Lynn and Wells-next-the-Sea. He asked, without explanation, if he and Cyril Southerland could come to see me in my office at Blickling. Usually any controversial issues at Brancaster would be dealt with over the telephone, or when the Managing Agent visited the National Trust's properties there, which included Scolt Head Island, 2150 acres of beach, and four and a half miles of tidal foreshore, sand dunes, marsh and saltings.

Cyril I knew as a Brancaster fisherman and shellfish merchant, dealing in whelks, mussels and oysters, all of which were once plentiful along that stretch of coast. His standing locally was already high before he became involved in the saga of the Royal West Norfolk Golf Club sea wall; and he was one of the few to emerge from that particular battle with praise from all sides.

The golf course at Brancaster occupies the dunes to the north of the village. On one side are the beach and the North Sea, and on the other a great expanse of salt-marsh, bought by the National Trust in 1967, shortly after the launch of its Enterprise Neptune coastal campaign. To the north-east is Scolt Head Island, which at low tide is separated from the beach by a narrow but dangerous channel, and which at high tide seems far out to sea. Much of the beauty of the coastline lies in the ever-changing sand dunes, accreting in some places but disappearing in others at an alarming rate, whenever wind and tide combine to create a storm surge. On one of these rapidly eroding stretches stands the clubhouse. Entirely understandably, members of the golf club were reluctant to see their building engulfed by the sea.

Over gin-and-tonics at the club bar, it must have all seemed very simple. Many of the members were and are extremely well-heeled, and would contribute generously to an appeal to construct new sea defences along the edge of the course and around the clubhouse. A well-disposed engineer drew up a scheme, proposing that large quantities of gravel, chalk and flint from a nearby quarry should be dumped on the beach, on the stretch in front of the clubhouse; and in 1995 it was duly presented to the parish council. Maroons bursting out at sea could not have produced a more energetic and united response.

The fishing villages of the north Norfolk coast may have lost much of their traditional

Cyril Southerland, a fisherman and shellfish merchant from Brancaster in Norfolk, who donated his motor fishing vessel, *Isabel Deborah*, to the National Trust in 1997.

livelihood, but they have kept their capacity for independent thinking and, if provoked, belligerence. Much of the coast also has the protection of most of the national and international conservation designations, from Area of Outstanding Natural Beauty and Heritage Coast, to Special Area of Conservation and Site of Special Scientific Interest. The Government agency responsible for ensuring that these labels meant something was the Nature Conservancy Council, later to become English Nature. Great stretches have also gradually been acquired by different conservation charities, including the National Trust, the Norfolk Naturalists' Trust (now the Norfolk Wildlife Trust), the Royal Society for the Protection of Birds, and the Norfolk Ornithologists' Association.

At Brancaster the issue of ownership is nicely complicated by the fact that, although much of the foreshore is owned by the National Trust, it is common land – indeed, there are large areas of submarine commons – jealously guarded by the Scolt Head and District Common Rightholders' Association, whose chairman, Brian Everitt, had a reputation for unusual zeal and vigour. Those promoting the golf club scheme had unwittingly united all these bodies in fierce opposition to a scheme that might have bought a few years' protection to the clubhouse, but which had scant regard for the natural beauty and importance of this stretch of coast. The villagers of Brancaster did not take kindly to the idea that the sandy beach which had long been enjoyed by locals and visitors should be covered with flints and gravel, which could be washed round into the harbour and the mussel lays.

What might have seemed to be a squabble between petty local interests, in fact touched on issues relating to a centuries-old conflict between those exercising long-established common rights and those who see common land as a potential asset to be exploited for private gain. Of course that was not how the members of the golf club perceived matters – they simply wanted to be able to go on playing golf at Brancaster – but their behaviour was calculated to arouse passions and confrontation.

[above] Scolt Head Island, off the north Norfolk coast, with Brancaster Harbour on the right and the North Sea on the left. The island was presented to the National Trust as a nature reserve in 1923 by the Norfolk and Norwich Naturalists' Society.

[right] Henry Blogg (1876–1954), coxswain of the Royal National Lifeboat Institution's Cromer Lifeboat in Norfolk, who launched his vessel 387 times, helped to save 873 lives, and was awarded the George Cross, the British Empire Medal, and seven RNLI medals for gallantry.

The need to protect common land was a cause which brought the founders of the National Trust together. As early as 1867 Robert Hunter had written:

> Is he [the owner of 'wastes'] entitled to shut them [the public] out even for the purpose of cultivation or improvement, when it is not clear that the results attained will be on the whole beneficial to the nation? On the highest principles, evidently not, for no private person is morally justified in self-aggrandisement at the expense of large numbers of his fellow creatures.[1]

Canon Hardwicke Rawnsley was a champion of the protection of public rights of way in the Lake District, and Octavia Hill devoted much of her life to securing open spaces in the countryside and towns, for public enjoyment. All three founders were constantly resisting appropriation of land by the wealthy.

Both the common rights-holders and the fishermen at Brancaster have a strong sense of mutual dependence and of the need to share resources. Few on the north Norfolk coast would dispute that the man who represents its values best is not Coke of Holkham, Humphry Repton, or one of the great banking dynasties of Barclays and Gurneys. Their hero is Henry Blogg (1876–1954), the coxswain of the

Cromer Lifeboat, awarded the George Cross, the British Empire medal, three RNLI Gold Medals and four RNLI Silver Medals for gallantry. His qualities were shown in innumerable rescues, sometimes in the most perilous of circumstances, and his generosity of spirit is legendary. Time and again Blogg put the needs of others before his own safety.

Other allegiances played a part. Since 1923, when Scolt Head Island was presented to the National Trust, generations of students had been brought to study the ecology of the dunes by Professor Alfred Steers, of the Department of Geography at Cambridge University, and then by Dr David Stoddart. An advisory committee, for many years chaired by Steers, assisted with the management of Scolt Head, dealing with issues such as predation by foxes and the invasion of the dunes by rapidly spreading *Rosa rugosa*. Something of the devotion of those serving on the Scolt Head committee can be gauged from Stoddart's letter of December 1992 to its secretary, John Morley, in which he apologised for failing to get to a meeting. He was at the time teaching in the Department of Geography at the University of California, Berkeley:

This is to report upon last week's total debacle. Which really began with you fixing the Scolt meeting on Thanksgiving Day, which here is even bigger than Christmas. Frequent-flier miles are blacked out before, during and after. However, I got the last opportunity on Monday to get myself to the east coast, and the first opportunity on Saturday to return from thence.

Well, there was a bit of enormously creative ticketing, at no small cost, to get me onwards. This was Washington Dulles to Newark, and then Virgin Atlantic to Gatwick. Trouble was that the flight to Newark was delayed two hours, and would have arrived after the Virgin left. Great panic. I actually got my suitcase off the Newark flight, and with microseconds to spare got myself onto a direct flight to Heathrow. At which point – with literally five minutes to go before take-off at the far end of the terminal – I found some clown had reloaded my suitcase to Newark, destined for Gatwick. We radioed the plane in flight and had the ground staff standing by at Newark, since fifteen minutes after the Newark flight arrived, a USAir took off for Heathrow. Well, I got to Heathrow (surcharge of $300), reported the missing bag, was advised to hang around, and an hour later the suitcase actually showed up – all my vests and underpants, etc. Then I got the bus to Cambridge. I got to the A11 turn-off to Norwich just after 11, and realised that by the time I got to Blickling you would all have buggered off to lunch. Coming back on Saturday I again had something creative – Gatwick to Baltimore, bus to DC, then to Washington National, flight to Dallas, onwards to Oakland. You won't believe it but the airport bus ex-Baltimore to DC burst into flames within 50 yards of departure and we all bailed out! I thought Christ Almighty, is anyone on my side? It took 29 hours door to door to get home, and the whole caper cost me $1200.

By the time I got back I was totally buggered. I had spent more time travelling than actually in England. And my dream of luncheon at the Jolly Sailors never materialised. My lady wife thinks I am out of my mind (but has done so for decades, of course).

Well, I have serious things to say about Scolt, which I would have declaimed had I been there. They will be for a subsequent letter. Sorry about all of this – I can only say one does one's best.[2]

There was more at stake over the future of the Brancaster dunes than a round of golf. The battle-lines were drawn. On the one side was a motley alliance of villagers, common rights-holders, academics and fishermen. On the other were the members of the golf club: moneyed, exclusive, confident of getting their own way, and with royal patronage. A public meeting held in Brancaster village school to discuss the issues rapidly turned acrimonious. At just the moment that tempers were frayed, the chairman asked if Cyril Southerland had any suggestions. He did. He proposed that it would be possible to slow the rate of erosion and buy a few more years for the clubhouse if sand could be trapped at the base of the dunes, to reduce the undercutting during winter surges. Instead of working against nature, he advocated working with the natural processes of the coast. Wooden posts should be driven into the beach at the edge of the dunes, in a zig-zag pattern, intended to break the impact of the waves. They would be stabilised with open-mesh netting, behind which sand would accumulate. A relatively short stretch could be constructed as a trial, and if it did not work, we could all think again.

Not the least attraction of the proposition was that it was based on local knowledge and well-tried practice. Not everyone was convinced. A member of the golf club's Sea Defence Committee asked if Mr Southerland (a fisherman all his life) 'had ever seen a storm?' But there was overwhelming support for a trial. In July 1996 a length of 200 metres was constructed. By the end of the winter a great ramp of sand had built up at the base of the dunes. Thereafter, a further stretch was added each year. By 2008 the scheme had been completely vindicated.

So it was more than just curiosity that made me anxious to respond to John and Cyril. The purpose of their visit was, they explained, to find out whether the Trust could prevent the destruction of *Isabel Deborah*, Cyril's boat. This motor fishing vessel had been built in 1949 by William Weatherhead and Sons of Cockenzie, East Lothian, at their yard in

The *Isabel Deborah*, Cyril Southerland's fishing boat, commissioned by his uncle, Cyril Loose, from William Weatherhead and Sons of Cockenzie, East Lothian, in 1949.

Cyril Loose (left) and his brother Ernie, aboard the *Isabel Deborah*, on which they worked together for many years.

Eyemouth, to a specification devised by Cyril Loose, a Brancaster fisherman and Cyril Southerland's uncle. The design is based on a Scottish ringnetter, but with a shallower draft to suit the fishing in and around Brancaster. After nearly half a century of hard and steady use, the hull of oak and pine was still sound. The mizzen sail originally positioned behind the wheelhouse was no longer usable, but otherwise the boat was very little altered. She had been named after Cyril Southerland's aunt.

The decision to commission the vessel from a Scottish yard, even though there were established boat-builders in King's Lynn and Sheringham, was not just because of the reputation of their shipwrights. The fishermen of north Norfolk worked the length of the east coast, and most knew the Scottish ports well. Many of the girls who filleted and packed the enormous quantities of herrings that came into Great Yarmouth and Lowestoft were from Scotland. The various fishing communities of the east coast often had closer relations with each other than they did with towns and villages inland.

Cyril had kept his uncle's papers and log, explaining how the boat came to be commissioned. During the Second World War, Cyril Loose had served in the Royal Navy in coastal minesweepers, which had taken him to areas of the North Sea well away from the fishing-grounds he was familiar with. He concluded that there was great potential for whelk-fishing much further away from Brancaster, provided a really strongly constructed boat was used. The boats built in Norfolk were derived from crab boats of clinker (overlapping) board construction. The Scottish boats were carvel built (with flush planks) on a heavier oak frame.In April 1949 Cyril Loose, his brother Ernie and brother-in-law Fred Southerland took the train up the east coast, stopping first at Berwick-on-Tweed. The fishing boats there had a draught of at least four-foot-six, which was too deep for the shallow waters around Brancaster. They continued up to Eyemouth, ten miles to the north, where they looked at boats built by Weatherhead and Sons. One particular fishing boat caught their eye, but it was 60 feet long, with a correspondingly deep draught. Loose made enquiries and found himself introduced to the foreman of the yard. Bluntly he asked whether they could build a boat with the same lines as the one they had admired, but scaled down to a length of 35 feet, and with a draught of only three feet and six inches. At this the foreman threw his hat on the ground and replied, 'Now you've got me,' and then, after a pause, 'go and have a cup of tea, and I'll think about it.'

The quotation, dated 27 April 1949, arrived at Brancaster the day after their return. The dimensions of the boat were to be exactly as Cyril Loose had requested. The hull would cost £1,250, the mizzen sail and rigging £100, and the thirty-horsepower engine £390. Weather-heads did not ask for so much as a down-payment; and by October the boat was ready for collection.

Cyril Loose's log records the journey back to Brancaster, which provided ample sea-trials. They left Eyemouth on 15 October, in a fresh breeze and a nasty swell. The next day the weather was kinder, and they made good progress to Scarborough, on the Yorkshire coast. As they rounded Flamborough Head on the 17th the weather deteriorated, and at 5am they found themselves in a full-scale storm, with the boat 'tossing and jumping'. By 6.30am the weather had improved, they cleared the Humber estuary, and by midday were 'making grand progress.' At 3pm the boat was on its mooring at Brancaster.

After he had taken over the boat from his uncle, Cyril Southerland found himself, from time to time, caught far out at sea in bad weather. He remembers one particularly fierce westerly, at force ten, when larger boats might well have broached. The design of *Isabel Deborah* coped well with the erratic waves of the Norfolk coast and the Wash. The boat's stern was pointed and canoe-shaped, allowing a following sea to sweep down both sides without pushing her sideways. Although *Isabel Deborah*'s engine was not powerful enough to drive her ahead of a breaking wave, she remained stable and, in Cyril's words, 'kept plodding on'.

In 1996 changes in fishing and boat regulations had led Cyril to decide that he should decommission *Isabel Deborah*. In other circumstances she might have been thought suitable for an honourable retirement as a pleasure boat. However, the Ministry of Agriculture, Fisheries and Food (MAFF) attached strict conditions to their terms for decommissioning. In order to secure compensation, the scheme stipulated that fishing boats had to be made unusable, either by burning them or by sawing them in half. The idea of a Viking-style funeral pyre on the Brancaster marshes did not appeal.

There was one provision in the MAFF regulations that might give *Isabel Deborah* a reprieve. Boats of sufficient historic interest could be preserved, provided they were formally accessioned by a registered museum. The purpose of John and Cyril's deputation was to ask whether the National Trust would agree to accept this unusual museum exhibit as a gift.

The responsible answer to their request should have been a polite 'no'. Historical vessels are notoriously difficult and expensive to maintain, even if, like HMS *Victory* or the *Cutty Sark*, they are kept in a dry dock. On at least two occasions the National Trust had become involved with boat preservation, and the experiences had been salutary. The first had been a characteristically imaginative scheme of the Trust's Regional Director in Cornwall, Michael Trinick, who worked with the National Maritime Museum to restore the Tamar barge *Shamrock*, which had been built in Plymouth in 1899 and was acquired as a hulk in 1973. The work of restoration had revealed that almost all the boat's structural timbers were in an advanced state of decay and needed complete replacement. The search for authentic cleats, blocks, ropes and rigging had involved scouring almost every shipyard in the west country. As the costs of the project soared, so relations between the Museum and the Trust had become

increasingly strained. In spite of these tensions, *Shamrock* was re-floated in 1979, and now acts as the centrepiece of the quay at Cotehele, where the surrounding buildings have been restored and are open to the public.

Far more contentious was the decision to acquire and restore *Gondola*, a steam yacht first launched on Coniston Water in the Lake District in 1859. The National Trust's committees were persuaded, somewhat reluctantly, to take on this vessel because she was such an interesting survival of the early years of tourism in the Lakes, as well as being an exceptionally elegant and beautifully furnished craft. If the Trust was prepared to invest in eighteenth-century Adam sideboards, why not the upholstery of Victorian pleasure craft? Appalled at the mounting financial commitment involved, the Finance Committee were un-amused to be asked by the agent responsible for the project, Gordon Hall, whether they would like to consider establishing a 'sinking-fund'. Any subsequent proposals involving boats were viewed with deep suspicion.

If National Trust history was not on the side of *Isabel Deborah*, neither were the practicalities of acquisition. The MAFF conditions were clear that only a museum registered as such by the Museums and Galleries Commission would be acceptable. As it happened, the National Trust had recently signed up to the registration scheme, but because over a hundred historic houses were likely to qualify, the process of completing the bureaucratic requirements had been started in the northern regions, and had not reached East Anglia.

Any or all of these obstacles could have been used to justify declining the offer of *Isabel Deborah*. But there were other considerations to be weighed up. The boat not only had an interesting history: it seemed to speak for a whole way of life that was disappearing from the Norfolk coast, but which had had an important impact on the Trust's properties there.

The first 'Watcher' on Scolt Head Island, following its acquisition by the National Trust in 1923, was a distinguished naturalist and photographer, Miss Emma Turner, who acted as a voluntary warden. After two years in the post, she persuaded the local committee to employ a full-time paid warden, and Charles Chesney was appointed. He was a Brancaster fisher-

The Victorian steam-powered yacht *Gondola* on Coniston Water in Cumbria, first launched in 1859, and acquired and restored by the National Trust in 1980.

man, and was pleased to take the job when he saw the price of whelks drop from ten shillings to two shillings a bag during the 1920s. In 1950 he was succeeded as warden by his son, Bob Chesney, also a fisherman, whose knowledge of the island and its birds was shared with thousands of naturalists, young and old. When the National Trust needed a new warden for Blakeney Point in 1981, again it was a local fisherman, Joe Reed, who was appointed and who, like Chesney, proved to be an outstanding naturalist and a brilliant communicator.

Norfolk's fishing communities were not beholden to the owners of large estates in the way that most inland villages in Norfolk were; unless, like the Upchers of Sheringham, they had provided them with a lifeboat. Over the years, the National Trust found that its coastal properties were often best looked after by a warden whom local fishermen regarded as one of their own. An outsider telling them what to do, or not do, could be met with breathtaking hostility.

One particular meeting, some twenty years ago, of the parish council of Morston – on the coast between Brancaster and Blakeney – comes to mind. The issue being debated was whether the National Trust, as owner of 589 acres of the Morston Marshes, should introduce a parking charge for cars left on its property near the creek. The intention was that the income should be shared between the Trust and the village, to make the proposal more acceptable. It would probably have been carried with little fuss, had its introduction not been advocated at considerable length by a councillor from neighbouring Blakeney. The longer she spoke, the more the hackles of the Morston members rose. They did eventually agree to the charge, but the Blakeney councillor's departure was greeted by the chairman with audible expletives so coarse as to be unrepeatable.

On the 31 March 2006 the minutes of the Blakeney Harbour Boatmen's Association reported the death of Major Andrew Athill, who had been president and was described, with rare understatement, as a 'larger than life character'. After a colourful army career, the Major had retired to Morston, where he grew oysters and ran a small sailing school, using a ragged flotilla of boats kept in the creek. He was known locally as 'Clanger', both because of his tendency to sound off like a ship's bell and because what he said might well prove to be a clanger. The Major was for many years the National Trust's honorary warden for the Morston

Marshes, where he kept an eye on everything, from over-wintering wildfowl to boats that might be in trouble out in Blakeney Pit. Like many others I have reason to be grateful to him, for coming to my rescue on a cold November evening after a capsize.

Major Athill's services to the National Trust included the organisation and umpiring of the annual Peter Grimes Challenge Cup, named after George Crabbe's dark and doomed Suffolk fisherman. Six sailing dinghies usually competed, three from Head Office – with the Trust's Director-General, Martin Drury, serving as Admiral one year – and three drawn from the staff of the East Anglia Region, on a date in October as close as possible to Trafalgar Day. In part it was a celebration of the heroic rector's son from Burnham Thorpe, just inland from Brancaster. Major Athill would present the (diminutive) cup at a fish-pie supper, giving pleasure to the home team by invariably referring not to Head Office, but to 'the London branch.'

How 'the London branch' and its committees would respond to the proposed acquisition of *Isabel Deborah* was far from certain. At least there was a chance that the Regional Committee for East Anglia might be sympathetic, given the significance of the Trust's relationship with some of the fishing communities. With the help of John Snelling and Cyril Southerland, a more or less plausible proposal was put together. *Isabel Deborah* would be accessioned by one of the National Trust's Northumberland properties (the registering as museums had reached that far), and then loaned back to Norfolk. An idea which particularly appealed was that the boat should be adopted by Cragside, the late-nineteenth-century house built by Richard Norman Shaw for the industrialist and arms-manufacturer, Sir William Armstrong, whose company transformed mid-nineteenth-century Newcastle, supplied ships for Queen Victoria's navy and developed the breech-loading guns that controlled the British Empire. The snag with Cragside was that it was miles inland and *Isabel Deborah* was hardly a battleship. A better suggestion was that she should be accepted by Lindisfarne Castle, perched on a rock in the North Sea at the end of a tide-washed causeway.

Sunset over the salt-marshes at Brancaster Staithe in Norfolk.

Having satisfied the MAFF regulations, the boat needed to be given a new role and a new life. As it happened, the timing of Cyril's intended gift could scarcely have been better. The National Trust had just secured funding, including a grant from the Millennium Commission, to set up an Activity Centre at Brancaster Staithe. The centre was to be in Dial House, once the home of the Chesney family, and bought from the Nature Conservancy Council in 1984, with bequests from Miss H.S.E. Smith and Mr Cyril E. Little, in memory of his wife, Mrs Dorothy Little. Although it had previously provided accommodation and laboratories for students, the building was to be re-equipped to cater for school and university parties, whether engaged in scholarly research or visiting the Norfolk coast for sailing and kayak lessons. *Isabel Deborah* could be used to take parties out to the National Nature Reserve at Scolt Head Island, and to explore the area around Brancaster harbour.

None of this would cut much ice with the region's Finance Committee unless it could be shown that the boat would not be a drain on central funds. John Snelling calculated that engine-servicing, painting and keel repairs would cost £1,650 a year. He then arranged for an article about *Isabel Deborah* to appear in the Brancaster parish magazine, which explained what was proposed and continued:

> The National Trust are not able to commit themselves to the full expense of the vessel's upkeep and would therefore like to see a local committee formed to administer the preservation project, raise funds or help in repairs and maintenance. If anyone considers this a worthy project and would like to be involved, please contact Cyril Southerland or John Snelling.

Octavia Hill, one of the three founders of the National Trust in 1895, used to say that 'gifts of time' were as important as gifts of money, and *Isabel Deborah* attracted both, with the Norfolk Centre of National Trust members contributing particularly generously.

On 31 May 2000 Richard Seppings, the Chairman of the National Trust *Isabel Deborah* Committee, was able formally to present the boat to the Brancaster Millennium Activity Centre. In fact she had been given to the Trust by Cyril Southerland three years earlier, but had since been re-equipped, repainted and fully licensed for her new role. There were trips out into the harbour for those attending the presentation.

That might be the moment on which to conclude the saga of *Isabel Deborah*. When Samuel Smiles wrote his great Victorian classic *Self-Help*, he was careful to end his accounts of humble endeavour at the moment of heroic achievement, ignoring the fact that many of his subjects slipped back into poverty. In the case of *Isabel Deborah*, she served several useful years, as intended, working out of Brancaster and providing an unusual and exciting experience for those staying at the Activity Centre. But the group maintaining her found that the costs of upkeep kept rising. She also proved to be too small to carry large parties, and this became a drawback. Reluctantly Cyril Southerland and the National Trust agreed that other ways of giving her a secure future should be explored. The upshot was that she made the journey back to Scotland, and joined the collection of boats being gathered together by the Scottish International Sailing Craft Association at Eyemouth. She had returned to the place where she was built, to be preserved permanently. The Brancaster solution may not have been a lasting one, but without a reprieve she might well have gone to that Viking funeral pyre.

17

THE AMBASSADORS

Lady Labouchere and Dudmaston;
Lord Bridges and Orford Ness

APPEARANCES CAN DECEIVE, in historic houses as in detective novels. Sometimes the deceit is little more than teasing: the gothic battlements on the gate lodge or the classical trophies in stucco in the great hall. But often there is more serious intent. At Kinloch Castle on the island of Rum the visitor is confronted by portraits of James VI and I, Charles II as Prince of Wales, and the laird himself, Sir George Bullough, full-length with kilt, sporran and shepherd's crook. It is too good to be true. Kinloch Castle, with its echoes of Balmoral, was built in 1897 with a fortune made from power-loom weaving in Lancashire. Sir George's grandfather, an inventor of spinning machinery, wore clogs all his life.

Often the reweaving of family history is a much more elaborate process. When in 1976 the National Trust found itself the owner of the Dunham Massey estate in Cheshire – the intended bequest from Roger, 10th and last Earl of Stamford had been known to the Chairman, but was otherwise a closely guarded secret – the initial assumption was that this was a largely early-eighteenth-century house, relatively complete and undisturbed. Gervase Jackson-Stops and I believed that what would be presented to the public was a Georgian sequence of rooms.

It was John Cornforth who sensed that its history, socially and decoratively, was a good deal more complicated. During the nineteenth century, two generations of the Grey family had been the subject of much-publicised scandals. In 1848 George, 7th Earl of Stamford married Elizabeth Billage, the daughter of the bootman at Trinity College, Cambridge; and then, two years after his first wife's death in 1854, Kitty Cocks, a captivating equestrienne from a London circus. His cousin and successor, Harry, 8th Earl of Stamford, had lived in South Africa with a black woman called Martha Solomon, and their illegitimate son was barred from inheriting the title. It therefore passed in 1890 to his nephew, William Grey, whose father was principal of St John's Theological College in Newfoundland, and who devoted his life to philanthropy. Cornforth's intuition proved correct: Dunham Massey had been recreated in the early twentieth century by the 9th Earl's wife, Penelope, Countess of Stamford, with advice from the London decorators, Percy Macquoid and Morant and Co, to look as though it had been untouched since the eighteenth century. The nineteenth-century history of the house had been expunged.

The Great Hall at Dunham Massey in Cheshire, a sixteenth-century moated house extensively remodelled and redecorated in the early eighteenth and twentieth centuries. It was bequeathed to the National Trust by Roger, 10th and last Earl of Stamford, in 1976.

Dudmaston, near Bridgnorth in Shropshire, is another house that is easy to misread. On the east side its plain red brick is glimpsed between the cedars and limes of a modest park, while the west front sits easily above grassy terraces which descend not to a lake, but to the 'Big Pool'. There is no forced grandeur about it. This is the house of a Shropshire squire, concerned with his woods, his game, his public service as a magistrate on the local bench, and the well-being of his tenantry. Nothing really prepares one for its interior.

The last squire to live at Dudmaston was Geoffrey Wolryche-Whitmore, who devoted his life to the estate and to forestry, serving as President of the Royal Forestry Society from 1944 to 1946. In 1952 he handed Dudmaston over to his niece, Rachel Labouchere (*née* Hamilton-Russell), on the understanding that on her death it would pass to the National Trust. Until the transformation of the house carried out in the 1960s by Sir George and Lady Labouchere, it would have been hard to sustain the case for Dudmaston meeting the Trust's criteria for acceptance, that it was of 'outstanding national importance'.

Dudmaston had never fully recovered from the excesses of Sir John Wolryche, who betted heavily on cock-fighting and horse-racing, and who drowned in 1723, in the early hours of the morning, while trying to cross the river Severn after the Chelmarsh races. When William Whitmore, a distant cousin, inherited the estate in 1775, he found the house empty, apart from 'an old pair of yellow breeches in a large antique oaken chest'.[1] The estate continued to be heavily mortgaged throughout the nineteenth century. Geoffrey Wolryche-Whitmore, who acquired Dudmaston from his father in 1921, was content to live in a house with little in the way of pictures and furniture of any real quality. Sir George and Lady Labouchere could therefore fill its rooms with their own collections, without displacing things which were historically important to the house. Their transformation of Dudmaston gave it an unexpected, international dimension.

Rachel Hamilton-Russell met George Labouchere in 1943. He had joined the diplomatic service in 1929. Having agreed to marry him, Rachel determined to join him in Sweden, where he was based from 1943 to 1946. On her first attempt to fly across the North Sea, the plane had to turn back because insufficient cloud-cover made it too vulnerable to enemy aircraft. She succeeded at the second attempt, and they were married in Sweden in 1943.

Sir George Labouchere had a long and distinguished career, with postings to China, Argentina, Austria and Hungary, before serving as the British Ambassador in Belgium from 1955 to 1960, and in Spain from 1960 to 1966. With suitably diplomatic skill he used these postings to buy works of art by artists of the country where he was resident, which were then displayed in the Embassy. Inspired by his experiences in the Far East, he collected antique and contemporary Chinese porcelain. For the Embassy in Brussels, he bought pictures by J. Milo in 1957 and René Guiette in 1959, both abstract painters. His purchases in Spain included work by Lucio Muñoz and the Catalan painter Antoni Tàpies. George handled the uneasy relationship with General Franco with considerable tact and an increasing mutual respect.[2] In fact his paintings by Tàpies – which are based on graffiti, with the appearance of

The late-seventeenth-century east front of Dudmaston in Shropshire, attributed to William and Francis Smith of Warwick, with a later attic storey added in 1826.

being abstract – have deeply felt, anti-government messages. Was he aware of how subversive they were?

Sir George bought the work of other early-twentieth-century painters and sculptors who he felt had an enduring place in European art: a small picture by Wassily Kandinsky, Sonia Delaunay's *Flamenco Singers* of 1916, and paintings by Jean Dubuffet, Max Ernst and Amedeo Modigliani. He also acquired sculpture by Henry Moore, Barbara Hepworth, Kenneth Armitage, and other English artists.

When Sir George retired in 1966, most of these works came to Dudmaston, where the old dining room and the adjoining room were transformed into galleries. His collecting was shaped by several considerations: there was its diplomatic value, his interest was genuine and well-informed, and in the 1960s contemporary art was, as he acknowledged, 'accessible financially'.[3] There was another factor. He did not have to compete with the outstanding collections Rachel had inherited from her Darby ancestors. She made no secret of the fact that she found incomprehensible much of the work that attracted him,[4] but both respected each other's area of specialist interest. It may also be that George felt the need to assert his own tastes. Although he was an ambassador, Rachel was the more forceful of the two. On one occasion, when on holiday, he returned from a street market with a rather flamboyant sunhat. Rachel took one look at it, and told him to take it back where it had come from.[5]

That episode may suggest someone who was bossy, even tiresome; but that could not be further from the truth. Rachel Labouchere's character was shaped by her Quaker ancestors and by the ideals of the Darby family of Coalbrookdale in Shropshire. Although not a member of the Society of Friends, she was drawn to aspects of the Quaker faith, which she found profoundly sympathetic.[6] Her grandmother, Alice Mary Wolryche-Whitmore, was a direct descendant of Abraham Darby II (1711–1763), who was largely responsible for the rapid expansion and prosperity of the Shropshire iron industry. Their Quaker beliefs provided the Darbys with a network of banking and industrial contacts in the Midlands, Bristol, East Anglia, and the United States. These religious and business associations were partly the result of the exclusion of Quakers from the universities of Oxford and Cambridge, from Parliament and the professions. Instead they became pioneers of industry, scientific research and modern banking.

Rachel's affinity with the Quaker world of the Darbys was influenced by her own education, or lack of it. She had wanted to go to Lady Margaret Hall, Oxford, but her schooling had not given her the necessary qualifications, and the idea of cramming for exams did not appeal. For someone of exceptional intelligence and historical imagination, this was a matter of lasting regret, and she may consequently have felt an intellectual outsider. The award of an honorary doctorate by Birmingham University, in acknowledgement of her books about the Darbys and her own role in the success of the Ironbridge Gorge Museum, made belated amends. She greatly admired the Darby women who played a vital role in the development of Coalbrookdale, largely running the business when their husbands were ill or died young. The diaries and journals of her forbears, Abiah Darby (1716–1793), Deborah Darby (1754–1810) and Adelaide Darby (1817–1899), fascinated her, partly because their Quaker connections led them to travel so widely in England, Wales, Ireland and the United States. She was to write books on all three.

In preparation for the Laboucheres' return to England in 1966, Dudmaston was given

Jan van Huysum, *Still Life of Fruit and Flowers*, 1742. The picture was inherited by Lady Labouchere from her cousin Muriel Cope Darby in 1935, accepted in lieu of inheritance tax in 1998 and allocated to Dudmaston, where it remains in the Library.

the ambassadorial treatment, with curtains and carpets supplied on the advice of the interior decorator Nina Campbell, then an assistant to John Fowler, and with furniture and pictures from the Darby collections. As Quakers, the Darbys did not collect figurative art, nor did they employ fashionable portrait painters to glorify their dynasty. But their scientific and botanical interests encouraged Francis Darby (1783–1850) to collect seventeenth- and eighteenth-century flower pieces by, among others, Jan van Huysum (1682–1749), Jan van Os (1744–1808), and Paul Theodorus van Brussel (1754–1795). Most of the pictures were Dutch, and appealed partly because the artists and their patrons were industrious and imbued

with the Protestant work ethic. These passed to Rachel on the death of her cousin Muriel Cope Darby in 1935, and so to the library and small dining room at Dudmaston.

Flower pieces are not to everyone's taste, and it would be easy to regard them as little more than superior decoration. To Rachel they meant much more than that. Almost all the flowers delineated with such skill were prized specimens, which would have been recognisable to the artist's Dutch patrons. The exotic variegated tulips, peonies and roses were collectors' items, and were sometimes even more valuable than the pictures recording their features so meticulously. Rachel treasured them for their scientific, historical and family interest, and was herself a dedicated botanical artist. Writing in 1980 of her collection of paintings and her love of flowers, she observed:

> In a life of travel it was the flowers by which a special place was often remembered, such as a glade in the forests of Sweden where 'Linnaea borealis' flowered with grace; or the lower slopes of the Purple Mountain near Nanking in China, down which showered in many thousands miniature red and white tulips ('Tulipa edulis'); or an upland in Castilla, a province of Spain, where the wild pink single paeony opened in the summer sun.[7]

When on leave from postings abroad, she attended the courses run at Flatford Mill in Suffolk by the Fields Study Council, where she was taught first by John Nash and then by Mary Grierson, the official botanical artist at Kew. The grand hostess of embassies would happily share a spartan dormitory with other students, and particularly enjoyed the expeditions to paint in the Suffolk garden of the artist and plantsman, Sir Cedric Morris, whose own work favoured plants with a strong formal quality, painted with a rich impasto.

Rachel's furniture was also of outstanding quality: Louis XV commodes, an English carpet woven with a Savonnerie design in about 1800, a *secrétaire à abattant* of the 1760s, amongst which were scattered some of George's twentieth-century drawings. Her Darby porcelain was also exquisite. The overall effect at Dudmaston was un-squirish, un-English, and visually most rewarding.

On George's retirement they both devoted themselves to Dudmaston, and engaged in relaxed, civilised discussions with the National Trust about the gift of the estate. Geoffrey Wolryche-Whitmore had been given to understand that the Trust would accept the house, probably with a view to it being occupied by a member of the family on a full repairing lease and with a minimum of public access. Rachel had other ideas. She wanted it to be seen and enjoyed by visitors, and was particularly keen that the garden – important for its historical associations with Thomas Shenstone's The Leasowes, one of the most influential eighteenth-century landscapes – should be restored and opened to the public. Her plans were supported by the Trust's Regional Director, Gerard Noel, and with characteristic diplomacy one of the paths in the garden was duly named 'Gerard's Walk'. When the Finance Committee reviewed his report on the future funding of the estate, its Chairman, Mark Norman, suspected him of collusion and accused him of being in love with Lady Labouchere.[8] The truth was that we all were.

There was good reason to be concerned about the finances of the property. Dudmaston was never likely to attract large numbers; the estate produced very little income; and Rachel was unable to provide a large endowment, because she felt she had other conservation obligations at Ironbridge. Noel was determined to steer Dudmaston into the hands of the National Trust, and was undaunted by the scepticism of its committees. It may have helped that the Regional Chairman, Gerald, 6th Earl of Bradford, had a family interest: the daughter of the 1st Earl had married William Wolryche-Whitmore in 1810, and the library at Dudmaston was reputedly modelled on the one at Weston Park. No less important was the ambassadorial skill and charm with which members of the Trust's committees were made welcome. Only rarely was her iron will revealed. Iron was, after all, what the Darbys brought to the Industrial Revolution.

Dudmaston became a National Trust property in 1978, and I spent much of the next two years helping the Laboucheres to arrange galleries of botanical drawings, modern pictures, and a display on the significance of the nineteenth-century pioneer of the computer, Charles Babbage, whose wife Georgiana was a Wolryche-Whitmore. The exhibits belonged to Rachel, and she knew their history and significance intimately. All I had to do was carry out her instructions to the letter, enjoy her and George's many kindnesses, and accept the more or less general applause. My role was largely fraudulent, but I loved every moment. Just occasionally I had to act nimbly, as happened over the future of Dale House in Coalbrookdale.

During the eighteenth century the Darbys occupied three plain, well-proportioned houses in Coalbrookdale, perched up on the hillside above the works and physically very close to them, as was customary with early industrialists. One of these, Sunniside, was demolished in the nineteenth century. Of the other two, Rosehill had been acquired from Telford Development Corporation with Rachel's support and was to be furnished with collections associated with the Darbys, donated by her. The other, Dale House, had been divided up into flats in the 1950s, had become very dilapidated and, once squatters had been evicted, was boarded up. Dale House was still owned by Telford Development Corporation, which had taken a leading

William Westwood, *Dale House and Rosehill viewed over the Upper Furnace Pool, Coalbrookdale*, showing two of the three eighteenth-century houses built by the Darby family, close to their iron-works at Ironbridge in Shropshire.

role in setting up the Ironbridge Gorge Museum, now a World Heritage Site. Lady Labouchere was the museum's president, and many of its fundraising events had been held at Dudmaston.

In September 1981, on one of my frequent visits to Dudmaston for some gentle gallery arranging, I encountered Rachel as I had never seen her before. She was very angry – contained but unmistakeable – and very agitated. Telford Corporation had put Dale House on the market, and no one, not even the brilliant director of the museum, Dr Neil Cossons, had thought (or had the courage) to tell her. We agreed there and then that we would go straight to Coalbrookdale. I was a member of the Ironbridge Gorge Museum Trust Executive Board, and I accompanied her in that capacity and as chauffeur.

My recollection is that we went straight to the museum office and spoke to a rather disconcerted Neil Cossons (shortly to become director of the National Maritime Museum in 1983, then of the Science Museum in 1986, and on retirement, as Sir Neil Cossons, chairman of English Heritage). We collected the keys of Dale House and before we left Rachel rang the chairman of Telford Development Corporation, Lord Northfield, who was given a succinct lecture on the significance of the two houses, both separately and together. Then we went to look at Dale House. The front door was padlocked and, once opened, access was obstructed and difficult. Undeterred, Rachel clambered in and, with characteristic thoroughness, went all over the house. She was, as usual, immaculately dressed in a tweed suit, which might have been more appropriate for a royal visit than for exploring the dark, derelict and squalid rooms of Dale House. On our return to the museum office, she asked to be put through to Lord Northfield, and told him that because of the importance of the house, she would be buying it herself, on behalf of the museum.

Can this be true? Is it a figment of my romantic imagination, fed by fondness and admiration? This is one of the few episodes that makes me regret not keeping a diary, because nothing except the outcome of our visit is recorded in the Ironbridge files. Just as I was concluding that I could not give such an unsubstantiated account, I happened to take off my shelves a copy of a book which Rachel had recommended to me, Arthur Raistrick's *Quakers in Science and Industry*, which has a picture of the Iron Bridge at Coalbrookdale as its frontispiece. For many years Raistrick acted as historical adviser to the Ironbridge Gorge Museum, and Rachel revered him. Tucked inside the book, and long forgotten, was a sheaf of papers, including a guidebook to Dale House and Rosehill of 1983, a typed explanation of their significance, and a letter from Rachel dated 30 May 1983, two years after we had moved from Shropshire to Norfolk. The letter begins:

This pamphlet is ready at last and tells the story of the Darby houses! It seems a long time since we climbed into Dale House. The roof there is on the way to complete renewal – also at Rosehill & at the latter most of the difficult work is almost finished. The County Council came up with £50,000 and there has been another grant the same but we still have to get more to finish properly I expect. Neil, who leaves for Greenwich at the end of next month, is very anxious that we should have your advice over the 'furnishing' of Rosehill – & also Dale House… I have some (very few) original curtains and materials, but we shall have to buy correctly. We are having a success with the American Quakers – a good line there now into those who are erudite and helpful… Elizabeth Fry (as Elizabeth Gurney) stayed at Dale House with the Richard Reynolds family – so that front door ushered in all the guests from 1718 onwards.

The account of Dale House had been typed by Rachel's secretary, and is worth quoting, because it reveals how her engagement with her Darby ancestors was both scholarly and deeply felt:

In 1715, Abraham Darby, who was then living at Madeley Court, began to build a house at Coalbrookdale just above the works. The house was still unfinished when he died in 1717, although a Quaker meeting had been held there shortly before his death…

It became customary for the Manager of the works to live at the Dale House. In 1763 Richard Reynolds took over the management and moved there from Ketley. In the same year he married his second wife Rebecca Gulson, and his family lived at Dale House until 1776 when Abraham Darby III entered the works.

She then explained how it had been the home to successive generations of the Darby family, when exactly they were visited by friends such as the prison reformer Elizabeth Fry and how they could watch the first iron bridge in the world being built. She continued:

Many American Friends came there, the first mentioned being Thomas Storey in 1735, a friend of William Penn. The house originally had a roof with dormer windows, but was first

Lady Labouchere on the steps of Rosehill at Coalbrookdale, Shropshire, in 1983.

altered to a parapet, probably in the latter part of the eighteenth century.... It is the most important historic house of all in Coalbrookdale.

The guide has an introduction signed *Rachel Labouchere* and a photograph of her opening the door of Dale House, still with its familiar padlock.[9] She was also photographed on the steps of Rosehill. Nowhere does the guide suggest that it was Lady Labouchere who bought the house for the museum, at the moment when the sale to a Shrewsbury builder was almost complete. Nor does the guide explain the underlying reason why Rachel was so determined that Dale House should be preserved. She would in private explain her belief that while industrial archaeology had become established as a popular, indeed fashionable subject for study, work on the influence of the Quakers remained neglected, as was reflected in the lack of interest in Dale House. It was the link between Quaker beliefs and industrial innovation that was the key to a full understanding of Coalbrookdale's success. In her efforts to correct the imbalance she was as much a passionate pioneer as her Darby ancestors.

The archives of the museum confirm the story and fill in some of the gaps.[10] On 16 September 1981 Lord Northfield wrote to Lady Labouchere saying that the museum had been given the opportunity to buy Dale House on 7 August and had declined the offer on the 19th (without letting the President know). He warned that the building was in very poor condition and that the offer from a Shrewsbury builder of £25,000 would have to be matched. He went on:

> I would be very unhappy to see you being left with a ruinous liability if you do buy this property but if, after a few days thought, you decide you would still like to proceed, then needless to say I will be delighted to ensure… you have it.

Rachel's response is recorded in her letter of 20th September to Neil Cossons:

> I am able, I am glad to say, to give this house to the Museum to complete the Quaker 'complex' up on the hill… we must get grants as well as Quaker money.

She wrote again two days later:

> I am buying Dale House for the Museum – I have accepted the terms Lord Northfield set out. It had nearly gone. It is a must for us and very historic.

To the Deputy Director, Stuart Smith, shortly to succeeed Cossons, she revealed why she felt so strongly:

> Dale House is the key house of all and is as important as the machines!

The reason why her gift of the property is not mentioned in the guide is that she eventually preferred to donate the £25,000 needed for purchase to the museum, which would then buy the building. Money for its restoration came from the National Heritage Memorial Fund and various Cadbury and other Quaker trusts. Rachel also wrote to Jennifer Jenkins, the Chairman of the Historic Buildings Council, which gave grants totalling £63,000 towards repairs.

In 1988 Rachel sent me a copy of her book, *Abiah Darby of Coalbrookdale*, which was largely devoted to edited extracts from Abiah's journal. Inside there is a card:

> Herewith, at last, my Abiah Darby. 'Deborah' is to follow – helped by American historians.
> We open phase 2 of Rosehill on 8th April – I have been busy on the contents.

Deborah Darby of Coalbrookdale, 1754–1810: her visits to America, Ireland, Scotland, Wales, England and the Channel Isles followed in 1993, dedicated to Dr Arthur Raistrick and Dr G. Frederick Williams: 'without their devoted and imaginative work the Ironbridge Gorge Museum would not have become a reality, nor would the original furnace have been saved for posterity.' The list of illustrations does not mention that the vignette on the title page, illustrating Dale House and Rosehill surrounded by a garland of wild flowers, is a watercolour by the author, Rachel Labouchere.

By then George was suffering from advanced dementia, and Rachel herself was seriously ill. She died on 22 March 1996 at Dudmaston, leaving instructions that the funeral was to be entirely private. Sir Joshua Rowley suggested that this was to spare George, now very confused, a large gathering of friends and associates. There were no children of their own; but in 1994 Rachel had provided a fund, in honour of Sir George Labouchere, for the advancement of Spanish studies at Oxford University, allowing young students to visit Spain. Her transcription of *The Private Journal of Adelaide Darby of Coalbrookdale, from 1833 to 1861* was edited by Emyr Thomas and published posthumously, in 2004.

Eighteenth-century artists in search of the sublime were frequent visitors to Coalbrookdale, which provided them with dramatic views of belching smoke, furnaces which were kept burning all hours of the day and night, and molten metal pouring into moulds. J.M.W. Turner was in Shropshire in 1794, and it may have been during this visit that he made the sketches on which his *Limekiln at Coalbrookdale* is based. It is one of his earliest surviving oil paintings, and seems to have been influenced by Rembrandt's *The Flight into Egypt*, which he would have seen when he was working for Sir Richard Colt Hoare of Stourhead, where the picture then hung.

The National Trust's involvement with Turner began inauspiciously. In the late 1890s the Executive Committee considered whether it should acquire the house in Chelsea where he had lived during his final years, and where he died in 1851.[11] Turner had constructed a railed enclosure on the roof, so he could sketch the Thames looking west, which he called 'the English view', or as it flowed east, known as 'the Dutch view'.[12] The reasons why the negotiations failed are unrecorded, and the house was subsequently altered and largely rebuilt.

Following the gift of Petworth House in West Sussex from Charles, 3rd Lord Leconfield in 1947, the Trust became the custodian of the greatest collection of Turners outside the national museums. The negotiations to transfer some of the contents of the house caused John Wyndham (Leconfield's nephew and heir) and the Trust's Chairman, Lord Crawford, immense frustration. They were dealing with the permanent secretary at the Treasury, Sir Edward (later Lord) Bridges, who in turn was advised by curators at the National Gallery and the Victoria and Albert Museum. They had recommended that only the finest pictures and sculpture should be accepted in lieu of tax, which would have broken up the collection, and that the valuation for what was to be acquired, including all the Turners, a head of *Aphrodite* by Praxiteles, and some of the furniture, should be £553,148. Crawford (a trustee of the National Gallery, National Portrait Gallery and British Museum) tried to explain to Bridges that the proposal to divide the collection was 'quite lunatic, quite indefensible, quite exasperating' and would 'absolutely wreck the house'. He was only partially successful; and on the valuation Bridges was unmoved. As Wyndham later wrote, the consequences of holding out for a fairer figure might have wrecked the whole deal. The outcome, in 1956, was agreement on the Treasury's terms: 'Whatever may happen to me or my family, Petworth House, its contents and its park should be preserved for posterity. I am glad.'[13] It was the first occasion that, using recent legislation, a country house collection had been successfully transferred to the National Trust in payment of death duties.

On other matters Bridges was extremely helpful to the National Trust. He assisted the Chancellor of the Exchequer, Hugh Dalton, with the setting up of the National Land Fund, greatly to the Trust's benefit. He also served on its Executive Committee, and was the chairman of its local Headley Heath and Box Hill committees. His wife was a Farrer, the family of lawyers who owned Abinger Roughs, transferred to the National Trust through the Land Fund in 1950. His son Thomas, 2nd Lord Bridges, British ambassador in Italy from 1983 to 1987, was to play an important part in the Trust's acquisition of Orford Ness, on the Suffolk coast, in 1993. It too was painted by Turner.

In the summer of 1824 Turner took a boat from Aldeburgh, down the river Ore towards Orford. An eight-mile shingle spit running from north to south separates the river from the sea. Where the spit narrows at both the northern and southern ends, Turner would have been close enough to the open sea to be able to spot the occasional passing sail. The central section of the Ness was punctuated then, as it is today, by a lighthouse. The one he saw was built in 1792, and was adopted by Trinity House in 1837. He would have been told how perilous this stretch of coast could be: in 1627 a dozen ships were wrecked in a single night off the Ness.

The sketchbook Turner had with him on that trip has page after page of very rapid pencil drawings, and these he translated into a series of finished watercolours: a peaceful scene near the Martello tower at Aldeburgh, now in Tate Britain; a wreck on the seaward side of the Ness, showing the same tower; a view from the Ness across to Orford church and castle; and then another shipwreck, just below the lighthouse. Turner's profound pessimism finds expression in this image of disaster, as it does in his poetry, which he called 'fallacies of hope'.

The 'pagodas' built at Orford Ness, in Suffolk, by the Atomic Weapons Research Establishment during the Cold War. Orford Ness was bought from the Ministry of Defence by the National Trust in 1993, with public grants and private donations, and is now a National Nature Reserve.

The lighthouse is a futile attempt to frustrate the fury of the sea. So too is the jury sail and, one senses, the efforts of the rowing boats trying to pull the vessel off the shingle. Turner's painting has a strange resonance today. The sea is eroding and rolling back the eastward side of the Ness so fast that the present lighthouse will almost certainly have gone within twenty years. The coast guard lookout and its ancillary buildings are similarly at risk. No doubt there will be calls to attempt to preserve or relocate them, but nature will have to take its course.

The protracted and often frustrated efforts to find a secure future for Orford Ness, after it was declared surplus to Ministry of Defence requirements in the 1970s, merited all of Turner's pessimism. The site had been purchased by the War Department in 1913, for bombing practice by the Royal Flying Corps. Until 1993 the general public was excluded, encouraging wild speculation about the weapons testing carried out there. In the space of 60 years this evolved from the dropping of hand-held bombs from the cockpits of bi-planes, to the testing of trigger mechanisms for atomic bombs. At Orford Ness some of the earliest experiments on the parachute were carried out. Between 1935 and 1937 Robert Watson-Watt began the first trials of an aerial defence system, later to be called radar; and their success altered the course of the Second World War. During the Cold War the Atomic Weapons Research Establishment used Orford Ness to test how extremes of temperature and vibration might affect their bombs. They built concrete chambers with raised roofs supported on columns, to avoid any unintended explosion being contained in an sealed space. Shingle was piled against the walls and heaped on the roof, so they looked like vast tumuli, distantly descended from the Sutton Hoo burial mounds a few miles down the coast. They became known as the 'pagodas'.

With the end of the Cold War, scientific work on the Ness ended. The Ministry of Defence allowed scrap-metal merchants to strip out the buildings, tear off the doors, and smash what was of no value to them. Their overloaded lorries broke the bridges which gave access over Stony Ditch, the tidal creek which divides the central section of the Ness. The combination of desolation, debris and weapons of mass destruction made it a threatening place for many of those who came to consider whether it might be a suitable acquisition for the National Trust.

What could not be disputed was the importance of its geomorphology, its vegetation and its birds. On its eastern side the shingle has, over many centuries, been piled by the sea into a succession of ridges, which not only make it possible to understand how the landform has evolved, but which also support rare plants, including sea campion and sea pea. That it is a Site of Special Scientific Interest, a Special Protection Area and a Special Area of Conservation has a certain irony: for most of the twentieth century it was in effect a laboratory devoted to destruction on an unprecedented scale.

There were other considerations. The National Trust had been established by Act of Parliament to protect places of historic interest and natural beauty. Its record in preserving the uplands, the coast and much beautiful countryside spoke for itself. But for much of the second half of the twentieth century, the history which it had chosen to safeguard was overwhelmingly that of the country house. It was the history of privilege, indulgence, and sometimes brilliant but frequently rather vapid decorative arts. To a large extent it was also the eighteenth-century history of the country house. The collections of mid-twentieth-century art at Dudmaston were very much an exception. In stark contrast, there were at Orford Ness monuments to the realities of twentieth-century history: unimaginable destruction, extermination as an industrial process, war directed as much at civilian populations as at opposing warriors. These considerations were stressed in the papers that went to the Trust's Properties Committee in February 1989.

For understandable reasons there were those who were strongly opposed to any involvement by the National Trust. The Trust's solicitor quite properly drew attention to the potential liabilities: unexploded ordnance, scores of derelict buildings, and – perhaps most serious of all – the possibility that the Trust could be held responsible if sea defences on the Ness failed and the towns of Orford and Aldeburgh were consequently flooded. The Director of Finance questioned whether the purchase price demanded by the Ministry of Defence could be justified, and was sceptical that the total acquisition cost, calculated to be £3.5 million, could be found.

Gradually, powerful advocates for acquisition emerged. The regional officer of the Nature Conservancy Council, John Morley, was always on hand to speak to representatives of the grant-aiding bodies about the conservation value of the Ness, and could be regarded as more objective than members of the Trust's staff. Another effective ally was Professor Keith Clayton, of the Department of Environmental Sciences at the University of East Anglia. For years he had been a voice in the wilderness, warning of the likely effects of global warming and sea-

Dennis Creffield, *Orford Ness: The A.W.R.E. Magazine and Orford Castle (Sunset) 1994 (No.2)*, commissioned by the National Trust's Foundation for Art, following the acquisition of Orford Ness in 1993.

level rise; and it was not until the early 1990s that politicians and others were just beginning to listen. The president of the Royal Geographical Society, Lord Chorley, had recently presented Clayton with the Society's Gold Medal. In 1991 Chorley, a mountaineer as well as a geographer, became Chairman of the National Trust. He was ready to be convinced that the shingle banks and salt marshes of the Ness might move, eroding and accreting as they had for centuries; but that this would only add to its scientific interest.

Locally, Lord Bridges was able to reassure those who were doubtful about the National Trust becoming responsible for the Ness. On their retirement from the embassy in Rome in 1987, Tom and Rachel Bridges had gone to live at Great House, Orford, just a few minutes' walk from the quay; and Tom had joined the Trust's regional committee for East Anglia. He presented the case for the charity's involvement on the basis of intimate knowledge of the area, not least gleaned from the river, on which he sailed a dinghy.

Visits to Orford Ness in the middle of winter were often problematical, because the weather could be extremely hostile and there was little shelter in its derelict buildings. When trustees of the National Heritage Memorial Fund came in 1992, its representatives were at first baffled and then extremely doubtful about support. During an excellent lunch at Great House there was the beginning of a thaw; and a generous grant was ultimately approved. A special allocation was also made by the Department of the Environment. Enterprise Neptune contributed its largest-ever donation of £500,000. That such a property was in part bought thanks to the generosity of thousands of nameless National Trust supporters seemed apposite. When Orford Ness was opened to the public in 1995, after 80 years of being a forbidden site and in the National Trust's centenary year, a celebratory party was held in the garden of Great House.

The response to Orford Ness has been unusual. It is as though poets and painters have taken up where the Suffolk poet George Crabbe and Turner had left off. One of the most thoughtful responses is in Christopher Woodward's book *In Ruins*.[14] He had been particularly struck by the Trust's decision to allow the concrete pagodas to deteriorate gradually, without attempting to prevent or even slow down the rate of decay. The reasons for this philosophy of non-intervention had been eloquently articulated by the Trust's Regional Archaeologist, Angus Wainwright, and its Assistant Historic Buildings Representative, Jeremy Musson.[15] The policy was also influenced by expediency: the pagodas were constructed of reinforced concrete, using sand with a high salt content which would make the corrosion of the steel ties unavoidable. Woodward related the experience of visiting Orford Ness to the ideas of the eighteenth-century picturesque: 'a perspective which … involved a meditation on time, transience and humanity.' He added, 'In a new and hopefully more peaceful century the ruins would crumble into extinction in exposure to the wind and waves, as if the earth was being purified by nature.'

Among the late twentieth-century artists who have produced memorable images of Orford Ness are Dennis Creffield, David Gentleman and John Wonnacott. There are evocations of its sense of isolation and desolation in W.G. Sebald's account of an extended walk through Suffolk, *The Rings of Saturn*,[16] and in Robert Macfarlane's *The Wild Places*.[17] Andrew Motion, the Poet Laureate, visited the Ness in 1996 and was inspired to write a long narrative poem, *Salt Water,* which describes how nature turns the most advanced technology to detritus; but then ends on a note of recovery:

> … Then the waves work up a big rage against ridge-tiles
> and breeze blocks, against doors, ventilation shafts, clocks,
> and moon-faced instrument panels no one needs any more.
>
> Then the wind gets to work. It breaks into laboratories
> and clapboard sheds, it rubs out everything everyone said,
> clenching its fingers round door jambs and window frames.
>
> Then the gulls come to visit, shuffling noisily
> into any old scrap-metal mess, settling on this for a nest,
> and pinning their bright eyes on the bare sky overhead.
>
> And in due season flocks of beautiful shy avocets –
> they also come back, white wings scissored with black,
> calling their wild call as though they felt human grief…[18]

The strange indifference of Orford Ness – with its extremes of tranquility and violence, its history and its light – continues to inspire painters, poets and writers.

THE SPIRITUALISTS
AND THE VOLUNTEER

Edith Pretty, the Tranmers and Sutton Hoo

Edith Pretty and two friends watching archaeologists excavating the ship-burial at Sutton Hoo in Suffolk, in 1939. Having purchased the estate in 1927, and following the death of her husband Frank in 1934, Edith Pretty encouraged Basil Brown to excavate on her land, leading to his discovery of the ship-burial in July 1939.

WHEN THE SALE PARTICULARS of farmland on the Deben estuary in Suffolk arrived, unsolicited, at the National Trust's regional office at Blickling Hall, it was scarcely surprising. The Trust had launched its East Anglia Coast and Country-side Appeal in 1986, principally to raise funds for the purchase of Sheringham, with the Prince of Wales as Patron. No secret had been made of its interest in acquiring land on the Suffolk estuaries. The National Trust already owned Kyson Hill, which looks across to Woodbridge in one direction and, in the other, down the Deben estuary as it makes its way south-easterly to the sea. The farmland in question was on the opposite side of the estuary to Kyson Hill, and the agents for the sale had quite reasonably supposed that the Trust might be a potential purchaser. The name of the estate had a certain resonance: Sutton Hoo.

A quick look at the map accompanying the particulars indicated that the site where the great Anglo-Saxon ship treasure had been discovered in 1939 was excluded from the sale, and so too was the woodland which fringed the burial mounds and ran down to the estuary. The farmland was going to be expensive and the areas of greatest interest to the Trust were not for sale. The particulars were filed and almost forgotten.

The possibility of some form of National Trust involvement at Sutton Hoo resurfaced in September 1990, thanks to Elisabeth and David Walters. For over 30 years Elisabeth had advised the Trust on architectural and planning issues (first as Elisabeth Beazley, then after marriage as Elisabeth Walters). Without her imagination and understanding of the needs of visitors, the showing of properties such as Plas Newydd, Erddig and Styal would have been far less successful. On David's retirement from the Royal Navy, they had moved to Suffolk, principally so that he could keep a boat on the Deben. They had bought the Old Primary School at Sutton, which was ideally placed for a Deben mooring. They followed the excavations of the ship burials at Sutton Hoo, renewed in 1983, with interest, and had got to know the archaeologist directing the dig, Professor Martin Carver, well. He was anxious to make contact with the National Trust, and Elisabeth and David were happy to act as intermediaries, inviting me to meet him for supper on 25 September, after which he was to show me the site.

At that time the approach to Sutton Hoo was unimpressive. Cars had to be left on the far side of the road from Woodbridge to Bawdsey, which was dangerous to cross.[1] Once over the road, visitors walked along the edge of featureless farmland to the site of the excavations. The paraphernalia of a major dig had the effect of overwhelming the Sutton Hoo burial mounds: as has been said, 'Suffolk's pyramids are… as unprepossessing as molehills.'[2] Archaeologists are preoccupied with data and material evidence; with some notable exceptions, they tend not to be concerned with aesthetics, which can get in the way of historical truth, nor with the romanticism of ancient places, which is subjective and so can be a distraction. A dig on the scale of the Sutton Hoo excavations of 1983 to 1993 reached the historical imagination through what looked like industrial processes.

On that late September evening, however, the mounds cast long shadows; and no one could fail to be touched by the knowledge Carver had gleaned from seven years of excavating the site, and by his passionate identification with its extraordinary significance. Clearly the campaign of excavation had been approached as a tactical, logistical exercise, consistent with Carver's military background, and had been executed with energy and precision. Temperamentally Carver was more a soldier than a politician.

The discovery in 1939 of the ship burial at Sutton Hoo revealed not only the richest treasure ever found on British soil, but also that a formative period of the nation's history had been misrepresented and misunderstood. The so-called 'Dark Ages' were shown to be a period of the very highest artistic accomplishment. The courts of Anglo-Saxon rulers were culturally cosmopolitan: included in the treasure were silver bowls from the eastern Mediterranean, coins minted in France, and weapons associated with royal burials in Sweden. Few sites better encapsulated the National Trust's twin obligations to preserve 'places of historic interest and natural beauty'. The treasure was both historically potent and exquisitely crafted.[3] The Deben estuary, on that autumn evening, was landscape of uncommon loveliness.

Having guided me round the site, Carver suggested that we might discuss, in one of the dig huts, what would happen to the site once the excavations were complete. There were problems, and despite Carver's considerable efforts to find a solution, they remained intractable. Only one quarter of the burial site had been excavated, and once the dig was complete it would be liable to damage by metal-detector enthusiasts, farm vehicles and rabbits. Although the family of the former owner, Edith Pretty, had retained the rights to excavation and to any finds, Sutton Hoo House and the area of the mounds was now the property of Mrs Annie Tranmer, who was guided by her solicitor, John Miller. Over many years Miller was scrupulous in reconciling obligations to the Tranmer family with a responsibility to the international community of those interested in Sutton Hoo.

That sense of responsibility, Carver explained, had not touched the government agencies charged with the protection of such places. English Heritage then had a policy of not taking what it called 'soft sites' – in other words, earthworks without substantial masonry – into guardianship and wanted nothing to do with Sutton Hoo. Carver's next line of inquiry was directed to the Capital Taxes Office. The Tranmers owed £350,000 in Estate Duty. Might Sutton Hoo be offered 'in lieu' of tax, and then transferred to a suitable body, perhaps one set up for this particular task? The district valuer was consulted, with a brief from the Capital Taxes Office that regard should only be had for the agricultural value of the site. It was protected under the Ancient Monuments Act, and so the only permissible agricultural use was occasional grazing. As far as any 'in lieu' solution was concerned, Sutton Hoo was virtually valueless.[4]

Carver had then tried to establish a value based on comparisons with historic archives. Sutton Hoo was in effect a document illuminated in gold and silver, the discovery of which had led to the rewriting of several centuries of our national history. Anglo-Saxon books and manuscripts fetched high prices – witness Lord Lothian's sales from Blickling – so why not put a comparable price on the value of the site of the richest Saxon burial? The Getty Trust and others were unconvinced.

The official indifference to the future of Sutton Hoo had left Annie Tranmer and John Miller discouraged. Carver too was utterly frustrated and increasingly worried that the Sutton Hoo Research Trust, set up to sponsor his excavation, might shortly have to leave this extremely fragile and vulnerable site unprotected. 'Would the National Trust help?' he asked, 'and would it be prepared to consider an approach to Annie Tranmer?' Although she was known to be unwell, both her daughter, Mrs Valerie Lewis, and John Miller were likely to be sympathetic. I said I would consult the Trust's advisors and write in the next few days.

The Chairman of the National Trust's Archaeology Panel, Professor Peter Fowler, felt it was right to explore the possibility of involvement, and so too did the region's archaeology adviser, Dr Peter Wade Martins. Both were concerned that earthworks were among East Anglia's most historic sites, and yet were, in practice, inadequately safeguarded. In early October I wrote to Carver to say that the Trust was in no doubt of Sutton Hoo's importance, that we believed we had the skills needed to safeguard the site in perpetuity, and that we were not short of experience in dealing with the various bodies that might feel proprietorial towards the site without actually being prepared to take it on. A letter also went to Mrs Annie Tranmer, suggesting that if she thought there was any useful role for the National Trust to play, she should not hesitate to let us know, and concluding:

> This is only the most tentative of enquiries, really just to offer assistance if that accords with your own wishes. The Trust does not normally seek involvement in property not in our own ownership, but Sutton Hoo is of such national and international importance that I thought you should at least know of our interest.[5]

There was no immediate answer, and that might have been the end of the matter.

Sutton Hoo has a history of unconventional solutions. It has also seen how obstructions

The purse lid from the ship-burial at Sutton Hoo.

and petty jealousies can be swept aside. The problems with which Carver was grappling were considerable, but not of the same urgency as those confronted by Mrs Edith Pretty, the owner of Sutton Hoo, in 1939. The earlier history of the site and its excavation had shown how imagination, improvisation and generosity can triumph over bureaucracy and self-interest. There were to be remarkable continuities.

Edith Pretty, who was born in 1883, inherited an industrial fortune from her parents, Robert and Elizabeth Dempster.[6] Her husband, Frank Pretty, came from an Ipswich family with various business interests, from silk underwear to steel, and had served with distinction in the First World War. They did not become engaged until after the death of Edith's father – she had been looking after him and travelling the world – and when they finally married in 1926, Frank Pretty was 47 and Edith 42. The following year, Edith bought the Sutton Hoo estate, and in 1929 she became a magistrate on the Woodbridge Bench. Happiness, then tragedy, came in quick succession. In 1930, at the age of 47, she had a son, Robert, and in 1934 Frank Pretty died of cancer.

After the death of her husband, Edith Pretty became more detached from Suffolk society and increasingly preoccupied with her young son. She regularly visited a well-known faith-healer and spiritualist, William Parish, in London, whom she had contacted shortly after Frank Pretty's cancer was first diagnosed. Edith supported Parish financially and was also a benefactor of another clairvoyant and faith-healer, Charles Toft, of Llanelli.[7] Her involvement with spiritualism did not, however, distract this highly intelligent and capable woman from the efficient management of her estate, her responsibilities as a magistrate, or her long-standing interest in archaeology.

Edith Pretty had spent her childhood at Vale Royal in Cheshire, a much altered seventeenth-century house built on the site of the largest Cistercian abbey in England.[8] When Robert Dempster took on the lease from Lord Delamere in 1907, the remains of the abbey had been almost entirely grassed over, although a few fragments had been incorporated in the house. Edith's father excavated the footings of the abbey walls and left them exposed, so making it possible to discern the plan of the great abbey church. He also fed his daughter's enthusiasm for antiquities by taking her, at the age of seventeen, to Pompeii, Syracuse, Athens, and to the excavations then being carried out in the Nile Valley, particularly those at Luxor. Of no less relevance to her future role at Sutton Hoo were journeys to Iceland, where they travelled over remote and inhospitable terrain using Icelandic ponies, and to Uppsala in Sweden, with its huge sixth-century burial mounds.[9]

Detail of a portrait of *Edith Pretty*, painted by Cor Visser in 1939, and presented to the National Trust by her family, to hang at Tranmer House on the Sutton Hoo estate.

Given this unusual upbringing, it is perhaps surprising that when she chose a home for herself and Frank shortly after their marriage, she should have bought Sutton Hoo House, which was less than twenty years old. It was well built, in a relaxed Arts and Crafts tradition, with well-proportioned rooms and superb views over the Deben, but architecturally undistinguished. Less surprising is her curiosity about a group of mounds, on an escarpment overlooking the Deben and clearly visible from the first floor, which led her to seek advice from Guy Maynard, the curator of Ipswich Museum, about the possibility of excavation. The person he recommended for the task was Basil Brown, a self-taught agricultural labourer turned archaeologist, who in his flat hat looked more like a Suffolk poacher than an academic. Indeed he brought something of a poacher's guile to the gentlemanly practice of archaeology.

During the summer of 1938, Brown was employed by Edith Pretty, on a wage of 30 shillings a week, to excavate one of the mounds which, as it turned out, had already been comprehensively plundered. He was assisted by John Jacob, an estate gardener, and William Spooner, the gamekeeper, so ensuring that Edith Pretty retained complete control of everything that happened. The following year Brown was engaged again, and by May had discovered a ship burial of unprecedented size, larger than any Saxon finds in Britain or any Viking ships found in Norway.

Basil Brown, a largely self-taught archaeologist, who was employed by Edith Pretty to excavate the mounds at Sutton Hoo in the summers of 1938 and 1939.

For Brown the discovery was a personal triumph. All the highly professional and distinguished archaeologists who have worked at Sutton Hoo since have paid tribute to his patience, skill, intuition and diligence. His achievement was all the more remarkable because he had left school at the age of twelve, and his later education was gleaned from books, some lent by two retired clergymen, and a correspondence course which earned him a 'Harmsworth Self-Educator Diploma'. In his free time he had taught himself four languages, and in 1932 had published a widely acclaimed book on astronomy. Edith Pretty, much of whose own education came from wide reading and travel, was quick to appreciate his qualities: both were independent-minded and not inclined to deference. A bond developed between them, which the extraordinary events of that summer of 1939 served to strengthen. Both rose above the jealousies of others, which could easily have flared into acrimony.

There was potential for ill-feeling the moment Mrs Pretty realised that she ought to inform the British Museum and the Office of Works of the scale of what was being uncovered. She had been advised to do this by Charles Phillips, a Cambridge archaeologist who had been invited to visit Sutton Hoo by Maynard. Almost immediately there was an instruction from the Office of Works to stop excavating, followed by the decision that Phillips should assume responsibility for the dig. At Mrs Pretty's insistence Basil Brown was taken on as his assistant. Phillips then set about gathering together a young and brilliant team of archaeologists.

Basil Brown, meanwhile, blithely ignored the order to cease excavating, and with Edith

Archaeologists working on the ship-burial at Sutton Hoo, showing the full length and breadth of the vessel; one of many colour photographs taken in 1939 by two schoolmistresses, Mercie Lack and Barbara Wagstaff.

Pretty's tacit agreement he continued to clear around what he had correctly deduced was the burial chamber. Her encouragement took the unusual form of suggesting that he might visit a well-known spiritualist, Mrs Florence Thompson, who happened to be visiting Woodbridge on 1 July. Their encounter is described in a letter of three days later, to his wife May:

> She certainly seemed very positive, always dresses in blue when on Spiritualist work. Another message for me which may wake things up… The message of all things was this. Some one is holding you up in your business, assert yourself. Now such a message coming at this particular time from a well-known medium, said to be always right, was quite enough to start Mrs Pretty into finding out why we could not excavate the burial, and what will happen now I don't know at all.[10]

There was to be tension and at least one major row, but the saga of Sutton Hoo was to conclude triumphantly.

The row arose because, understandably, Ipswich Museum, and particularly its president James Reid Moir, were being pushed aside. The discoveries from the excavation in 1938 had been given by Mrs Pretty to Ipswich, but the involvement of the British Museum meant that future finds were likely to go to London. When first appointed, Phillips had said that he was 'quite content to be regarded as the agent of Ipswich Museum',[11] as well as the Office of Works; but his naturally autocratic style rapidly asserted itself.

The relationship between Phillips and Reid Moir had been strained before the Sutton Hoo discoveries brought things to a head. Both were involved with the Prehistoric Society of East Anglia, of which Reid Moir – the manager of a tailoring business in Ipswich – was an authoritative and highly respected member. Phillips and one of the archaeologists he recruited to Sutton Hoo, Stuart Piggott, had pressed for the Society to expand and modernise, so leading to lasting resentment. A confusion of Maynard's making, over dates for a visit to Sutton Hoo in July, resulted in open hostility, with Reid Moir describing Phillips as 'over-riding, bumptious and tactless – a typical product of modern Cambridge'; while Phillips referred to the 'overbearing and belligerent' Reid Moir, who was, he granted, 'a good bespoke tailor'.[12]

There might easily have been a still more serious breakdown between Phillips and Brown, had it not been for Mrs Pretty's discreet but firm interventions. By the time Phillips returned to Sutton Hoo on 10 July with his carefully chosen team, Brown had revealed the outline of the burial chamber and had concluded that its contents were intact. At this point Phillips decided that the excavation of the chamber itself should be carried out by Stuart Piggott, a future professor of archaeology at Edinburgh, his wife Peggy, and W.F. ('Peter') Grimes, later to be director of the Institute of Archaeology, assisted at crucial moments by other highly experienced and trusted professional archaeologists. This was a bitter blow for Brown, and one which caused life-long disappointment and resentment. Someone more sensitive than Phillips might have handled things differently. It was left to Edith Pretty to insist that as the gold and cloisonné enamel buckles, the silver dishes and weapons were uncovered, they would be carried in boxes to Sutton Hoo House by Basil Brown, accompanied by William Spooner, the gamekeeper, armed with a shotgun.[13]

Not surprisingly, the treatment of Brown at this phase of the excavation has been seized on by Phillips's detractors.[14] What can be overlooked is that the treasure and the ship were buried in sand, and there had already been one major trench collapse before Phillips took control. He was generous in his praise for Brown's achievements, referring to his 'great competence in what he had done',[15] and later acknowledging that it was his decision to excavate from within the outline of the ship, rather than cutting through it, that 'made such a major contribution to the success of the 1939 excavation'.[16] Conscious of the responsibility on his shoulders, and concerned that Brown had something of a reputation for excavating 'like a terrier after a rat',[17] Phillips made the decision that the uncovering of the contents of the chamber should be entrusted to the young and lithe Stuart and Peggy Piggott, and to Grimes, who did much of the work lying on their stomachs. He himself was of Suffolk corn-milling stock, was heavily built, and largely directed operations from the terrace at the edge of the excavated area.[18] However disappointing to Brown, and inadequately explained, Phillips's decision to entrust the burial chamber to others was a reasonable one.

By the end of July almost all the finds were packed and ready for transfer to the British Museum for initial assessment. On 29 July the story, leaked by Guy Maynard, was in the national press, much to Phillips's dismay and anger. By 31 July the treasure had all been transported to London, and two policemen had been employed – at Mrs Pretty's expense – to protect the burial site from opportunist treasure hunters.

The recovery of the treasure without mishap and in the space of just a few weeks was an extraordinary achievement. The weather had been kind and occasional showers had scarcely impeded the work of recording this fragile, friable site. The satisfactory completion of the excavation can be attributed to the restraint and calm good sense shown by Edith Pretty and Basil Brown, and to Charles Phillips's outstanding abilities as an archaeologist and administrator. What now had to be resolved was the ownership of the treasure.

Under English law, treasure which has been buried with the intention of recovery belongs to the Crown. Treasure which was meant to remain buried belongs to the landowner. In normal circumstances the archaeologists involved at Sutton Hoo might have been expected to argue that an intent to recover was not impossible, in which case the Crown, as owner, might be expected to deposit the treasure in the British Museum, perhaps with some exhibits loaned to the Ipswich Museum. But there was nothing that was normal about Sutton Hoo.

A Treasure Trove Inquest was heard on 14 August 1939 in Sutton village hall by the North Suffolk coroner, Lionel Vulliamy, assisted by a former director of the British Museum, Sir George Hill. Basil Brown, Guy Maynard, Charles Phillips and Stuart Piggott were the main witnesses. All maintained that there could never have been any thought of concealment or of disturbing so grand a burial once a mound had been piled around it. It says much for their respect for Edith Pretty that they were, in effect, presenting the case for the landowner, rather than for the Crown. The fourteen-man jury, which included the village schoolmaster, a smallholder, the local blacksmith and the licensee of the Plough Inn at Sutton, retired to consider their verdict. Their conclusion was that the burial did not constitute treasure trove. The gold and silver finds, of incalculable value, were the property of Edith Pretty.

Over the next four days Mrs Pretty consulted William Parish and Charles Phillips. In his diary Phillips records a discussion with Parish, in which he suggested that 'the time has come for your client to make a very generous gesture.'[19] His entry for 13 August reads:

> In the evening I had an important conversation with Mrs Pretty in which she announced her intention of presenting all the finds to the nation and authorised me to get the British Museum officials to publish this fact without delay.[20]

The treasure, which had been on display during the inquest, was packed away and dispatched back to London. Four weeks later war was declared. The Sutton Hoo treasure again disappeared underground, to a tunnel between Holborn and Aldwych. Basil Brown did his best to protect the excavated mound by cutting and pulling bracken over it.

A year later, in December 1940, Edith Pretty received a letter from the Prime Minister's office, asking whether she would accept the appointment of Commander of the Order of the British Empire.[21] She wrote back without delay, declining the honour, and prompting her sister to call her 'a goose'.[22] In 1942 Sutton Hoo House and the burial ground were requisitioned for army training: tanks were driven over the mounds, which were also used as a firing range. To escape from the disturbance, Edith Pretty went to stay with William and Peggy Parish in Surrey, and while there she unexpectedly developed a blood clot on the brain. She died on 17 December in Richmond Hospital.

There have been suggestions that, unlike Edith Pretty, the community of academic archaeologists treated Basil Brown ungenerously. That could certainly not be said of Rupert Bruce-Mitford who, as assistant keeper and then Keeper, Medieval and Later Antiquities at

the British Museum until his retirement in 1975, was responsible for the treasure itself and for publishing the finds in three magisterial volumes. In 1970 he wrote to Brown, saying that he had 'decided to print your log and diary in full in the big Sutton Hoo publication,' assuring him that 'you come out of it all very well, and will achieve immortality.'[23] Bruce-Mitford was both an inspiring teacher of the young, and unfailingly kind to Brown in his final years. In 1966, at Bruce-Mitford's instigation, Brown was given a civil list pension of £250 a year in recognition of his work at Sutton Hoo.

Unfortunately, a spirit of generosity and imagination had been conspicuously absent in the 1980s, when Martin Carver tried to enlist the help of government agencies with the long-term protection of the burial ground. When he eventually turned to the National Trust in the autumn of 1990, it was to an organisation with a record of looking after its archaeological sites which was at best patchy.

In its early years, the Trust had acquired some of the most important archaeological sites in the country. One of the founders of the National Trust, Canon Hardwicke Rawnsley, had championed the purchase of Castlerigg Stone Circle, near Keswick in Cumbria, in 1913. Stonehenge Down in Wiltshire was bought in 1928 after a public appeal. Considerable stretches of Hadrian's Wall in Northumberland, including Housesteads Fort, were given to the Trust in 1930. Avebury in Wiltshire, one of the largest henge monuments and stone circles in the British Isles, was purchased in 1943. But after the Second World War priorities changed, and resources were concentrated on the protection of the coast – almost inadvertently the Trust found itself responsible for much cliff-top archaeology – and country houses. Some of these, such as Stourhead in Wiltshire, had been the home of noted antiquarians, but that was not why they were accepted by the Trust. Archaeological sites became the Cinderellas of the Trust's estates.

Standing stones at Avebury in Wiltshire, one of the largest henge monuments and stone circles in the British Isles, dating from 3000 to 2000 BC. Most of the 912-acre site was bought by the National Trust in 1943, with help from the Pilgrim Trust and Mr I.D. Margary.

They appealed to James Lees-Milne for their romantic associations, but it may be a symptom of his self-confessed agoraphobia that he rarely visited them. When he did go to Avebury in 1942 he irritated his companion, Eardley Knollys, with his 'lack of enthusiasm and disrespect for the ugly stones' and concluded: 'To hell with archaeology!'[24] Robin Fedden wrote engagingly in his books about some of the great archaeological monuments of the Near and Middle East, but his descriptions of the important sites in the Trust's ownership are, by comparison, scanty. Although distinguished archaeologists such as Sir Cyril Fox and Sir Mortimer Wheeler sat on the Trust's committees, it was left to a tireless amateur from Southend-on-Sea, Miss Phyllis Ireland, to compile adequate descriptions of the archaeological sites owned by the Trust.

Part of the problem was that neither the National Trust's 'boots' (the Land Agents) nor its 'lilies' (the aesthetes) felt comfortable with archaeology. When the Trust began to employ its own professional archaeologists in the 1980s, and to enlist honorary advisers in each region, they were at first answerable to the Historic Buildings Secretary, and were then shuffled across to the Chief Agent's department. Sutton Hoo was to be a test of what the Trust's commitment to archaeology really amounted to.

Looking after the historic landscape of Sutton Hoo in the long-term would be, in some respects, a more exacting task than carrying out intensive excavations. There was a temptation to say that, once the dig was completed, the burial ground should be allowed to regain its aura of ancient mystery and would rapidly revert to undulating Suffolk heath. That solution was only superficially attractive. Undisturbed it would not be: rabbits would quickly take over the role of excavators, with metal-detector enthusiasts not far behind. There was also a more fundamental problem. The owners of Sutton Hoo had been encouraged to involve government agencies, but in the face of their supine response, all serious negotiations went into abeyance. Such was the situation when Mrs Annie Tranmer died in 1993.

The future of the Sutton Hoo estate was now in the hands of Annie Tranmer's trustees: her daughter, Valerie Lewis, and her solicitor, John Miller. It was a substantial inheritance.

View of the Sutton Hoo burial mounds at dawn. The site, with its adjoining woodlands and the early twentieth-century house bought by Edith Pretty in 1927, was given to the National Trust in 1998.

Leslie Tranmer came from an impoverished background and made no secret of his humble origins. After the Second World War he set up a plumbing business, supplying heating pipes to the Nissen huts at British army bases in Germany. He found that it made sense to store large quantities of copper piping, which he either used himself or was able to supply to the building trade. As the business prospered, so Tranmer diversified into baths, wash-basins, and central heating, operating from Martlesham and Ipswich.

It was while he was living at Shotley, near Ipswich, that he asked a local solicitor, John Miller, to help him with the diversion of a right of way near his house, which was going to a public enquiry. Miller handled the case with tact and skill, so securing the diversion without upsetting most local people. Tranmer appreciated his entirely frank advice: thereafter Miller became a counsellor for the family and close personal friend, as well as being their solicitor. After they moved from Shotley to Sutton Hoo, he guided them over the major decisions which arose from Leslie's business success. Like many self-made men, Leslie Tranmer could be blunt and assertive, but he knew the value of good professional advice. He appointed Miller one of the three directors of the Tranmer Group.

By the 1960s the Tranmer Group had expanded so successfully that it was decided to go public and float it on the Stock Exchange. The family became very wealthy in consequence. But the work of fitting-out army buildings had left Leslie with mesothelioma, a lung cancer caused by handling asbestos. Before he died in 1973 he appointed his wife and Miller to be his executors. When Annie died twenty years later, she left her estate, including Sutton Hoo, to Valerie and to John Miller, to be used for charitable purposes.

There was no particular expectation that a solution would be found for the estate which protected its archaeology. Indeed, Leslie Tranmer had been so incensed by the damage caused by rabbits that he had wanted to plough up all the land which was not actually scheduled. By contrast, Valerie was interested in its historical significance, and was intrigued when her husband Nigel discovered a battered, but richly decorated, Saxon bucket in fields near the house. But it was due to Miller that plans to give Sutton Hoo a secure future now began to take shape. As he wrote later:

> … the preservation, protection and securing for the public of this real treasure has been my utter concern since Leslie Tranmer died in 1973. I regard it as the high point of my life's work.[25]

One of their first decisions was to put their inheritance into what became the Annie Tranmer Charitable Trust.

Like Carver, Valerie Lewis and John Miller had been frustrated by the long drawn-out and ultimately fruitless discussions over a possible 'in lieu' agreement, and their dealings with central and local government had left them disenchanted. They were now relieved to be able to explore an alternative solution, and to meet representatives of the National Trust at Sutton Hoo.

Leslie and Annie Tranmer, who owned Sutton Hoo after the Second World War. Following their deaths in 1973 and 1993, the estate was left to their daughter Valerie Lewis and their family solicitor John Miller, to be used 'for charitable purposes.'

Valerie Lewis lived in a modest house in Woodbridge, and after her mother's death, Sutton Hoo House had been cleared of furniture. The meeting was in a largely empty room, with a sense of the whole estate being in limbo. The impression was misleading. As trustees, Valerie Lewis and John Miller had now decided that they were prepared to make a gift to the National Trust of the burial ground, Top Hat Wood (which screened the site from the Deben), the rest of the land, and Sutton Hoo House itself. Whether the Trust could accept their generous offer would depend on whether it could find ways of protecting the mounds, maintaining a substantial building in the middle of the site, and providing public access which would not involve pedestrians crossing a dangerous road and then walking up a busy farm track. A satisfactory solution was bound to be expensive and would be likely to depend on an application to the Heritage Lottery Fund, then just beginning to find its feet. Proposals for the future of the site would have to satisfy both the Trust's committees and the HLF that it was to be safeguarded effectively and would be financially self-supporting.

One of Carver's ideas for the site was that a cast of the ship, possibly in concrete, should be placed in the mound where the treasure was found. When Bruce-Mitford led a British Museum re-excavation of the site in 1965, a full-scale cast had been taken of the outline of the ship, articulated by the prominent lines of rivets, so there were no technical reasons why this should not be done. There were, however, questions of principle and aesthetics. The National Trust's initial thoughts were to prefer an exhibition hall alongside the stables of Sutton Hoo House, in which the cast could be displayed. If sufficient numbers of visitors could be attracted to the site, it would be possible to employ the staff needed to supervise and protect the burial ground. Sutton Hoo House itself could be used as a field-study and activity centre, making similar provisions to those being planned by the Trust at the Dial House at Brancaster, which was to be largely funded by the Millennium Commission.

These proposals, when submitted to the Heritage Lottery Fund, immediately encountered formidable obstacles. A special adviser to the trustees, Sir David Wilson – a former director of the British Museum and a distinguished specialist in Anglo-Saxon studies – was strongly critical of the plans. Some years before, he had been involved in a joint exhibition with the National Maritime Museum, at which a section of the Sutton Hoo ship cast had been shown, in his view unsatisfactorily. Relations between the two museums over the exhibition had also been strained. Wilson had been left with a strong prejudice against exhibitions using ship casts.

The HLF's trustees were influenced by his reservations, but before making their decision, they agreed to inspect the cast themselves. A delegation that included Lord Rothschild and Dame Jennifer Jenkins, then acting as a special adviser, visited the British Museum store, where the huge sections of plaster of paris casts were stacked forlornly on metal storage racks. They were unimpressed, and the National Trust was told to think again; but the principle of a grant was affirmed. Valerie Lewis and John Miller were now sufficiently reassured to proceed with the gift of the property to the Trust.

The decision not to display a cast of the ship may have been disappointing, but it brought benefits. The National Trust was forced to think rigorously and imaginatively about the different ways in which the significance of Sutton Hoo could be explained to visitors. There were no exhibitions of comparable material in Britain, but major museums with similar artefacts had been built in Norway, Sweden and Denmark. The Trust's Chief Archaeological Adviser, Dr David Thackray, who had championed the acquisition of Sutton Hoo, led an expedition to the Baltic, taking with him the East Anglia region's Historic Buildings Representative, David Adshead, its Archaeologist, Angus Wainwright, and the Sutton Hoo project manager, Richard Hill.

They visited Roskilde, near Copenhagen, where Viking ships had been so well preserved in situ that it has been possible to construct replicas which can be sailed on the fjord adjoin-

The *Sæ Wylfing* under sail, a half-scale replica of the ship excavated at Sutton Hoo in 1939.

ing the museum. They followed the footsteps of Edith Pretty, to the University Museum in Uppsala in Sweden, where there are seventh-century helmets with decoration so close in detail to the one found at Sutton Hoo that the same moulds may have been used. The new museum building at Gamla Uppsala, close to royal burial mounds roughly contemporary with Sutton Hoo, was a rich source of ideas and relevant exhibition techniques. At Valsgärde – where Bruce-Mitford had excavated – there is a cemetery of ship-graves close to the river, in beautiful, unspoilt countryside, which served as a reminder that the ancient site itself, without all the trappings of heritage interpretation, is a most precious exhibit, and one easily spoilt. The visit produced a greatly improved brief for the Trust's architects, Joanna van Heyningen and Birkin Haward, who themselves made an excursion to related Scandinavian sites.

The solution for the care and display of Sutton Hoo which finally found favour with Valerie

Lewis and John Miller, with the Heritage Lottery Fund, and with the many other grant-aiding bodies, involved two new buildings close to the stables, an exhibition with a carefully researched replica of the burial chamber as a centrepiece, and the use of Sutton Hoo House for holiday cottages, for study rooms, and for educational activities. The burial ground itself was to be reached by a footpath, which looks down to the estuary from where the great ship was dragged to its final resting place. The mounds would simply be roped off. In order that the whole site could be easily seen, a wooden viewing platform was to be built, tucked into the edge of Top Hat Wood.

The construction of the new buildings and the creation of the exhibitions coincided with the publication of Seamus Heaney's translation of the Anglo-Saxon masterpiece *Beowulf*, which won the Whitbread Book of the Year Prize in 1999. David Adshead and I had heard Heaney talk about his work on the translation at a lecture in the British Museum, when he spoke most eloquently and amusingly about his first encounter with the Sutton Hoo treasure. Although the exhibition hall was not due to be completed for many months, I wrote to ask whether he would consider speaking at the opening ceremony. Understandably, Heaney did not commit himself, nor did the National Trust press him beyond occasional reports on progress with the project. When he was told that Sutton Hoo would be ready to open in March 2002, the Nobel Laureate confirmed that he would be there.

The early morning of 13 March was grey but dry. Heaney had been staying at Sutton Hoo House the night before, and we had agreed that he should be left to walk alone to the burial ground, before he was shown the new exhibition. When all the guests were assembled in the reception building, he was invited to talk about *Beowulf* and Sutton Hoo. He began with a quotation in Anglo-Saxon, and then, in his own translation, described how, at the end of the poem, there is an account of the burial of the king of the Geat people, who construct a great mound:

> … a marker that sailors could see from far away… it was their hero's memorial; what remained from the fire they housed inside it, behind a wall as worthy of him as their workmanship could make it.

Heaney then made a generous comparison:

> What we celebrate today is a new stage in the construction and celebration of a heroic memorial; we are housing a history behind walls as worthy of it as our workmanship can make them. The opening of the site at Sutton Hoo, the erection of new buildings, the recreation of ancient arms and regalia by an exercise of immemorial skills, the exhibition of these objects and of some of the original treasure *in situ* – all this constitutes a significant act of repossession.26

The significance which Heaney drew out of what had happened at Sutton Hoo might also apply to other places which benefactors had steered into the safekeeping of the National Trust. He proposed that the opening of the exhibition at Sutton Hoo should be seen as 'a re-articulation, a restitution of its cultural and historical meaning, and a reawakening of regard for its material existence'. Most of those in his audience would have been vaguely aware that the reawakening of the past was what drew them to such places. But only a great poet could articulate it so clearly:

> The flow of life, in other words, is not always a matter of the current running away. It can also involve backwash and replenishment, a marvellous retrieval of time and tide…

Rather than name all the scholars, benefactors, curators and fundraisers who had made important contributions at Sutton Hoo, he singled out just two:

> It would be impossible to enumerate all the vanished faces which are being assumed into the new pattern, but the shades of the ancient denizens of Sutton Hoo are bound to be hovering close, the ones that Edith Pretty is said to have witnessed in her day, haunting the crests of the burial mounds… We must also call to mind, deliberately and gratefully, the gazing face of Mrs Pretty herself and the face too of that vigilant *genius loci*, Basil Brown. Brown, as we all know, was the amateur archaeologist whose intuition and native skills were crucial to the discovery and right treatment of the great finds in 1939. He was the ship-wright of our earth ship, the man whom we might also name the mound-warden or the hoard-watcher or call by any of those honorific kennings that the Beowulf poet bestowed on the gold-guarding dragon.

Heaney concluded by suggesting that the doling out of gold, helmets and horses by King Hrothgar, described in Beowulf, recalls and prefigures the generosity of all those who had made the Sutton Hoo project possible, particularly the trustees of the Annie Tranmer Charitable Trust.

Valerie Lewis did not want any recognition for herself. However, she did ask that Sutton Hoo House should be renamed Tranmer House, as a tribute to her mother. Both before and after the opening of Sutton Hoo, she regularly worked with the volunteers who assisted with the clearing of brambles from the woodland and other practical tasks around the estate. Most of the other volunteers had no idea that she was in fact the donor of the property, or that the Annie Tranmer Charitable Trust had made substantial contributions to the project. They were simply puzzled when she was helping with the removal of an old, redundant fence, and remarked: 'Oh, I remember putting this in, years ago.'

One of the most carefully planned parts of the exhibition hall was the Treasury, a relatively small room with high security protection. On a visit to the site in 2000, the director of the British Museum, Dr Robert Anderson, agreed to the periodic loan of pieces of the treasure back to Sutton Hoo. These rotating exhibitions would ensure that the finds were looked at afresh, in a different context from the display in the British Museum. When planning the exhibitions, the expectation was that around 60,000 people might visit. In 2002 there were over 200,000 visitors to Sutton Hoo. As John Miller, who had retained the shooting rights for his lifetime, ruefully remarked, all those visitors had done nothing to improve his shoot.

The loans also honoured the intentions of Edith Pretty, shortly after she gave the treasure to the nation. She had hoped that a temporary exhibition of the finds could be mounted in Suffolk, but the war had intervened. Now, over 60 years later, her wish was fulfilled.

19

THE FRENCH HAIRDRESSER

Tyntesfield and a Public Appeal

T HE PUBLICATION IN 1971 of Mark Girouard's book, *The Victorian Country House*, surprised, even shocked, many who thought of themselves as civilised admirers of English domestic architecture. To those who persisted in regarding most post-Regency architecture as an aberration, Girouard's book was a revelation: his scholarship was as impeccable as the illustrations – mostly drawn from the archives of *Country Life* – were poetic and evocative. The photographs of Anthony Salvin's Peckforton Castle in Cheshire, of Woodchester Park in Gloucestershire, and of the ruinous but romantic Bayons Manor in Lincolnshire gave the lie to assumptions that the great houses of the Victorians were monstrosities. There was, however scant treatment of a building that was largely inaccessible. Tyntesfield, near Bristol, is mentioned only briefly.[1]

Girouard's book prompted questions at the National Trust's Properties Committee, the Chairman of which, Lord Rosse, had been involved in the formation of the Victorian Society in 1958.[2] There was an uncomfortable realisation that the very first house to be given to the Trust, in 1937, under the Country Houses Scheme, had been Wightwick Manor, the home of a Wolverhampton industrialist built in 1887. Since then the Trust had acquired scores of Georgian buildings, but only one country house – Sir Charles Barry's Cliveden – by an outstanding Victorian architect. The upshot was that Girouard was asked to draw up a list of houses which merited National Trust protection, if ever they were offered for sale or as a gift.

During the next thirty years the list was reviewed and revised as buildings either found a secure future or had their contents dispersed. Girouard had put Norman Shaw's Cragside, in Northumberland, top of his list, and in 1977 it was transferred to the Trust through National Land Fund procedures – though not to universal enthusiasm. When the Properties Committee discussed its merits, John Julius Norwich, the Chairman of the Trust's Arts Panel and revered for his contributions to the World Monuments Fund and Venice in Peril, described it as an 'architectural cat's-cradle'. It was only because of the unshakeable resolve of the Trust's local Honorary Historic Buildings Representative, Sheila Pettit, that its acquisition was finally approved. Standen in Sussex, the finest surviving building by Philip Webb, was bequeathed to the Trust by Miss Helen Beale in 1973. In the late 1980s and 1990s there were no more major transfers of Victorian buildings to the Trust, but that was partly because the stream of country house acquisitions generally was drying up.

Feliks Topolski, *Rosalie, Lady Mander, c.*1940, wife of Sir Geoffrey Mander who donated Wightwick Manor, near Wolverhampton, to the National Trust in 1937.

The south front of Cragside in Northumberland, designed by Richard Norman Shaw and built for the industrialist and arms manufacturer, Sir William (later 1st Lord) Armstrong, in 1864. The house and its estate were transferred to the National Trust in lieu of death duties in 1977.

When Angus Stirling succeeded Sir Jack Boles as Director-General in 1983, it was at a moment of opportunity: the National Heritage Memorial Fund was well-disposed to the National Trust, membership numbers were increasing rapidly, and legacy income brought confidence and optimism. Stirling sensed a favourable wind in the Trust's sails and set his course accordingly. He encouraged family and school visits to properties, reinvigorated Enterprise Neptune, and championed a string of acquisitions, including Fountains Abbey and Studley Royal in Yorkshire in 1983; Belton House in Lincolnshire in 1984; Calke Abbey in 1985 and Kedleston the following year, both in Derbyshire, where there was an exceptionally energetic and capable Regional Director, James Turner; and Sheringham in Norfolk in 1987. Then there was a pause.

Between 1991, when the National Heritage Memorial Fund passed Chastleton House in Oxfordshire over to the National Trust, and 2002 no buildings of outstanding architectural importance were acquired. It looked increasingly as though the phase of the Trust's intervention to save country houses at risk was over, and the organisation had adopted other priorities. There were changes externally which helped to explain the shift. Under Margaret Thatcher's Conservative governments taxation for the private estate-owner had been greatly reduced, and many no longer needed to turn to the Trust. Government ministers were unsympathetic. Nicholas Ridley, when Secretary of State for the Environment, advocated that the free market should apply as much to country houses as to the rest of the economy, and if owners had fallen on hard times, their homes should be sold on to those who could afford to maintain them. In 1992, when the future of Pitchford Hall – 'the most splendid piece of black-and-white building in Shropshire' as Pevsner described it – was in doubt, the Secretary of State for National Heritage, David Mellor, blocked the efforts of English Heritage, the National Heritage Memorial Fund, and the National Trust to find a solution. Its contents were sold and it continues to be inaccessible to the general public.

The lead statue of *Bacchus* and the Temple of Piety at Studley Royal, North Yorkshire. The water-gardens, laid out by John Aislabie between 1716 and 1740, and incorporating the medieval ruins of Fountains Abbey as a dramatic focal point, were bought by the National Trust in 1983, with grants from public organisations and subscriptions to a public appeal.

Some of the reasons for the change were, however, internal. During the 1990s the Trust became increasingly embroiled in the issue of hunting, which involved resolutions at the Annual General Meetings in 1988, 1990 and 1993. At the last of these the Trust was out-manoeuvred by the League Against Cruel Sports, which used the wording in the National Trust Act of 1907 – that there was a statutory duty to preserve the 'natural aspects, features, animal and plant life' of its properties – to support demands for the issue of cruelty in the hunting of deer to be scientifically investigated. Sir Angus Stirling, as he had become, concluded that the pressure for a report would become irresistible. The Trust duly abandoned the policy that had stood it in good stead for half a century: that ethical and moral issues were a matter for Parliament. When Professor Patrick Bateson was appointed to lead the research, the Trust embarked on a course that could and ultimately did lead to the conclusion that the hunting of deer with dogs was cruel. That in turn would be likely to result in a ban, unless a Labour government was elected and made hunting illegal before the Trust was forced to act.

Another major distraction concerned the organisation of the National Trust, and particularly the future of its head office, which had spread out of buildings in Queen Anne's Gate in Westminster into satellites in London and the west country. In 1988 the Secretary of the Trust, David Beeton, was charged with finding a solution, and identified Corsham Court in Wiltshire as a possible location out of London, but with good rail communications. The Bath Academy of Art was leaving extensive nineteenth-century buildings, which could readily be adapted to offices, and which adjoined an outstanding house with an important picture collection. Discussions over the future of Corsham Court had been initiated by Paul, 4th Lord Methuen and James Lees-Milne in 1936, and were now resumed with his nephew, Anthony, 6th Lord Methuen. There seemed the possibility of solving two problems at a stroke. Reactions to the proposal were initially favourable, but then support wavered. Eventually the staff who would have been affected were delighted to be told that proposals for a move from London were to be set aside, and instead the Trust would concentrate on the celebration of its first hundred years, due in 1995. Stirling was to stay on beyond the normal retirement age of 60, for what was to be a triumphant centenary year.

His successor, Martin Drury, and the new Chairman, Charles Nunneley, who took over from Lord Chorley in 1996, moved promptly to address the issues they had inherited. Bateson's report, unsurprisingly, found there was strong scientific evidence that deer pursued by hounds experienced considerable, measurable distress, concluding that this amounted to cruelty. With a minimum of delay the Trust's Council announced that the hunting of deer on its properties should cease. The decision was bitterly resented, particularly in the west country. Both Drury and Nunneley found themselves committed to a long drawn-out, energy-sapping, and unwinnable campaign to placate the Trust's critics, many of them previously well-disposed and generous.

At the same time Drury was considering how to improve the management and effectiveness of the Trust. Organisational change can be a tedious subject, laden with the jargon of professional consultants, and difficult to relate to the core purposes of a body such as the National Trust. Different ways of working are only a means to an end, and for a century the Trust had rarely had to revise its structures and procedures radically. By the mid-1990s, however, the need for change was generally accepted by staff, and was being urged by the Trust's committees.

In July 1996 Drury reported to the Executive Committee that he proposed to look again at the question of head office location, and 'the need to provide for the Trust's requirements into the next century'. The review concluded that the financial benefits of a move out of London were significant, but 'until a decision is made on how head office should be structured and how many staff it requires, it would not be sensible to incur the very high costs of relocation or to invest in a change of premises.'[3] Drury accepted this and most of the other recommendations of the review. He initiated a fundamental reappraisal of how the National Trust could be better organised centrally and regionally. A root-and-branch reorganisation of the Trust was already underway in 2001, when Fiona Reynolds, previously director of the CPRE and then director of the Women's Unit in the Cabinet Office, took over as Director-General from Drury. As a passionate conservationist, it was an opportunity she had dreamt of for years. At 43 she had age on her side, and she knew the Trust well from serving on a regional committee. Reynolds realised that changes talked about for over ten years now needed decisive implementation.

Wholesale reorganisation for a body such as the National Trust is, for most staff, utterly disorientating and demoralising. The uncertainty, the disruption to families, and the possibility of redundancy mean that the process becomes all-consuming and a constant distraction from what at other times would be matters of the highest priority. It was at this moment of turmoil for the Trust, in July 2001, that the reclusive Richard, 2nd Lord Wraxall, died unexpectedly in his small, plain bedroom at Tyntesfield.

Tyntesfield had been placed second by Mark Girouard in his list of the six outstanding Victorian houses which most deserved preservation. Two other houses on the list – Thoresby Hall in Nottinghamshire by Anthony Salvin and Mentmore in Buckinghamshire by

The west front of Tyntesfield in north Somerset, designed by John Norton of Bristol in 1863 for William Gibbs. Following the death of his descendant, Richard, 2nd Lord Wraxall, in July 2001, the National Trust acquired the house and its contents in 2002, with contributions from national organisations, two substantial anonymous donations, and over 77,000 separate subscriptions to a public appeal.

Joseph Paxton – had in the intervening years lost most of their contents. Girouard was unequivocal: 'I feel quite confident in saying that there is now no other Victorian country house which so richly represents its age as Tyntesfield.'[4] But the odds were heavily stacked against its preservation.

Lord Wraxall had prepared a will stipulating that the estate should be divided between his father's descendants. By the time he died there were nineteen of them, making it inevitable that everything had to be sold. His executors were legally bound to secure the highest possible values, and instructed Christie's and their agents, Savills, accordingly. They then set a deadline: if the National Trust was interested, it would have to make its best offer by the end of March 2002.

The very thought of preserving such a place at huge public expense provoked a hostile reaction in some influential quarters. Writing in *The Architects' Journal* Martin Powley described Tyntesfield as a 'mixture of grandeur, squalor and junk', piled up in this 'storage husk of a house'. It was like a 'dinosaur in its death throes', and the money spent on its conservation would be better directed to building hospitals, he insisted (as if there would ever be a simple choice between the two).[5] The initial response of the Trust's committees was to be dismayed by the probable costs involved, which looked likely to exceed £40 million. Doubts were also expressed by the Trust's Head of Gardens, Mike Calnan, and by the chairman of the Gardens Panel, Anna Pavord, about the significance of the grounds. Even more serious was the reaction of the English Heritage director for the south-west, who questioned whether Tyntesfield possessed 'sufficient merit to warrant a major campaign in support of public ownership'.[6] This was reflected in the listing of the house by English Heritage as Grade II*, rather than Grade I.

During the first half of 2002 it became increasingly clear that those who questioned the interest and value of Tyntesfield were seriously out of tune with shifting public taste. The

The dining room at Tyntesfield.

monster of fifty years earlier had become the precious endangered species in a new century. Tyntesfield may have been built from the profits of importing guano – the droppings of seabirds accumulating many feet deep on islands off the Pacific coast of South America, which could be used as an agricultural fertiliser – but its architecture, decoration, and furniture spoke of the High Anglican allegiances and conspicuous philanthropy of the Gibbs family. The architect of the house was John Norton, the designer of many churches around Bristol, who submitted his designs for Tyntesfield in 1863. For the chapel (the largest attached to an English country house), William Gibbs turned to Arthur Blomfield, son of the Bishop of London. Although their buildings evoke the spirit of the age, neither was an architect of the first rank. Perhaps posterity's greatest debt to them is that in 1862 first Norton and then Blomfield encouraged a young architectural assistant with literary ambitions, Thomas Hardy.

Among other ecclesiastical buildings funded by William Gibbs are St Michael and All Angels at Paddington and William Butterfield's chapel at Keble College, Oxford. The gothic towers of Tyntesfield, with subsidiary clusters of bays and turrets rising out of sleeping beech woods, were intended to have more the appearance of a medieval monastery than the palace of a millionaire industrialist. Tyntesfield is a house that turns away from statements about classical learning, the lure of the Mediterranean or frivolous entertainment. Instead it is a monument to Victorian aspirations to self-improvement and piety.

Such sentiments had been profoundly unfashionable for most of the twentieth century. That disdain had been expressed in the dynamiting and destruction of so many great nineteenth-century buildings, most spectacularly the Duke of Westminster's Eaton Hall in Cheshire. But by 2002 public opinion had changed. Perhaps Margaret Thatcher's enthusiasm for Victorian values played a part. In academic and conservation circles much Georgian decoration had come to be regarded by a young generation of architectural historians as predictable, repetitive and often rather dull. That could never be said of Tyntesfield, which

The east facade of Eaton Hall, Cheshire, in 1901. Originally a seventeenth-century house, it was substantially rebuilt in the late nineteenth century by Alfred Waterhouse for Hugh, 1st Duke of Westminster,and demolished in 1961.

was less Jane Austen's Pemberley, in *Pride and Prejudice*, and more J.K. Rowling's Hogwarts, in the Harry Potter novels then gripping public imagination.

The potential for harnessing the latent enthusiasm for this Victorian masterpiece was not lost on Marcus Binney's SAVE Britain's Heritage. Binney rapidly put together a generously illustrated publication called *The Tyntesfield Emergency*, to which Girouard, Peter Howell of the Victorian Society, Jennifer Jenkins and Martin Drury contributed essays. Simon Jervis, who was on the point of retiring as the National Trust's Director of Historic Properties, wrote on 'The Grand Ensemble'. David Lambert, of the Garden History Society, explained why the surrounding landscape was of outstanding historical interest. In a characteristically belligerent piece the architectural historian John Harris proclaimed: 'Let there be no WAVERERS.' The message penetrated the office of English Heritage. The chief executive, Simon Thurley, and the chairman, Sir Neil Cossons, appalled that they might be seen to have abetted the destruction of the house, rapidly muzzled their regional director and signalled that representations to have Tyntesfield listed Grade I would be considered sympathetically.

There was still an argument to be won within the National Trust. With Jervis's departure early in 2002, the Trust's Architectural Adviser, Tim Knox, became the champion for Tyntesfield. A scholar with an unusual eye for both quality and the exotic, Knox was an eloquent lecturer and a writer. There were many others within the Trust who brought expertise to the evaluation of Tyntesfield, but it was Knox who articulated its importance to the committees and to grant-aiding bodies.

For Fiona Reynolds the timing was in some ways problematical and in others advantageous. She was trying to lead the National Trust through a period of great upheaval. Several members of the management board were unenthusiastic about Tyntesfield, and at least one – Simon Murray, a Territory Director – was hostile. He had started his career with the Trust in the East Midlands, where he had made an outstanding success of Mr Straw's House, the

Mendips, in the Liverpool suburb of Woolton, the childhood home of John Lennon, built in 1933 and acquired by the National Trust in 2002.

semi-detached, terraced house of a Worksop grocer, given to the Trust in 1990. Murray had subsequently advocated that the Trust should try to acquire a greater variety of historic properties, including a cinema in Stockport, and the childhood home of John Lennon in Liverpool. 'Tyntesfield is just the sort of building we ought not to be associating ourselves with,' he told the management board. Reynolds herself, although by training a geographer and landscape historian, was ready to listen carefully to the case for preservation and from the outset saw that Tyntesfield could be used to demonstrate the Trust's wider social purposes.

There were, however, other considerations. It was ten years since the National Trust had acquired a property of major architectural distinction, and Reynolds was well aware that her own appointment as Director-General had been interpreted as an indication that the Trust might in future turn more to countryside and environmental conservation, and away from concern for the built heritage. This unjust perception had been strengthened by changes resulting from the organisational review which she was promoting. In the new structure the old historic buildings department was to cease to exist, and its staff were to be absorbed into a new conservation department, with a former land agent as its director. The 'lilies' were being trampled by the 'boots'. One consequence of this was that no member of the Trust's management board was academically or professionally qualified to speak for historic properties. The changes were also to result in a reduction in the numbers of curatorial staff based in regional offices and in conservation staff being spread more thinly around the country and the Trust's collections.

For some of those with long memories, the proposal that the Trust should economise on its historic buildings staff was familiar. When Lord Gibson became Chairman in 1977, he had found that there was a presumption that having a member of staff in each region who was qualified to advise on the care of buildings and collections 'was a luxury the Trust could not afford'.[7] Gibson's response had been to insist that the curatorial arm of the organisation should be strengthened. He now set about making the case all over again, and found Reynolds responsive. She was also tackled by Gibson's successor, Dame Jennifer Jenkins, who had chaired committees at the CPRE, was a powerful ally, and could be a formidable opponent. Jenkins understood the need for effective curatorship from her years as chairman of the Historic Buildings Council and she was dismayed by what was happening to the National Trust's historic buildings department. There was widespread relief when, in response to these pleas, Reynolds announced that, although the care of buildings would continue to be a part of the responsibilities of the conservation department, the Director of Historic Properties would have a place on the management board.

In 2002 I had retired from the post of Regional Director in East Anglia, after 21 years, and when the number of regions was reduced from fourteen to eleven. Now that the Director of Historic Properties was to be a member of the management board, the post was a much more attractive one, and I duly applied for it. I took up the reins in May 2002, when the department was still in disarray and the future of Tyntesfield was hanging in the balance.

Meanwhile something unexpected and rather extraordinary was happening in response to the SAVE campaign. Tyntesfield had become a sensation and was constantly in the pages of the national press. This may have partly been due to the Hogwarts factor. But a still more potent media fantasy was at work. In April the papers were full of the story that Tyntesfield had attracted the singer Kylie Minogue as 'the perfect retreat from the burdens of fame'.[8] Local people were up in arms. 'It's nothing against her personally, but we value our peace and quiet in this neck of the woods. The last thing we want is thousands of fans coming down here,' one resident was quoted as saying. A 'Kylie Out' campaign was launched, and signs demanding that she stay away appeared at the entrance to the estate. The more her agents flatly denied her rumoured interest, the more they fanned the flames of publicity. The fate of Tyntesfield had become, in Knox's words, 'a death struggle between the flaxen-haired superstar and the heritage fogies'.[9]

It would be pleasing to be able to record that this publicity masterstroke had been devised in the appeal office of the National Trust's 'Save Tyntesfield' campaign. A more prosaic explanation is that the rumour started as a joke in the local pub. What is indisputable is that an obscure, seemingly unfashionable building had become a hotly disputed trophy, which thousands of people wanted to see preserved by the National Trust. The numbers contributing to the appeal sailed past the 50,000-mark, with two anonymous donors giving £4 million and £1 million respectively. By July 2002 over 77,000 separate donations had been received, many from people not normally associated with the Trust. The message was not lost on its staff and committees: the public loved great houses, preferably rambling, romantic and gothic ones.

The most surprising donor I encountered was in a barber's on the outskirts of Norwich. David Barritault moved from Angoulême in central France to Norfolk when his girlfriend,

The east front of Red House, in Bexley-heath, south London, designed by Philip Webb in 1859 for William Morris, and purchased by the National Trust in 2003.

Dr Flore Depient, took a job at the Institute of Food Research, based near the University of East Anglia. He cut hair rather better than he spoke English, but in due course he found out that I worked for the National Trust. On days off, he told me, they visited their favourite Trust properties, particularly Blickling and Felbrigg. 'Have you managed to save the house near Bristol?' he asked me, between snips. 'We have sent in our donation.'

The scale of public response to Tyntesfield encouraged the trustees of the National Heritage Memorial Fund to give support on an unprecedented scale. When their chairman, Dame Liz Forgan, and the director, Anthea Case, came to see the house, they needed little persuading of its importance. One of Forgan's special interests is the work of Augustus Welby Pugin. The sight of the lot numbers attached not just to the furniture by J.D. Crace, who worked with Pugin on the Palace of Westminster, but also to the crucifix and altar vessels in the chapel made a powerful impression. The NHMF gave £17.4 million to Tyntesfield – normally its annual expenditure for three years – making it the largest grant in its history. The Art Fund bought the contents of the chapel. On 31 July 2002 the National Trust was able to announce that its offer for the house had been accepted by the executors, and it had taken possession of the estate. Four years later the Heritage Lottery Fund approved a grant of £20 million towards continuing conservation, the educational work being undertaken, and for an endowment. Those thousands of contributors to the appeal, most of them nameless and expecting no recognition, had provided the key to securing unprecedented levels of grant.

There was for me an uncomfortable sequel. When reporting to the Trust's committees on the rarity of Tyntesfield, great play had been made of the Girouard list. What made Tyntesfield so important, they were told, was that few, if any, other houses of the 1860s, of comparable importance, had survived: this was an opportunity never to recur. The case had

Sir Edward Burne-Jones, *The Wedding Banquet of Sir Degravaunt* (detail), one of three wall-paintings commissioned by his friend William Morris for the Upstairs Drawing Room at the Red House.

been accepted. Then, less than six months later, came the news that Red House, designed for William Morris by Philip Webb, was coming on the market. Unlike Tyntesfield, the building was extremely well-known in this country and abroad, it was an acknowledged masterpiece, and its creator had been a significant influence on the founders of the National Trust. To complete my embarrassment, William and Janey Morris had moved into Red House in April 1860, and had immediately begun decorating it. The two houses were, to all intents and purposes, exactly contemporary. Rather lamely it was pointed out that one was a country house estate on a grand scale, and the other a four-bedroom dwelling in the London suburbs.

Perhaps because the costs looked relatively modest compared to Tyntesfield, the committees were forgiving. There may even have been a rekindled enthusiasm for historic buildings. Certainly the purchase of Red House was completed in 2003, thereby making the Trust the guardian of Philip Webb's first and, with Standen, last house. Other important country houses have followed: Agatha Christie's house, Greenway, overlooking the river Dart, in 2000, Godolphin in Cornwall in 2007, and Seaton Delaval in Northumberland in 2009. The ten-year drought had been followed by, if not a flood, at least a steady stream of great buildings taken into permanent protection by the Trust.

Reassured by the public's appetite for such acquisitions, the National Trust has reaffirmed its commitment to 'places of historic interest' as well as to 'natural beauty'. What has changed during the period that Fiona Reynolds has been Director-General has been the extent to which those properties are used to engage visitors in their care. Tyntesfield has provided an opportunity to involve the public in a variety of conservation activities, both inside and outside the house, working under the supervision of qualified, professional staff. The role of volunteers, working in gardens, woods and the Trust's buildings, has so expanded that projects which would not have been contemplated a few years ago are now practicable. In 2008 over 50,000 volunteers were committed to carrying out regular work for the Trust. Its properties are being used to teach local children what is involved in growing their own vegetables, often in under-used kitchen gardens such as the one at Tyntesfield. 'We want to inspire a new generation of young people to connect with the land and grow food,' Reynolds has said of these initiatives.

The response, nationally and indeed internationally, to the call to preserve Tyntesfield took everyone by surprise. But the generosity of a French hairdresser should not be seen as altogether extraordinary. After all, British artists from John Constable to Francis Bacon have found their work more enthusiastically received in Paris than in their home country. The gothic architecture from which Tyntesfield derives was invented in France; and it was to French ecclesiastical buildings that Blomfield looked for the design of the chapel at Tyntesfield.

THE REWARDS OF GENEROSITY

A T THE VERY FIRST MEETING of the National Trust's Executive Committee in February 1895, the Secretary, Canon Hardwicke Rawnsley, was able to report the offer of a piece of coastal property as a gift. The land was a gorse-covered hillside amounting to no more than four and a half acres above Barmouth and overlooking Cardigan Bay on the Merioneth coast. The donor was Mrs Fanny Talbot, an admirer of Ruskin who had contacted Rawnsley because she had 'long wanted to secure for the public for ever the enjoyment of Dinas Oleu'; and she believed that the newly-formed National Trust would 'never vulgarise it, or prevent wild nature from having its own way'.[1]

Several of the properties acquired in the Trust's early years were straightforward gifts, but many more were bought after public appeals. The first coastal property in England was Barras Nose, near Tintagel in Cornwall, purchased by subscription in 1897. The Trust's appeal letters were usually drafted by Rawnsley and then passed to Octavia Hill, who would sometimes amend them with suggestions, such as: 'I thought perhaps it would be well to dwell a little on the breeze and beauty of the space as well as on its historical and poetical side…'[2]

Public appeals have continued to be a vital source of support, not just for the money raised but for the opportunities they give to engage the general public. As Octavia Hill expressed it at the inaugural meeting in 1894, 'the trust, like St Francis of old, would be strong in its poverty, and, like him, would appeal for gifts.'[3] However, both she and the first chairman, Sir Robert Hunter, appreciated the need for a secure legal foundation and special powers granted by Parliament. The National Trust Act of 1907, which Hunter drafted, gave the newly formed organisation the ability to hold land inalienably. This meant that, once designated 'inalienable', property could only be taken away from the Trust, against its wishes, with the express consent of Parliament. This statutory provision was unprecedented and remains unique to the National Trust. It was the first expression of Parliament's willingness to see the Trust develop and grow as a charity independent of government control and funding, yet with support through enlightened legislation.

The largesse heaped on the National Trust has come in many different forms. It has received gifts of land and property, often in conjunction with financial contributions from very large numbers of supporters and making use of tax incentives which successive governments have been far-sighted enough to grant. That combination of support accounts

Dinas Oleu, five acres of gorse-covered cliffland, overlooking Barmouth and the Mawddach Estuary, donated to the National Trust by Mrs Fanny Talbot as its first property in 1895.

for the National Trust's extraordinary success. By the time the centenary of the National Trust Act was celebrated in 2007 the organisation had a membership of 3.5 million, looked after 617,500 acres of land in England, Wales and Northern Ireland, was guardian of 37,000 buildings, 4,000 historic monuments, and 235 gardens and landscape parks. As a parable it is a latter-day Feeding of the Five Thousand. The generosity it represents is on an almost unimaginable scale.

The various ways in which the government has enabled the National Trust and other conservation organisations to protect and make available to the public beautiful countryside, works of art and historic buildings have been touched on in earlier chapters. Usually these provisions have been made because a minister or civil servant has responded to a specific need in an enlightened and imaginative way (and usually with dire warnings and obstruction from the Treasury). The most significant pieces of legislation are the various National Trust Acts;[4] Hugh Dalton's creation of the National Land Fund in 1946; the grants for historic buildings, as recommended by Sir Ernest Gowers and delivered through the Historic Buildings and Ancient Monuments Act of 1953; the provisions of the Finance Act of 1972, secured by the Trust's then Director-General, Sir Frederick Bishop, that all gifts and legacies to the Trust and other specified charities should be free of tax; and the transforming of the National Land Fund into the National Heritage Memorial Fund in 1980.

Whenever such government support has been offered, there have been those who have predicted that the inevitable consequence of accepting help from the government would be loss of independence. There were strongly worded exchanges of letters at the time of the Gowers Report, with Harold Nicolson writing to the Chairman, Lord Crawford:

I feel that the moment we accept the principle of being subsidised by the government, we lose our voluntary character and enter the corridor which leads to a government department.[5]

Why have those fears proved unfounded? There has been at least one government minister, Richard Crossman, who in the 1960s thought the National Trust should be nationalised, but the Prime Minister, Harold Wilson, had more sense. Why should any sensible government wish to squander so much public goodwill and generosity for the satisfaction of trying to meet similar aims out of taxation?

There was, however, a price to pay; and it took a subtler form. With the advent of the National Land Fund and then the National Heritage Memorial Fund, the National Trust was able to put together funding arrangements for major acquisitions which included an element of gift from the former owner, grants from charitable trusts, a public appeal, and a substantial contribution from the government, either by foregoing tax through the in-lieu procedures, or by a grant, or both. Not surprisingly, the different parties saw the outcome in their own different ways. The donor and his or her family tended to regard acquisition by the Trust as the consequence of their generosity. Those who had contributed to a public appeal might reasonably feel that they had enabled the Trust to assume ownership. And the grant-aiding bodies would frequently wish to be cast in the role of saviour. Usually all parties could, with some justification, feel proprietorial.

Inevitably, tensions and jealousies could and did arise; and if allowed to fester, developed into acrimonious public rows. In the early 1970s the correspondence pages of *The Times*

Sudbury Hall, in Derbyshire, painted with its formal gardens in the second half of the eighteenth century. The seventeenth-century house, with its principal contents, was transferred to the National Trust in lieu of death duties in 1967, with an endowment donated by John, 10th Lord Vernon.

The Great Staircase at Sudbury Hall in Derbyshire.

and other papers were taken up with the heated controversy surrounding the National Trust's treatment of Sudbury Hall in Derbyshire, and in particular the work carried out there by John Fowler. The house had been transferred in 1967 through the National Land Fund, with grants towards maintenance from the Historic Buildings Council and Derbyshire County Council, and John, 10th Baron Vernon providing an endowment. Although never reconciled to the treatment of Sudbury after he ceased to live there, Lord Vernon, with considerable magnanimity, bequeathed important contents to the Trust which he had previously removed from the house. In the same county Henry Harpur-Crewe behaved with great generosity and public spirit over the transfer of Calke Abbey, but he too felt increasingly that he was not sufficiently involved and consulted. His complaints were like small-arms fire compared with the broadsides from Lord Scarsdale of Kedleston Hall, again in Derbyshire.

Before the National Trust was ever involved at Kedleston – one of Robert Adam's most assured and exquisitely realised classical houses – Francis, 3rd Viscount Scarsdale was in very public dispute with his own family about the future of the estate. He had inherited the house, park and 4,300 acres of farmland from his cousin in 1977, but with it a tax liability of £2.25 million. His eldest son, Peter Curzon, was left ten per cent of the estate's total value, which was £20 million. To secure his share, Peter urged that Kedleston should be sold. Lord Scarsdale was adamant that it should not be, and to his great credit a solution was found which kept it all together. In 1987 he gave the house and park to the National Trust, with a contribution towards an endowment. A total of £2.5 million was needed to carry out repairs, £10 million to purchase the contents, and £5.9 million to put the house on a secure financial footing, making a total cost of £18.4 million. Most of this came from a special allocation from the government, channelled through the National Heritage Memorial Fund, and from a public appeal.

Lord Scarsdale had translated his deep affection for the house into an act of great generosity. As the nephew of George Nathaniel, Marquess Curzon of Kedleston – Viceroy of India and a considerable benefactor of the National Trust – he had honoured his forebear's wishes, expressed in a supplement to his will, that 'my executors and heirs at Kedleston will see it preserved in good hands'. Lord Scarsdale continued to occupy the 23 rooms in the family wing, had the use of two staff flats, was allowed to hold parties in the state rooms, and retained the shooting in the park, all rent free. What was not achieved was a harmonious relationship with the Trust, and in particular with its regional staff. By 1994 disputes about the rearrangement of furniture, changes in the garden, and the redecoration of Adam's state rooms

[below left] Detail of the south front of Kedleston Hall in Derbyshire, designed by Robert Adam in the 1760s. The hall and park were given to the National Trust by Francis, 3rd Viscount Scarsdale in 1987.

[below right] Breakfast in the Hall at Kedleston, following the Hunt Ball in 1955.

had spilled into the press, with Scarsdale accusing the Trust of 'vandalism and sacrilege'. While he complained about lack of consultation, the Trust protested that he had chosen to ignore genuine efforts to communicate and explain. At this stage the general public weighed in.

The *Times Magazine* of 22 October 1994 carried a long article entitled 'When an Englishman's home is the nation's castle'. The author was Adam Nicolson, whose father Nigel had given Sissinghurst to the National Trust. He could understand both points of view and was even-handed in his treatment of Scarsdale and the Trust. Nicolson's discussions with other donor families confirmed that the way the Trust organised its staff, with a division between the agents who managed properties and the historic buildings staff who dealt with aesthetic and conservation matters, meant that donors, 'at the receiving end of decisions, rarely know who made them or how'. He concluded that 'all complaints could be read as a symptom of powerlessness'.

At Kedleston that powerlessness was the consequence of Lord Scarsdale's personal efforts to prevent the break-up of the house and its collections, achieved with considerable personal sacrifice. So far, so admirable. But all was not well. Nicolson related how two National Trust members, Alan and Valerie Greathead, had had an upsetting visit to Kedleston. They had been asked at the entrance to be careful of sheep on the drive. As they were approaching the house, a Range Rover came up behind them, flashing its lights and trying to overtake on the grass verge. An altercation followed. Alan Greathead's explanation – that he was trying to comply with the notices asking visitors to drive slowly – prompted the retort: 'You don't have to tell me about that. This is my home and it has been for twenty years.' Immediately after the visit, Mr and Mrs Greathead instructed their solicitor to change their wills. The National Trust was to have been the sole beneficiary of their estate, worth at least £200,000, but no longer. The explanation they gave for the change was that 'we cannot consciously do anything which will enable people such as Lord Scarsdale to act in such an arrogant way towards the public who now provide for the upkeep of the property.'

During the last 30 years there have been fewer outright gifts of great houses and an increasing tendency to strike a hard commercial bargain when property passes to the Trust. In the 1970s the Douglas Pennant family encouraged the return to Penrhyn Castle of the finest of their pictures, including a Rembrandt and Jan Steen's *Burgomaster of Delft*, previously loaned to the National Gallery of Wales in Cardiff. Then, following the death of Lady Janet Douglas Pennant, the Steen was sold in 2004 for £8.5 million to the Rijksmuseum in Amsterdam, and the Rembrandt, currently valued at between £32 million and £46 million, is also on loan there. Without government intervention and support, such sums are beyond the National Trust's reach.

The hardening of attitudes has also been evident at Chirk Castle, on the Welsh borders. When the castle was transferred to the Trust through National Land Fund procedures in 1981, it was on the basis of an agreement that the Historic Buildings Council for Wales would fund repairs to the building – it was in a precarious state – and the Myddelton family would leave the principal contents on long loan, in expectation that they would be offered in lieu of tax by successive generations over the next hundred years. It was a solution for which Colonel Ririd Myddelton fought particularly hard, and which involved years of frustrating negotiation with the Welsh Office. When its civil servants were at their most indecisive, Colonel Myddelton remarked to me: 'You go down to Cardiff to give them one of your courteous National Trust taps on the shoulder. I shall follow, with a kick up their backsides.' Eventually the tactic worked.

Twenty years later the Myddelton family were being advised to challenge the loan agreement with a view to selling the most precious pictures and furniture in the castle. The suggestion that there might be a moral obligation to respect both the letter and the spirit of the agreement which had kept Chirk Castle and its contents together prompted the retort from Christian that this was not 'practical politics'.[6]

This attitude is strikingly different from the belief of the Dalyell family that the House of the Binns belongs 'to the people of Scotland', or the Countess of Enniskillen's conviction that 'Florence Court belongs to everyone.' Most recent negotiations with the National Trust over the transfer of works of art associated with an historic house have often started with an assumption by the owners and their advisors that they are assets to be realised at full market value. There are, however, useful inducements to encourage owners to sell to museums or to the Trust, the most significant of which are the tax exemptions for private treaty sales, with the added incentive of a *douceur*, which gives part of the benefit of the saving in tax to the seller.

These arrangements, valuable though they have been, are insufficient to prevent the dispersal of many great collections, with the owner persuaded by the leading salerooms that the greatest financial benefit can be secured from an auction on the premises. Among the most prominent of these was the auction at Easton Neston, in Northamptonshire, in May 2005. Easton Neston was remodelled by Nicholas Hawksmoor in about 1700, incorporating earlier work by Sir Christopher Wren. The building is of supreme architectural importance, and had been cared for in an exemplary way by Christian, Lady Hesketh, who died in 2006. Scarcely a murmur of public concern was heard when the house was sold by Lord Hesketh and the contents dispersed.

The Hesketh family had owned another historic house, Rufford Old Hall, in Lancashire. In 1936 Thomas, 1st Baron Hesketh gave the house, with an endowment, to the National Trust. The family continued to take a close interest in it, his daughter-in-law Christian Hesketh making the long journey from Easton Neston to Rufford to attend meetings of the local committee supervising its upkeep. There was some consolation in the sale of the Easton Neston collections when the Trust was able to buy, thanks to the generosity of several benefactors, a large

The Great Hall at Rufford Old Hall, Lancashire, probably built between 1530 and 1550. The house was given to the National Trust in 1936 by Thomas, 1st Lord Hesketh, with an endowment.

landscape by the rare Mechelen artist, Gommaer van der Gracht, marine paintings by Francis Swaine, several family portraits, archives and a Dutch cabinet, all of which were recorded at Rufford Old Hall in the 1920s. The fate of Easton Neston and of Rufford is in striking contrast; and the changing attitudes in one family revealing.

Should there be greater inducements to keep great collections together and to encourage gifts to museums? In a positive and potentially significant initiative in 2003 the Chief Secretary to the Treasury, Paul Boateng, with the encouragement of the Minister for the Arts, Estelle Morris, commissioned Sir Nicholas Goodison to produce a review entitled *Securing the Best for our Museums: Private Giving and Government Support*. The Chief Secretary's advisory panel included the directors of three national museums, trustees and notable benefactors of museums, and representatives of the Historic Houses Association and the National Trust (most of whose great houses are registered as museums). The report, published in 2004, made 45 recommendations, including the proposal that owners of pre-eminent objects should be able to offer them in lieu of tax and with the benefit of the *douceur* during their lifetimes; and also that donors of such objects should be allowed to offset the gross value of their gift against income before liability to income tax. These and the other recommendations would enable museums to acquire many of those objects which they are now powerless to prevent going overseas. Disappointingly, the government chose to adopt those recommendations which involved fine-tuning existing provisions, but have not acted on those that might have enabled museums and the National Trust to compete for acquisitions with institutions in Europe and the United States.

There are those who have argued that state aid to help museums or the National Trusts to acquire what has previously been private – and usually aristocratic – property is an undesirable, even pernicious, form of nationalisation. Those criticisms took an extreme form in an article written by the philosopher Roger Scruton in *The Times* of 11 February 1984, entitled 'Out with the Stately, Enter the State', which referred to 'the dead hand of the National Trust over these once glorious institutions', to its 'ghoulish tendencies', and to the transformation of great houses into mausolea. *The Times* published a response of mine, and a long and excellent letter from James Lees-Milne, which set out to refute the charge that a building, once in the hands of the National Trust, becomes 'eternally fossilised'. The irony of Lees-Milne's defence was that when he came to publish *People and Places: Country House Donors and the National Trust* in 1992, he concluded a gloomy epilogue with the assertion that the houses he had helped to save were now 'lovingly and adeptly preserved in aspic by the National Trust'.[7] He also asserted that the descendants of donors have tended to find that the arrangements for occupation 'did not work'. Lees-Milne implied that as the expectations of visitors increased, so have the strains on the relationship, to the point that 'fewer and fewer families live in their old homes'. This is true of Upton, Chirk, Greys Court and Wallington. There are other properties such as Penrhyn, Stourhead and Dyrham where the donor family made the decision to move out at the time of the transfer; and others such as Felbrigg and Scotney where there were no children to take up occupation. In those cases the alternative to ownership by the Trust would probably have been another in the long line of country house sales and dispersals. What is surprising is not so much the number of cases where the

William Hogarth, *The Hervey Conversation Piece*, portraying John, Lord Hervey (in a grey coat holding his key as Vice-Chamberlain of the King's Household), surrounded by a group of his Whig friends. The painting hangs in the smoking room at Ickworth in Suffolk.

family have left, but the many instances where donor families have managed to continue living in a house which is both their home and a property of the National Trust.

There is one house where the relationship failed completely. The Trust had considerable misgivings about allowing Victor, 6th Marquess of Bristol to move into the east wing at Ickworth after he was released from prison in 1941, having served two years of a three-year sentence. At a time when the nation was struggling for survival, there was little appetite for reminders of the lurid press reports of the robberies with which he had been involved. The Trust eventually concluded that it was morally bound by the Memorandum of Wishes agreed with his aunt, which gave the head of the family a right of occupation rent free. By 1979 Victor Bristol had decided that in London it was 'no longer safe to walk the streets', and he moved permanently to Monte Carlo with its attractive rates of taxation and where 'there is no crime rate'.[8]

Whatever reservations Victor may have had about the National Trust's position at Ickworth, it was nothing compared to his hostility to his eldest son John. When he was married in 1984 his father took the trouble to put an announcement in *The Times* saying that he would not be attending the wedding 'owing to a prior engagement in London'. He did nevertheless leave his son a Suffolk estate of 7,000 acres and nearly £19 million.

John Bristol's decline was as relentless as anything depicted in 'The Rake's Progress'. What distinguished him from the subject of Hogarth's engravings was that drugs destroyed his health while homosexual hangers-on wasted his fortune. His presence at Ickworth began to put the safety of the public at risk. When under the influence of drugs he had a head-on collision on the entrance drive with a car full of children. His Irish wolfhounds attacked visitors who subsequently had to have hospital treatment. Raids by the police on the east wing resulted in the seizure of drugs and, after several warnings and opportunities for treatment, consequent jail terms. All this meant that he was persistently breaching the terms of a lease which he would have had to forfeit if he had not been overtaken by debt. His attendance at meetings involving his trustees and the National Trust became increasingly unpredictable. When he did appear it was all too evident that his life was disintegrating: he still had cold, cruel eyes, but the mouth no longer relaxed habitually into a sneer. He was intent on using his inheritance to hasten his own destruction. On one occasion he arrived half dressed and so late that those representing him had dispersed. As his hands were shaking uncontrollably, the Trust's regional chairman, Lord Hemingford, tried to help him insert his cuff links. When told that his trustees had gone to lunch, he left the house and pursued them at speed in his Porsche.

In 1996 he decided that he would sell the furniture and pictures in the East Wing that had not been part of the original transfer to the Trust. A two-day sale raised nearly a million pounds but repaired his finances only temporarily. He also removed from Ickworth an Italian eighteenth century fireplace that he claimed was his property. The Trust established that it had been there since the early twentieth century and it was duly reinstated. Eventually, in 1998, his trustees proposed a payment from the National Trust to reflect some of the value of the lease, which was then surrendered. Bristol died the following year, aged 44, of 'multi-organ failure attributable to chronic drug abuse'.[9] His great aunt's conviction that the gift of Ickworth to the Trust gave it a necessary protection from the weaknesses of successive generations of Herveys has been vindicated. The east wing at Ickworth is now a successful hotel and the main house and park attract over 100,000 visitors a year.

Elsewhere the inevitable tensions, irritants and occasional exasperations in the relationship of donor families with the Trust have been surmounted. The Wyndhams are very much a presence at Petworth, the Carew-Poles at Antony, the Sackville-Wests are living at Knole, and the Nicolsons are still at Sissinghurst, where the pitfalls and attractions of involvement with the Trust have been the subject of television programmes and a book by Adam Nicolson, *Sissinghurst: An Unfinished History*. What is curious and misleading is the criticism that without a donor family in residence, ownership by the Trust is a death sentence. Take Blickling as an example: the permanent staff includes a trained conservator to look after the collections; there are six gardeners and two woodsmen; managers and assistants run the shop and restaurant; a direct works building team is also used at other nearby properties; and in a converted barn on the estate, the textile conservation studio takes work from both Trust properties and privately-owned houses, and has an international reputation. Over a hundred volunteers assist in the house and garden. Far from being dead, this particular hand of the National Trust has active and nimble fingers. While it is undeniable that the role of the building has changed, it is still a rich and varied one, involving many people who are enriched by both the cultural and social life of the house.

The National Trust has always regarded itself as a refuge of last resort. Most of those who gave their estates to the Trust did so because the alternative seemed to be decay and, sooner or later, the dispersal of their family collections. Frequently it was because taxation – with death duties raised to 75% in Hugh Dalton's budget of 1946 – meant that the stark alternatives were sale or the offer of the estate *in lieu* of tax. When owners decided, after sounding out the Trust, that they preferred to find their own solutions, the charity was relieved rather than disappointed.

In September 1945 James Lees-Milne had tentative discussions with the Coke family solicitor about Holkham Hall in Norfolk, but they were not pursued. How much better that Edward, 7th Earl of Leicester continued to live there, running the estate in an exemplary way, taking advice from the late John Cornforth and Sheila Stainton (retired from the National Trust), and managing the park to a higher standard than the Trust normally achieves. Mark Norman, as chairman of the Trust's finance committee in the 1960s and '70s, used to warn that it was its country houses which might ultimately bankrupt the organisation, and he hoped that the stream of acquisitions would slow down. His wish has been granted.

No one could sensibly dispute that a house still being lived in by a family long associated with it has an enhanced historical resonance, a sense of continuing vitality. To acknowledge this need not imply that any other form of ownership renders the house lifeless and soulless. That would be an historical nonsense, because houses have often changed hands down the centuries, and been transmogrified and revitalised.

That the rediscovery of the past can represent a new and valid life for an evolving historic property was articulated memorably by Seamus Heaney at Sutton Hoo. The same theme of transformation and renewal is the subject of T.S. Eliot's poem, 'Little Gidding', in which he asserts that:

> We cannot revive old factions,
> We cannot restore old policies
> Or follow an antique drum…

But that is not the end of the matter:

> … history may be servitude,
> History may be freedom. See, now they vanish,
> The faces and places, with the self which, as it could, loved them,
> To become renewed, transfigured, in another pattern.[10]

There was no tidy thesis that I wanted to substantiate when I embarked on these portraits of benefactors; nor do I want to categorise those who have given generously in ways which might lessen their individuality. However, as the chapters began to take shape, I could not help thinking that some donors have things in common with others, that their backgrounds and circumstances may have given them a predisposition to generosity; and that shared values meant that the pursuit and possession of material things mattered less to them than others might suppose.

Many of the National Trust's benefactors did not have close family to inherit things that were precious to them. Some were childless. Consideration of philanthropy and childlessness prompted Francis Bacon to write that 'the noblest works and foundations have proceeded from childless men, which have sought to express the images of their minds, where those of their bodies have failed'.[11] Very often the sons who might have inherited had been killed in the First or Second World Wars. Stourhead in Wiltshire would probably not belong to the National Trust if the son of Sir Henry and Lady Hoare had not been a casualty of the Great War. Like other gifts to the Trust, Stourhead was to be a perpetual memorial. Another was Newark Park, a sixteenth-century hunting lodge, remodelled by James Wyatt in the 1790s, in a remote part of the Cotswolds, which was given to the Trust in 1949 by Mrs C.A. Power-Clutterbuck in memory of her son, James Edward, who had been killed in the First World War. The house has been repaired and revived in recent years by a sympathetic and generous tenant, Robert Parsons. Many benefactors have been spinsters. Others were bachelors, which may or may not mean that they were homosexual. Some were and did not conceal it. Those who were discreet had good reason to be so. It was in the homophobic 1950s that Scotland Yard considered prosecuting Benjamin Britten and Peter Pears because their relationship was illegal. In 1953 John Gielgud, recently knighted, was arrested for importuning. As society has changed, so have assumptions of homosexuality. In the case of Wyndham Ketton-Cremer, his close friend Anthony Powell, who was a frequent visitor to Felbrigg, presents a subtler picture, writing in his memoirs about the shy undergraduate he had known at Balliol:

> One longed for him to get drunk, swear, fall
> down, break a window, even if he remained (as he
> always did) uncommitted to sex. No such
> outbreak ever took place. Probably he knew what
> was best for himself.

Powell acknowledged that Ketton-Cremer 'read the proofs of my books, never without making improvements' and that his suggestions 'sometimes indicated that, anyway inwardly, he was not as innocent as some might suppose.'[12] The future of the Felbrigg inheritance did not worry Ketton-Cremer while his gregarious brother Richard was alive. *Felbrigg: The Story of a House* is dedicated 'To the memory of my Father, my Mother and my Brother.'

Sir Winston Churchill's desk in the Study at Chartwell in Kent. The house, garden and park were bought by a group of Churchill's friends, and given to the National Trust in 1946 with an endowment for maintenance.

When in 1946 a group of Winston Churchill's friends bought his house, garden and park at Chartwell and gave it to the National Trust, it was to be an expression of gratitude to the former Prime Minister and a testament to the sacrifices made in the war. Several of those I have written about were soldiers, or served in the armed forces. The awareness of mutual dependence, of comradeship, the acceptance that health and life itself may be sacrificed in a moment, is likely to affect, in varying ways, attitudes to the accumulation and retention of personal wealth. My conversations with donors such as Lord Anglesey of Plas

Newydd, Colonel Charles Brocklehurst of Hare Hill in Cheshire, Colonel Ririd Myddelton of Chirk Castle, and Sir Joshua Rowley of the Tendring Hall estate in Suffolk, suggested that their military service shaped their thinking about other forms of service. The same was true of Sir John Carew-Pole DSO, Andrew Devonshire MC and Nigel Nicolson.

I have also been struck by how many of the National Trust's benefactors are women; and how the organisation itself has been shaped by women, starting with Octavia Hill, and continuing with others such as its first gardens adviser, Ellen Field, and Phyllis Ireland who transformed its attitudes to archaeology. Many women have been influential on its committees, including the Trust's chairman, Dame Jennifer Jenkins, and Selina Balance, who chaired its architectural panel. The Trust's first donor in 1895 was Mrs Fanny Talbot. Without the positive, imaginative response of wives, widows and daughters, the Country Houses Scheme in England, Scotland, Wales and Northern Ireland would have achieved far less. This is a book about heroines at least as much as it is about heroes. They include Octavia Hill's band of young female helpers, Teresa Berwick, Rosalie Mander, Eleanor Dalyell, Edith Pretty and Valerie Lewis, Nancy Enniskillen, Sybil Bedingfeld (the donor of Oxburgh Hall in Norfolk), Matilda Talbot who gave Lacock Abbey and village in Wiltshire, and many more. When I think of them I am reminded that the word 'heroine' is Greek in origin and means 'demi-goddess'.

Since the post was created in 1968, there have been six Director-Generals of the National Trust. The first woman to be appointed, Fiona Reynolds, has since 2001 implemented a reordering of the Trust's governance, the relocation of its head office from London to Swindon, and a reorganisation of its staff structures. Reynolds has raised awareness of the range of the Trust's obligations and activities among politicians, the press and the nation at large. In a rapidly changing world these changes of perception have enabled the Trust to renew and extend its commitment to preserving places of natural beauty and historic significance.

Among my other portraits there are an actor and the daughter of an artist. Communities of artists are often interdependent, as willing to exchange ideas as painters often exchange pictures. Of course there are cases of painters who have allowed themselves to become consumed with jealousy. One example is Sir Alfred Munnings, a meretricious painter himself, who developed an intense dislike for both the work of Stanley Spencer and the artist himself. Munnings contrived to borrow some of Spencer's drawings from a London exhibition, had them photographed, and then passed the material over to the police, urging a prosecution under the obscenity laws. Sir Gerald Kelly and Walter Sickert persuaded the Director of Public Prosecutions to drop the case, and then ensured that Munnings, as a past President of the Royal Academy, was officially censured by its Council, who assured Spencer of their regret and 'readiness to assist him if further attacks of the kind were made on him'.[13] Sickert had been one of those who had supported Spencer in the face of earlier criticism, writing that his work 'will rank among the masterpieces of all generations'.[14] His greatest achievement, the Sandham Memorial Chapel murals in Hampshire, was given to the National Trust in 1947. The circumstances of the commission followed an unusual course. It was originally Spencer's own idea to paint a cycle of paintings recording his experiences in 1918, while serving with the army as a medical orderly in Macedonia. He showed the designs to John and Mary Behrend, who 'felt at once that we would like to do something about this castle in the air' and who had the chapel built to accommodate his paintings. Mary Behrend's brother, Lieut. H.W. Sandham, had died in 1919 from illness contracted in Macedonia and she was wanted to com-

memorate him. Spencer's paintings were initially the result of enlightened patronage, which had the added purpose of providing a family memorial.[15]

In his own reckless, indulgent way Sickert was true to his own dictum: 'The thing is to give, give, give. You always get back more than you give.' At a time when his own finances were a dire shambles, he decided to auction his *Raising of Lazarus* of 1929 (the year Costanza Hulton recovered his portrait of Signor de Rossi from Venice) for the benefit of Sadler's Wells, which he did on the stage of the theatre, and to much public acclaim, for 380 guineas. No wonder that his friends and admirers, including Teresa Berwick, would not let him die in penury.

It is no coincidence that the National Trust itself grew out of the involvement of its founders in the efforts to protect common land. These were, quite clearly and openly, campaigns to use the law to prevent property shared for a communal benefit from being enclosed and appropriated by private landowners. In my chapter on the fishing communities of the north Norfolk coast and their generosity of spirit, the shared interest in common land and its protection was a powerful bond. Something of the same idealism was shown when the Fell and Rock Climbing Club bought Great Gable in the Lake District in 1923, as a memorial to its members killed in the First World War, and presented it to the National Trust.

An assumption of many fundraisers is that donors expect acknowledgement, and the more generous they have been, the more prominent should be the record of their gifts. Yet the biblical virtue of doing good by stealth surfaces again and again. The anonymous benefactor to the appeal to protect the park at Stowe is one example. Simon Sainsbury is another.

One of the most generous recent gifts to the Trust was also one of the most self-effacing.

Stanley Spencer's murals in the Sandham Memorial Chapel at Burghclere in Berkshire, built by Mr and Mrs John Louis Behrend in 1926–27 in memory of her brother, Lieutenant Henry Willoughby Sandham, who died in 1919 of an illness contracted during the First World War. The chapel was given to the National Trust by the Behrends in 1947 with an endowment.

Great Gable viewed from the shores of Wastwater in Cumbria. In 1923 the Fell and Rock Climbing Club bought the summit of Great Gable for the National Trust as a memorial for those of its members killed in the First World War. Wastwater formed part of the 31,215-acre Leconfield Commons transferred to the Trust in lieu of death duties in 1979, the largest acquisition ever made in the Lake District.

In 2008 the public learnt that Richard Broyd was giving three country houses to the Trust. He had rescued Bodysgallen Hall – a largely seventeenth-century house near Llandudno – in 1980 and had made it into a thriving hotel. In the 1970s Middleton Hall near York, built in 1699, was being used as a strip club until it too was acquired by Broyd's Historic House Hotels. Hartwell House near Aylesbury, which in 1809 had been leased to the exiled Louis XVIII of France, also came with the gift, which was one of the most generous in the Trust's history. All three houses, which are in excellent condition, will continue to be managed by Historic House Hotels, prompting Broyd to remark that he had 'joined the middle management of the Trust'.[16]

Another unexpected feature of this assembly of portraits is just how important the continuities seem to have been. Most accounts of the founding of the National Trust rightly stress how much influence F.D. Maurice and the Christian Socialists had on Octavia Hill and Robert Hunter. Nonconformity marched hand-in-hand with radicalism in the late nineteenth century, and both left their mark on the Trust in its early years. The ideals of the Unitarians and the Quakers continued to influence the Trust, as the gifts of Quarry Bank Mill and Dudmaston show. The Beale family, donors of Standen, were Unitarians, like many of the great philanthropists of Victorian Birmingham. Quite rightly, the Regional Director responsible for launching the museum at Styal, Gerard Noel, was determined to see that Norcliffe Chapel, built by Samuel Greg in 1822, was brought under the wing of the Trust for long-term protection. Somehow he managed to persuade the finance committee that it did not represent an onerous financial commitment. That was in 1979, and in his long career was as near as

Noel ever came to perjury. Norcliffe Chapel is as much part of the story of Styal as the Apprentice House, Quarry Bank House (acquired by the Trust in 2006), and the Mill itself.

The influence of Nonconformity and Unitarianism on donors is a reminder of just how many of those who gave their property to the Trust were not from long-established landed families, but had acquired their wealth from nineteenth-century industrial enterprises. This is true of the donors of Anglesey Abbey, Bodnant, Dudmaston, Cragside, Felbrigg, Standen, Wightwick and many more. A family like the Herveys may have had a long history of involvement in politics and the established church, but the endowment of Ickworth came from railways. Unlike their counterparts in many countries in Europe, the English aristocracy was constantly renewing itself by marrying into industrial wealth and by the ennobling of successful industrialists, so providing the wealth which in due course could be transferred into gifts to the Trust. Where there were links with nineteenth-century commerce and industry, there were also likely to be associations with Nonconformity.

Ruskin's followers found, as did the supporters of Sir Richard Acland's Common Wealth Party, that communal forms of land-ownership are difficult to sustain. That has been so down the centuries. Because of the way it was established, the National Trust proved to be one way of promoting shared ownership of property for the benefit of society as a whole. Its success depends on being business-like without being like business. In recent years it has, like so many organisations, found itself drawn towards the structures and jargon of American-inspired business management practice. Their acceptance has not been uncritical. The Trust staff in East Anglia agreed a few years ago that they functioned best when combining the aspirations of a *corps de ballet* with those of a workers' co-operative. Octavia Hill would have nodded understandingly (she called her assistants 'workers'); and James Lees-Milne might have welcomed the one model, if not the other.

However, this may be a moment to pause. These studies of benefactors have not been based on the premise that they were acting out some political philosophy, still less had been so moulded by their family, educational or class background that they were pre-conditioned to be generous, any more than a different upbringing might have groomed them for a life of self-serving greed. Writers on the horrors of the twentieth century have identified the banality, the very commonness of evil. The same applies, surely, to generosity: it is, in a way that should be reassuring, commonplace, banal even. There is an infinite variety to the benefactors delineated here.

The last century witnessed destruction on a colossal scale. The impulse to destroy, to disperse, to obliterate has been all too evident. But the urge to create, to rescue and to share has not been extinguished. Contemplating the building of Dumfries House in the 1750s, the 5th Earl of Dumfries observed that ''tis certainly a great undertaking, perhaps more bold than wise, but necessity has no law'. The Prince of Wales wrote that the efforts in 2007 to prevent the dispersal of its collections had been another 'great undertaking' that had proved irresistible.[17]

Spontaneous generosity can be another irresistible urge, as was observed by one of the Trust's most down-to-earth benefactors, Beatrix Potter. She was also someone who understood that generosity brings its own rewards. After she purchased the Monk Coniston estate of 4,000 acres in the Lake District in 1930, with the intention of passing it over to the Trust, she was asked to assume responsibility for running the whole area. She described this as 'interesting work at other people's expense'. As well as being an enlightened hill-farmer, she was a biologist, artist and writer, so conforming to some of the models of generosity suggested earlier in this chapter. When she congratulated the Chairman of the National Trust, John Bailey, on the success of the public appeal for funds for Monk Coniston, she concluded:

> Those of us who have felt the spirit of the fells reckon little of passing praise; but I do value the esteem of others who have understanding. It seems that we have done a big thing; without premeditation; suddenly; inevitably – what else could one do?[18]

During the recession caused by the banking crisis of 2008, the National Trust was faced with a likely decline in membership, a fall in the value of its investments, and uncertainty over whether there would be fewer visitors to its properties. It seemed the worst possible time to have to contemplate a campaign to safeguard the future of Sir John Vanbrugh's great house of Seaton Delaval, just north of Newcastle, in Northumberland, following the death of Edward, 22nd Lord Hastings. The house was scarred by a calamitous fire in 1822 and the central section is still a blackened shell. The reputation of the builder's family is scarcely less black: in 1775 the last of the line, intent on abusing a laundry maid, died from a kick in the groin. Vices which Vanbrugh might have hesitated to depict in one of his plays were acted out at Seaton Delaval.

There were grave misgivings about launching a major appeal, not least because it was thought that people in and around Blyth, which had grown and contracted with the fortunes of Bates Colliery, might think that other community provisions were a higher priority. This assumption may have been typical of what Vanbrugh, relishing the gale that greeted his arrival in August 1721, called 'the tame sneaking south of England'.[19] What had not been forgotten was the warm and generous support, twenty years earlier, for the Trust's campaign to clean up the coastline of County Durham, where the sandy beaches had been turned black with coal waste from Easington Colliery. At Seaton Delaval a similar response showed just how much pride there was locally in this most romantic and theatrical of houses, and how strong the wish to be involved in its transfer to the Trust. It was as though there was a subliminal recollection of the feelings expressed in the inscription over the west door of Staunton Harold church in Leicestershire, which was given to the National Trust in 1954 by Robert, 12th Earl Ferrers. The tribute reads:

> In the year 1653 When all things Sacred were throughout ye nation Either demolisht or profaned Sir Robert Shirley, Barronet, Founded this church; Whose singular praise it is To have done the best things in ye worst times And hoped them in the most callamitous.

To those who rallied to the plea to give a secure future to Seaton Delaval, it must have seemed one of the best things, at the worst time. In December 2009 the house passed to the Trust.

A new act in an unpredictable drama is about to begin.

NOTES

CHAPTER 1:
INTRODUCTION:
THE DONORS' LUNCH
(PAGES 10–21)

1. Republished in Simon Jenkins, *The Selling of Mary Davies* (London, 1993), 99.
2. This was true of Barrow Cadbury (1862–1958), as was made clear by his grand-daughters, Catherine Hickinbotham and Philippa Southall, in an interview recorded by the author and Samantha Wyndham on 25th March 2010 and deposited with the Barrow Cadbury Trust.
3. See also Lewis Hyde, *The Gift: How the Creative Spirit Transforms the World* (Edinburgh, 2006).
4. Matthew Sturgis, *Walter Sickert: A Life* (London, 2005), 143.
5. David Cannadine, *In Churchill's Shadow* (London, 2002), 243.
6. Robert Hunter, *The Preservation of Commons* (1867), 358–9.
7. Text of Sir Charles Trevelyan's broadcast in the National Trust's archives.
8. Recalled by Gerard Noel and relayed to the author in a letter of 8th October 2009. Dalton's words to him were: 'Try to nationalise the countryside and they will be up in arms, but call it a charity and they will throw it at us.'
9. See Jennifer Jenkins, *From Acorn to Oak* (London, 1994): chapter 6, on Dalton's attitude to nationalisation and the Trust, and page 136.
10. Jenkins, *From Acorn to Oak*, 137.
11. Transcripts of all the speeches are in the National Trust's archives.
12. The same view is expressed in Andrew Devonshire, *Accidents of Fortune* (Norwich, 2004), 48. An account of another, subsequent donor's lunch is in Adam Nicolson, *Sissinghurst: an Unfinished History* (London, 2008), 153.

CHAPTER 2:
THE PUBLICAN AND
THE MASKED LADIES
(PAGES 22–37)

1. Jonah Jones, *Clough Williams-Ellis: The Architect of Portmeirion* (Bridgend, 1996), 179.
2. The image may have come to him from one of Conan Doyle's hugely popular *Tales of Adventure*, called *The Sealed Room*, which describes 'the red brick tentacles of the London octopus engulfing the surrounding countryside'.
3. Information from Peggy Pollard's

nieces, Kitty Turnbull and Jean Gladstone, in an interview recorded for the National Trust sound archive, 22 October 2008.
4. The copy is now in the possession of Claire Riche, who kindly showed it to me.
5. Kitty Turnbull and Michael Maine interview, 22 October 2008.
6. Quoted in Sue Herdman, 'The Cloaked Crusaders,' *National Trust Magazine*, Spring 2008, p.26.
7. The 'Boo' has been deposited by the National Trust in the Wiltshire County Record Office in Chippenham.
8. Clough Williams-Ellis, *On Trust to the Nation* (London, 1947), 168.
9. I am grateful to Richard Haslam for drawing my attention to the masque, which is among Clough's papers in the National Library of Wales.
10. Clough Williams-Ellis, *Architect Errant* (London, 1971), 226.
11. Clough Williams-Ellis, *England and the Octopus* (new ed., Glasgow, 1975), 3–4.
12. Williams-Ellis, *England and the Octopus*, 4–5.
13. I am grateful to Michael Maine for letting me have copies of letters in his possession, written by Clough Williams-Ellis to Peggy Pollard.
14. Williams-Ellis, *England and the Octopus*, 3.
15. Williams-Ellis, *Architect Errant*, 227.

CHAPTER 3:
THE EDITOR AND
THE STATESMAN
(PAGES 38–51)

1. Christopher Hussey, *The Picturesque: Studies in a Point of View* (London, 1927), 287.
2. John Cornforth, ' The Husseys and the Picturesque,' *Country Life*, 10 May 1979, 1438
3. I am grateful to Lady Gibson for information about the Husseys.
4. Christopher Hussey, 'Large ideas for small estates,' *Country Life*, 5 April 1930, 500.
5. J.R.M. Butler, *Lord Lothian (Philip Kerr) 1882–1940*, (London, 1960), 144.
6. Norman Rose, *The Cliveden Set: Portrait of an Exclusive Fraternity* (London, 2000), 40.
7. Butler, *Lord Lothian*, 53.
8. Rose, *The Cliveden Set*, 57.
9. Butler, *Lord Lothian*, 51.
10. Butler, *Lord Lothian*, 144.
11. Butler, *Lord Lothian*, 145.
12. Lord Lothian, *English Country Houses: The Case For Their*

Preservation (printed by the National Trust, 1934).
13. Oliver Garnett, 'Reaping the Benefits', in *Apollo: Houses and Collections Annual 2008*, 10. I am grateful to him for drawing my attention to the significance of this purchase by Hussey.
14. Chorley memoirs, in National Trust archives.
15. Lothian, *England's Country Houses*, 4.
16. Rose, *The Cliveden Set*, chapter 7.
17. Michael Astor confirmed that his mother's letters showed the relationship to be platonic, in *Tribal Feelings*, (1963), 143. See also Rose, 58.
18. Letter of 2 September 1992 to the National Trust's chairman, Lord Chorley, copied to the author.
19. Letter of 29 November 1935, in the Lothian archives deposited in the Record Office in Edinburgh: GD 40/17/311.
20. Lothian papers, Edinburgh Record Office, GD 40/17/405/453.
21. Butler, *Lord Lothian*, 317.
22. Butler, *Lord Lothian*, 313.
23. Lothian, *English Country Houses*.
24. Rose, *The Cliveden Set*, 40.

CHAPTER 4:
THE DIARIST
(PAGES 52–67)

1. James Lees-Milne, *The Milk of Paradise: Diaries 1993–1997* (London, 2005), 234.
2. This chapter was written in 2007 without the benefit of Michael Bloch's *James Lees-Milne: The Life* (London, 2009). His approach to his subject is different to mine and I was reassured to find that much of the material I have used does not appear in his book. I decided to leave the chapter largely unaltered, as an alternative view of a complex and engaging man.
3. Charles Darwent, 'Our Man of the Moment,' *Perspectives*, January 1995.
4. James Lees-Milne, *The Milk of Paradise*, 262.
5. 'Controversy could be left to History but he intended to be one of the historians', in John Keegan, *Churchill* (London, 2002), 160.
6. Anon., 'James Lees-Milne's Heavenly Diary', *Private Eye*, January 1998, 24.
7. Letter from Sir Francis Nicholls, whose father served on the Trust's committees, sent to the author on 11 May 1999.
8. James Lees-Milne, *People and Places: Country House Donors and the*

National Trust (London, 1992), 10.
9. Harold Nicolson, *Diaries and Letters 1930–1964*, abridged volume (Harmondsworth, 1980), 60.
10. Victoria Glendinning, *Vita: The Life of Vita Sackville-West* (London, 1983), 86.
11. Alastair Forbes, 'The Honours of the House', *Times Literary Supplement* (10 October 1975), 1191.
12. Michael Trinick, 'Provenance Remembered,' published in Merlin Waterson, *A Cornish Bastion: The Work of Michael Trinick* (Lanhydrock, 2006), 45.
13. James Lees-Milne, *Holy Dread* (London, 2001), note on 224.
14. Forbes, 'The Honours of the House', 1190.
15. James Lees-Milne, *Ancestral Voices: Diaries 1942–1943* (London, 1975), 214.
16. Charles Darwent, 'Our Man of the Moment,' *Perspectives*, January 1995, 22.
17. James Lees-Milne, *Prophesying Peace: Diaries 1944–1945* (London, 1977), 19.
18. Lees-Milne, *Prophesying Peace*, 214.
19. James Lees-Milne, *A Mingled Measure* (London, 1994), 25.
20. Lees-Milne, *Ancestral Voices*, 171.
21. James Lees-Milne, *Caves of Ice* (London, 1983), 197.
22. James Lees-Milne, *Holy Dread* (London, 2001), 125.
23. Lees-Milne, *Holy Dread*, 225.
24. James Lees-Milne, *Ancient as the Hills* (London, 1997), 31

CHAPTER 5:
THE AGENTS
(PAGES 68–87)

1. With Lothian papers in the Scottish Record Office: SRO 9040/17/311
2. Mark Norman's recollections, written during a holiday in Madeira in March 1984, are unpublished. A copy is in the National Trust's archives.
3. James Lees-Milne (ed.), *The National Trust: A Rcord of Fifty Years' Achievement* (London, 1945), x.
4. Anne Acland, *A Devon Family* (London, 1981), 153.
5. From copies of correspondence supplied by Sir John Acland, September 1993.
6. Quoted by John Acland in a letter of 3 September 1993 to the author.
7. Information supplied by Tam Dalyell MP.
8. Transcript of interview with Tony Lord recorded by Samantha Wyndham.
9. Interview recorded and transcribed

by Samantha Wyndham, November 1992.

10. James Lees-Milne, *Ceaseless Turmoil* (2004), 238.

11. Michael Trinick, 'The Daunting Task', *National Trust Magazine*, Spring 1985.

12. Michael Trinick papers in the National Trust's Lanhydrock office.

13. Michael Trinick, 'Occasional Papers – Rubbish Dumps'.

14. Michael Trinick, from a talk given to the National Association of Decorative and Fine Arts Societies in 1986.

15. Michael Trinick, 'What the National Trust has done at Lanhydrock,' talk given to the Lanhydrock Women's Institute, 1986; text in Lanhydrock archives.

16. *Ibid.*

17. Michael Trinick, 'The Development of National Trust Houses in Cornwall,' lecture given to the Attingham Study Week, 1993.

18. Michael Trinick, 'Occasional Paper No.7: Stories from the Past – Two That Got Away,' 1993, unpublished.

19. Michael Trinick, 'Occasional Paper No.4: Provenance Remembered,' 1993, unpublished.

20. Letter from Michael Trinick to Canon Hamer, 13 January 1983, Lanhydrock archives.

21. Richard Crossman, *Diaries* (London, 1976), vol.2, 458.

22. Letter to the author, on my being made regional director for East Anglia, 17 January 1981.

23. Michael Trinick, interview recorded by Samantha Wyndham.

24. Copies of these letters were kindly passed on to me by Martin Drury, when he was sorting papers in the Director-General's office.

25. Michael Trinick in an interview with Samantha Wyndham, November 1992, unpublished transcription.

CHAPTER 6:

THE 'HEIR OF TAILYIE'

(PAGES 88–99)

1. Roy Strong, Marcus Binney, John Harris, *The Destruction of the Country House*, exhibition catalogue (Victoria and Albert Museum), 1974, 101.

2. Ian Gow, *Scotland's Lost Houses* (London, 2006), 19.

3. Gow, *Scotland's Lost Houses*, 10.

4. Conversations with the author on 17 March and 13 April 2007.

5. Butler, *Lord Lothian*, 185

6. Letter from Tam Dalyell of 21 November 1999, quoted in Douglas Bremner, *For the Benefit of the Nation* (Edinburgh, 2001), 298.

7. The correspondence is in the House

of the Binns files in the archives of the National Trust for Scotland.

8. David Steel, *Against Goliath* (London, 1989), 24.

9. Letter from Tam Dalyell to the author, 6 April 2007.

10. John Cornforth, *The Country Houses of England 1948–1998* (London, 1998) 52.

11. NTSA, archives box JD 171, letter of 13 November 1945, quoted in Michael Moss, *The Magnificent Castle of Culzean and the Kennedy Family* (Edinburgh, 2002), 264

12. Michael Moss, *Culzean*, 267

13. Michael Moss, 'Reinventing Culzean,' *Apollo*, November 2004, 92

14. Moss, *Culzean*, 267

15. Moss, *Culzean*, 264

16. Reported in *The Guardian*, 7 April 1993

CHAPTER 7:

THE PAINTER'S DAUGHTER AND THE BIOGRAPHER

(PAGES 100–117)

1. Martin Drury told me about this exchange, which was prompted by his article 'The Early Years of the Country Houses Scheme,' *National Trust Magazine*, Autumn 1987. His subsequent research showed that in fact neither house was the first property to take advantage of the scheme. Old Devonshire House, which was given by Major Benton Fletcher with a collection of musical instruments, preceded them but was destroyed in the Second World War.

2. The Trust owes Lady Mander and Arthur Grogan a great debt for enriching these two houses. In making them literary and artistic shrines, they transformed them in ways their original owners may not have intended.

3. Some of this material is taken from my article, 'Lady Berwick, Attingham and Italy', in Gervase Jackson-Stops (ed.), *National Trust Studies 1981*, 43–68.

4. Costanza Hulton's unpublished memoir is among the papers which, at Lady Mander's suggestion, were deposited by Lady Berwick at the Ashmolean Museum; they have since been transferred to the Bodleian Library.

5. *Ibid.*

6. Sickert's letters to Costanza Hulton, with Lady Berwick's notes, were also given by her to the Ashmolean Museum, and are now in the Bodleian Library.

7. Costanza Hulton, unpublished memoir, Bodleian Library.

8. Information from Lady Mander, 1980.

9. Cousens, *op.cit.*, 47.

10. Sarah Kay, *Attingham Park*

(unpublished 2006), 17.

11. H. Dixon ('The Druid'), *Saddle and Sirloin or English Farm and Sporting Worthies* (1870).

12. The Duke of Wellington's name occurs in the Attingham Visitors' Book in 1953. Lady Berwick carefully annotated her copy of Mario Praz's *The House of Life* (London, 1956).

13. I was myself guilty of encouraging this assumption in my article on Lady Berwick in *National Trust Studies 1981*, 43–68.

14. James Lees-Milne, *People and Places* (London, 1992), 56.

15. Notes by Lady Berwick, with the drawings given to the Ashmolean Museum in 1972. Thérèse Lessore was in fact Sickert's third wife. Dr Wendy Baron has kindly informed me that the portrait of Gioconda was exhibited at Temple Newsam in 1942, and was sold at Sotheby's in 1944. Its present whereabouts are unknown.

16. In the case of Gwen Ffrangcon-Davies, it was an inscribed etching, *Woman on a Staircase*, of 1928–29.

17. The drawing was among those given to the Ashmolean Museum in 1981.

18. Costanza Hulton memoir, Bodleian Library.

19. James Lees-Milne, *People and Places: Country House Donors and the National Trust* (London, 1992), 57.

20. Letter of September 1919, quoted in Kay, 9.

21. Notes by Claud Bicknell, solicitor to Sir Charles Trevelyan, July 1993; copy in National Trust archives.

22. David Cannadine, *G.M. Trevelyan* (London, 1992), 11–13.

23. Laura Trevelyan, *A Very British Family: The Trevelyans and Their World* (London, 2006), 132.

24. The extract from Lady Mander's letter was sent to me in October 1991 by Belinda Cousens, because she thought it would amuse me.

25. From an obituary written for *The Times*, which was not published but was passed on to me by Charles Brocklehurst.

26. Another version of this painting, dated 1925, was exhibited at the Imperial War Museum in 2005, in the exhibition entitled *William Orpen: Politics, Sex and Death*. I am grateful to Alastair Laing for clarifying that there are two versions of this picture.

CHAPTER 8:

THE PLANTSMEN

(PAGES 118–135)

1. The Gregs of Styal, also Unitarians, put their industrial concerns into the hands of those sons who had

proven business skills.

2. James Lees-Milne, *Caves of Ice* (London, 1983), 52.

3. Aberconway, Henry Duncan McLaren, *Dictionary of National Biography*, vol. 35, 728.

4. Charles, 3rd Lord Aberconway, obituary in *The Times*, 5 February 2003; and *Dictionary of National Biography*, vol. 35, 728.

5. James Lees-Milne, *Midway on the Waves* (London, 1985), 154.

6. John Gaze, *Figures in a Landscape* (London, 1988), 166.

7. Recalled by Peter Borlase, the former head gardener at Lanhydrock in Cornwall, and recounted in John Sales's foreword to *Recollections of Great Gardeners* by Graham Stuart Thomas (London, 2003), p.16.

8. Related to the author by Richard Ayres, 22 February 2007.

9. Related to the author, 1981.

10. Thomas, *Recollections*, 135.

11. Thomas, *Recollections*, 138.

12. Graham Stuart Thomas, *Gardens of the National Trust* (London, 1979), 173.

13. Paula Weideger, *Gilding the Acorn* (London, 1994), p.217.

14. Writing to the author on 22 September 1993, Aberconway stated: 'Pochin was not a radical politician.'

15. An account of her achievements and generosity was published in *Nature*, No. 448, (August 2007) and in the King's College Cambridge Annual Report, 2008, 67.

16. W.B. Yeats, *Collected Poems*, (London, 1969), p.225.

17. Thomas Hardy, *The Complete Poems* (New Wessex Edition, London, 1976), 160.

18. John Sales in his foreword to Graham Stuart Thomas's *Recollections of Great Gardeners*, 32.

19. Sales, foreword to Thomas, *Recollections*, 14.

20. Thomas, *Gardens of the National Trust*, 176.

21. Jacq Barber, 'The Quiet Gardener', *National Trust Magazine*, Spring 2009, 46.

CHAPTER 9:

THE BANKERS

(PAGES 136–153)

1. Gillian Darley, *Octavia Hill* (London, 1990), 176.

2. Miriam Rothschild, *Dear Lord Rothschild: Birds, Butterflies and History* (London, 1983); republished as *Walter Rothschild: The Man, the Museum and the Menagerie* (London, 2008), 90.

3. Rothschild, *Walter Rothschild*, 87.

4. Rothschild, *Walter Rothschild*, 225.

5. 'Miriam Rothschild' (obituary), *The*

Guardian, 22 January 2005, 25.

6. Jennifer Jenkins and Patrick James, *From Acorn to Oak Tree: The Growth of the National Trust 1895–1994*, (London, 1994), 36–37.

7. Rothschild, *Walter Rothschild*, 287.

8. Mrs James de Rothschild, *The Rothschilds at Waddesdon Manor* (London, 1979), 118.

9. Rothschild, *The Rothschilds*, 118.

10. Rothschild, *The Rothschilds*, 126.

11. Rothschild, *The Rothschilds*, 132.

12. Related to the author by Nicholas Baring, 17 March 2009.

13. Related by Baring.

14. Mark Norman, unpublished memoir, 1984, in National Trust archives, 1.

15. Norman memoir, 2.

16. Norman memoir, 4.

17. John Smith *et al.*, *The Landmark Handbook* (London, 1995), v.

18. Smith, *The Landmark Handbook*, iii.

19. Appendix to a letter to the author, 22 September 1993, headed 'Aberconway's account of a quarrel with the National Trust.'

20. 'Aberconway's account'.

21. National Trust archives, quoted in Merlin Waterson, *The National Trust: The First Hundred Years* (London, 1994), 168.

22. Letter to the author, 20 January 1994.

23. Letter from Christian Smith to the author, 14 March 2007.

24. Jenkins and James, *From Acorn to Oak Tree*, 203.

25. Letter to the author, 15 November 1994. The offending passage on his resignation was in my book, *The National Trust: The First Hundred Years*, 160.

26. The break was a matter of great sadness to me; I had written a report for him on the preservation of the historic dockyard at Portsmouth, and exchanged letters and cards frequently.

27. Related to the author by Lord Rothschild, July 2008, and confirmed in a letter of 6 August 2009.

28. Quoted in 'Tearing down the fences' (no author cited), *Broadleaf*, Spring 2008, 17.

29. Rothschild, *The Rothschilds*, 164.

30. Rothschild, *The Rothschilds*, 164.

CHAPTER 10:
THE MILL OWNER AND THE WOODLANDER
(PAGES 154–165)

1. Mary B. Rose, *The Gregs of Styal* (London, 1978), 21–28.

2. Friedrich Engels, *The Condition of the Working Class in England* (London, 1969), 214.

3. Interview recorded by Samantha Wyndham, transcript in National

Trust archives.

4. Interview recorded by Wyndham.

5. Interview recorded by Wyndham.

6. Interview recorded by Wyndham.

7. Interview recorded by Wyndham.

8. Noted by the author at Ebworth, July 2006.

9. W.H. Auden, *A Selection by the Author* (Harmondsworth, 1958), 164.

CHAPTER 11:
THE MILITARY HISTORIAN
(PAGES 166–183)

1. The Marquess of Anglesey F.S.A., *One-Leg: The Life and Letters of Henry William Paget, First Marquess of Anglesey, K.G. 1768–1854* (London, 1961), 159.

2. Nigel Nicholson, *Long Life* (London, 1997), 1.

3. *The Dictionary of National Biography*, supplement (Oxford, 1975), 2659.

4. James Lees-Milne, *People and Places: Country House Donors and the National Trust* (London, 1992), 209.

5. Gervase Jackson-Stops, 'Rex Whistler at Plas Newydd,' *Country Life*, 4 August 1977, 286.

6. Arthur Jones, *Britain's Heritage: The Creation of the National Heritage Memorial Fund* (London, 1985), 207, quoting from the *Annual Report of the Trustees of the NHMF*, 1980–81.

7. Robert Hewitson, *The Heritage Industry* (London, 1987), 32.

CHAPTER 12:
THE ACTOR
(PAGES 184–199)

1. The archives of the Yorke family of Erddig are in the Clwyd County Record Office at Hawarden. The accounts of theatricals are quoted in my book, *The Servants' Hall: The Domestic History of a Country House* (London, 1980), 58.

2. Relayed to the author by Colonel Ririd Myddelton of Chirk Castle.

3. Relayed by Philip Yorke and in Merlin Waterson, *The Servants' Hall*, 88.

4. Geoffrey Veysey, *Philip Yorke: Last Squire of Erddig* (Wrexham, 2003), 18.

5. Relayed to the author.

6. Veysey, *Philip Yorke*, 21.

7. Veysey, *Philip Yorke*, 22.

8. Veysey, *Philip Yorke*, 26.

9. Oliver Garnett, *Erddig*, National Trust guidebook (1995), 28.

10. Erddig MSS, Clwyd County Record Office, Hawarden.

11. Veysey, *Philip Yorke*, 30.

12. Veysey, *Philip Yorke*, 33.

13. Veysey, *Philip Yorke*, 37.

14. A copy of the letter was given to

John Cornforth, who quoted it in his book, *The Inspiration of the Past* (Harmondsworth, 1985), 218.

15. Thomas Hardy, *The Complete Poems* (London, 1981), 485.

16. Keith Miller, 'Love and Other Areas,' *Times Literary Supplement*, 28 March 2008, 19.

17. Veysey, *Philip Yorke*, 94.

18. Harold Nicolson, *Comments, 1944–1948* (London, 1948), 248. The essay is entitled 'The National Trust'.

19. Albinia Lucy Cust, *Chronicles of Erthig on the Dyke* (London, 1914), Vol. I, 220.

20. Merlin Waterson, *Elihu Yale*, in *The Smithsonian*, October 1977, 91.

21. Nigel Dennis, *Cards of Identity* (Chicago, 1955), 292, 296.

22. Adam Mars-Jones, *Lantern Lecture* (London, 1981), 17.

23. Typescript retained by the author.

24. Galen Strawson, in the *Times Literary Supplement*, 9 October 1981.

25. Keith Miller, 'Love and other areas', *Times Literary Supplement*, 28 March 2008.

26. Garnett, *Erddig*, 26.

27. Correspondence with the author, May 1990.

CHAPTER 13:
THE SQUIRE, THE SCHOOLMASTER AND SPECIAL INTELLIGENCE
(PAGES 200–217)

1. R.W. Ketton Cremer, *A Norfolk Gallery* (London, 1948), p.212

2. His poems are listed in Stephen Clark and John Gretton, *R.W. Ketton-Cremer: An Annotated Bibliography* (1995), 27.

3. R.W. Ketton-Cremer, *Felbrigg: The Story of a House* (London, 1962), 250.

4. Ketton-Cremer, *Felbrigg*, 257.

5. Ketton-Cremer, *Felbrigg*, 290.

6. Lees-Milne, *Ancestral Voices*, 55.

7. Related to the author by the present Lord Egremont.

8. Sir Brinsley Ford, 'Staying at Felbrigg as a Guest of Wyndham Ketton-Cremer', *National Trust Year Book* (1977–78), 58.

9. Ford, 'Staying at Felbrigg', 60.

10. National Trust Sheringham files, held at regional office.

11. Repton's *Red Book* for Sheringham is owned by the National Trust and is on loan to the library of the Royal Institute of British Architects.

12. National Trust Sheringham files, held at the regional office.

13. National Trust Sheringham files, held at the regional office.

14. Letter passed on to the author by Lady Harrod, and now in the National Trust Sheringham files at the regional office.

CHAPTER 14:
THE TRAITORS, THE COUNTESS AND MR BOND
(PAGES 218–237)

1. Terence Dooley, *The Decline of the Big House in Ireland: A Study of Irish Landed Families 1860–1960* (Dublin, 2001), 71.

2. Dooley, *The Decline of the Big House*, chapter 4: 'Causes and Effects of Landlord Indebtedness, 1877–1914'.

3. Iris Origo, *Images and Shadows* (London, 1970), 61.

4. Wyndham has other claims to a place in history. He championed Rodin's work in England and organised the purchase by the South Kensington Museum of his *Saint John the Baptist Preaching*. Rodin's bust of George Wyndham was completed in 1905, two years after the passing of his Irish Land Act.

5. Dooley, *The Decline of the Big House*, 171.

6. Dooley, *The Decline of the Big House*, 287.

7. The destruction of Shanbally Castle is described in Randal MacDonnell, *The Lost Houses of Ireland*, (London, 2002), 191.

8. Steve Benson, *I Will Plant Me a Tree* (London, 2002), 50.

9. Quoted in MacDonnell, *The Lost Houses*, 196.

10. W.B. Yeats, *The Collected Poems of W.B. Yeats* (London, 1969), 263.

11. There is an evocative account of Lissadell in Mark Bence-Jones, *Life in an Irish Country House* (London, 1996), 170.

12. Unpublished interview of Dick Rogers by Samantha Wyndham, 30 June 1993.

13. Information from Peter Marlow, who was present.

14. Lyn Gallagher and Dick Rogers, *Castle, Coast and Cottage: The National Trust in Northern Ireland* (Belfast, 1986), 139.

15. Unpublished interview with Peter Marlow by Samantha Wyndham, 29–30 June 1993.

16. The fullest account of the house is by Gervase Jackson-Stops, *Country Life*, 30 June 1983, 1768, and 7 July 1983, 20.

17. Unpublished interview of John Lewis-Crosby by Samantha Wyndham, 30 June 1993.

18. Information supplied by Professor Ronald Buchanan, formerly National Trust chairman for Northern Ireland Regional Committee.

19. Information supplied by David Goode; and an account in John Gaze, *Figures in a Landscape* (London, 1988), 285.

20. The return of the contents of

Florence Court is described in Ian B. McQuiston, 'The Palingenesis of Florence Court' in *Avenues to the Past: Essays Presented to Charles Brett*, edited by Terence Reeves-Smyth and Richard Oram (Belfast, 2003), 213. I am grateful to McQuiston for providing additional information; and to Professor Ronald Buchanan for letting me see all the correspondence which passed between him and Lady Enniskillen.

21. The verdict is in *Ireland Observed* by Maurice Craig and the Knight of Glin (Cork, 1970), 54.

CHAPTER 15:
THE GROCER
(PAGES 238–249)

1. Andrew Wilson (ed.), *The Simon Sainsbury Bequest to Tate and the National Gallery* (London, 2008), 19.
2. Related to the author by Stewart Grimshaw, June 2008.
3. Related to the author by Dame Rosalind Savill, March 2009.
4. Related to the author by Stewart Grimshaw, June 2008.
5. David Gentleman, *Artwork* (London, 2002), 86–89.
6. I am grateful to Martin Drury for his account of the rescue of Canons Ashby; and have also drawn on an interview with Gervase Jackson-Stops, recorded in 1993.
7. Christopher Gibbs, 'A Search for Beauty', in Andrew Wilson (ed.), *The Simon Sainsbury Bequest to Tate and the National Gallery* (London, 2008), 15.

CHAPTER 16:
THE SHELLFISH MERCHANT
(PAGES 250–261)

1. Robert Hunter, *The Preservation of Commons* (1867), 358–89.
2. Letter given to the author by John Morley.

CHAPTER 17:
THE AMBASSADORS
(PAGES 262–277)

1. Merlin Waterson, *Dudmaston* (London, 1980), National Trust guidebook, 29.
2. Both Sir George and Lady Labouchere admired the way Franco planned the return to a constitutional monarchy in Spain. In an interview with me in 1993 (of which there is a transcript), Rachel referred to this aspect of Franco's rule as 'very wise'.
3. George Labouchere, *Contemporary Art at Dudmaston* (London, 1980), 5.
4. Lady Labouchere's interview with

Merlin Waterson, 1993: 'In a room of modern art, I couldn't tell one from another.'
5. The story was related by Sir Joshua Rowley, who used to holiday with the Laboucheres.
6. See introductory note to Rachel Labouchere, *Deborah Darby* (London, 1993).
7. Rachel Labouchere, *Botanical Prints and Drawings at Dudmaston* (London, 1980), 4.
8. Letter of 13 October 2009 from Gerard Noel to the author.
9. The newsletter of the Friends of the Ironbridge Gorge Museum, Summer 1982, notes that the National Heritage Memorial Fund had made a grant of £20,000 towards the acquisition of Dale House: 'Thanks to the grant, and to generous financial help from Lady Labouchere… the Museum will now be able to complete the purchase of the building.'
10. I am grateful to Librarian and Archivist of Ironbridge, John Powell, for locating this correspondence and for help with photographs.
11. Minutes of the Executive Committee, in National Trust archives.
12. John Gage, *J.M.W. Turner: A Wonderful Range of Mind* (London, 1987), 153.
13. Lord Egremont, *Wyndham and Children First* (London, 1969), p.204.
14. Christopher Woodward, *In Ruins* (London, 2001), 221–26.
15. Angus Wainwright, 'Orford Ness', in David Morgan Evans, Peter Salway and David Thackray (eds), *The Remains of Distant Times* (Woodbridge, 1996), 198–210.
16. W.G. Sebald, *The Rings of Saturn* (London, 1995), 231.
17. Robert Macfarlane, *The Wild Places* (London, 2007), 241–263.
18. Andrew Motion, *Selected Poems 1976–1997* (London, 1998), 117

CHAPTER 18:
THE SPIRITUALISTS AND
THE VOLUNTEER
(PAGES 278–293)

1. There was at least one serious accident in the 1980s.
2. Peter Sagar, *Ostengland* (Köln, 1990), published as *East Anglia* (London, 1994), 192.
3. There is abundant literature on Sutton Hoo. The most useful introduction is Martin Carver's *Sutton Hoo: Burial Ground of Kings?* (London, 1998).
4. Carver, *Sutton Hoo*, 159–61.
5. Correspondence held in the National Trust's files at its East Anglia Regional Office.
6. Mary Skelcher and Chris Durrant,

Edith Pretty: From Socialite to Sutton Hoo (Leiston, 2006).
7. Skelcher and Durrant, *Edith Pretty*, 63–66.
8. Nikolaus Pevsner and Edward Hubbard, *The Buildings of England: Cheshire* (Harmondsworth, 1971), 366.
9. Skelcher and Durrant, *Edith Pretty*, 14.
10. Quoted in Robert Markham, *Sutton Hoo Through the Rear View Mirror* (Ipswich, 2002), 26.
11. Markham, *Sutton Hoo*, 20.
12. Markham, *Sutton Hoo*, 34.
13. Markham, *Sutton Hoo*, 29.
14. Most recently by John Preston in the *Seven* supplement of *The Sunday Telegraph*, 29 April 2007, 23; and in his novel, *The Dig* (2007), in which some facts, dates and names are respected, but not others.
15. Letter from Phillips to Maynard, 28 June 1939, quoted in Markham, 25.
16. Chris Durrant, *Basil Brown: Astronomer, Archaeologist, Enigma* (Leiston, 2004), 24.
17. Carver, *Sutton Hoo*, 5.
18. Preston's assertion that Phillips was 'unable to do any of the digging himself: he was too fat' is contradicted by the photographs of him taken during the dig.
19. Skelcher and Durrant, *Edith Pretty*, 65.
20. Skelcher and Durrant, *Edith Pretty*, 58.
21. Not Dame of the British Empire, as stated in Carver, *Sutton Hoo*, 22.
22. Skelcher and Durrant, *Edith Pretty*, 60.
23. Durrant, 45.
24. Lees-Milne, *Ancestral Voices*, 43.
25. Letter to the author of 26 March 2006.
26. Typescript in the author's possession.

CHAPTER 19:
THE FRENCH HAIRDRESSER
(PAGES 294–305)

1. In the 1971 edition there is a short entry on Tyntesfield in the 'Catalogue of Country Houses' at the back. The edition of 1979 has a full illustrated account of the house.
2. As had Lord Esher and John Fowler. Both John Cornforth and James Lees-Milne wrote enthusiastically about Victorian buildings.
3. *The National Trust: Head Office Location Review*, unpublished report, December 1996.
4. SAVE Britain's Heritage, *The Tyntesfield Emergency* (London, 2002), 2.
5. Martin Powley, 'Country Houses or Hospitals,' *The Architects' Journal*, 27 June 2002, 18, and 5 September 2002, 24.
6. Notes of the meeting of the

Tyntesfield Action Group, 28 March 2002.
7. Unpublished report by the secretary and the chief finance officer of the National Trust, 1976.
8. 'The Unwanted Neighbour', *Metro*, 15 April 2002, 9.
9. Unpublished lecture by Tim Knox, 'Tyntesfield: the Rescue of a High Victorian Dream', given in the Purcell Room at London's South Bank Centre, February 2003.

CHAPTER 20:
THE REWARDS OF
GENEROSITY
(PAGES 306–323)

1. Waterson, *The National Trust*, 38.
2. Gillian Darley, *Octavia Hill: A Life* (London, 1990), 301
3. Waterson, *The National Trust*, 37.
4. The dates of the National Trust Acts are 1907, 1919, 1937, 1939, 1953 and 1971. The various amendments and additions to Hunter's original Act did not change its fundamental provisions or principles, which have stood the test of a century astonishingly well.
5. Jenkins and James, *From Acorn to Oak Tree*, 153.
6. Letter from E.A. Manisty of Christie's to the author, 26 May 2004.
7. James Lees-Milne, *People and Places* (London, 1992), 221
8. Michael De-la-Noy, *The House of Hervey: A History of Tainted Talent* (London, 2001), 209
9. De-la-Noy, *The House of Hervey*, 229.
10. T.S. Eliot, *The Complete Poems and Plays* (London, 1969), 195–96.
11. Quoted in Keith Thomas, *The Ends of Life: Roads to Fulfilment in Early Modern England* (Oxford, 2009), 258 and ff.
12. Anthony Powell, *To Keep the Ball Rolling: The Memoirs of Anthony Powell – Volume I: Infants of the Spring* (London, 1976), 163.
13. Maurice Collis, *Stanley Spencer: A Biography* (London, 1962), 216.
14. Collis, *Stanley Spencer*, 117.
15. George Behrend, *Stanley Spencer at Burghclere* (London, 1964), 62. I am grateful to Oliver Garnett for reminding me of the significance of the Sandham Memorial Chapel.
16. A remark to the author at Garsington, 14 June 2009.
17. Marcus Binney, *Dumfries House* (London, 2008), 1.
18. Susan Denyer, *Beatrix Potter and her Farms* (London, 1992), 29.
19. James Lees-Milne, *English Country Houses: Baroque* (London, 1970), 184.

THE GROWTH OF THE NATIONAL TRUST, 1895–2010, AND SOME OF THE PROPERTIES ACQUIRED

* Gift
¶ Public subscription/appeal
  or bought with bequests
† Acquired with government grants
  or in lieu of tax

1895

ACREAGE: 5

MEMBERSHIP: 100

The National Trust is registered under the Companies Act.

PROPERTY ACQUISITIONS INCLUDED:
Dinas Oleu, Gwynedd*
Alfriston Clergy House, East Sussex¶
Barras Nose, Cornwall¶
Wicken Fen, Cambridgeshire*

1900

PROPERTY ACQUISITIONS INCLUDED:
Long Crendon Courthouse, Buckinghamshire¶
Brandelhow, Cumbria¶
Old Post Office, Tintagel, Cornwall¶

1905

ACREAGE: 1,500

MEMBERSHIP: 500

The National Trust Act (1907).

PROPERTY ACQUISITIONS INCLUDED:
Barrington Court, Somerset¶

Paycocke's, Coggeshall, Essex

Mam Tor, Edale, Derbyshire

1910

PROPERTY ACQUISITIONS INCLUDED:
Grange Fell, Borrowdale, Cumbria¶
Blakeney Point, Norfolk*
Castlerigg Stone Circle, Cumbria¶
Box Hill, Surrey*

1915

ACREAGE: 6,000

MEMBERSHIP: 700

PROPERTY ACQUISITIONS INCLUDED:
Dodman Point, Cornwall*
Kinver Edge, Staffordshire*

1920

PROPERTY ACQUISITIONS INCLUDED:
Scafell Mountain Group, Cumbria*
Lyveden New Bield, Northamptonshire¶
Leith Hill, Surrey*
Scolt Head Island, Norfolk¶
Hatfield Forest, Essex*
Chedworth Roman Villa, Gloucestershire¶
Paycocke's, Coggeshall, Essex*
Farne Islands, Northumberland¶

1925

ACREAGE: 21,000

MEMBERSHIP: 850

Council for the Protection of Rural England (CPRE) founded in 1926.

PROPERTY ACQUISITIONS INCLUDED:
Ashridge Estate, Hertfordshire¶
Tattershall Castle, Lincolnshire*
Bodiam Castle, East Sussex*
Stonehenge Down, Wiltshire¶
Tennyson Down, Isle of Wight*

1930

The National Trust for Scotland formally constituted in 1931.
The Marquess of Lothian's speech on the plight of country houses at the National Trust's Annual General Meeting in 1934.

PROPERTY ACQUISITIONS INCLUDED:
Montacute, Somerset*
Housesteads Fort, Hadrian's Wall, Northumberland*
Monk Coniston Estate, Cumbria*¶
Little Solsbury Hill, Somerset*
Runnymede, Surrey*
Assembly Rooms, Bath*
Shalford Mill, Surrey*
Longshaw Estate, Derbyshire¶
Dovedale, Derbyshire*
Old Town Hall, Newtown, Isle of Wight*
East Riddlesden Hall, West Yorkshire*

1935

ACREAGE: 50,000

MEMBERSHIP: 4,850

The National Trust Act (1937).

PROPERTY ACQUISITIONS INCLUDED:
Aberglaslyn Pass, Gwynedd*
Lizard Downs, Cornwall*
Easedale, Cumbria*
Buttermere, Cumbria¶
Wilderhope Manor, Shropshire*
Rufford Old Hall, Lancashire*
Wordsworth House, Cockermouth, Cumbria¶
White Park Bay, Co. Antrim¶
Little Moreton Hall, Cheshire*
Wightwick Manor, Staffordshire*

Malham, North Yorkshire

Smallhythe Place, Kent*
Sutton House, Hackney, London⁹
Quarry Bank Cotton Mill & Styal
    Village, Cheshire*
Houghton Mill, Cambridgeshire⁹
Great Langdale, Cumbria⁹

1940

PROPERTY ACQUISITIONS INCLUDED:
Dolaucothi Estate, Dyfed*
Bateman's, East Sussex*
Max Gate, Dorset*
Packwood House, Warwickshire*
Wallington, Northumberland*
Cliveden, Buckinghamshire*
Blickling Hall, Norfolk*
Woolsthorpe Manor, Lincolnshire*
Flatford Mill & Willy Lott's House,
    Suffolk*
West Wycombe Park, Buckinghamshire*
Great Chalfield Manor, Wiltshire*
Avebury Stone Circles, Wiltshire⁹
Lindisfarne Castle, Northumberland*
Lacock Abbey & Village, Wiltshire*
Killerton, Devon*
Holnicote Estate, Somerset*
Polesden Lacey, Surrey*
Blaise Hamlet, Bristol*
Hill Top, Sawrey, Cumbria*
Speke Hall, Lancashire*
Mam Tor, Edale, Derbyshire*
Gunby Hall, Lincolnshire*
Shaw's Corner, Ayot St Lawrence,
    Hertfordshire*

1945

ACREAGE: 112,000
MEMBERSHIP: 7,850
*The National Land Fund is established
in 1946.*
The National Parks Act (1949).
PROPERTY ACQUISITIONS INCLUDED:
Hatchlands Park, Surrey*
Malham Tarn, North Yorkshire*
Chartwell, Kent*
Charlecote Park, Warwickshire*
Coughton Court, Warwickshire*
Stourhead, Wiltshire*
Hughenden Manor, Buckinghamshire*
Cotehele, Cornwall†
Attingham Park, Shropshire*
Knole, Kent*
Clumber Park, Nottinghamshire⁹
Hidcote Manor Garden, Gloucestershire*
Petworth House, West Sussex*
Sandham Memorial Chapel, Hampshire*
Lyme Park, Cheshire*
Buckland Abbey, Devon⁹
Ham House, Surrey*
Alderley Edge, Cheshire*
Hardy's Cottage, Higher Bockhampton,
    Dorset⁹
Townend Farm, Troutbeck, Cumbria†
Lytes Cary Manor, Somerset*
Upton House, Warwickshire*
Osterley Park, Middlesex*
Arlington Court, Devon*
Mussenden Temple, Downhill, Co.
    Londonderry*
Bodnant Garden, Gwynedd*
Newark Park, Gloucestershire*
Buscot Park, Oxfordshire*

Hardy's Cottage, Higher Bockhampton, Dorset

Snowshill Manor, Gloucestershire

1950

*The Gowers Report on the maintenance
of historic houses is published in 1950.*
*The Historic Buildings and Ancient
Monuments Act (1953).*
PROPERTY ACQUISITIONS INCLUDED:
Acorn Bank Garden, Cumbria*
Ascott, Buckinghamshire*
Brockhampton Estate, Herefordshire*
Sizergh Castle, Cumbria*
Plas-yn-Rhiw, Gwynedd*
Oxburgh Hall, Norfolk*
Guildhall of Corpus Christi, Lavenham,
    Suffolk*
Snowshill Manor, Gloucestershire*
Castle Coole, Co. Fermanagh†
Compton Castle, Devon*
Nunnington Hall, North Yorkshire*
Penrhyn Castle & Ysbyty Estate†
Powis Castle, Powys*
Winkworth Arboretum, Surrey*
Bredon Barn, Worcestershire*
Tintinhull House & Garden, Somerset*
Lanhydrock, Cornwall*
Hanbury Hall, Worcestershire*
Castle Ward, Co. Down†
Derrymore House, Co. Armagh*
Florence Court, Co. Fermanagh*
Staunton Harold Church, Leicestershire*
St Michael's Mount, Cornwall*
Trerice, Cornwall⁹
Dunsland House, Devon⁹
Sheffield Park Gardens, East Sussex⁹
Uppark, West Sussex*

1955

ACREAGE: 218,000

MEMBERSHIP: 55,658

PROPERTY ACQUISITIONS INCLUDED:

Trelissick, Cornwall*
Boscastle Harbour, Cornwall*
Clandon Park, Surrey*
Nostell Priory, West Yorkshire*
Claydon House, Buckinghamshire*
Washington Old Hall, Co. Durham⁵
Coleshill, Oxfordshire*
Mottisfont Abbey, Hampshire*
Gunwalloe Church Cove, Cornwall⁵
The Vyne, Hampshire*
Ickworth, Suffolk*†
Great Barn, Great Coxwell, Oxfordshire*
Rowallane, Co. Down†
Ashdown House, Oxfordshire*
Croft Castle, Herefordshire*†
Bradenham Village & Estate,
    Buckinghamshire*
Saltram, Devon†
Springhill, Co. Londonderry*†
Waddesdon Manor, Buckinghamshire*
Berrington Hall, Herefordshire*†
Benthall Hall, Shropshire*
Beningbrough Hall, North Yorkshire†
Hardwick Hall, Derbyshire†
Ardress House, Co. Armagh†

Giant's Causeway, Co. Antrim

Corfe Castle Estate, Dorset

1960

The National Trust's Ulster Coastline Appeal is launched in 1962.

PROPERTY ACQUISITIONS INCLUDED:

Melford Hall, Suffolk†
Dyrham Park, Gloucestershire†
Tatton Park, Cheshire†
Trengwainton, Cornwall*
Farnborough Hall, Warwickshire*†
Clevedon Court, Somerset*†
Antony House, Cornwall*
Dunstanburgh Castle, Northumberland*
Giant's Causeway, Co. Antrim*†
Ormesby Hall, Cleveland*
Brownsea Island, Dorset†
Moseley Old Hall, Staffordshire*
River Wey Navigation, Surrey*
Wakehurst Place, West Sussex*

1965

ACREAGE: 328,500

MEMBERSHIP: 157,581

The National Trust's Enterprise Neptune coastline appeal is launched in 1965.

PROPERTY ACQUISITIONS INCLUDED:

Branscombe, Devon†
Emmetts Garden, Kent*
Sissinghurst Castle Garden, Kent*†
Long Mynd, Shropshire⁵
Conwy Suspension Bridge, Gwynedd*
Brecon Beacons, Powys*
Anglesey Abbey, Cambridgeshire*
Brancaster, Norfolk⁵
Sudbury Hall, Derbyshire*†
Shugborough Hall, Staffordshire*†
Formby, Lancashire⁵
Dunwich Heath, Suffolk⁵
Wellbrook Beetling Mill, Co. Tyrone*
Westbury Court Garden,
    Gloucestershire*
Lundy, Devon⁵
Felbrigg Hall, Norfolk*
Greys Court, Oxfordshire*

1970

The National Trust's Royal Oak Foundation is launched in 1973 to raise funds in the USA.

'The Destruction of the Country House' exhibition is held at the Victoria & Albert Museum in 1974.

PROPERTY ACQUISITIONS INCLUDED:

Scotney Castle Garden, Kent*
Brimham Rocks, North Yorkshire*
Great Hangman, Devon*
Gawthorpe Hall, Lancashire*
Knightshayes Court, Devon*
Rievaulx Terrace & Temples, North
    Yorkshire⁵
Erddig, Clwyd*
Gibside Chapel, Co. Durham*
Standen, West Sussex*
Castle Drogo, Devon*
St David's Head, Dyfed⁵
Theatre Royal, Bury St Edmunds,
    Suffolk*

1975

ACREAGE: 383,000

MEMBERSHIP: 539,285

PROPERTY ACQUISITIONS INCLUDED:

The Needles, Isle of Wight⁵
Middle Littleton Tithe Barn,
    Worcestershire*
Dunster Castle, Somerset*
Dunham Massey, Cheshire*
Plas Newydd, Anglesey*
Stiffkey Saltmarshes, Norfolk⁵
Mount Stewart, Co. Down*
Stackpole, Dyfed†
Fontmell Down, Dorset⁵
Bellister, Northumberland*
Wimpole Hall, Cambridgeshire*
Hare Hill, Cheshire*
Dudmaston, Shropshire*

Cragside, Northumberland*†
Crown Liquor Saloon, Belfast¶
Basildon Park, Berkshire*
The Argory, Co. Armagh*
Leconfield Commons, Cumbria†
White Horse Hill, Uffington,
    Oxfordshire*

1980

The National Heritage Memorial Fund is established in 1980.

PROPERTY ACQUISITIONS INCLUDED:
Monk's House, Rodmell, East Sussex¶
Baddesley Clinton, Warwickshire†
Canons Ashby, Northamptonshire*
Wenlock Edge, Shropshire¶
Kinder Scout, Derbyshire¶
Corfe Castle Estate, Dorset*
Kingston Lacy, Dorset*
Chirk Castle, Clwyd†
Aberdulais Falls, West Glamorgan*¶
St David's Commons, Dyfed¶
Hod Hill, Dorset¶
Fountains Abbey & Studley Royal, North
    Yorkshire¶†
Belton House, Lincolnshire*†
Cadair Idris, Gwynedd¶
Abergwesyn Common, Powys¶†

Upper Wharfedale, North Yorkshire

Greenway, Devon

1985

ACREAGE: 533,000

MEMBERSHIP: 1,322,996

PROPERTY ACQUISITIONS INCLUDED:
Ightham Mote, Kent*
Roseberry Common, Cleveland¶
Calke Abbey, Derbyshire*¶†
Hinton Ampner, Hampshire*
Sherborne Park, Gloucestershire*
Kedleston Hall, Derbyshire*
Crom Estate, Lough Erne, Co.
    Fermanagh†
Cape Cornwall, Cornwall*
Workmans Wood, Gloucestershire*
Sheringham Park, Norfolk¶†
Upper Wharfedale, North Yorkshire*
Biddulph Grange Garden, Staffordshire¶†
Copt Hall, Essex¶
Llanerchaeron Estate, Dyfed*

1990

PROPERTY ACQUISITIONS INCLUDED:
Dinefwr Park, Carmarthenshire¶†
Grange Barn, Coggeshall, Essex*
Mr Straw's House, Worksop,
    Nottinghamshire*
Stowe Landscape Gardens,
    Buckinghamshire*¶†
A La Ronde, Devon¶
Cherryburn, Northumberland*
Chastleton House, Oxfordshire¶†
Mourne Mountains, Co. Down†
Patterson's Spade Mill, Co. Antrim¶†
Orford Ness, Suffolk¶†
2 Willow Road, Hampstead, London¶†

1995

ACREAGE: 580,000

MEMBERSHIP: 2,290,000

The Heritage Lottery Fund is established in 1995.

PROPERTY ACQUISITIONS INCLUDED:
Croome Park, Worcestershire¶†
Rosedene, Worcestershire¶
20 Forthlin Road, Liverpool (Sir Paul
    McCartney's childhood home)*
Sutton Hoo, Suffolk*
The Homewood, Surrey*
Sunnycroft, Wellington, Shropshire*

2000

PROPERTY ACQUISITIONS INCLUDED:
Godolphin, Cornwall¶
Mendips, Liverpool (John Lennon's
    childhood home)*
Greenway, Devon*
The Workhouse, Southwell,
    Nottinghamshire¶
Tyntesfield, Somerset¶†
Red House, Bexleyheath, London¶
Divis & the Black Mountain, Co.
    Antrim¶
Mr. Hardman's Photographic Studio,
    Liverpool*
Back to Backs, Inge Street & Hurst Street,
    Birmingham¶

2005

ACREAGE: 623,945

MEMBERSHIP: 3,392,000

PROPERTY ACQUISITIONS INCLUDED:
Bodysgallen Hall, North Wales*
Middlethorpe Hall, North Yorkshire*
Hartwell House, Buckinghamshire*
Seaton Delaval, Northumberland*¶†

The Workhouse, Southwell, Nottinghamshire

SELECT BIBLIOGRAPHY

Aslet, Clive, *The Last Country Houses* (London, 1982)

Anglesey, The Marquess of, *One Leg: The Life and Letters of Henry William Paget* (London, 1960)

Beard, Geoffrey, *Attingham: The First Forty Years, 1952–1991* (London, 1991)

Binney, Marcus, and Kit Martin, *The Country House: To Be or Not to Be* (London, 1982)

Bloch, Michael, *James Lees-Milne: A Life* (London, 2009)

Bremner, Douglas, *For the Benefit of the Nation: The National Trust for Scotland: The First 70 Years* (Edinburgh, 2001)

Butler, J.R.M., *Lord Lothian (Philip Kerr) 1882–1940* (London, 1960)

Calnan, David, *Rooted in History: Studies in Garden Conservation* (London, 2001)

Cannadine, David, *The Decline and Fall of the British Aristocracy* (London, 1990)

Cannadine, David, *G.M. Trevelyan* (London, 1992)

Carver, Martin, *Sutton Hoo: Burial Ground of Kings?* (London, 1998)

Clemenson, Heather A., *English Country Houses and Landed Estates* (London, 1982)

Cornforth, John, *Country Houses in Britain: Can they Survive?* (London, 1974)

Cornforth, John, *The Country Houses of England 1948–1998* (London, 1998)

Cornforth, John, *The Inspiration of the Past: Country House Taste in the Twentieth Century* (Harmondsworth, 1958)

Cornforth, John, *The Search for a Style: Country Life and Architecture, 1897–1935* (London, 1988)

Dakers, Caroline, *Clouds: The Biography of a Country House* (London, 1993)

Dutton, Raph, *The English Country House* (London, 1935)

Dutton, Raph, *A Hampshire Manor: Hinton Ampner* (London, 1968)

Egremont, Lord, *Wyndham and Children First* (London, 1969)

Evans, David Morgan; Peter Salway; David Thackray, '*The Remains of Distant Times': Archaeology and the National Trust* (London 1996)

Fedden, Robin, *The Continuing Purpose* (London, 1968)

Gaze, John, *Figures in a Landscape: A History of the National Trust* (London, 1988)

Girouard, Mark, *The Victorian Country House*, 2nd edn (London, 1981)

Gow, Ian, *The Lost Houses of Scotland* (London, 2006)

Harris, John, *No Voice from the Hall: Memories of a Country House Snooper* (London, 1998)

Harris, John, *Echoing Voices: More Memories of a Country House Snooper* (London, 2002)

Haslam, Richard, *Clough Williams-Ellis,* (London, 1996)

Hewison, Robert, *The Heritage Industry: Britain in a Climate of Decline* (London, 1987)

Hussey, Christopher, *The Picturesque: Studies in a Point of View* (London, 1927)

Jackson-Stops, Gervase (ed.), *The Treasure Houses of Britain: Five Hundred Years of Private Patronage and Art Collecting* (New Haven and London, 1985)

Jenkins, Jennifer, and Patrick James, *From Acorn to Oak: The Growth of the National Trust, 1895–1994* (London, 1994)

Jones, Arthur, *Britain's Heritage: The Creation of the National Heritage Memorial Fund* (London, 1985)

Jones, Jonah, *Clough Williams-Ellis: The Architect of Portmeirion* (Bridgend, 1996)

Ketton-Cremer, R.W., *Felbrigg: The Story of a House* (London, 1962)

Ketton-Cremer, R.W., *A Norfolk Gallery* (London, 1947)

Lees-Milne, James, *Diaries, 1975–1905: Vols 1-12* (London)

Lees-Milne, James, *Fourteen Friends* (London, 1996)

Lees-Milne, James, *The National Trust: A Record of Fifty Years' Achievement* (London, 1945)

Lees-Milne, James, *People and Places: Country House Donors and the National Trust* (London, 1992)

Lowenthal, David, *The Past is Another Country* (Cambridge, 1985)

Mauss, Marcel, *The Gift: The Form and Reason for Exchange in Archaic Societies* (London, 1990)

McDonnell, Randall, *The Lost Houses of Ireland* (London, 2002)

Moss, Michael, *The 'Magnificent Castle' of Culzean and the Kennedy Family* (Edinburgh, 2002)

Newby, Howard (ed.), *The National Trust: The Next Hundred Years* (London, 1995)

Nicolson, Adam, *Sissinghurst: An Unfinished History* (London, 2008)

Nicolson, Nigel, *A Long Life* (London, 1997)

Raistrick, Arthur, *Quakers in Science and Industry* (Newton Abbott, 1968)

Robinson, John Martin, *The Country House at War* (London, 1989)

Robinson, John Martin, *The Last Country Houses* (London, 1984)

Rose, Mary, *The Gregs of Styal* (London, 1978)

Rose, Norman, *The Cliveden Set: Portrait of an Exclusive Fraternity* (London, 2000)

Rothschild, Miriam, *Walter Rothschild: The Man, the Museum and the Menagerie* (London, 2008)

Rothschild, Mrs James de, *The Rothschilds at Waddesdon Manor* (London, 1978)

Sayer, Michael, and Hugh Massingbird, *The Disintegration of a Heritage: Country Houses and their Collections* (Norwich, 1993)

Strong, Roy, Marcus Binney and John Harris (eds), *The Destruction of the Country House, 1875–1975* (London, 1974)

Sturgis, Matthew, *Walter Sickert: A Life* (London, 2005)

Thomas, Graham Stuart, *Gardens of the National Trust* (London, 1979)

Thomas, Graham Stuart, *Recollections of Great Gardeners* (London, 2003)

Tinniswood, Adrian, *A History of Country House Visiting: Five Centuries of Tourism and Taste* (Oxford and London, 1989)

Trevelyan, G.M., *Must England's Beauty Perish? A Plea on Behalf of the National Trust* (London, 1929)

Waterson, Merlin (ed.), *The Country House Remembered: Recollections of Life Between the Wars* (London, 1985)

Waterson, Merlin, *A Cornish Bastion: The Work of Michael Trinick* (Lanhydrock, 2006)

Waterson, Merlin (ed.), *The National Trust: The First Hundred Years* (London, 1994)

Weideger, Paula, *Gilding the Acorn: Behind the Façade of the National Trust* (London, 1994)

Whistler, Laurence, *The Laughter and the Urn: The Life of Rex Whistler* (London, 1985)

Williams, Raymond, *Culture and Society, 1780–1950* (London, 1958)

Williams, Raymond, *The Country and the City* (London, 1973)

Williams-Ellis, Clough, *Architect Errant* (London, 1971)

Williams-Ellis, Clough, *England and the Octopus* (London, 1928)

Williams-Ellis, Clough, *On Trust for the Nation* (London, 1947)

Williams-Ellis, Clough (ed.), *Britain and the Beast* (London, 1937)

Wright, Patrick, *On Living in an Old Country* (London, 1985)

INDEX

Page numbers in *italics* refer to illustrations